Praise for
A Swim in a Pond in the Rain

"[Saunders] offers one of the most accurate and beautiful depictions of what it is like to be inside the mind of the writer that I've ever read—that state of heightened alertness, lightning-quick decisions."
—*The New York Times Book Review*

"Saunders is a gentle giant in American letters. . . . Why does fiction matter now? The answer, Saunders finds, lies in understanding reading to be a kind of life skill—for understanding our position in the world, for arbitrating truth."
—*The Wall Street Journal*

"This book is a delight, and it's about delight too. . . . [*A Swim in a Pond in the Rain* is] very different from just another 'how to' creative writing manual, or just another critical essay. . . . One of the pleasures of this book is feeling [Saunders's] own thinking move backwards and forwards, between the writer dissecting practice and the reader entering in through the spell of the words, to dwell inside the story."
—*The Guardian*

"It's the next best thing to sitting in the room with [Saunders]. Academic but accessible, these stories and related essays will especially be of interest to fiction die-hards, but also to anyone interested in new ways of seeing and understanding the world."
—*Time* (100 Must-Read Books of 2021)

"When my faith in humanity falters (often, these days), I reach for either a drink or a George Saunders story. His fiction is the dressing room mirror that finds us naked and vulnerable, capturing us humans at our most embarrassing, selfish, lazy or lovelorn. Saunders's gift, though, is that he never condemns his characters—or us—but instead pleads for patience and grace, daring readers to forgive each other our awfulness and to live with kindness on our minds. His latest book is nonfiction but still thrums with empathy as Saunders, who also teaches creative writing at Syracuse University, unpacks the short stories of four Russian writers—Tolstoy, Chekhov, Turgenev and Gogol—exploring how they too used verbs, nouns and adjectives to paint and plead for our shared humanity. It's a must-read for writers, and for the rest of us humans."

—NPR (Best Books of the Year)

"It is like reading with a wise, kind and thoughtful teacher by your side who points out details in the language and the plot."

—St. Louis Public Radio (Best Books of the Year)

" 'The part of the mind that reads a story is also the part that reads the world,' George Saunders writes in *A Swim in a Pond in the Rain*. It's perhaps the truest distillation of Saunders's visionary life and work, encapsulating the characteristic generosity and humanity of his artistic outlook. Saunders has spent over two decades teaching creative writing in Syracuse University's MFA program, where his most beloved class explores the nineteenth-century Russian short story in translation. In *A Swim in a Pond in the Rain*, Saunders has distilled decades of coursework into a lively and profound master class, exploring the mechanics of fiction through seven memorable stories by Chekhov, Tolstoy, Turgenev, and Gogol. In these warm, sublimely specific essays, Saunders's astounding powers of analysis come into full view, as does his gift for linking art with life. By becoming better readers, Saunders argues, we can become better citizens of the world."

—*Esquire* (Best Books of the Year)

"Lively, edifying . . . another generous, funny, and stunningly perceptive book from one of the most original and entertaining writers alive."

—*Vanity Fair*

"A true gift to writers and serious readers . . . With infectious enthusiasm and generosity of spirit, Saunders delves into seven stories that he calls the 'seven fastidiously constructed scale models of the world.' . . . While the genesis of *A Swim in a Pond in the Rain* can be found in the creative writing classroom—and writers at any level of their careers will glean priceless pearls from nearly every page—the genius of Saunders's book, and his clear intention in offering it up, is to elucidate literature for the engaged reader, deepening the reading experience. It is also a blueprint for a greater engagement with humanity."   —*BookPage* (starred review)

"Superb mix of instruction and literary criticism . . . Saunders's generous teachings—and the classics they're based on—are sure to please."
                                        —*Publishers Weekly* (starred review)

BY GEORGE SAUNDERS

FICTION

CivilWarLand in Bad Decline
Pastoralia
The Very Persistent Gappers of Frip
The Brief and Frightening Reign of Phil
In Persuasion Nation
Tenth of December
Fox 8
Lincoln in the Bardo

NONFICTION

The Braindead Megaphone
Congratulations, by the Way
A Swim in a Pond in the Rain

A Swim in a Pond in the Rain

A Swim in a Pond in the Rain

IN WHICH
FOUR RUSSIANS
GIVE A MASTER CLASS ON
WRITING, READING,
AND LIFE

George Saunders

RANDOM HOUSE
New York

2022 Random House Trade Paperback Edition

Published in the United States by Random House, an imprint and division of
Penguin Random House LLC, New York.

RANDOM HOUSE and the HOUSE colophon are registered trademarks of
Penguin Random House LLC.

Originally published in hardcover in the United States by Random House,
an imprint and division of Penguin Random House LLC, in 2021.

LIBRARY OF CONGRESS CATALOGING-IN-PUBLICATION DATA
Names: Saunders, George, author. | Gogol', Nikolaĭ Vasil'evich, 1809–1852.
Nos. English (Struve) | Chekhov, Anton Pavlovich, 1860–1904. Kryzhovnik. English
(Yarmolinsky) | Chekhov, Anton Pavlovich, 1860–1904. Na podvode. English
(Yarmolinsky) | Chekhov, Anton Pavlovich, 1860–1904. Dushechka. English
(Yarmolinsky) | Turgenev, Ivan Sergeevich, 1818–1883. Pevtsy. English (Magarshack) |
Tolstoy, Leo, graf, 1828–1910. Alësha Gorshok. English (Brown) | Tolstoy, Leo, graf,
1828–1910. Khoziain i rabotnik. English (Maude and Maude)
Title: A swim in a pond in the rain: in which four Russians give a master class on
writing, reading, and life / by George Saunders.
Description: New York: Random House, 2021. | Includes texts of seven short stories. |
Includes bibliographical references.
Identifiers: LCCN 2020031045 (print) | LCCN 2020031046 (ebook) |
ISBN 9781984856036 (paperback) | ISBN 9781984856043 (ebook)
Subjects: LCSH: Gogol', Nikolaĭ Vasil'evich, 1809–1852. Nos. | Chekhov, Anton
Pavlovich, 1860–1904. Kryzhovnik. | Chekhov, Anton Pavlovich, 1860–1904. Na
podvode. | Chekhov, Anton Pavlovich, 1860–1904. Dushechka. | Turgenev, Ivan
Sergeevich, 1818–1883. Pevtsy. | Tolstoy, Leo, graf, 1828–1910. Alësha Gorshok. |
Tolstoy, Leo, graf, 1828–1910. Khoziain i rabotnik. | Short stories, Russian—19th
century—History and criticism. | Short stories, Russian—19th century—History and
criticism—Study and teaching. | Reader-response criticism—United States.
Classification: LCC PG3097 .S28 2021 (print) | LCC PG3097 (ebook) |
DDC 891.708—dc23
LC record available at lccn.loc.gov/2020031045
LC ebook record available at lccn.loc.gov/2020031046

Printed in the United States of America on acid-free paper

randomhousebooks.com

68975

Book design by Simon M. Sullivan

To my students at Syracuse, past, present, and future

And in grateful memory of Susan Kamil

Ivan Ivanych came out of the cabin, plunged into the water with a splash and swam in the rain, thrusting his arms out wide; he raised waves on which white lilies swayed. He swam out to the middle of the river and dived and a minute later came up in another spot and swam on and kept diving, trying to touch bottom. "By God!" he kept repeating delightedly, "by God!" He swam to the mill, spoke to the peasants there, and turned back and in the middle of the river lay floating, exposing his face to the rain. Burkin and Alyohin were already dressed and ready to leave, but he kept on swimming and diving. "By God!" he kept exclaiming, "Lord, have mercy on me."

"You've had enough!" Burkin shouted to him.

—ANTON CHEKHOV, "Gooseberries"

Contents

A Swim in a Pond in the Rain

We Begin

For the last twenty years, at Syracuse University, I've been teaching a class in the nineteenth-century Russian short story in translation. My students are some of the best young writers in America. (We pick six new students a year from an applicant pool of between six and seven hundred.) They arrive already wonderful. What we try to do over the next three years is help them achieve what I call their "iconic space"—the place from which they will write the stories only they could write, using what makes them uniquely themselves—their strengths, weaknesses, obsessions, peculiarities, the whole deal. At this level, good writing is assumed; the goal is to help them acquire the technical means to become defiantly and joyfully themselves.

In the Russian class, hoping to understand the physics of the form ("How does this thing work, anyway?"), we turn to a handful of the great Russian writers to see how they did it. I sometimes joke (and yet not) that we're reading to see what we can steal.

A few years back, after class (chalk dust hovering in the autumnal air, old-fashioned radiator clanking in the corner, marching band practicing somewhere in the distance, let's say), I had the realization that some of the best moments of my life, the moments during which I've really felt myself offering something of value to the world, have been spent teaching that Russian class. The stories I teach in it are constantly with me as I work, the high bar against which I measure my own. (I want my stories to move and change someone as much as these Russian stories have moved and changed me.) After all these years, the texts feel like old friends, friends I get to introduce to a new group of brilliant young writers every time I teach the class.

So I decided to write this book, to put some of what my students and

I have discovered together over the years down on paper and, in that way, offer a modest version of that class to you.

Over an actual semester we might read thirty stories (two or three per class), but for the purposes of this book we'll limit ourselves to seven. The stories I've chosen aren't meant to represent a diverse cast of Russian writers (just Chekhov, Turgenev, Tolstoy, and Gogol) or even necessarily the best stories by these writers. They're just seven stories I love and have found eminently teachable over the years. If my goal was to get a non-reader to fall in love with the short story, these are among the stories I'd offer her. They're great stories, in my opinion, written during a high-water period for the form. But they're not all equally great. Some are great in spite of certain flaws. Some are great *because* of their flaws. Some of them may require me to do a little convincing (which I'm happy to attempt). What I really want to talk about is the short story form itself, and these are good stories for that purpose: simple, clear, elemental.

For a young writer, reading the Russian stories of this period is akin to a young composer studying Bach. All of the bedrock principles of the form are on display. The stories are simple but moving. We care about what happens in them. They were written to challenge and antagonize and outrage. And, in a complicated way, to console.

Once we begin reading the stories, which are, for the most part, quiet, domestic, and apolitical, this idea may strike you as strange; but this is a resistance literature, written by progressive reformers in a repressive culture, under constant threat of censorship, in a time when a writer's politics could lead to exile, imprisonment, and execution. The resistance in the stories is quiet, at a slant, and comes from perhaps the most radical idea of all: that every human being is worthy of attention and that the origins of every good and evil capability of the universe may be found by observing a single, even very humble, person and the turnings of his or her mind.

I was an engineering student in college, at the Colorado School of Mines, and came to fiction late, with a particular understanding of fiction's purpose. I'd had a powerful experience one summer, reading *The Grapes of Wrath* at night, in an old RV in my parents' driveway in Amarillo, after long days working in the oil fields as what was called a "jug hustler." My fellow workers included a Vietnam vet who, there in the middle of the prairie, periodically burst into the voice of an amped-up radio host ("THIS IS WVOR, AMARILLO!") and an ex-con, just out of jail, who, every morning, in the van on the way to the ranch where we were working, would update me on the new and perverse things he and his "lady" had tried sexually the night before, images that have stayed with me ever since, sadly.

As I read Steinbeck after such a day, the novel came alive. I was work-ing in a continuation of the fictive world, I saw. It was the same Amer-ica, decades later. I was tired, Tom Joad was tired. I felt misused by some large and wealthy force, and so did Reverend Casy. The capitalist behe-moth was crushing me and my new pals beneath it, just as it had crushed the Okies who'd driven through this same Panhandle in the 1930s on their way to California. We too were the malformed detritus of capital-ism, the necessary cost of doing business. In short, Steinbeck was writ-ing about life as I was finding it. He'd arrived at the same questions I was arriving at, and he felt they were urgent, as they were coming to feel urgent to me.

The Russians, when I found them a few years later, worked on me in the same way. They seemed to regard fiction not as something decora-tive but as a vital moral-ethical tool. They changed you when you read them, made the world seem to be telling a different, more interesting story, a story in which you might play a meaningful part, and in which you had responsibilities.

We live, as you may have noticed, in a degraded era, bombarded by facile, shallow, agenda-laced, too rapidly disseminated information bursts. We're about to spend some time in a realm where it is assumed that, as the great (twentieth-century) Russian short story master Isaac Babel put it, "no iron spike can pierce a human heart as icily as a period in the right place." We're going to enter seven fastidiously constructed scale models of the world, made for a specific purpose that our time maybe doesn't fully endorse but that these writers accepted implicitly as the aim of art—namely, to ask the big questions: How are we sup-posed to be living down here? What were we put here to accomplish? What should we value? What is truth, anyway, and how might we recognize it? How can we feel any peace when some people have everything and others have nothing? How are we supposed to live with joy in a world that seems to want us to love other people but then roughly separates us from them in the end, no matter what?

(You know, those cheerful, Russian kinds of big questions.)

For a story to ask these sorts of questions, we first have to finish it. It has to draw us in, compel us to keep going. So, the aim of this book is mainly diagnostic: If a story drew us in, kept us reading, made us feel respected, how did it do that? I'm not a critic or a literary historian or an expert on Russian literature or any of that. The focus of my artistic life has been trying to learn to write emotionally moving stories that a reader feels compelled to finish. I consider myself more vaudevillian than scholar. My approach to teaching is less academic ("Resurrection, in this context, is a metaphor for political revolution, an ongoing concern in the Russian zeitgeist") and more strategic ("Why do we even need that second return to the village?").

The basic drill I'm proposing here is: read the story, then turn your mind to the experience you've just had. Was there a place you found particularly moving? Something you resisted or that confused you? A moment when you found yourself tearing up, getting annoyed, thinking anew? Any lingering questions about the story? *Any answer is acceptable.* If you (my good-hearted trouper of a reader) felt it, it's valid. If it confounded you, that's worth mentioning. If you were bored or pissed off: valuable information. No need to dress up your response in literary language or express it in terms of "theme" or "plot" or "character development" or any of that.

The stories were, of course, written in Russian. I offer the English translations that I've responded to most strongly or, in some cases, the versions I first found years ago and have been teaching from since. I don't read or speak Russian, so I can't vouch for their faithfulness to the originals (although we'll do some thinking about that as we go). I propose that we approach the stories as if they were originally written in English, knowing that we're losing the music of the Russian and the nuance they would have for a Russian reader. Even in English, shorn of those delights, they have worlds to teach us.

The main thing I want us to be asking together is: What did we feel and where did we feel it? (All coherent intellectual work begins with a genuine reaction.)

Once you've read each story, I'll provide my thoughts in an essay, in which I'll walk you through my reactions, make a case for the story, offer some technical explanations for why we might have felt what we felt, where we felt it.

I should say here that I expect a given essay won't mean much if you haven't read the corresponding story. I've tried to pitch the essays to someone who's just finished reading and has a reaction fresh in her mind. This is a new kind of writing for me, more technical than usual. I hope the essays are entertaining, of course, but as I was writing, the term "workbook" kept coming to mind: a book that will be work, sometimes hard work, but work that we'll be doing together, with the intention of urging ourselves deeper into these stories than a simple first read would allow.

The idea here is that working closely with the stories will make them more available to us as we work on our own; that this intense and, we might say, forced acquaintance with them will inform the swerves and instinctive moves that are so much a part of what writing actually is, from moment to moment.

So, this is a book for writers but also, I hope, for readers.

Over the last ten years I've had a chance to give readings and talks all over the world and meet thousands of dedicated readers. Their passion for literature (evident in their questions from the floor, our talks at the signing table, the conversations I've had with book clubs) has convinced me that there's a vast underground network for goodness at work in the world—a web of people who've put reading at the center of their lives because they know from experience that reading makes them more expansive, generous people and makes their lives more interesting.

As I wrote this book, I had those people in mind. Their generosity with my work and their curiosity about literature, and their faith in it, made me feel I could swing for the fences a little here—be as technical, nerdy, and frank as needed, as we try to explore the way the creative process really works.

To study the way we read is to study the way the mind works: the way it evaluates a statement for truth, the way it behaves in relation to another mind (i.e., the writer's) across space and time. What we're going to be doing here, essentially, is watching ourselves read (trying to reconstruct how we felt as we were, just now, reading). Why would we want to do this? Well, the part of the mind that reads a story is also the part that reads the world; it can deceive us, but it can also be trained to accuracy; it can fall into disuse and make us more susceptible to lazy, violent, materialistic forces, but it can also be urged back to life, transforming us into more active, curious, alert readers of reality.

Throughout, I'll be offering some models for thinking about stories. No one of these is "correct" or sufficient. Think of them as rhetorical trial balloons. ("What if we think about a story this way? Is that useful?") If a model appeals to you, use it. If not, discard it. In Buddhism, it's said that a teaching is like "a finger pointing at the moon." The moon (enlightenment) is the essential thing and the pointing finger is trying to direct us to it, but it's important not to confuse finger with moon. For those of us who are writers, who dream of someday writing a story like the ones we've loved, into which we've disappeared pleasurably, and that briefly seemed more real to us than so-called reality, the goal ("the moon") is to attain the state of mind from which we might write such a story. All of the workshop talk and story theory and aphoristic, clever, craft-encouraging slogans are just fingers pointing at that moon, trying to lead us to that state of mind. The criterion by which we accept or reject a given finger: "Is it helping?"

I offer what follows in that spirit.

IN THE CART

Anton Chekhov

(1897)

A PAGE AT A TIME

THOUGHTS ON "IN THE CART"

───────

Years ago, on the phone with Bill Buford, then fiction editor of *The New Yorker,* enduring a series of painful edits, feeling a little insecure, I went fishing for a compliment: "But what do you *like* about the story?" I whined. There was a long pause at the other end. And Bill said this: "Well, I read a line. And I like it . . . enough to read the next."

And that was it: his entire short story aesthetic and presumably that of the magazine. And it's perfect. A story is a linear-temporal phenomenon. It proceeds, and charms us (or doesn't), a line at a time. We have to keep being pulled into a story in order for it to do anything to us.

I've taken a lot of comfort in this idea over the years. I don't need a big theory about fiction to write it. I don't have to worry about anything but: Would a reasonable person, reading line four, get enough of a jolt to go on to line five?

Why do we keep reading a story?

Because we *want to*.

Why do we want to?

That's the million-dollar question: What makes a reader keep reading?

Are there laws of fiction, as there are laws of physics? Do some things just *work* better than others? What forges the bond between reader and writer and what breaks it?

Well, how would we know?

One way would be to track our mind as it moves from line to line.

A story (any story, every story) makes its meaning at speed, a small structural pulse at a time. We read a bit of text and a set of expectations arises.

"A man stood on the roof of a seventy-story building."

Aren't you already kind of expecting him to jump, fall, or be pushed off?

You'll be pleased if the story takes that expectation into account, but not pleased if it addresses it too neatly.

We could understand a story as simply a series of such expectation/resolution moments.

For our first story, "In the Cart," by Anton Chekhov, I'm going to propose a one-time exception to the "basic drill" I just laid out in the introduction and suggest that we approach the story by way of an exercise I use at Syracuse.

Here's how it works.

I'll give you the story a page at a time. You read that page. Afterward, we'll take stock of where we find ourselves. What has that page done to us? What do we know, having read the page, that we didn't know before? How has our understanding of the story changed? What are we expecting to happen next? If we want to keep reading, why do we?

Before we start, let's note, rather obviously, that, at this moment, as regards "In the Cart," your mind is a perfect blank.

IN THE CART

———

y drove out of the town at half past eight in the morning.

The paved road was dry, a splendid April sun was shedding warmth, but there was still snow in the ditches and in the woods. Winter, evil, dark, long, had ended so recently; spring had arrived suddenly; but neither the warmth nor the languid, transparent woods, warmed by the breath of spring, nor the black flocks flying in the fields over huge puddles that were like lakes, nor this marvelous, immeasurably deep sky, into which it seemed that one would plunge with such joy, offered anything new and interesting to Marya Vasilyevna, who was sitting in the cart. She had been teaching school for thirteen years, and in the course of all those years she had gone to the town for her salary countless times; and whether it was spring, as now, or a rainy autumn evening, or winter, it was all the same to her, and what she always, invariably, longed for was to reach her destination as soon as possible.

She felt as though she had been living in these parts for a long, long time, for a hundred years, and it seemed to her that she knew every stone, every tree on the road from the town to her school. Here was her past and her present, and she could imagine no other future than the school, the road to the town and back, and again the school and again the road.

Now your mind is not so blank.

How has the state of your mind changed?

If we were sitting together in a classroom, which I wish we were, you could tell me. Instead, I'll ask you to sit quietly a bit and compare those two states of mind: the blank, receptive state your mind was in before you started to read and the one it's in now.

Taking your time, answer these questions:

1. Look away from the page and summarize for me what you know so far. Try to do it in one or two sentences.

2. What are you curious about?

3. Where do you think the story is headed?

Whatever you answered, that's what Chekhov now has to work with. He has, already, with this first page, caused certain expectations and questions to arise. You'll feel the rest of the story to be meaningful and coherent to the extent that it responds to these (or "takes them into account" or "exploits them").

In the first pulse of a story, the writer is like a juggler, throwing bowling pins into the air. The rest of the story is the catching of those pins. At any point in the story, certain pins are up there and we can feel them. We'd better feel them. If not, the story has nothing out of which to make its meaning.

We might say that what's happened over the course of this page is that the path the story is on has narrowed. The possibilities were infinite before you read it (it could have been about anything) but now it has become, slightly, "about" something.

What is it about, for you, so far?

What a story is "about" is to be found in the curiosity it creates in us, which is a form of caring.

So: What do you care about in this story, so far?

It's Marya.

Now: What is the flavor of that caring? How, and where, were you made to care about her?

—

In the first line, we learn that some unidentified "they" are driving out of some town, early in the morning.

"The paved road was dry, a splendid April sun was shedding warmth, **but** there was still snow in the ditches and in the woods. Winter, evil, dark, long, had ended so recently; spring had arrived suddenly; **but** neither the warmth nor the languid transparent woods, warmed by the breath of spring, nor the black flocks flying in the fields . . ."

I've bolded the two appearances of the word "but" above (and yes, I phrase it that way to avoid saying, "I bolded the two buts above") to underscore that we're looking at two iterations of the same pattern: "The conditions of happiness are present, **but** happiness is not." It's sunny, **but** there's still snow on the ground. Winter has ended, **but** this offers nothing new or interesting to . . . and we wait to hear who it is, taking no solace in the end of this long Russian winter.

Even before there's a person in the story, there's an implied tension between two elements of the narrative voice, one telling us that things are lovely (the sky is "marvelous" and "immeasurably deep") and another resisting the general loveliness. (It would be, already, a different-feeling story, had it started: "The paved road was dry, a splendid April sun was shedding warmth, and although there was still snow in the ditches and the woods, it just didn't matter: winter, evil, dark, long, had, at long last, ended.")

Halfway through the second paragraph, we find that the resisting element within the narrative voice belongs to one Marya Vasilyevna, who, failing to be moved by springtime, appears in the cart at the sound of her name.

Of all the people in the world he might have put in this cart, Chekhov has chosen an unhappy woman resisting the charms of springtime. This could have been a story about a happy woman (newly engaged, say, or just given a clean bill of health, or a woman just naturally happy), but Chekhov elected to make Marya *unhappy*.

Then he made her unhappy in a particular flavor, for particular reasons: she's been teaching school for thirteen years; has done this trip to town "countless times" and is sick of it; feels she's been living in "these parts" for a hundred years; knows every stone and tree on the way. Worst of all, she can imagine no other future for herself.

This could have been a story about a person unhappy because she's been scorned in love, or because she's just received a fatal diagnosis, or because she's been unhappy since the moment she was born. But Chekhov chose to make Marya a person unhappy *because of the monotony of her life.*

Out of the mist of every-story-that-could-possibly-be, a particular woman has started to emerge.

We might say that the three paragraphs we've just read were in service of *increased specification.*

Characterization, so called, results from just such increasing specification. The writer asks, "Which particular person *is* this, anyway?" and answers with a series of facts that have the effect of creating a narrowing path: ruling out certain possibilities, urging others forward.

As a particular person gets made, the potential for what we call "plot" increases. (Although that's a word I don't like much—let's replace it with "meaningful action.")

As a particular person gets made, the potential for meaningful action increases.

If a story begins, "Once there was a boy who was afraid of water," we expect that a pond, river, ocean, waterfall, bathtub, or tsunami will soon appear. If a character says, "I have never once in my life been afraid," we might not mind it so much if a lion walks in. If a character lives in perpetual fear of being embarrassed, we have some idea of what might need to happen to him. Likewise with someone who loves only money, or confesses that he has never really believed in friendship, or who claims to be so tired of her life that she can't imagine another.

When there was nothing in the story (before you started reading it) there was nothing that wanted to happen.

Now that Marya is here, unhappy, the story has become restless.

The story has said of her, "She is unhappy and can't imagine any other life for herself."

And we feel the story preparing itself to say something like "Well, we'll see about that."

Paused here for what I expect you are finding an unreasonable amount of time, at the end of the first page of an eleven-page story, we're at an interesting place.* The story is under way. The first page has radically narrowed the concerns of the story; the rest of the story must now address (use, exploit) those concerns and not any others.

If you were the writer, what would you do next?

As a reader, what else would you like to know?

* One of the features of this page-at-a-time exercise: the better the story, the more curious the reader is to find out what's going to happen and the more annoying the exercise is.

. . .

She had lost the habit of thinking of the time before she became a schoolmistress and had almost forgotten all about it. She had once had a father and mother; they had lived in Moscow in a big apartment near the Red Gate, but all that remained in her memory of that part of her life was something vague and formless like a dream. Her father had died when she was ten years old, and her mother had died soon after. She had a brother, an officer; at first they used to write to each other, then her brother had stopped answering her letters, he had lost the habit. Of her former belongings, all that remained was a photograph of her mother, but the dampness in the school had faded it, and now nothing could be seen on it but the hair and the eyebrows.

[2]

When they had gone a couple of miles, old Semyon, who was driving, turned round and said:

"They have nabbed an official in the town. They have sent him away. They say that he and some Germans killed Alexeyev, the mayor, in Moscow."

"Who told you that?"

"They read it in the papers, in Ivan Ionov's house."

And again there was a long silence. Marya Vasilyevna thought of her school, of the examinations that were coming soon, and of the girl and the four boys whom she was sending up for them. And just as she was thinking about the examinations she was overtaken by a landowner named Hanov in a carriage with four horses, the very man who had acted as examiner in her school the previous year. As he drew alongside he recognized her and bowed.

"Good morning," he said. "Are you driving home, madam?"

. . .

So, I ended my last section by asking what else you wanted to know.

What I wanted to know was: How did Marya get here, in this crummy life?

Chekhov answers in the first paragraph of this page: she's here because she has to be. She grew up in Moscow, in a big apartment, with her family. But then her parents died, she fell out of touch with her only sibling, and now she's alone in the world.

A person could have "gotten here" by being born out here, in the sticks, or by being an idealistic young woman dedicated to rural improvement who broke off her engagement with her conventional, citified fiancé and fled to the countryside. But here's how Marya got here: her parents died and financial necessity compelled her.

And all she has left of her family is that sad photograph, in which her mother is just hair and eyebrows.

So Marya's life is not just monotonous but lonely.

When we talk about fiction, we tend to use terms like "theme," "plot," "character development," and "structure." I've never, as a writer, found these very useful. ("Your theme's no good" gives me nothing to work with, and neither does "You might want to make your plot better.") These terms are placeholders, and if they intimidate us and block us up, as they tend to do, we might want to put them aside and try to find a more useful way to think about whatever it is they're placeholding for.

Here, Chekhov gives us an opportunity to reconsider the scary term "structure."

We might think of structure as simply: an organizational scheme that allows the story to answer a question it has caused its reader to ask.

Me, at the end of the first page: "Poor Marya. I already sort of care about her. How did she get here?"

Story, in the first paragraph of its second page: "Well, she had some bad luck."

We might imagine structure as a form of call-and-response. A question arises organically from the story and then the story, very considerately, answers it. If we want to make good structure, we just have to be aware of what question we are causing the reader to ask, then answer that question.

(See?

Structure's easy.

Ha, ha, ha.)

We've known, from the first line of the story ("**They** drove out of the town at half past eight in the morning") that someone else is there in the cart with Marya. Halfway down the page we learn that this is "old Semyon" and wait for Semyon to exhibit some characteristics. ("Who are you, Semyon, and what are you doing in this story?") If his answer is "I'm here to drive the cart," that's not good enough. A million peasants could drive this cart. We're waiting to find out why Chekhov chose this specific peasant to do it.

So far, the story has declared itself to be about, approximately: a woman unhappy with the monotony of her life, a life forced on her by necessity. Semyon, by suddenly appearing, has become, whether he likes it or not, an element of that story and, therefore, doesn't get to just drive the cart while gazing out at the scenery. He has to do something for this particular story, the one with (bored, unhappy) Marya in it.

So, what do we learn about Semyon?

Not much, not yet. He's old, he's driving (she's seated behind him, we realize). He tells her some news: the mayor of Moscow has been assassinated. Marya's response ("Who told you that?") feels remonstrative and impatient (she doubts him). Semyon heard it read aloud, from a newspaper, in a teahouse. (This implies that he can't read.) And although Marya is skeptical, Semyon is actually correct: Nikolay Alekseyev, the mayor of Moscow, was, in fact, shot, in his office, by a deranged person, in 1893.

Marya's reaction? She goes back to thinking of her school.

We don't know what to make of any of this yet, but our minds quietly file it under "Semyon, Stuff About," and "Marya, Stuff About." Our expectation, given the extreme frugality of the form, is that the stuff in those files will prove meaningful later.

In the penultimate paragraph of this page, Marya's thoughts about her students and the upcoming exams are interrupted when the cart is "overtaken by a landowner named Hanov in a carriage with four horses, the very man who had acted as examiner in her school the previous year."

Let's pause here a second. How did your mind "receive" Hanov into the story?

I recall here a phrase from old movies: "What do you take me for?"

What did you take Hanov for? What did you think he was here in the story to do?

There should be a name for this moment in a story when, a situation having been established, a new character arrives. We automatically expect that new element to alter or complicate or deepen the situation. A man stands in an elevator, muttering under his breath about how much he hates his job. The door opens, someone gets in. Don't we automatically understand that this new person has appeared to alter or complicate or deepen the first man's hatred of his job? (Otherwise, what's he doing here? Get rid of him and find us someone who *will* alter, complicate, or deepen things. It's a story, after all, not a webcam.)

Having understood Marya as "she who is unhappy with the monotony of her life," we're already waiting for some altering presence to arrive.

And here comes Hanov.

This is the big event of the page, and notice this: having made Marya on its first page, the story didn't stay static for long at all. (We didn't get a second page merely explicating her boredom.) This should tell us something about the pace of a story versus the pace of real life: the story is way faster, compressed, and exaggerated—a place where something new always has to be happening, something relevant to that which has already happened.

The main way fiction writing is taught at Syracuse (and at most MFA programs) is by way of the workshop model. Six students come together once a week, having read work by two of their number, and we all discuss that work in a technical way. We've each read the stories at least twice and line-edited them and provided some pages of commentary.

Then the fun begins.

Before we launch into our in-class critique, I'll sometimes ask the workshop to come up with what I call the "Hollywood version" of the story—a pithy one- or two-sentence summary. It's no good to start making suggestions about a story until we've agreed on what it's trying to do. (If a complicated machine showed up in your yard, you wouldn't start altering it and "improving" it until you had some idea of its intended function.) The "Hollywood version" is meant to answer the question "What story does this story appear to want to be?"

This is done in the way artillery fire is directed, at least in my imagination: an initial shot, followed by a series of adjustments for precision.

An unhappy woman is going somewhere in a cart.

A schoolteacher, Marya Vasilyevna, unhappy because she's been teaching too long, is on her way home from a trip to town.

A schoolteacher, Marya Vasilyevna, unhappy because she's been teaching too long, bored with the monotony of her life, alone in the world, teaching only out of necessity, is on the way home from a trip into town.

Marya, a bored, lonely schoolteacher, runs into a man named Hanov.

Actually, she runs into a *wealthy* man named Hanov (he's "a landowner" after all, and has those four horses).

Notice that, in spite of the fact that we are literary sophisticates, engaged in a deep reading of a Chekhov masterpiece, we feel the sudden appearance of Hanov to be a potential nineteenth-century Russian meet-cute:

A lonely schoolteacher runs into a wealthy landowner, who, we feel, might transform her depressing life.

Put a little more crassly:

Lonely woman encounters possible lover.

Where might the story go from here?

Scan your mind, make a list.

Which of your ideas feel too obvious? That is to say: Which, if Chekhov enacts them, will disappoint you by responding too slavishly to your expectations? (Hanov, on the next page, drops to one knee and proposes.) Which, too random, won't be responding to your expectations at all? (A spaceship comes down and abducts Semyon.)

Chekhov's challenge is to use these expectations he's created but not too neatly.

No pressure.

. . .

This Hanov, a man of about forty, with a worn face and a lifeless expression, was beginning to age noticeably, but was still handsome and attractive to women. He lived alone on his large estate, was not in the service, and it was said of him that he did nothing at home but pace from one end of the room to the other, whistling, or play chess with his old footman. It was said, too, that he drank heavily. And indeed, at the examination the previous year the very papers he had brought with him smelt of scent and wine. On that occasion everything he wore was brand-new, and Marya Vasilyevna had found him [3] very attractive and, sitting next to him, had felt embarrassed. She was used to seeing cold, hardheaded examiners at the school, but this one did not remember a single prayer, did not know what questions to ask, was exceedingly polite and considerate, and gave only the highest marks.

"I am on my way to visit Bakvist," he continued, addressing Marya Vasilyevna, "but I wonder if he is at home."

They turned off the highway onto a dirt road, Hanov leading the way and Semyon following. The team of four horses kept to the road, slowly pulling the heavy carriage through the mud. Semyon changed his course continually, leaving the road now to drive over a hillock, now to skirt a meadow, often jumping down from the cart and helping the horse. Marya Vasilyevna kept thinking about the school, and wondering whether the arithmetic problem at the examination would be hard or easy. And she was annoyed with the Zemstvo office, where she had found no one the previous day. What negligence! For the past two years she had been asking them to discharge the janitor, who did nothing, was rude to her, and cuffed the boys, but no one paid any attention to her.

. . .

Although we might feel a little guilty for, just now, expecting this to be a love story, reading the first paragraph of this page, we see that Marya's thinking along the same lines. Hanov (she observes) has a worn face and a lifeless expression and is beginning to age but is still "attractive to women." He lives alone, is wasting his life (he does nothing but play chess and drink). Last year, when he came to her school, his papers smelled of wine. Surely this must have irritated and horrified her? Well, no, actually: his papers smelled of "*scent* and wine," and Marya had found him "very attractive" and, sitting next to him, had felt "embarrassed," which we read as "embarrassed by the feelings she was having because of his proximity."

Let's look at the last sentence in that first paragraph for a little insight into how Chekhov makes characters. We learn that Marya "was used to seeing cold, hardheaded examiners at the school." This sets us up to expect that Hanov will be the opposite (warm and softhearted, say). We carry that assumption of warmth and softheartedness into the next bit of text, where it's affirmed (he was "exceedingly polite and considerate") but also complicated. If Hanov is warm and softhearted, he's also clueless and disorganized and incapable of an adult level of discrimination (he doesn't remember "a single prayer," gives only the highest marks).

So a broad character (a handsome rich man) is cross-painted with contradictory information (he is, yes, handsome and rich, but he's also a bumbler, and we feel his alcoholism to be a function of his bumbling, a form of inattention or denial). The person that emerges is complex and three-dimensional. We wonder about him, rather than having him neatly in our pocket, and we're not sure if we want Marya interested in him or not.

Hanov announces the purpose of this trip in a way that completes this portrait of an amiable doofus: he's taking this long drive through the mud to visit a friend, but he has no idea whether that friend is even home.

The carts turn off the highway. In a lesser story, Marya's thoughts would be only of Hanov. But Chekhov remembers the Marya he's made. She's lived here a long time. She knows Hanov and he knows her. She's already, we suspect, thought about Hanov as a possible savior before. So, her mind returns easily and naturally to the school, and we might now recall that this is just what it did after Semyon's assassination anecdote, earlier. She's twice now retreated from the world to thoughts of the school (and we're that much more sensitized to future occurrences). Why does she do this? What does this tell us about her that we might need to know?

We put this aside for now. But notice that, even as we do, we're again enacting an expectation of efficiency—if it turns out that this tendency of hers isn't somehow used later, we will feel it (slightly) as wasteful.

Yes: it's a harsh form, the short story.

Harsh as a joke, a song, a note from the gallows.

. . .

It was hard to find the chairman at the office and when you did find him, he would say with tears in his eyes that he had no time; the inspector visited the school once in three years and had no understanding of anything connected with it, since he had formerly been employed in the Finance Department and had obtained the post of school inspector through pull; the School Board met very rarely and no one knew where; the Trustee was a half literate peasant, the owner of a tannery, stupid, coarse, and a bosom friend of the janitor's—and heaven knows to whom she could turn with complaints and inquiries.

[4]

"He is really handsome," she thought, glancing at Hanov.

Meanwhile the road was growing worse and worse. They drove into the woods. Here there was no turning off the road, the ruts were deep, and water flowed and gurgled in them. Twigs struck them stingingly in the face.

"How's the road?" asked Hanov, and laughed.

The schoolmistress looked at him and could not understand why this odd fellow lived here. What could his money, his interesting appearance, his refinement get him in this Godforsaken place, with its mud, its boredom? Life granted him no privileges, and here, like Semyon, he was jogging slowly along an abominable road and suffering the same discomforts. Why live here, when one had a chance to live in Petersburg or abroad? And it seemed as though it would be a simple matter for a rich man like him to turn this bad road into a good one so as to avoid having to endure this misery and seeing the despair written on the faces of his coachman and Semyon? But he merely laughed, and apparently it was all the same to him, and he asked nothing better of life. He was kind, gentle, naïve; he had no grasp of this coarse life, he did not know it, any more than he had known the prayers at the examination. He presented nothing to the schools but globes, and sincerely regarded himself as a useful person and a prominent worker in the field of popular education. And who had need of his globes here?

. . .

Marya continues to think of the school and its corrupt administration, and the fact that there is no one for her to turn to—

And then thinks, with no transition, self-interrupting: "He is really handsome." So, even though she's dismissed Hanov, she's been watching him (his broad, wealthy back swaying there, just ahead, in that expensive fur coat) and, we might say, pretending to think about the school while really thinking of him, or trying not to think of him.

That self-interruption is a beautiful thing. It says: the mind can be two places at once. (Many trains are running simultaneously in there, consciousness aware of only one at a time.)

Note the little burst of pleasure we feel as we recognize ourselves in Marya. (Ever had a light, persistent, unrequited, indefensible semi-crush?) He's not for her, she knows it, she never seriously considered him anyway, and yet her mind keeps being lured back to him, like a dog to the alley behind a good-smelling restaurant.

Notice how impatient your reading mind is or, we might say, how alert it is. It knows where we are: Marya, lonely and unhappy, has encountered a potential antidote in Hanov. Like an obsessed detective, the reading mind interprets every new-arriving bit of text purely in this context, not interested in much else.

And yet here, in the third paragraph, it seems that, whether we want one or not, we're going to get a description of the road.

Why does a story even need these types of descriptions? Why did Chekhov decide to pull us out of the central action and describe the world outside the cart? One of the tacit promises of a short story, because it is so short, is that there's no waste in it. Everything in it is there for a reason (for the story to make use of)—even a brief description of a road.

So, as we enter this description, we're asking, somewhere in the back of our reading mind: How is this description of a road going to turn out to be essential, i.e., not wasteful?

Earlier, we asked if there might exist certain "laws" in fiction. Are there things that our reading mind just responds to? Physical descriptions seem to be one such thing. Who knows why? We like hearing our world described. And we like hearing it described specifically. ("Two men in green sweaters were playing catch beside a wrecked car" is better than "I drove through this area that was sort of bland and didn't notice much.") A specific description, like a prop in a play, helps us believe more fully in that which is entirely invented. It's sort of a cheap, or at least easy, authorial trick. If I am trying to put you in a certain (invented) house, I might invoke "a large white cat, stretching itself out to what seemed like twice its normal length" on a couch in that house. If you see the cat, the house becomes real.

But that's only part of the move. That cat, having been placed in that particular story, is now, also, a metaphorical cat, in relation to all of the other dozens (hundreds) of metaphorical elements floating around in the story.

And that cat now has to do some story-specific work. Or, we might say, it's *going to be* doing some story-specific work, whether it chooses to or not, by its very presence in the story; the question is what work it's going to be asked to do and how well it will do it.

Here, the road's "growing worse." A particular authorial choice; it would be a different story if the road were getting wider and drier and opened into a meadow awash with new flowers. What does it "mean," that the road is growing worse? Why did Chekhov choose to make the road worse? That's a good question, one that might be best answered by you, dear reader, via this method: hold the two models up in your mind (road growing worse vs. road growing better) and feel the ways in which "worsening road" is better. Or feel the way that the two choices are *different*. We can try to articulate the reasons why a worsening road is a better choice than an improving road, or vice versa—but for now let's just note that Chekhov did two things in this paragraph: he remembered where he'd put us (in a cart passing through some woods in early spring), then described conditions there with specificity ("The ruts were deep, and water flowed and gurgled in them").

So, this is both a realistic description (it's spring, snow melts, roads get muddy) and a little poem that adjusts our understanding of the story.

Roughly speaking, we understand this description to indicate: "a steadily degrading situation." The road is "growing worse and worse." They are driving "into the woods." There's "no turning off." There's a cost to this trip (those twigs in the face).

This falls on us differently (with more foreboding, say) than a description in which they drove "out of the woods and into the bright sunshine" to find that "the road widened welcomingly" and "low-hanging flowers brushed against her cheeks softly as the cart gently rolled past a joyful peasant wedding."

Both of these descriptions would fulfill a sort of preparatory function—we would feel Chekhov using the description to set us up for whatever is to come.

What's strange is this: had Chekhov decided to send them past that joyful peasant wedding, this would have changed the rest of the story. Or: the rest of the story would have had to change, to take that more positive description into account and render it cogent to the larger, evolving entity.

A story is an organic whole, and when we say a story is good, we're saying that it responds alertly to itself. This holds true in both directions; a brief description of a road tells us how to read the present moment but also all the past moments in the story and all those still to come.

Hanov has money. He could live anywhere. But here he is, right where Marya is: on a muddy provincial road, one that he, at least, could repair, only it would never occur to him to do so. "But he merely laughed, and apparently it was all the same to him, and he asked nothing better of life." Why is he so passive? If she had power, she'd do something with it. She completes this turn against him at the end of the page, remembering the stupid globes he gives to the school, a gift that allows him to think of himself, incorrectly, as an enlightened, useful person.

Let's ask our three questions again, and I'll give you my approximate answers:

1. Look away from the page and summarize for me what you know so far.

A lonely woman is in the presence of someone who, we expect, may become a friend or lover or, in some way, relieve her loneliness.

2. What are you curious about?

They seem to have known each other a long time, with no sparks. So, what might bring them together today (if they've never been brought together before)? Also, do I even want them together? I sort of do, I guess, and the story seems to be dangling that possibility in front of me. But by the end of the page, Marya seems to be leaning away from him.

3. Where do you think the story is headed?

I don't know. I know what "the issue" is but don't see how it's going to get resolved. This uncertainty is producing a not-unpleasant tension. I feel that something has to happen that will present an opportunity for Hanov to provide comfort to Marya, to assuage her loneliness. Maybe they will just become friends or share some small moment of closeness that has the effect of (slightly) relieving Marya's unhappiness.

Here, an announcement: to avert the possibility of you abandoning my book this early in the game due to annoyance, we'll now start reading two pages at a time.

. . .

"Hold on, Vasilyevna!" said Semyon.

The cart lurched violently and was about to turn over; something heavy fell on Marya Vasilyevna's feet—it was her purchases. There was a steep climb uphill over a clayey road; noisy rivulets were flowing in winding ditches; the water had gullied the road; and how could one drive here! The horses breathed heavily. Hanov got out of the carriage and walked at the edge of the road in his long coat. He was hot.

"How's the road?" he repeated, and laughed. "This is the way to smash your carriage." [5]

"But who tells you to go driving in such weather?" asked Semyon in a surly voice. "You ought to stay home."

"I'm bored at home, grandfather. I don't like staying home."

Next to old Semyon he seemed well-built and vigorous, but there was something barely perceptible in his gait which betrayed him as a weak creature, already blighted, approaching its end. And suddenly it seemed as though there were a whiff of liquor in the woods. Marya Vasilyevna felt frightened and was filled with pity for this man who was going to pieces without rhyme or reason, and it occurred to her that if she were his wife or his sister she would devote her whole life to his rescue. His wife! Life was so ordered that here he was living in his great house alone, while she was living in a God-forsaken village alone, and yet for some reason the mere thought that he and she might meet on an equal footing and become intimate seemed impossible, absurd. Fundamentally, life was so arranged and human relations were complicated so utterly beyond all understanding that when you thought about it you were terrified and your heart sank.

"And you can't understand," she thought, "why God gives good looks, friendliness, charming, melancholy eyes to weak, unhappy, useless people—why they are so attractive."

"Here we must turn off to the right," said Hanov, getting into his carriage. "Good-by! All good wishes!"

And again she thought of her pupils, of the examination, of the janitor, of the School Board; and when the wind brought her the sound of the receding carriage these thoughts mingled with others. She wanted to think of beautiful eyes, of love, of the happiness that would never be . . .

His wife? It is cold in the morning, there is no one to light the stove, the janitor has gone off somewhere; the children come in as soon as it is light, bringing in snow and mud and making a noise; it is all so uncomfortable, so unpleasant. Her quarters consist of one little room and a kitchen close by. Every day when school is over she has a headache and after dinner she has heartburn. She has to collect money from the children for firewood and to pay the janitor, and to [6] turn it over to the Trustee, and then to implore him—that overfed, insolent peasant—for God's sake to send her firewood. And at night she dreams of examinations, peasants, snowdrifts. And this life has aged and coarsened her, making her homely, angular, and clumsy, as though they had poured lead into her. She is afraid of everything and in the presence of a member of the Zemstvo Board or of the Trustee, she gets up and does not dare sit down again. And she uses obsequious expressions when she mentions any one of them. And no one likes her, and life is passing drearily, without warmth, without friendly sympathy, without interesting acquaintances. In her position how terrible it would be if she were to fall in love!

. . .

The cart nearly tips. We find out that Marya has made some purchases in town. (These purchases are now an element of the story. What use, we wonder, will be made of them?) Hanov repeats the dumb joke he made on the previous page, Semyon turns on him ("But who tells you to go driving in such weather," he says, in a "surly" voice), and Hanov's gentle response to this insult from someone beneath him in status (Semyon is a peasant, Hanov a wealthy landowner) tracks satisfyingly with what Marya has told us about Hanov: he's a pushover, spineless, an easy grader.

Marya thinks she smells liquor in the woods. She pities Hanov, who is "going to pieces without rhyme or reason," and thinks that, if she were his wife or sister, she'd devote "her whole life" to his rescue. But that's impossible. "Fundamentally, life was so arranged and human relations were complicated so utterly beyond all understanding that when you thought about it you were terrified and your heart sank."

Then, as if he's just heard Marya ruling out their marriage, Hanov rides right out of the story.

Marya barely seems to notice, confirming our sense that she doesn't really consider him a romantic possibility. (She doesn't think, "Oh no, he's gone, I failed to interest him!") Her mind returns to the school (she thinks of "her pupils, of the examination, of the janitor, of the School Board"). This is now the third time she's done this—withdrawn from the real world into worry about the school. It's a habit with her (her default rumination, a measure of how she's been trained and reduced by this life of toil).

One of the accomplishments of this story is Chekhov's representation of the way a lonely mind works. Marya's just musing here, doing the sort of light fantasizing we do when we imagine winning the lottery or becoming a senator or telling off someone who hurt our feelings back in high school. Although the story sets us up to feel that Marya might (might) be open to Hanov, it also gives us plenty of reasons to understand this as both impossible and not to be desired. He's a drunk, an idler, past the age for reformation. He doesn't seem interested in Marya, or in anybody—he's likely had plenty of chances to marry before but never has. And Marya is, actually, kind of prideful; even as she's assessing him, we feel her thinking that, if they did get together, he'd prove a handful and a disappointment.

And yet . . .

Chekhov has her do something lovely: she hears "the sound of the receding carriage" and suddenly wants to think of "beautiful eyes, of love, of the happiness that would never be. . . ."

She thinks, again, of being his wife (not his sister this time).

She's already ruled out this possibility, just a few paragraphs earlier. But here it comes again. ("His wife?") The float that is her heart keeps bobbing back up. And it's sad—her mind returns to Hanov not because he's a great guy or her soulmate but because (1) there's nobody else around (that is, in her world) and (2) her loneliness is so extreme.

She's lonely, he's nearby. He's nearby, and though he's not lonely, exactly, it seems he could use some help.

But if you've ever tried to act as a matchmaker, you know that even two extremely lonely people continue to have standards. We can't presume to speak for them. In this case, Marya and Hanov have already spoken for themselves. Their situation is not: two people ripe for love suddenly meet for the first time. It's: two people, not exactly ripe for love (who, if they were going to become involved, would have done so years ago), meet again.

Nobody's expecting anything to happen and, in fact, it would be kind of weird if it did.

In the long paragraph at the end of page 6, she addresses her own question ("His wife?") with a dismal recounting of her actual life: the snow, the mud, the discomfort, her tiny room, her headaches, her heartburn, her constant need to beg for funds; this degrading life that has "aged and coarsened her." Though she is obsequious, "no one likes her," the poor dear.

For most of its length, the paragraph seems to be saying, "How ridiculous, to think that this wealthy man would marry such a drudge as I." Then, in its last line ("In her position how terrible it would be if she were to fall in love!"), it says something worse: yes, she's beneath him, but also, her life, as difficult as it is, has no room in it for love, even if he were interested.

Which, apparently, he isn't.

———

Einstein once said: "No worthy problem is ever solved in the plane of its original conception."*

The story has just written itself out of the plane of its original conception, by removing Hanov as a possible antidote for Marya's loneliness.

What now?

We might think of a story as a system for the transfer of energy. Energy, hopefully, gets made in the early pages and the trick, in the later pages, is to use that energy. Marya was created unhappy and lonely and has become more specifically unhappy and lonely with every passing page. That is the energy the story has made, and must use. There's vestigial evidence in Marya's thoughts that she wouldn't be averse to an overture from Hanov. She considers him handsome and attractive and has an urge to save him from himself. Although the story has been telling us all along that a relationship isn't likely (it won't happen today because it's never happened before) we've still been rooting for it to happen—we've been rooting for Marya.

We want what she wants: for her not to be so lonely. The energy of the story is being stored in our hope that she'll find some relief.

Chekhov, in these first five pages, built a door and indicated that he wanted us to go through it. Over that door is a sign: "Hanov Might Assuage Marya's Loneliness." Every time we've felt Marya's loneliness, we've glanced hopefully over at that door. Now that door has been shut and locked.

Or, actually, it's vanished.

Chekhov has, with Hanov's exit, denied himself the obvious, expected source of resolution. Who knows how Chekhov arrived at this decision, practically speaking, but we can observe what he *did:* he got rid of Hanov. Now there's no danger that the story will take that easy route.

This is an important storytelling move we might call "ritual banality avoidance." If we deny ourselves the crappo version of our story, a bet-

* Apparently this is a misquote of what Einstein actually said, which was "Let the people know that a new type of thinking is essential if mankind is to survive and move toward higher levels." But years ago a student relayed this to me in the form above and, no offense to Einstein, I thought my student's version was brilliant and have been using it ever since.

ter version will (we aspirationally assume) present itself. To refuse to do the crappo thing is to strike a de facto blow for quality. (If nothing else, at least we haven't done *that*.)

We might think of it this way: Chekhov already "has" the benefit of our expectation of a romantic development between Marya and Hanov. We've already pre-imagined that development. So he doesn't have to go there. He can go *past* it, to whatever the next and presumably more sophisticated solution turns out to be (he can force his own hand, so to speak), just by taking Hanov out of the story. (If there were a big bowl of candy in your kitchen and that was all you were eating, one way of forcing yourself to eat something better would be to throw the candy away.)

When I try to explain this notion to my students, I invoke these bracelets we used to make back in the late 1960s, when I was in grade school ("love beads," we sweet little ChicagoLand hippies-in-training called them). You put a bead on, then pushed it all the way back to the knot in the string. This cleared the way for new beads.

Just so in a story: we should always be pushing the new bead to the knot. If you know where a story is going, don't hoard it. Make the story go there, now. But then what? What will you do next? You've surrendered your big reveal. Exactly. Often, in our doubt that we have a real story to tell, we hold something back, fearing that we don't have anything else. And this can be a form of trickery. Surrendering that thing is a leap of faith that forces the story to attention, saying to it, in effect, "You have to do better than that, and now that I've denied you your trick, your first-order solution, I know that you will."

Consider a story that, in its last lines, reveals that the narrator has been paralyzed all along (and just happened to neglect to mention it).

Consider a story in which, late in the game, the narrator is revealed to be not, after all, a person walking through the Lincoln Park Zoo but *a tiger within it* (!) (but all clues that this was the case had been carefully concealed, to maximize the reveal; the other animals kept calling our tiger "Mel," and talking to him about the White Sox and so on).

A work of art moves us by being honest and that honesty is apparent in its language and its form and in its resistance to concealment.

Marya's dilemma is still in effect. She's still lonely and bored. By removing the first-order solution (Hanov), Chekhov has made his story more ambitious. In its early pages it said, "Once there was a lonely person." It might have gone on to say, "And isn't it wonderful? That lonely person met another lonely person and now neither is lonely." By declining to go there, the story now begins asking a more profound question: "What if a lonely person can find no way out of her loneliness?"

This is where, to me, the story starts to feel big. It's saying: loneliness is real and consequential and there is no easy way out of it for some of us who are in it and sometimes there's no way out at all.

We care about Marya, we expected Hanov to help her, and suddenly he's gone.

Now what?

. . .

"Hold on, Vasilyevna!"

Another steep climb.

She had begun to teach school from necessity, without feeling called to it; and she had never thought of a call, of the need for enlightenment; and it always seemed to her that what was most important in her work was not the children, not enlightenment, but the examinations. And when did she have time to think of a call, of enlightenment? Teachers, impecunious physicians, doctors' assistants, [7] for all their terribly hard work, do not even have the comfort of thinking that they are serving an ideal or the people, because their heads are always filled with thoughts of their daily bread, of firewood, of bad roads, of sickness. It is a hard, humdrum existence, and only stolid cart horses like Marya Vasilyevna can bear it for a long time; lively, alert, impressionable people who talk about their calling and about serving the ideal are soon weary of it and give up the work.

Semyon kept on picking out the driest and shortest way, traveling now across a meadow, now behind the cottages, but in one place the peasants would not let them pass and in another the land belonged to the priest and so they could not cross it, in yet another Ivan Ionov had bought a plot from the landowner and had dug a ditch round it. They kept turning back.

They reached Nizhneye Gorodishche. Near the teahouse, on the dung-strewn, snowy ground, there stood wagons loaded with great bottles of oil of vitriol. There were a great many people in the teahouse, all drivers, and it smelled of vodka, tobacco, and sheepskins. The place was noisy with loud talk and the banging of the door which was provided with a pulley. In the shop next door someone was playing an accordion steadily. Marya Vasilyevna was sitting down, having tea, while at the next table some peasants were drinking vodka and beer, sweaty with the tea they had had and the bad air.

"Hey, Kuzma!" people kept shouting confusedly. "What's doing?"

"The Lord bless us!" "Ivan Dementyich, that I can do for you!" "See here, friend!"

A little pockmarked peasant with a black beard, who was quite drunk, was suddenly taken aback by something and began using foul language.

"What are you cursing about, you there?" Semyon, who was sitting some way off, remarked angrily. "Don't you see the young lady?"

"The young lady!" someone jeered in another corner.

"The swine!"

"I didn't mean nothing—" The little peasant was embarrassed. "Excuse me. I pays my money and the young lady pays hers. How-de-do, ma'am?"

[8]

"How do you do?" answered the schoolmistress.

"And I thank you kindly."

Marya Vasilyevna drank her tea with pleasure, and she, too, began turning red like the peasants, and again she fell to thinking about firewood, about the janitor . . .

"Wait, brother," came from the next table. "It's the school-ma'am from Vyazovye. I know; she's a good sort."

"She's all right!"

The door was banging continually, some coming in, others going out. Marya Vasilyevna went on sitting there, thinking of the same things all the time, while the accordion went on playing and playing behind the wall. There had been patches of sunlight on the floor, they shifted to the counter, then to the wall, and finally disappeared altogether; this meant that it was past midday. The peasants at the next table were getting ready to leave. The little peasant went up to Marya Vasilyevna somewhat unsteadily and shook hands with her; following his example, the others shook hands with her at parting, and filed out singly, and the door squeaked and slammed nine times.

. . .

At the top of page 7, the process of characterization through specification continues.

Marya becomes, again, a slightly more specific Marya. (The story form reminds us that a human being is never static or stable. The form demands that the writer honor this. If a character keeps doing or saying the same thing, keeps occupying the same position, we will feel this as static, a repeated beat—a failure of development.) Here, we learn that Marya is not a person called to teach. She was forced into it by financial necessity. It has "always" seemed to her that the examinations were what mattered (not the children, not enlightenment). We note the continually increasing particularity of this person Chekhov is making, the extent to which she has just departed from a first-order, clichéd, overworked, idealistic teacher. She is not, never has been, a teacher for the love of it. This is part of what has worn her down, this absence of love for her work. She started out not full of hope but disliking the work: understanding it as beneath her, something at which it was possible to fail, rather than as something she might do out of love.

Chekhov is averse to making pure saints or pure sinners. We saw this with Hanov (rich, handsome bumbler and drunk) and we see it now with Marya (struggling noble schoolteacher who has constructed her own cage through joyless complicity in her situation). This complicates things; our first-order inclination to want to understand a character as "good" or "bad" gets challenged. The result is an uptick in our attentiveness; subtly rebuffed by the story, we get, we might say, a new respect for its truthfulness. Here we'd just about settled into a simple view of Marya as a completely innocent, blameless victim of a harsh system. But then the story says, "Well, hold on; isn't one quality of a harsh system that it deforms the people within it and makes them complicit in their own destruction?" (Which is another way of saying: "Let's not forget that Marya is a human being, and complicated, and susceptible to error.")

Hers is still a sad situation, but now we understand that she contributed to it, by not having the wherewithal to rise to the occasion of the work. I revise her slightly in my mind: she's limited, a bit less capable.

On the other hand, what kind of Russia is this that compels a person to work a job to which she has no calling, and be so reduced by it? To have to collect funds and teach in a drafty room and get no support from the community? How could anyone love that life? (I find myself thinking of Terry Eagleton's assertion that "capitalism plunders the sensuality of the body.")

Just imagine the many Maryas who have existed, all over the world, their best selves sacrificed to exigency, whose grace suffered under the pressure of being poorly suited to the toil required of them to make a living. (Maybe, like me, you've been one of them yourself.)

As we've been saying, the story form is ruthlessly efficient. Everything in a story should be to purpose. Our working assumption is that nothing exists in a story by chance or merely to serve some documentary function. Every element should be a little poem, freighted with subtle meaning that is in connection with the story's purpose.

Honoring this principle—let's call it the Ruthless Efficiency Principle (REP)—as our cart enters a town (Nizhneye Gorodishche), we find ourselves asking, "What is the purpose of this town?" And because it is a town in a story, the only possible answer is: "This town is here to do some work the story needs it to do." So what we should actually ask is: "What is the purpose of *this* town? Why this town, and not another?"

Watch your mind as you read this paragraph toward the end of page 7, to see what Chekhov wants us to notice:

They reached Nizhneye Gorodishche. Near the teahouse, on the dung-strewn, snowy ground, there stood wagons loaded with great bottles of oil of vitriol. There were a great many people in the teahouse, all drivers, and it smelled of vodka, tobacco, and sheepskins. The place was noisy with loud talk and the banging of the door which was provided with a pulley. In the shop next door someone was playing an accordion steadily.

Now, this is a good description—that door pulley makes it come especially alive for me—but it's also a pointed description. As we follow Marya inside, Chekhov wants to convey something to us. As we read, scanning for implication, we find ourselves collecting "negative" words, like "dung-strewn," "vitriol," "smelled," "noisy," "loud," and "banging." Adding in the party sounds and the perpetual droning accordion, we conclude that Chekhov wants to communicate: *this is a rough place*.

Consider this differently flavored version:

> Near the teahouse, on the white, snowy ground, stood wagons loaded with generous containers of oranges and apples, shipped from exotic, faraway places. There were a great many people in the teahouse, all drivers, and it smelled of tea and something baking in a tremendous oven at one end of the room. The place was noisy with happy talk, and the constant joyful opening and closing of the door made for a festive, welcoming feeling. In the shop next door, someone was playing a lighthearted dance tune on an accordion.

Such a town could exist, has existed somewhere, but Chekhov didn't need that one.

So: a lonely woman, discontented with her life, which she feels is beneath her, walks into a rough place, a place into which, in the life she was meant to have had, she would never have set foot.

The movie producer and all-around mensch Stuart Cornfeld once told me that in a good screenplay, every structural unit needs to do two things: (1) be entertaining in its own right and (2) advance the story in a non-trivial way.

We will henceforth refer to this as "the Cornfeld Principle."

In a mediocre story, nothing much will happen inside the teahouse. The teahouse is there to allow the writer to supply local color, to tell us what such a place is like. Or something might happen in there, but it won't mean much. Some plates will fall and get broken, a ray of sunlight will come randomly through the window to no purpose, just because rays of sunlight do that in the real world, a dog will run in and run out, because the writer recently saw a real dog do that in a real teahouse. All of this may be "entertaining in its own right" (lively, funny, described in vivid language, etc.) but is not "advancing the story in a non-trivial way."

When a story is "advanced in a non-trivial way," we get the local color *and* something else. The characters go into the scene in one state and leave in another. The story becomes a more particular version of itself; it refines the question it's been asking all along.

So, what happens here?

A "pockmarked peasant" swears. (This falls into the category of local color.) Then Semyon reacts to the swearing by calling the peasant's attention to Marya's presence. ("Don't you see the young lady?")

In workshop, we talk a lot about "raising the stakes" of a story. Semyon just did this. There was a bare wire labeled "Marya" and a bare wire labeled "Peasants in a Teahouse" and electricity was coursing through each but they were laid out parallel to one another, several feet apart.

Semyon, by reacting to the swearing, just crossed them. Marya and those gathered peasants had nothing to do with one another, were not in relation. Now they do, and are.

Someone "jeers" at Semyon's characterization of Marya: "The young lady!" (Meaning both: "You call her *young*?" and "You call her a *lady*?")

Suddenly the room is full of tension. Marya has been insulted twice: indirectly, by the initial swearing, and directly, by the jeer. We feel the potential for this room of peasants to turn on this "elite" schoolteacher. Who's there to defend her?

The tension gets defused by that sweet little pockmarked peasant, whom I always imagine looking like Sleepy of the Seven Dwarfs (doffing his hat, in my mind, as he apologizes). Marya accepts his apology. "How do you do?" she says stiffly, afraid, maybe, that this will escalate further.

So: a close call, one that underscores Marya's tenuous position among the rabble. Had that swearing peasant been a different swearing peasant, it could have been worse. (It will be worse, in about twenty years, when the Russian Revolution breaks out and some of these same peasants march up the road and seize Hanov's estate.)

What is Marya's reaction? She drinks her tea "with pleasure." She could have done so "with shaking hands" or "near tears." But no. Maybe, it occurs to us, this isn't such an unusual experience for her. (We took it harder than she did.) She's likely been in this teahouse many times before, on other trips to and from town. Maybe this low-level taunting has happened before?

Our understanding of Marya has been refined again. This is not the story of a woman only just now falling in the world. It is the story of someone who fell some time ago and is so used to her fallen state that she's no longer particularly outraged about it. She fell, is still falling, may fall further still. She's nearly a peasant herself.

Has the scene fulfilled the Cornfeld Principle? I think it has. Though she has previously presented herself, through her inner monologues, as a woman fallen into a life among the rabble, we maybe didn't really believe her. Now we do. In those monologues (as in, I suppose, all of our inner monologues) she retained control, by subtly judging Semyon and Hanov, and through the very act of intelligent reflection. But now we've seen how precarious her position really is. In fact, it's worse than she knows. She's become blind to how far she's fallen—but now we know.

Imagine a person walking along a street thinking it might be time to buy a new suit. This one he's wearing is pretty great, and people are always complimenting it, but what the heck, he should treat himself. On his way to the store, he passes some teenagers, who make a joke about how old-fashioned and crappy his suit is.

We feel pity for him, but we also suddenly see his suit.

Having seen the difference between Marya's internally narrated version of herself and her actual position in the world, I find myself feeling more tenderness for her, and more protective of her. This more complicated, endangered Marya is the one I take with me to the end of the story.

Which is now (take heart) three pages away.

. . .

"Vasilyevna, get ready," Semyon called to her.

They drove off. And again they went at a walking pace.

"A little while back they were building a school here at this Nizh-neye Gorodishche," said Semyon, turning round. "There were wicked doings then!"

"Why, what?"

"They say the chairman pocketed a cool thousand, and the Trustee another thousand, and the teacher five hundred."

"The whole school only cost a thousand. It's wrong to slander people, grandfather. That's all nonsense." [9]

"I don't know. I only repeat what folks say."

But it was clear that Semyon did not believe the schoolmistress. The peasants did not believe her. They always thought she received too large a salary, twenty-one rubles a month (five would have been enough), and that she kept for herself the greater part of the money that she received for firewood and for the janitor's wages. The Trustee thought as the peasants did, and he himself made something on the firewood and received a salary from the peasants for acting as Trustee—without the knowledge of the authorities.

The woods, thank God, were behind them, and now it would be clear, level ground all the way to Vyazovye, and they had not far to go now. All they had to do was to cross the river and then the railway line, and then they would be at Vyazovye.

"Where are you going?" Marya Vasilyevna asked Semyon. "Take the road to the right across the bridge."

"Why, we can go this way just as well, it's not so deep."

"Mind you don't drown the horse."

"What?"

"Look, Hanov is driving to the bridge, too," said Marya Vasil-yevna, seeing the four-horse team far away to the right. "I think it's he."

"It's him all right. So he didn't find Bakvist in. What a blockhead he is. Lord have mercy on us! He's driving over there, and what for? It's all of two miles nearer this way."

They reached the river. In summer it was a shallow stream, easily forded and usually dried up by August, but now, after the spring floods, it was a river forty feet wide, rapid, muddy, and cold; on the bank, and right up to the water, there were fresh wheel tracks, so it had been crossed there.

"Giddap!" shouted Semyon angrily and anxiously, tugging violently at the reins and flapping his elbows as a bird does its wings. "Giddap!"

The horse went into the water up to its belly and stopped, but at once went on again, straining its muscles, and Marya Vasilyevna felt [10] a sharp chill in her feet.

"Giddap!" she shouted, too, standing up. "Giddap!"

They got to the bank.

"Nice mess, Lord have mercy on us!" muttered Semyon, setting the harness straight. "It's an affliction, this Zemstvo."

Her shoes and rubbers were full of water, the lower edge of her dress and of her coat and one sleeve were wet and dripping; the sugar and flour had got wet, and that was the worst of it, and Marya Vasilyevna only struck her hands together in despair and said:

"Oh, Semyon, Semyon! What a fellow you are, really!"

. . .

A word here about variation.

Back in the cart, Semyon again begins to gossip, this time about some "wicked doings" in the town they've just left. Earlier, Semyon was correct in a bit of gossip he was passing along (about the assassination of the mayor of Moscow) and Marya didn't believe him/wasn't interested. Here, it seems, he's *in*correct, and she *is* interested, and corrects him. It might have been the case that, both times, Semyon was passing along incorrect gossip and Marya was interested and corrected him. Again, Chekhov's instinct seems to be toward variation, against stasis. One of his gifts is an ability to naturally impose variety on a situation that a lesser writer would leave static.

Because of the variation in his presentation, we're able to read Semyon two ways at once: as a nineteenth-century Russian version of a conspiracy theorist, always willing to believe the worst of anyone in power, and as someone who, though he lives in the same low milieu as Marya, has managed to maintain a lively (although erratically precise) interest in the things going on around him.

Marya, on the other hand, isn't interested in "world events," only in what is local and might affect her already tenuous status in the community. (And after that experience in the teahouse, we don't blame her.) This also explains the tendency we've observed for her mind to always be turning back to the school. It's a self-protective, border-assessing move. She's obsessing about the one thing over which she might actually still have some control.

Notice, too, that we're reading Semyon and Marya against one another. They're like two dolls in a box, fallen into different postures. He's interested in the world; she's not. He speculates; she doesn't. They both distrust the system (although for different reasons). He's a peasant; she nearly is. And so on.

And, actually, there are three dolls in there: Marya, Semyon, and Hanov. Without even meaning to, we're continually scanning the three for similarities and differences. We group Marya and Semyon together because they're from the same town and are in the same cart; Marya and Hanov together because they're younger and of a higher social class than Semyon and are a possible (although apparently not all that possible) couple; Semyon and Hanov together because both of them represent "people less intelligent than Marya, with whom she must cope." But each person is also solitary in his or her own way: Marya the only woman, Semyon the only peasant, Hanov the only landowner.

A story is not like real life; it's like a table with just a few things on it. The "meaning" of the table is made by the choice of things and their relation to one another. Imagine these things on a table: a gun, a grenade, a hatchet, a ceramic statue of a duck. If the duck is at the center of the table, surrounded closely by the weapons, we feel: that duck is in trouble. If the duck, the gun, and the grenade have the hatchet pinned down in one corner, we may feel the duck to be leading the modern weaponry (the gun, the grenade) against the (old-fashioned) hatchet. If the three weapons are each hanging precipitously over one edge of the table and the duck is facing them, we might understand the duck to be a radical pacifist who's finally had enough.

That's really all a story is: a limited set of elements that we read against one another.

Well, at least from here (middle of page 9), the trip will be easy. They're literally out of the woods, all level ground ahead. Chekhov gives us a simple, useful-for-visualization-purposes map of the landscape to come: "All they had to do was to cross the river and then the railway line."

There's a bridge nearby but Semyon has a plan. He'll ford the river, which is "not so deep," saving them some time. Hanov reappears in the story, hypercautiously (prudently?) headed for the bridge. Note that Marya doesn't give Hanov a thought (no reawakening of hope, no quickening heartbeat). This confirms our idea that her ruminations about Hanov have been idle, not really serious.

From the timing, Semyon concludes that Hanov, the "blockhead," didn't, after all, find his friend at home. So, Hanov's whole trip has been a waste.

They reach the river.

Before we let Semyon urge the horse forward, let's ask: Why did Chekhov go to the trouble of creating this river? He could have just run the cart straight into town, across a stretch of dry road. It must be the case that something useful to his purpose is going to happen during the crossing. (A linked pair of writing dictums: "Don't make things happen for no reason" and "Having made something happen, make it matter.")

"In summer [the river] was a shallow stream . . . but now . . . it was a river forty feet wide." So: it will be a challenge to cross. And yet, wheel marks indicate that someone has recently crossed it. This moment feels like a test of competence between Semyon and Hanov. Which version of reality is correct: (A) "Semyon, a smug peasant, dismissing the more intelligent gentry, tries to cross an unfordable river with disastrous results" or (B) "Semyon, a man of the people, to save time, reasonably does what others like him have recently done, unlike that clueless gentleman Hanov, who wastes his time playing it safe for no reason"?

Marya has no say in the matter, and is going to have to just sit there bearing the brunt of whatever happens, even though she's the main character and the smartest, most self-aware person in the story.

It's touch-and-go at first. Water comes rushing into the cart. They make it across and Semyon (conspiracy theorist to the end) blames . . . the local government (the "Zemstvo"). It's "an affliction" to live here. ("It's not me, it's this *town*!") Meanwhile Hanov continues, we imagine, to plod toward the bridge.

Who wins? Well, Semyon, sort of, but Marya's shoes are full of water, her dress is wet, and worst of all, the sugar and flour (her "purchases"), on which she's presumably just spent a good portion of her paycheck, are ruined.

"Oh, Semyon, Semyon!" she says. "What a fellow you are, really!"

This is such a sad moment: the one humble pleasure she sought (if we can consider acquiring basic staples for one's tiny room "a pleasure"), even that, she can't have.

Hanov has wasted a day on a trip with no tangible result.

So has Marya.

Above, we asked why Chekhov went to the trouble of putting this river into the story. He did it, apparently, to ruin Marya's purchases.

And why did he need to do that?

We carry that question forward.

As a young writer I once got a rejection that was full of praise but concluded with this: "It's fast and funny and wild . . . but we aren't sure it's a *story*." That was, you know . . . maddening. (I felt: If it's fast and funny and wild, isn't that enough, you dopes?) But I understand now. A short story is not just a series of events, one following after another. It's not a lively narrative that briskly continues for a number of pages, then stops. It's a narrative that compels us to finish reading it, yes, but that, in the midst of itself, somehow rises or expands and becomes . . . enough.

When I was a kid, Lipton had a TV commercial with the catchphrase "Is it soup yet?"

We're always asking, of a work we're reading (even if it's one of our own): "Is it *story* yet?"

That's the moment we're seeking as we write. We're revising and revising until we write the text up, so to speak, and it produces that "now it's a story" feeling.

One good way to investigate what causes that feeling: experimentally truncate a good story before the point where its creator actually ended it. Just cut it off and observe your reaction to that imposed ending. The resulting feeling will tell us something about what's missing. Or, conversely, about what the remaining text does supply, once we read it, that completes the transformation from "narrative" to "story."

So, how about we end the story right here, at the end of the section we've just read, like so:

"Oh Semyon, Semyon! What a fellow you are, really!"

THE END.

Go back to the beginning and scan through the story, ending it there. How does that strike you? What does the story, ended that way, seem to be "saying"? What is it lacking? (What bowling pins are still in the air?)

The feeling I get is: "No, not a story yet."

Let's see if we can figure out why.

Earlier, we suggested that the simplest statement of the story's idea of itself was:

Lonely woman encounters possible lover.

We've moved past that now, to something like:

Lonely woman encounters possible lover, who might assuage her loneliness but doesn't, and she (and we) realize that this was an empty hope anyway, and then she's borderline humiliated in a teahouse, and the ostensible purpose for her trip (her purchases) is negated.

THE END.

Truncated like this, the story feels anecdotal and harsh: *a series of bad things happen to a nice lady we like and then she goes back home in worse shape than when she left.* (This describes millions of days that have been lived in the real world, but it isn't "a *story*.")

In workshop we sometimes say that what makes a piece of writing a story is that something happens within it that changes the character forever. (That's a bit Draconian, but let's go with it as a starting place.) So, we tell a certain story, starting at one time and ending at another, in order to frame that moment of change. (We don't tell the story of the week before those three ghosts show up to haunt Scrooge, or Romeo's tenth-birthday party, or that period in Luke Skywalker's life when not all that much was going on.)

Why did Chekhov choose to narrate this day in Marya's life? To ask it another way: What has changed, today, for Marya? Is she a different person from the woman we met on the first page? It doesn't seem like it. Has anything new happened to her? I don't think so. She's met Hanov many times before and, as mentioned, we suspect she's had romantic and hopeful thoughts about him before, but things are going nowhere with him and she knows this very well. She was insulted in the teahouse but took it in stride, and although this reaction changed our view of her, and therefore felt like an escalation, it didn't change her view of herself. (We know this because of the way she drank her post-insult tea "with pleasure" and returned immediately to thinking about the school.)

What we're really asking is: What might happen (what needs to happen) over the remaining seven paragraphs to elevate this into a *story*?

It's kind of exciting to pause here and admit that, as things stand, it's not a story. Not yet. And I'm going to claim, right now, that by the end, it's going to be a great story.

So, there's something essential to learn here about the form itself: whatever converts *not yet a story* into *great story* is going to happen any minute now, over this next (last) page.

. . .

The barrier was down at the railway crossing. An express was coming from the station. Marya Vasilyevna stood at the crossing waiting for the train to pass, and shivering all over with cold. Vyazovye was in sight now, and the school with the green roof, and the church with its blazing crosses that reflected the setting sun; and the station windows were aflame, too, and a pink smoke rose from the engine. . . . And it seemed to her that everything was shivering with cold.

Here was the train; the windows, like the crosses on the church, reflected the blazing light; it hurt her eyes to look at them. On the platform of one of the first-class carriages a lady was standing, and Marya Vasilyevna glanced at her as she flashed by. Her mother! [11] What a resemblance! Her mother had had just such luxuriant hair, just such a forehead and that way of holding her head. And with amazing distinctness, for the first time in those thirteen years, she imagined vividly her mother, her father, her brother, their apartment in Moscow, the aquarium with the little fishes, everything down to the smallest detail; she suddenly heard the piano playing, her father's voice; she felt as then, young, good-looking, well-dressed, in a bright warm room among her own people. A feeling of joy and happiness suddenly overwhelmed her, she pressed her hands to her temples in ecstasy, and called softly, imploringly:

"Mama!"

And she began to cry, she did not know why. Just at that moment Hanov drove up with his team of four horses, and seeing him she imagined such happiness as had never been, and smiled and nodded to him as an equal and an intimate, and it seemed to her that the sky, the windows, the trees, were glowing with her happiness, her triumph. No, her father and mother had never died, she had never been a schoolmistress, that had been a long, strange, oppressive dream, and now she had awakened . . .

"Vasilyevna, get in!"

And suddenly it all vanished. The barrier was slowly rising. Marya Vasilyevna, shivering and numb with cold, got into the cart. The carriage with the four horses crossed the railway track, Semyon followed. The guard at the crossing took off his cap.

"And this is Vyazovye. Here we are." ✦

The railway barrier is down (a train is about to pass). Across the tracks they see home, the village of Vyazovye. Chekhov describes specific buildings, including Marya's enslaving workplace, "the school with the green roof," at a specific moment of the day: sundown. What does the setting sun do to buildings? It lights them up. Which parts, specifically? The crosses and the station windows. (Note the difference between this and "The town lay before them, looking just like every other small Russian village.")

Here comes the train. Chekhov remembers that he's just said that the sun, going down, lights things up. So, the windows on the train get lit up too. The result: Marya can't look directly at them. She looks, instead, at a first-class platform. And sees . . . her mother. (Note the tight causality in here, one thing causing the next.) Immediately, Chekhov corrects (has Marya correct) this misperception: "What a resemblance!" Is she reasonable in mistaking this woman for her mother? Yes. Chekhov proves it, via specificity. What is similar? The woman's hair, her forehead, the way she holds her head.

This causes a rush of forgotten memories: "for the first time in those thirteen years," she vividly imagines her early life in Moscow.

Hold this paragraph up against that earlier paragraph in which she recalled her childhood (first paragraph, page 2). In that description, there was no aquarium with its little fishes, no piano, no singing, no associated feeling of well-being. When she thought back to her childhood earlier (just a few hours ago), all she could honestly recall was "something vague and formless like a dream." Now her mind is full of specifics. That vague version of her childhood has been corrected. These recalled details alter her view of herself. She was once someone else, someone with a home, someone who was loved, someone "young, good-looking, well-dressed, in a bright warm room among her own people," someone safe and cared for.

She is overwhelmed by "a feeling of joy and happiness."

"Mama!" she calls, and starts to cry and "she did not know why."

If we've been waiting for an end to her unhappiness, here it is. Relief has arrived in the form of a memory. She recalls who she once was. She *is* who she once was.

Will this new state of happiness abide? (Will it change her forever?)

We see why Chekhov has told us the story of this day, and not another. This didn't happen to her yesterday or on any previous day over those thirteen nightmarish years.

Just today, for the first time.

It might be useful to pause here and read those two paragraphs about her childhood in sequence. Look at the overlap (Moscow, an apartment) but also the additions in the second iteration: the aquarium, the piano, the love, the sense of belonging. That's escalation. Had Chekhov given the same description both times, that would be stasis. ("I went to the store and it was hot in there and I saw Todd. Later, I went to the store and it was hot in there and I saw Todd.") Having recalled those memories, Marya is literally not the same person she was just seconds before. And we feel this as an escalation; suddenly, the person she used to be (beloved, special, cared for) wakes up into this scary new reality. We feel the shock of it. ("I'm a near-peasant teacher in a crummy provincial school? What? Me? *Marya?*") but we also feel her joy at being restored to herself, to her real self.

I love this new, suddenly elated Marya. (I see how miserable she's been all those years, and how brave.)

We've said that a story is a system for the transfer of energy. Energy made in the early pages gets transferred along through the story, passed from section to section, like a bucket of water headed for a fire, and the hope is that not a drop gets lost.

Note the beautiful, dominoes-falling effect of the causation here: the early energy of our pity for Marya (which made us hope she would get some relief, which we mistakenly thought might come from Hanov) was deepened by this terrible day, a day that culminated in the ruining of her purchases, and the cumulative pain of the day caused her to mistake a stranger for her mother, which, in turn, caused her to remember who she used to be, which gave her the first instant of happiness we've seen her experience the whole time we've known her, poor thing, which is to say, since the beginning of the story.

She's been rejuvenated, remade into that carefree, happy, hopeful young girl she used to be. She's like a superhero whose powers have suddenly returned.

And here, I always feel that this harsh world she's been living in is about to receive a correction.

I hope so, anyway.

Hanov pulls up. Whatever time Semyon saved by fording the river has been erased by their need to wait for the train to pass, and it's all a wash: Hanov is just as clever as Semyon and vice versa, i.e., not very. Nobody, in this Russia, is clever enough to defeat the generalized tedium—gentry and peasants equally inept, the Maryas of the world, who see things somewhat clearly, caught in the middle.

Seeing Hanov, Marya "imagined such happiness as had never been, and smiled and nodded to him as an equal and an intimate" (both of which she has earlier, on page 5, in nearly identical language, rejected as impossible).

"And it seemed to her that the sky, the windows, the trees, were glowing with her happiness" and also, oddly, with "her triumph." What is her "triumph"? Well, she's been restored to the girl she once was. Her parents haven't died, she has "never been a schoolmistress." No degradation has occurred. It was all "a long, strange, oppressive dream," from which she has now awakened.

She is happy again, proud again, a full human being again, at last.

She's happy, but still alone. (But is she still lonely?)

Here, a few lines from the end, can you imagine a version of the story in which this sudden confidence, this new sense of herself as someone worth loving, changes her so much that Hanov notices the difference, and sees her as if for the first time, and—

Well, I bet you can. I can. I do, every time I get here.

But no.

Semyon calls for her to "get in," i.e., "get back into this cart that is your actual life." Suddenly "it all vanished." The story has already told us that a relationship between them is impossible, and it is, it still is. There's not another mention of Hanov, only of his carriage: "The carriage with the four horses crossed the railway track." There is that strange and somehow perfect detail of the guard taking off his cap to her. ("Welcome back, madam, to your loneliness.")

And they're home, and the story's over.

How sad, how sad, how utterly truthful.

Why couldn't Hanov have been charmed?

Well, the best answer is that the story is more beautiful if he's not. If he were charmed, this would imply that the only reason he hasn't been charmed before is that Marya's never been this happy before (never before this attractive). In other words, the story would be understood to be saying, "All Marya had to do to be loved was be *more*." That's a less interesting story, even a trivial one. Besides, it contradicts what's already been made clear: these two aren't meant for one another. No amount of happiness glow is going to bridge the gap between them, and it would feel false, and forced, if it did.

Does Hanov acknowledge this change in her? He doesn't seem to. Either he misses that smile-and-nod or he notices but it inspires nothing in him—not a cheerful goodbye or a return nod-and-smile, much less a declaration of love. Is it possible that he doesn't notice the change? Sure, and, if so, all of those "Hanov is a doofus" moments pay off. (This is a guy so oblivious, he doesn't notice it when a woman has just shucked off thirteen years of misery.)

In any event, Marya doesn't care. Her attention is not on Hanov, but on the sky, the windows, and the trees, which are glowing with her happiness, and on the "triumph" of her sudden restoration to her true self.

What has happened to her is profound, and has nothing to do with Hanov: something long-dead just flickered back alive in her.

And the light we imagine in her eyes at that moment is where all the energy the story has created is being held.

We've said that a story frames a moment of change, saying, implicitly: "This is the day on which things changed forever." A variant of that says, "This is the day on which things almost changed forever, but didn't." Before the moment at the train tracks, "In the Cart" was a variant of that variant, saying, "This is the day on which it appeared that things might have changed forever, but then they didn't, because they never could have, of course" (the story of a brief, deceptive welling up of hope). At the train tracks, the story becomes: "This is the day on which things did, in fact, change forever, but in a way we didn't expect, that might be for better and might be for worse."

If we feel we are nothing and have always been nothing, that's one story. But if we feel that we are nothing and then, in one miraculous instant, remember that, once, we were something—is that a happier story or a sadder one?

Well, depends.

We wonder (the story has caused us to wonder): What will be the aftereffects of Marya's momentary feeling of power and confidence? Has this experience "changed her forever"? Will she still feel that way tomorrow? Will the knowledge that she was once young and beloved stay alive in her and inflect the way she lives?

The penultimate paragraph disposes us to think not; the phrase "shivering and numb with cold" indicates a reversion to her previous state, especially read against the fact that, at her peak moment of happiness, things were "glowing," a word we associate with warmth.

But one feature of a beautifully ended story is that we can imagine the lives of the characters continuing on beyond it. I can imagine this experience making Marya's life better, existing as a secret place she sometimes returns to as she rushes around that dismal schoolhouse. I can also imagine it making her life worse: a recurring taunt, a reminder of how far she's fallen.

And I can imagine the saddest outcome of all, consistent with her life so far: after a few more weeks (months, years) of this dulling life, she forgets about her moment of illumination at the train tracks entirely, the way she once forgot about that childhood aquarium.

What makes this such a human-scaled and heartbreaking description of loneliness, real loneliness, loneliness as it actually occurs in the world, is that we've watched Marya go through all of this from a position inside her. A story with less internality might have produced a simple feeling of pity ("Oh, that poor, lonely person"). We'd understand Marya as the Lesser Other. But the story's virtuosic internality implicates her, even as it draws us in. She's not a perfect person who is lonely. She's an imperfect person who is lonely. We feel pity for lonely imperfect Marya in the same way we would feel pity for someone lonely and imperfect we loved, or for imperfect (lonely) us.

—

We might think of a story this way: the reader is sitting in the sidecar of a motorcycle the writer is driving. In a well-told story, reader and writer are so close together that they're one unit. My job as the writer is to keep the distance between motorcycle and sidecar small, so that when I go right, you go right. When I, at the end of the story, take the motorcycle off the cliff, you have no choice but to follow. (I haven't, so far, given you any reason to distance yourself from me.) If the space between motorcycle and sidecar gets too great, when I corner, you fail to hear about it, and fall out of relationship with me and get bored or irritated and stop reading and go off to watch a movie. Then there's no character development or plot or voice or politics or theme. There's no anything.

Chekhov has kept us so close to Marya that we've essentially become her. He gave us no reason to put any emotional distance between ourselves and Marya and, on the contrary, has described the working of her mind so well that he seems at times to have been describing the workings of our minds. We are Marya and Marya is us, but us in a different life, one in which we are irremediably lonely.

Does the story solve the problem of loneliness? Suggest a solution? No. It seems to say that such loneliness has always been with us and always will be. As long as there's love, there'll be people who aren't loved. As long as there's wealth, there'll be poverty. As long as there's excitement, there'll be dullness. The story's conclusion, essentially, is: "Yes, that's how it is in this world."

But the true beauty of a story is not in its apparent conclusion but in the alteration in the mind of the reader that has occurred along the way.

Chekhov once said, "Art doesn't have to solve problems, it only has to formulate them correctly." "Formulate them correctly" might be taken to mean: "make us feel the problem fully, without denying any part of it."

We really feel Marya's loneliness now. We feel it as our own. We know, if we didn't before, that loneliness beyond relief is possible, and is all around us, in people showing no outward signs of it, as they go into town, pick up their checks, head quietly home (or stand in line at the post office, or sit in a car at a stoplight, singing with the radio).

Over the course of these eleven pages, the blank mind with which you began has been filled with a new friend, Marya, who, if my experience is any indication, will stay with you forever. And next time you hear someone described as "lonely," you may, because of your friendship with Marya, find yourself more inclined to think of that person tenderly, even though you haven't met her yet.

AFTERTHOUGHT #1

Should the teachers among us want to try a shorter in-class version of this annoying one-page-at-a-time exercise, I'd recommend using a Hemingway story called "Cat in the Rain." What I do is photocopy the whole story (around twelve hundred words), then cut it into six "pages" of approximately two hundred words each. Have everybody silently read the first page, then ask, as we did above: (1) What do you know so far? (2) What are you curious about? and (3) Where do you think the story is headed? (What bowling pins are in the air?)

Toward the end of the story, pick a place at which to truncate it and ask the "Is it *story* yet?" question.

Doing this exercise, students get a real sense of how constructed and exaggerated a story really is. This little story offers a great chance to talk, in particular, about escalation. It's quiet but never sits still. There's a subtle escalatory development in just about every paragraph.

To review: a story is a linear-temporal phenomenon.

Actually, that's any work of art. We know what we think of a movie even a few minutes in. We step up to a painting with a blank mind, look at it, and the mind fills up. In a concert hall, we're either riveted right away or wondering what that guy in the balcony's texting about.

A story is a series of incremental pulses, each of which does something to us. Each puts us in a new place, relative to where we just were. Criticism is not some inscrutable, mysterious process. It's just a matter of: (1) noticing ourselves responding to a work of art, moment by moment, and (2) getting better at articulating that response.

What I stress to my students is how empowering this process is. The world is full of people with agendas, trying to persuade us to act on their behalf (spend on their behalf, fight and die on their behalf, oppress others on their behalf). But inside us is what Hemingway called a "built-in, shockproof, shit detector." How do we know something is shit? We watch the way the deep, honest part of our mind reacts to it.

And that part of the mind is the one that reading and writing refine into sharpness.

We can do this page-at-a-time exercise using other art forms as well.

For example, there's a sequence in the film *Bicycle Thieves* that starts about fifty-four minutes in. The events in that sequence are: A father and his son are searching for the father's stolen bicycle. A lead they're following slips away, because of a mistake the father makes. When the son asks him about this, the father slaps the son, who starts crying. The father tells the son to wait on a bridge while he goes down to search by the river.

Then the father hears some commotion: a boy is apparently drowning. He thinks, and we think, that it might be the son. But no: the son appears at the top of a long flight of stairs, on the bridge, just where he was told to wait.

Father and son walk along the river. Feeling bad about that slap, the father checks his wallet, then proposes an extravagance: they'll go for pizza. At the restaurant, they're seated near a wealthy family. The son curiously observes a rich boy his age. Noting this, the father, moved to honesty, opens up to the boy. (The wound of the slap is healed.)

In class, watching this sequence over and over, we start noticing things we missed the first time through. For example: When the father and the son are walking sadly along the river, the boy walks on one side of a tree, the father on the other. But as they approach the next tree, the boy swerves over, and father and son pass on the same side of it. (We read this as "possible reconciliation pending?") A truck full of celebrating soccer fans goes past (they, unlike the father and the son, are happy). The father notices his son noticing the young men in the truck and this, we suspect, combined with the shame he feels about that slap, produces the idea of taking the boy to a restaurant. (But first, he checks his wallet.) As this sweet little scene of reconciliation plays out, behind them in the frame is a loving couple, looking out at the river.

It's a lesser sequence without those trees, that truck full of happy fans, that wallet check, that loving couple.

One of the pleasures of this exercise is watching my students as they start to realize that, yes, wow, the director, Vittorio De Sica, really did take that much care. Every aspect of every frame has been carefully considered and lovingly used, and this is part of the reason the sequence moved them the first time they watched it. That is: De Sica was taking responsibility for every single thing in his film.

Of course he was. *Bicycle Thieves* is a great work of art and De Sica is an artist, and that's what an artist does: takes responsibility.

THE SINGERS

Ivan Turgenev

(1852)

THE SINGERS

―――――

The small village of Kolotovka, which once belonged to a lady nicknamed in the neighborhood "Mistress Trouncer," because of her vicious and uncontrollable temper (her real name is not recorded), and now owned by some Petersburg German, lies on the slope of a bare hill cleft from top to bottom by a terrible ravine. Yawning like a chasm, this ravine winds its torn and eroded way across the very middle of the village street, dividing the poor little village in two, worse than any river (for a river could at least be bridged). A few spindly willows cling precariously to its sandy sides; at the bottom, dry and reddish like copper, lie huge flagstones of shale. A cheerless sight—no doubt about it—and yet the road to Kolotovka is well known to the people in the neighborhood: they go there readily and often.

At the very top of the ravine, a few yards from the spot where it begins as a narrow crack in the ground, a small square peasant's cottage stands solitary, apart from the others. It is thatched and has a chimney; a single window, like a watchful eye, looks toward the ravine and, lighted up from within on winter evenings, can be seen from afar through the dim frosty haze, shining like a guiding star to many a peasant who happens to be driving that way. Over the door of the cottage is nailed a little blue board; the cottage is a country pub, known as the Cozy Corner. In this pub, drinks are in all probability sold no cheaper than the fixed price, but it is much better attended than all similar establishments in the neighborhood, and the reason for that is the publican Nikolai Ivanych.

Nikolai Ivanych was once a slender, curly-headed and rosy-cheeked lad, but now he has grown into an inordinately fat and gray-haired man with a bloated face, a pair of sly, genial little eyes, and a fleshy forehead with deep furrows running right across it. He has lived in Kolotovka for over twenty years. Nikolai Ivanych is a wide-awake, resourceful fellow, as indeed most publicans are. Without being particularly amiable or talkative, he has the knack of attracting and keeping customers, who somehow feel at ease sitting in front of his counter, under the calm and affable, though rather watchful, eye of their phlegmatic host. He has a great deal of common sense, and he is well acquainted with the mode of life of the landowner, the peasant, and the tradesman; in difficult circumstances he could give good advice, were it not for the fact that as a cautious man and an egoist he prefers to keep his own counsel and guide his customers (and only those he particularly favors) out of trouble's way by rather obscure and indirect hints, dropped, as it were, in passing. He is an excellent judge of what a true Russian considers to be either interesting or important: of horses and cattle, timber, bricks, crockery, textiles, leather, singing, and dancing. When there are no customers he can usually be seen sitting like a sack on the ground in front of his cottage, his thin legs tucked up under him, exchanging pleasantries with every passer-by. He has seen much in his life, outlived more than a dozen of the small landowners who used to drop in for a glass of vodka; he knows everything that happens for a hundred miles round but never breathes a word about it and does not ever let on that he knows what even the most astute district police officer does not so much as suspect. All he does is keep mum, chuckle to himself quietly, and busy himself with the glasses.

[2]

His neighbors respect him: one of them, a certain Shcherepenko, a civil servant of the rank of a general and one of the most influential landowners in the neighborhood, always bows to him courteously when driving past his little cottage. Nikolai Ivanych is a man of influence too: he forced a well-known horse thief to return a horse stolen from one of his acquaintances; he made the peasants of a neighboring village listen to reason when they refused to accept a new agent; and so on. However, it would be a mistake to think that he did it all out of love of justice, or out of zeal for the welfare of his neighbors. No! He was simply trying to nip in the bud anything that might disturb his peace of mind.

Nikolai Ivanych is married and has children. His wife, a brisk, sharp-nosed, and quick-eyed tradeswoman, has also put on a good deal of weight lately, just like her husband. He defers to her judgment in everything, and she keeps a tight hand on the purse-strings. Rowdy drunkards are afraid of her; she dislikes them, for there is little profit and a lot of noise from them; she would much rather deal with the silent and gloomy ones. Nikolai Ivanych's children are still small; the first all died, and those who survived resemble their parents: it makes one feel good to look at the clever little faces of these healthy children.

It was an unbearably hot July day when, scarcely able to drag one foot after the other, I walked slowly, accompanied by my dog, up the Kolotovka ravine in the direction of the Cozy Corner. The sun was blazing away in the sky with a kind of fury; it was scorchingly, piteously hot; the air was saturated with choking dust. The rooks and crows, their feathers gleaming in the sunlight, gazed dolefully at the passers-by, their beaks gaping, as though begging them for sympathy; the sparrows alone did not seem to mind and, fluffing up their feathers, went on chirping more furiously than ever as they kept fighting each other along the fences, flying up from the dusty road in flocks and hovering in gray clouds over the green hemp fields. I was tortured by thirst. There was no water anywhere near: in Kolotovka, as in many another steppe village, there are no springs or wells, and the peasants drink a sort of liquid filth from the pond— but who would give the name of *water* to that horrible hogwash? I was thinking of asking Nikolai Ivanych for a glass of beer, or kvas.

It must be admitted that at no season of the year does Kolotovka present a cheerful sight; but it arouses a particularly mournful feeling when the blazing July sun glares down with its pitiless rays upon the half-crumbling brown roofs, the deep ravine, the scorched, dust-laden common on which some lean, long-legged chickens are wandering about despondently, the gray aspen-timbered shell of a former mansion, grown over with nettles, weeds, and wormwood, and the pond, black and almost incandescent, covered with goose feathers, with its fringe of half-dried mud and its lopsided dam; near the dam, on the fine, trampled, cinder-like earth, sheep, hardly able to draw their breath and sneezing from the heat, crowd sorrowfully

[*3*]

together and with dismal patience hang their heads low, as though waiting for the moment when this unbearable sultriness will pass at last.

Barely dragging my feet, I drew near at last to Nikolai Ivanych's cottage, as usual making the children stare in intense amazement at me and arousing in the dogs a feeling of indignation expressed by vicious and hoarse barking which seemed to tear their insides and make them choke and cough. Suddenly a tall, bare-headed man in a frieze overcoat with a blue belt round the waist appeared in the doorway of the country pub. He looked like a house-serf; his thick gray hair rose untidily over his thin wrinkled face. He was calling somebody with rapid movements of his arms, which were quite obviously swinging out much farther than he intended. It was clear that he had already had a drop too many.

[4]

"Come on, come on," he babbled, "come on, Blinker, come on! Good heavens, you're just crawling along! It isn't nice at all, old fellow. Not nice at all. They're waiting for you here and you're crawling along. Come on, come on now!"

"All right, I'm coming, I'm coming," a quavering voice cried, and a short, stout, lame fellow appeared from behind a peasant's cottage on the right. He wore a fairly clean farm laborer's cotton coat, with only one sleeve; a high, pointed hat, pulled straight over his forehead, gave his round, pudgy face a cunning, sardonic look. His little yellow eyes darted about; a restrained, forced smile never left his thin lips; and his nose, long and pointed, was thrust forward impudently, like a rudder. "I'm coming, my dear fellow," he went on, limping in the direction of the pub. "Why are you calling me? Anyone waiting for me?"

"Why am I calling you?" the man in the frieze overcoat cried reproachfully. "What a funny fellow you are, to be sure, Blinker! You're called to a pub and you ask why? There are all sorts of excellent fellows waiting for you: Yashka the Turk, the Wild Gentleman, and the contractor from Zhizdra. Yashka and the contractor have made a bet: they've wagered a quart of beer to see who wins— I mean who sings best—see?"

"Yashka's going to sing?" the man nicknamed Blinker cried excitedly. "You're not telling a lie, Booby?"

"No, I am not!" Booby replied with dignity. "It's you who're talking a lot of nonsense. Of course he's going to sing if he's made a bet, you stupid insect, you twister, you!"

"Oh, come along, you ninny," said Blinker.

"Come, give me a kiss at least, my dear fellow," Booby babbled, flinging his arms out wide.

"Get away with you, you great milksop!" Blinker replied contemptuously, elbowing him aside, and they both, stooping, went in through the low doorway.

The conversation I had overheard greatly aroused my curiosity. More than once rumors had reached me of Yashka the Turk as the best singer in the neighborhood, and all of a sudden I was given the chance to hear him in competition with another master. I redoubled my steps and entered the pub. [5]

I don't expect many of my readers have had occasion to look into a country pub, but we sportsmen go everywhere. The arrangement of these country pubs is very simple. They usually consist of a dark passage and a large room divided in two by a partition, behind which no customer is allowed to go. A big oblong opening is cut in this partition above a broad oak table. On this table or counter vodka is sold. Sealed bottles of different sizes stand side by side on shelves immediately opposite the opening. In the front part of the room are benches, two or three empty barrels, and a corner table put at the disposal of the customers. Village pubs are mostly rather dark, and on their timbered walls you hardly ever see any brightly colored popular prints, without which very few peasant cottages are complete.

When I went into the Cozy Corner a fairly large company was already assembled there.

Behind the counter, as was only to be expected, and filling almost the whole width of the opening, stood Nikolai Ivanych, in a gay cotton shirt, and with a lazy smile on his chubby cheeks, pouring out two glasses of vodka with his pudgy white hand for the two friends, Blinker and Booby, who had just come in. His sharp-eyed wife could be seen behind him in the corner near the window. In the middle of the room stood Yashka the Turk, a lean, slender man of twenty-three, wearing a long-skirted blue nankeen coat. He looked like a dashing factory hand and, so far as I could judge, his health was nothing to boast about. His sunken cheeks, large, restless gray eyes, straight nose with thin, mobile nostrils, his white receding forehead with light brown curls thrust back from it, his large but handsome and expressive lips—his whole face revealed an impressionable, passionate nature. He was in a state of great excitement: he blinked, breathed irregularly; his hands trembled as though he were feverish—and, as a matter of fact, he had a fever, that sudden, shaking fever which is so familiar to all who speak or sing in public.

Beside him stood a man of about forty, broad-shouldered, with broad cheekbones, a low forehead, narrow Tartar eyes, a short, flat nose, a square chin, and black, shiny hair, hard as bristles. The expression of his face, swarthy with a leaden hue, and especially of his pale lips, might almost have been called ferocious, if it had not been so calmly reflective. He hardly stirred and just kept looking round slowly like an ox from under the yoke. He wore a sort of threadbare frock coat with shiny copper buttons; an old black silk handkerchief was wrapped round his massive neck. He was nicknamed the Wild Gentleman.

[6]

Yashka's competitor, the contractor from Zhizdra, sat right in front of him on the bench under the icons. He was a short, thickset man of about thirty, pock-marked and curly-headed, with a blunt, tipped-up nose, lively brown eyes, and a scanty beard. He was looking round boldly, with his hands tucked under him, carelessly swinging and tapping his feet, on which he wore smart boots with trimmings. He had on a thin new peasant's overcoat of gray cloth with a velveteen collar, against which a strip of scarlet shirt, buttoned up tightly round his throat, stood out sharply.

In the opposite corner a peasant in a threadbare grayish coat with an enormous hole on the shoulder sat at a table to the right of the door. The sunlight came through the dusty panes of the two small windows in a fine yellowish shaft of light and seemed unable to dispel the habitual darkness of the room; all the objects in it were dimly illuminated, their outlines blurred. On the other hand, it was almost cool in the room, and the moment I crossed the threshold the sensation of closeness and sultriness fell from my shoulders like a heavy load.

My arrival—I could see it—at first disconcerted Nikolai Ivanych's guests a little; but, observing that he bowed to me as to an old acquaintance, they set their minds at rest and paid no more attention to me. I ordered some beer and sat down in the corner beside the little peasant in the torn coat.

"Well," Booby cried suddenly, after having drained a glass of vodka at one gulp, accompanying his exclamation with those strange gesticulations without which he evidently could not utter a single word, "well, what are we waiting for? Let's begin, eh, Yashka?"

"Yes, yes, let's begin," Nikolai Ivanych echoed approvingly.

"Let's begin, by all means," the contractor said coolly and with a self-confident smirk. "I'm ready."

"Me—too," Yashka declared with a catch in his voice.

"Well then, begin, my lads, begin," Blinker squeaked.

But notwithstanding this unanimously expressed wish, neither of them began; the contractor did not even stir from his bench; they all seemed to be waiting for something to happen.

"Begin!" the Wild Gentleman said sharply and sullenly.

Yashka gave a start. The contractor got up, pushed down his belt, and cleared his throat. "Who's to begin?" he asked in a slightly changed voice, addressing himself to the Wild Gentleman, who was still standing motionless in the middle of the room, his thick legs planted wide apart and his powerful arms thrust almost to the elbows into the pockets of his billowing wide trousers.

"You, Contractor, you," Booby babbled. "You, my lad."

The Wild Gentleman glanced at him frowningly. Booby uttered a faint squeak, faltered, threw a hasty glance at the ceiling, wriggled his shoulders, and fell silent.

"Draw for it," said the Wild Gentleman with deliberation, "and put the quart of beer on the counter."

Nikolai Ivanych bent down, picked up, grunting, the quart from the floor and put it on the table.

The Wild Gentleman glanced at Yashka and said, "Well?"

Yashka fumbled in his pockets, found a half-copeck piece, and marked it with his teeth. The contractor took out a new leather purse from the skirt of his coat, slowly undid the strings, and, pouring out a lot of small change into his hand, chose a new half-copeck

[7]

piece. Booby held out his battered old cap with its loose and broken peak; Yashka threw his half-copeck into it, and so did the contractor.

"You choose," said the Wild Gentleman, addressing Blinker.

Blinker smirked with a self-satisfied air, took the cap in both hands and began shaking it.

A dead hush fell for a moment upon the room; the coins chinked faintly against each other. I looked round attentively: every face expressed strained anticipation; even the Wild Gentleman half closed his eyes; my neighbor, the little peasant in the torn coat, also craned his neck inquisitively. Blinker thrust his hand into the cap and drew out the contractor's half-copeck; there was a general sigh. Yashka [8] flushed, and the contractor passed his hand through his hair.

"I said it was you, didn't I?" cried Booby. "I said so!"

"All right, all right, stop your cackle!" the Wild Gentleman observed contemptuously. "Begin!" he went on, nodding to the contractor.

"What shall I sing?" asked the contractor, with mounting excitement.

"Anything you like," replied Blinker. "Just think of something and sing it."

"Yes, of course, anything you like," added Nikolai Ivanych, slowly folding his arms across his chest. "We have no right to tell you what you should sing. Sing any song you like. Only, mind, sing it well, and we shall afterward decide without fear or favor."

"Aye," Booby put in, licking the rim of his empty glass, "so we shall—without fear or favor."

"Let me first clear my throat a little, friends," said the contractor, passing his fingers along the inside of the collar of his coat.

"Come now, don't waste time—begin!" the Wild Gentleman said forcefully and dropped his eyes.

The contractor thought for a moment, shook his head, and stepped forward. Yashka stared fixedly at him.

But before proceeding with the description of the contest itself, it may be as well to say a few words about each of the characters of my story. The circumstances of life of some of them I already knew when I met them in the Cozy Corner; I found out all about the rest subsequently.

Let us begin with Booby. His real name was Eugraph Ivanov, but no one in the neighborhood ever called him anything but Booby, and he referred to himself by the same nickname, so well did it fit him. And, to be sure, it seemed to go perfectly with his insignificant, perpetually worried features. He was a dissolute, unmarried house-serf, whom his masters had long since given up as beyond redemption and who, having no job of any kind and receiving no wages whatever, nevertheless found means of making merry at someone else's expense. He had a great many acquaintances who treated him to drinks and to tea without themselves knowing why, for, far from being amusing in company, he made everybody sick and tired of his senseless chatter, his unbearable importunity, his feverish fidgetings, and his ceaseless, unnatural laughter. He could neither sing nor dance, and he had never been known to utter an intelligent, let alone sensible, word: he just babbled and talked a lot of nonsense—a regular booby! And yet there was not a single drinking party for forty miles round at which his spindle-shanked figure did not turn up among the guests; people had become so used to him that they tolerated his presence as a necessary evil. It is true, they treated him with contempt; but the Wild Gentleman alone could check his absurd outbursts. [9]

Blinker was not at all like Booby. His nickname, too, fitted him well, though he did not blink more than anyone else; it is a well-known fact that the Russians are past-masters at giving nicknames. In spite of my efforts to unearth as many details of his past as possible, there remained for me—as well as for many others, I suppose—many dark spots in his life, places which, to use a literary cliché, were shrouded in mystery. All I could discover was that at one time he had been coachman to an old, childless lady, had run away with the team of three horses entrusted to his care, disappeared for a whole year, and, no doubt convinced by experience of the disadvantages and hardships of a vagrant's life, returned, now a lame cripple, thrown himself at his mistress's feet, and, having made amends for his crime by many years of exemplary conduct, won his way back into her favor and at last earned her full confidence; he had been appointed bailiff and, on his mistress's death, had somehow or other gained his freedom, registered as a member of the tradesmen's class, leased melon fields from the neighbors, grown rich, and now lived in clover. He was a man of great experience, knew which side his bread was buttered on, was neither good nor bad, but very calculating; a man who had been through the mill and who understood people and knew how to make use of them. He was cautious and at the same time resourceful, like a fox; talkative as an old woman, but never let out a secret, while making everybody else speak his mind freely; still, he never posed as a simpleton, as many cunning fellows of his kind do, and in fact he would have found it difficult to pretend: I have never seen shrewder and more intelligent eyes than his tiny, cunning "peepers."* They never just looked; they were always reconnoitering and spying. Blinker would sometimes spend whole weeks in thinking over some apparently simple enterprise, and at other times suddenly make up his mind to undertake some desperately daring business deal, and you'd think he'd be ruined; but no! his deal had come off and all was plain sailing again. He was lucky, and he believed in his luck, believed in omens. He was, in general, highly superstitious. He was not liked, because he did not care what happened to others, but he was respected. His entire family consisted of one small son who was the apple of his eye and who, brought up by such a father, would probably go far. "Little Blinky is the very spit of his father," the old men were already saying of him in an undertone as they sat gossiping on the mounds of earth outside their cottages on summer evenings; and everyone understood what that meant, and there was no need to say more.

[10]

Of Yashka the Turk and the contractor there is not much to be said. Yashka, nicknamed the Turk because he really was descended from a captured Turkish woman, was at heart an artist in every sense of the word, but was employed as a dipper in a paper-mill; as for the contractor, about whom, I'm afraid, I found out nothing, he appeared to me to be a highly resourceful and smart tradesman. But of the Wild Gentleman it is worth speaking at somewhat greater length.

---

* The people of Oryol Province call eyes "peepers," in the same way that they call a mouth a "gobbler." AUTHOR.

The first impression the appearance of this man made was one of barbaric, ponderous, but irresistible strength. He was clumsily built—"rough-hewn," as we say—but he exuded rude health, and, strangely enough, his bearlike figure was not without a certain peculiar kind of grace, which was perhaps the result of his absolute, calm confidence in his own strength. It was difficult to decide at first glance to what social class this Hercules belonged; he did not look like a house-serf or a tradesman or a retired and impoverished scrivener or a pugnacious, huntin' small country squire: he did indeed seem to be an exceptional case. Nobody knew from where he had descended on our district; it was said that he belonged to the class of free smallholders and had previously been in government service somewhere, but nothing definite was known about it; and indeed there was no one to find it out from, certainly not from the man himself: there was no more surly and taciturn man in the world. Neither could anyone say positively what he lived on: he was engaged in no trade; he visited no one; he scarcely knew anyone; and yet he had money—not much money, it is true, but he certainly had some money. He conducted himself not so much modestly—there was nothing modest about him—as quietly; he lived as though he never noticed anyone round him and he most certainly wanted nothing from anyone. [11]

The Wild Gentleman (this was his nickname; his real name was Perevlesov) enjoyed enormous influence in all the district; he was obeyed instantly and eagerly, although he had no right whatever to give anyone orders—but then, he never made the slightest claim on the obedience of people with whom he happened to come in contact. He spoke and was obeyed: power always claims its due. He hardly ever drank, had no dealings with women, and was passionately fond of singing. There was much that was mysterious about this man; it was as if tremendous forces were sullenly hidden within him, as though he knew that, once aroused, once let loose, they must destroy themselves and everything they touched; and I am sadly mistaken if some such explosion had not already happened in that man's life and that, taught by experience and having just escaped destruction, he was now holding himself inexorably under iron control. What struck me particularly about him was the mixture of a sort of innate natural ferocity with a similarly innate nobility—a mixture such as I have never come across in any other person.

And so the contractor stepped forward, half closed his eyes, and began to sing in a very high falsetto. His voice was quite sweet and agreeable, though a little husky; he played with it, twirled it about like a top, dwelt lovingly and with abandon on the high notes, with constant downward trills and modulations and constant returns to the top notes, which he held and drew out with a special effort, stopped, then suddenly took up his previous tune with a sort of rollicking, arrogant boldness. His transitions were sometimes rather daring, sometimes rather amusing; they would have given the connoisseur great pleasure; they would have greatly shocked the German. It was a Russian *tenore di grazia, tenor léger*. He sang a gay dance tune whose words, so far as I could make them out among the endless embellishments, extra consonants, and exclamations, were as follows:

[12]

A little plot of land, my love,
I'll sow,
A little scarlet flower, my love,
I'll grow.

He sang, and everyone listened to him with rapt attention. He evidently felt that he was dealing with experts and that was why he simply put his best leg forward, as the saying goes. And, indeed, in our part of the country people are good judges of singing, and it is not for nothing that the large village of Sergeyevskoye, on the Oryol Highway, is renowned throughout all Russia for its especially agreeable and harmonious singing.

The contractor sang for a long time without arousing any particular enthusiasm in his hearers; he missed the support of a choir; at last, after one particularly successful transition, which made even the Wild Gentleman smile, Booby could not restrain himself and uttered a cry of delight. We all gave a start. Booby and Blinker began to take up the tune in an undertone, humming, calling out, "Well done! Hold it, you dirty rascal! Hold it—higher, higher, you villain!

Up, up! Make it hotter, hotter, you dirty dog, you cur, the devil take you!" and so on. Behind the counter Nikolai Ivanych shook his head to right and left approvingly. At length Booby began stamping, dancing about, and twitching his shoulder, and Yashka's eyes blazed like coals, and he shook all over like a leaf and smiled confusedly. The Wild Gentleman alone did not change countenance and remained motionless as before; but his gaze, fixed on the contractor, softened a little, though his lips kept their contemptuous expression.

Encouraged by these signs of general satisfaction, the contractor let himself go in good earnest and went off into such flourishes, such tongue-clickings and drummings, such frantic throat play, that when, at last exhausted, pale, and bathed in hot perspiration, he threw himself back and let out a last dying note, a loud burst of general exclamation was the instantaneous response of his audience. [23] Booby threw himself on his neck and fell to smothering him in his long bony arms; Nikolai Ivanych's fat face flushed, and he seemed to have grown younger. Yashka shouted like a madman, "Well done, well done!"—and even my neighbor, the peasant in the torn coat, could bear it no longer and, striking his fist on the table, exclaimed, "*A-ha!* Good, damn good!" and, turning his head, spat with conviction.

"Well, my lad, you've given us a treat!" Booby cried, not without letting the exhausted contractor out of his embrace. "A real treat, and that's the truth! You've won, my dear fellow, you've won! Congratulations—the quart is yours! That fellow Yashka can't touch you. I'm telling you—he can't touch you. You must believe me!" And he again pressed the contractor to his bosom.

"Let him go, for heaven's sake," Blinker said with annoyance. "Let him go, you leech! Let him sit down on the bench here. Can't you see how tired he is? Oh, what a silly fool you are, my lad, what a silly fool! Why are you still sticking to him like a leaf from the whisk in a bath-house?"

"Why, of course, let him sit down and I'll drink to his health," replied Booby, going up to the counter. "It's on you, old fellow," he added, turning to the contractor.

The contractor nodded, sat down on the bench, pulled a towel out of his cap, and started wiping his face. Booby emptied his glass with eager haste and, as is the custom with confirmed drunkards, grunted and looked sad and preoccupied.

"You sing well, my boy, you sing well," Nikolai Ivanych observed graciously. "Now it's your turn, Yashka, dear fellow. Don't be nervous, mind. We shall see who's best, we shall. But the contractor sings well. Aye, so he does."

"He does that," observed Nikolai Ivanych's wife, glancing at Yashka with a smile.

"Aye, he does that!" my neighbor repeated in an undertone.

"Eh, you savage woodlander!"* Booby suddenly shouted and, walking up to the peasant with the hole in the shoulder of his coat, pointed a finger at him, began jumping up and down, and went off [14] into a jarring laugh. "Woodlander, woodlander! Ha, gee-up, wood savage! What brings you here, wood savage?" he shouted through his laughter.

The poor peasant looked embarrassed and was about to get up and depart hurriedly, when all of a sudden the brasslike voice of the Wild Gentleman resounded through the room. "What kind of disgusting animal is that?" he said, grinding his teeth.

"I—I didn't mean anything," Booby muttered. "I—I didn't—er—I just——"

"All right then, shut up!" said the Wild Gentleman. "Yashka, begin!"

Yashka touched his throat with his hand. "I'm afraid I—I don't quite—er—I mean, I don't rightly know—er—I don't quite——"

"For goodness' sake, man, don't be afraid. You ought to be ashamed of yourself! You're not trying to wriggle out of it, are you? Sing as God tells you." And the Wild Gentleman looked down and waited.

Yashka said nothing, glanced round, and covered his face with his hand. They all fixed their eyes on him, especially the contractor, whose face, through its usual expression of self-confidence and the

---

* The inhabitants of the Southern wooded districts, a long woodland belt beginning on the borders of the Bolkhovsk and the Zhizdrinsk districts, are known as woodlanders. They are distinguished by many peculiarities in their way of life, their customs and language. They are called savages because of their suspicious and harsh natures. AUTHOR.

triumph of his success, betrayed a faint unconscious anxiety. He leaned against the wall and again tucked his hands under him, but he no longer swung his legs. At last Yashka uncovered his face. It was as pale as a dead man's; his eyes glowed faintly through their lowered lashes. He took a deep breath and began to sing.

His first note was faint and uneven and seemed to come not from his chest but from somewhere far away, just as though it had come floating into the room by accident. This trembling, ringing note had a strange effect on us all; we glanced at one another, and Nikolai's wife suddenly drew herself up to her full height. This first note was followed by another, firmer and more drawn out, but still perceptibly trembling like a string, when, ringing out loudly after being suddenly plucked by a strong finger, it wavers with a last fast-fading trill; after the second came a third note, and, gradually warming up and broadening, the mournful song flowed on uninterruptedly. [15]

"Across the fields many a path is winding," he sang, and we all felt entranced and thrilled. I must confess I have seldom heard such a voice: it was a little broken and had a sort of cracked ring; at first, indeed, there seemed to be an unhealthy note in it; but there was in it also genuine deep passion, and youthfulness and strength and sweetness, and a sort of charmingly careless, mournful grief. A warmhearted, truthful Russian soul rang and breathed in it and fairly clutched you by the heart, clutched straight at your Russian heartstrings. The song expanded and went flowing on. Yashka was evidently overcome by ecstasy: he was no longer diffident; he gave himself up entirely to his feeling of happiness; his voice no longer trembled—it quivered, but with the barely perceptible inner quivering of passion which pierces like an arrow into the hearer's soul, and it grew continually in strength, firmness, and breadth. I remember once seeing in the evening, at low tide, a great white seagull on the flat sandy shore of the sea which was roaring away dully and menacingly in the distance: it was sitting motionless, its silky breast turned toward the scarlet radiance of sunset, only now and then spreading out its long wings toward the familiar sea, toward the low, blood-red sun; I remembered that bird as I listened to Yashka. He sang, completely oblivious of his rival and of all of us, but visibly borne up, like a strong swimmer by the waves, by our silent, passionate attention. He sang, and every note recalled something that was very near and dear to us all, something that was immensely vast, just as though the familiar steppe opened up before you, stretching away into boundless distance.

I could feel tears welling up in my heart and rising to my eyes; suddenly I became aware of dull, muffled sobs. I looked round—the publican's wife was weeping, her bosom pressed against the window. Yashka threw a quick glance at her and his song rose even higher and flowed on more sweetly than before. Nikolai Ivanych looked down; Blinker turned away; Booby, overcome by emotion, stood with his mouth stupidly gaping; the coarse, ignorant little peasant was quietly whimpering in a corner, shaking his head as he muttered bitterly to himself; down the iron countenance of the Wild Gentleman, from beneath his beetling brows, slowly rolled a heavy tear; the contractor had raised a clenched fist to his forehead and never stirred.

I do not know how the general suspense would have been broken if Yashka had not suddenly ended on a high, extremely thin note—just as if his voice had broken. No one uttered a sound; no one even stirred; everyone seemed to be waiting to see if he would sing again; but he opened his eyes as if surprised at our silence, cast a questioning glance round at us all, and saw that victory was his.

"Yashka," said the Wild Gentleman, putting a hand on his shoulder and—fell silent.

We all stood there as though benumbed. The contractor got up quietly and went up to Yashka. "You—it's yours—you've won," he said at last with difficulty and rushed out of the room.

His quick, decided movement seemed to break the spell; everyone suddenly began talking loudly, joyfully. Booby leapt up into the air, spluttered, and waved his arms like the sails of a windmill; Blinker went up limping to Yashka and began kissing him; Nikolai Ivanych stood up and announced solemnly that he would add another quart of beer on his own account; the Wild Gentleman kept laughing a sort of good-natured laugh which I had never expected to hear from him; the poor little peasant, wiping his eyes, cheeks, nose, and beard on both his sleeves, kept on repeating in his corner, "It's good, aye, it's good all right! Aye, I'm a son of a bitch if it ain't!" And Nikolai's wife, flushed all over, got up quickly and went out of the room.

Yashka enjoyed his victory like a child; his whole face was transfigured; his eyes, in particular, simply shone with happiness. He was dragged across to the counter; he called to the poor little peasant who had been crying to come over too, sent the publican's little son to fetch the contractor, and the revels began. "You'll sing to us again," Booby kept saying, raising his arms aloft, "you'll go on singing to us till the evening."

I cast another glance at Yashka and went out. I did not want to stay—I was afraid to spoil my impression. But the heat was still as unbearable as before. It seemed to hang over the earth in a thick, heavy layer; through the fine, almost black dust, little bright points [17] of light seemed to whirl round and round in the dark blue sky. Everything was hushed; there was something hopeless, something oppressive about this deep silence of enervated nature. I made my way to a hayloft and lay down on the newly mown but already almost dried grass. For a long time I could not doze off; for a long time Yashka's overpowering voice rang in my ears; but at last heat and fatigue claimed their due and I sank into a deep sleep. When I awoke, it was dark; the grass I had heaped all round me exuded a strong scent and felt a little damp to the touch; through the thin rafters of the half-open roof, pale stars twinkled faintly. I went out. The sunset glow had died away long ago and its last trace could be just distinguished as a pale shaft of light low on the horizon; but through the coolness of the night one could still feel the warmth in the air which had been so glowing-hot only a short while before, and the breast still yearned for a cool breeze. There was no wind, no cloud; the sky all round was clear and translucently dark, quietly shimmering with countless, hardly visible stars. Lights gleamed in the village; from the brightly lit pub nearby came a discordant and confused uproar through which I seemed to recognize Yashka's voice. At times there were wild bursts of laughter.

I went across to the window and pressed my face against the pane. I saw a rather sad, though lively and animated, scene: everyone was dead drunk—everyone, beginning with Yashka. He was sitting bare-chested on a bench and, humming in a hoarse voice some popular dance tune, lazily plucked and fingered the strings of a guitar. Strands of moist hair hung over his terribly pale face. In the middle of the pub, Booby, completely unstrung and coatless, was leaping about on his haunches as he danced in front of the little peasant in the grayish coat; the little peasant, in his turn, was laboriously stamping and scraping with his exhausted feet, and, smiling stupidly through his tousled beard, kept waving a hand as if to say, "I don't care!" Nothing could have been funnier than his face; however much he tried to lift his eyebrows, his heavy lids would not stay up, drooping over his scarcely visible, bleary eyes which, nonetheless, kept their sweet, sugary expression. He was in the delectable condition of complete intoxication when every passer-by, looking at his face, would be quite sure to say, "You're in a fine pickle, old fellow, in a fine pickle!" Blinker, red as a lobster, his nostrils dilated as far as they would go, was laughing sardonically from a corner; Nikolai Ivanych alone, as befits a good publican, remained as imperturbable as ever. Many new faces had collected in the room, but there was no sign of the Wild Gentleman.

[18]

I turned round and walked away quickly down the hill on which Kolotovka stands. At the foot of this hill lay a broad valley; covered as it was with vaporous waves of evening mist, it seemed vaster than ever and appeared to merge with the darkened sky. I was walking with great strides down the road along the ravine when suddenly, from a long distance away in the valley, there came the ringing voice of a boy calling, "Antropka-a! Antropka-a!" in obstinate, tearful desperation, drawing out the last syllable a long time.

He was silent for a few moments and then began to call again. His voice carried clearly in the motionless, lightly dozing air. He must have called Antropka's name thirty times at least, when suddenly from the opposite side of the meadow, as though from a different world, there came a hardly audible reply. "Wha-a-at?"

The boy's voice called at once with joyful desperation, "Come here, you little devil!"

"What fo-o-or?" answered the other after a long pause.

"'Cause Dad wants to give you a good hiding!" the first voice called promptly.

The second voice made no further reply, and the little boy started calling for Antropka again. His cries, growing more infrequent and fainter, still reached my ears when it had grown completely dark and I was rounding the corner of the wood that surrounds my village, about four miles away from Kolotovka.

"Antropka-a-a!" I still seemed to hear in the air full of the shadows of the night. ✦

THE HEART OF THE STORY

THOUGHTS ON "THE SINGERS"

Year after year, at the beginning of our class on "The Singers," I ask my students for their first reactions to this story, which I consider a masterpiece, and an awkward silence falls over the room. Finally, someone will just say it: "I kind of felt . . . well . . . I guess I was just wondering what was up with all of the *digression* in this story." Emboldened, someone else will chime in: "Yeah, why the endless physical descriptions of every living thing within a two-mile radius of the Cozy Corner?" A third person: "It's so *slow*. Does Turgenev really have to tell us *everything* about *everyone*?"

Then there's some relieved collective laughter and I know it's going to be a good class.

A story with a problem is like a person with a problem: interesting.

As we read a story (let's imagine) we're dragging along a cart labeled "Things I Couldn't Help Noticing" (TICHN). As we read, we're *noticing*—surface-level, plot-type things ("Romeo really seems to like Juliet"), but quieter things too: aspects of the language, say ("Tons of alliteration in the first three pages"), structural features ("It's being told in reverse chronological order!"), patterns of color, flashbacks or flash-forwards, changes in point of view. I'm not saying that we're *consciously* noticing. Often, we're not. We're "noticing" with our bodies and our quality of attention and may overtly "notice" only afterward, as we analyze the story.

What we're adding to our TICHN cart are, let's say, "non-normative" aspects of the story—aspects that seem to be calling attention to themselves through some sort of presentational excess.

If you closely observe your reading mind, you'll find that as you encounter an excess in a story (some non-normative aspect), you enter into a transactional relationship with the writer. When Kafka writes, "Gregor Samsa woke up one morning from unsettling dreams . . . changed in his bed into a monstrous vermin," you don't say, "No, he didn't, Franz," and throw the book across the room. You add "impossible incident: man just turned into bug" to your TICHN cart, then enter a period of "waiting to see." What's Kafka going to do with that? Your reading state has been affected. You are, let's say, "beginning to resist." You have "registered a mild objection." But we readers will tolerate all kinds of reading states, even negative-seeming ones: periods of boredom, of perplexity, periods during which we are really hating Character X and wondering if the writer knows just how much. What we are saying, essentially, is: "Well, Franz, that bug thing is excessive but I'm going to allow it. Proceed. What are you going to do with that thing I couldn't help noticing? I hope you're going to make it pay off."

When a writer subjects us to a non-normative event—a physical implausibility, the use of markedly elevated language (or markedly vernacular language), or a series of lengthy digressions in a Russian pub in which the people keep freezing in midaction for several pages so that each can be described at length, in turn—he pays a price: our reading energy drops. (We get suspicious and resistant.) But if it doesn't drop fatally, and if, later, we see that this was all part of the plan—if what seemed a failure of craft turns out to be integral to the story's meaning (that is, it seems that he "meant to do that")—then all is forgiven and we might even understand the profitable exploitation of that apparent excess as a form of virtuosity.

The goal is not to keep the TICHN cart empty and thus write a "perfectly normal" story. A story that approaches its ending with nothing in its TICHN cart is going to have a hard time ending spectacularly. A good story is one that, having created a pattern of excesses, notices those excesses and converts them into virtues.

Here's a place to ask a simple question: How do we know a story is good?

I once heard the writer and comic artist Lynda Barry cite a neurological study that said that when we get to the end of a story, a short lyric poem, or a joke, the brain performs an instantaneous retro-assessment for efficiency. If, as I tell the one about the duck who walks into a bar, I interject a fifteen-minute digression about the duck's child-hood that turns out to have nothing to do with the punch line, your brain notes this as an inefficiency and, at the end, you laugh less.

On what basis does the mind assess for efficiency?

It assumes that everything in the joke is there to serve the punch line, to make it more powerful.

We might think of a story as a kind of ceremony, like the Catholic Mass, or a coronation, or a wedding. We understand the heart of the Mass to be communion, the heart of a coronation to be the moment the crown goes on, the heart of the wedding to be the exchanging of the vows. All of those other parts (the processionals, the songs, the recitations, and so on) will be felt as beautiful and necessary to the extent that they serve the heart of the ceremony.

So, one way to approach a story—to evaluate how good it is, how graceful and efficient—is to ask, "What is the heart of you, dear story?" (Or, channeling Dr. Seuss, "Why are you bothering telling me this?")

That is: "When all is said and done, what do you claim to live by, story? I need to know this so I can see how well your non-normative aspects are serving the heart of you."

The heart of "The Singers" is, of course, the singing contest. That's what the story is "about," what it has to offer, what its component parts are there to serve. (The "Hollywood version" of "The Singers" would be something like: "Two men have a singing contest in a Russian pub. One wins, one loses.")

But we might notice—well, I'm pretty sure you *did* notice—that the contest doesn't even start until we've waded through eleven long, somewhat meandering pages.

So, by the earlier-mentioned Ruthless Efficiency Principle, we have a right, a responsibility, even, to ask: What are those first eleven pages *for*? Do they earn their keep? Are they worth the struggle?

"The Singers" is a story of an ancient variety, in which A and B meet in a contest of skills and one of them wins. (Think: *The Iliad* or *The Karate Kid* or *Rocky,* or any movie with a gunfight in it.)

What gives this type of story its meaning? If we just say it that way ("A and B meet in a contest of skills"), why do we care who wins? We don't. We can't. A is equal to B is equal to A is equal to B. Nothing is at stake if the contestants are identical. If I say: "Two guys got in a fight in a bar across from my house and, guess what? One of them won!"—that's not meaningful. What would make it meaningful is knowing who those guys were. If A is a saintly, gentle person and B a real stinker, and B wins, the story will be felt to mean something like "Virtue does not always prevail." If A has trained for the fight by eating only celery and B by eating only hot dogs, A's victory might be read as an endorsement of celery.

Given that the heart of this story is the singing contest, with Yashka and the contractor starring as "A" and "B," respectively, we might reasonably expect that those eleven pages preceding the singing are there, at least in part, to tell us something about Yashka and the contractor (i.e., what they "stand for"), so that when one of them wins, we'll be able to interpret the outcome.

But here's an interesting feature of the story: although it is, to understate it politely, "rich with description," we find, in those eleven pages, that although for everyone else in the Cozy Corner, Turgenev seems to have an inexhaustible source of backstory, he actually doesn't have much to say about his two main characters that would serve to distinguish one from the other (and make the contest meaningful). Yashka is a nervous local boy and the contractor is an outsider. Yashka, "a dipper in a paper-mill," has "an impressionable, passionate nature" and seems to be the best singer in the village. As for the contractor: we get a little physical description of him on page 6 and the vague assertion, later, that he appeared to be "a highly resourceful and smart tradesman." Beyond that, "of Yashka the Turk and the contractor there is not much to be said."

So when, after those first eleven pages, we ask, "What are the characteristics of these two singers that will make the outcome meaningful?," we still don't know, and have to look to the contest itself.

For now, let's do what you may have wished Turgenev had done: skip those first eleven pages and get right to the singing.

As the contractor starts singing (after the break at the top of page 12) we read along, looking for indications of how he's doing—looking, that is, for indications of how Turgenev wants us to think he's doing. (When Rocky takes a hit and goes down on one knee, we understand this to mean: "He seems to be losing!")

We're told that the contractor starts off in "a very high falsetto . . . quite sweet and agreeable" (i.e., "he's doing well and may win"). The next passage tells us (via phrases like "played with," "twirled it about," "lovingly and with abandon," and "rollicking, arrogant boldness") that he's confident and loose—a casual virtuoso. His transitions "would have given the connoisseur great pleasure." He's chosen "a gay dance tune," full of "endless embellishments, extra consonants, and exclamations," even the lyrics of which convey aspiration and confidence: "A little plot of land, my love, / I'll sow; / A little scarlet flower, my love, / I'll grow." Everyone listens "with rapt attention."

Our sense is that the contractor is killing it and will be hard to beat.

The whole experience of reading fiction might be understood as a series of "establishings" ("the dog is sleeping"), stabilizations ("he is really sleeping deeply, so deeply that the cat just managed to walk across his back"), and alterations ("Uh-oh, he woke up").

Here, it's established that the contractor is doing well, seems to be in the process of winning. Turgenev lets us stabilize there, then provides an alteration: "The contractor sang for a long time *without arousing any particular enthusiasm in his hearers*" (italics mine). The contractor is now, we might say, "encountering a difficulty." He's good, he's accomplished, and yet not much is happening to the audience emotionally. We read this as: "News flash: actually, this guy may lose."

Turgenev's introduction of this complication allows us to know the contractor better. He is, approximately: the guy who, though flashy, leaves people cold. (This starts to answer our question "Who is A?") This problem having been established, Turgenev issues a new status report, indicating that the contractor has solved the problem . . . by going even flashier. "After one particularly successful transition," there's a ripple of excitement: the Wild Gentleman smiles; Booby utters a cry of delight and then, with Blinker, starts humming along. Yashka, waiting in the wings, confirms the power of the contractor's performance: his "eyes blazed like coals, and he shook all over like a leaf and smiled confusedly." Only the Wild Gentleman is not convinced (he does "not change countenance"), though his gaze softens a little.

Encouraged, the contractor "let himself go," and what does this mean, for him? It means more flash: flourishes, tongue clickings, drummings, throat play. Having encountered a problem ("I'm not moving my audience"), he finds a fix ("Go flashier!"). He concludes, to a "loud burst of general exclamation." Booby pronounces him the winner. Nikolai Ivanych, the owner of the tavern, reminds everyone that the contest isn't over yet, although he concedes that "the contractor sings well."

Let's review the performance. The contractor's gifts are primarily technical. His singing is described in terms of technique, and he has an effect on the audience in two places: first after that "particularly successful transition" and again at the end, via that "throat play."

Again, specificity makes character. Turgenev has the contractor sing in a specific way (he's a "shredder," in guitar terms, amazing his audience via technical prowess), and through this, the contractor became a particular guy, and now stands for something.

Now it's Yashka's turn. The story can go in one of two ways: Yashka can lose (and it becomes a story about that, the tarnishing of this local legend and, presumably, how he handles it) or he can win. The story is now asking, by implication: What quality might Yashka have that will allow him to defeat the contractor's highly technical singing? Every time I read this story, as Yashka steps up for his turn, I find myself wondering anew, "How can Yashka win? The contractor was so *good.*" The story has become a referendum on . . . something. We're not sure what yet. But we know that, on one side of the ballot, is Technical Prowess. (And to be clear, I'm not saying that, after a first read, we're really even aware of this. I think, actually, we're not. We just have a feeling that the contractor has set a high bar, and we are wondering, "Jeez, how is Yashka going to top that?")

And now (on page 15) we again closely watch Turgenev describe some singing, to see what he wants us to make of it.

Yashka starts nervously: "his first note was faint and uneven." It seems to have "come floating into the room by accident" (the opposite of technical prowess). We may feel: "Uh-oh. Yashka's choking." But then: "This trembling, ringing note had a strange effect on us all; we glanced at one another, and Nikolai's wife suddenly drew herself up to her full height."

His song is mournful. Its lyrics, held up against those of the contractor's song, are less confident, more admitting of ambiguity: "Across the fields many a path is winding." (Because we're still wondering how Yashka can win, this line might suggest some gentler, Russian version of: "There's more than one way to skin a cat.")

Yashka's singing is not perfect; his voice is broken and cracked, and it has "an unhealthy note in it," but also "genuine deep passion, and youthfulness and strength and sweetness." Soon, Yashka is "overcome by ecstasy." He seems to lose awareness of himself and his audience, gives "himself up entirely to his feeling of happiness." And we recall that at a parallel moment (the moment of greatest power in his performance), the contractor "let himself go in good earnest" and produced that memorable series of flourishes and tongue clickings. He didn't lose himself, or forget about his audience, or surrender to a feeling; sensing victory, he unleashed a higher-level arsenal of charming tricks. (He acted *at* his audience, rather than *upon* them.)

Then something lovely happens, in the story and in Turgenev's telling of it. Just after Yashka gives "himself up entirely to his feeling of happiness," the narrator suddenly comes back into the story as a personal presence after a long absence (he's been mostly gone since that moment at the top of page 7 when he noticed himself being noticed). Inspired by Yashka's singing, he remembers something: "a great white seagull." At the word "seagull," we might visualize "soaring seagull, flying overhead," but no, the seagull the narrator remembers is "sitting motionless," and somehow, in that moment of correction, I always see the seagull clearly, "its silky breast turned toward the scarlet radiance of sunset, only now and then spreading out its long wings toward the familiar sea, toward the low, blood-red sun."

We might, at this point, recall some earlier birds in the story, those "doleful" rooks and crows, those "fighting" sparrows, back on page 3. This seagull is a freer species of bird, far from this crummy, sweltering little town, out in some cool, clean ocean air. Unlike those local birds, it's not suffering; it appears powerful and at ease; it even seems, in the spreading of its wings, to see and acknowledge beauty (i.e., the sunset). And who has brought it to the narrator's mind? Yashka. How? With his singing.

Yashka "sang, and every note recalled something that was very near and dear to us all." Whatever just happened, it's happened to all of them. Each of them has recalled something like the narrator's seagull. Nothing like this happened while the contractor was singing. He amazed, but did not transport them. The contractor's performance was described in terms of what he could do, Yashka's in terms of what he caused his listeners to feel.

Yashka evoked the seagull, but he also *is* the seagull: in touch with beauty, briefly stepping out of his expected character. The seagull is "sitting motionless" instead of flying; Yashka has ceased being a paper dipper and become an artist, even in this crappy little town.

General sobbing breaks out.

Yashka wins.

What I've just described is, as we've said, the heart of the story. It takes up about five pages of a total of nineteen and, as mentioned, doesn't get started until page 12.

So, what work were those first eleven pages doing?

We might think of a story as a candy factory. We understand that the essence of candymaking is . . . making that piece of candy right there. As we walk around the factory, we expect everything in the place—every person, every phone, every department, every procedure—to be somehow related to, or "about," or "contributory to" that moment of candymaking. If we stumble on an office labeled "Center for the Planning of Steve's Wedding," we sense inefficiency. It may be that the planning of Steve's wedding will prove beneficial to the making of that piece of candy, but it's a stretch. If we close down that office, our candymaking becomes, de facto, more efficient. (Steve may feel differently.) The candy factory becomes a more beautiful candy factory because it has become a more efficient candy factory.

Or imagine we're bouncers, roaming through Club Story, asking each part, "Excuse me, but why do you need to be in here?" In a perfect story, every part has a good answer. ("Well, uh, in my subtle way, I am routing energy to the heart of the story.")

Our evolving, rather hard-ass model of a story says that every part of it should be there for a reason. The merely incidental ("this really happened" or "this was pretty cool" or "this got into the story and I couldn't quite take it out again") won't cut it. Every part of the story should be able to withstand this level of scrutiny, a scrutiny that, we should note, is to be administered generously, lest our story become too neat and mathematical.

So, let's walk through those first eleven pages, asking, as we go: What are you guys doing to benefit the heart of the story?

Because I'm a former engineer, let me list the bits constituting those eleven (possibly extraneous, currently under investigation) pages below. And also, I am going to *italicize* the bits in which meaningful action occurs, to distinguish them from bits that are merely descriptive.

No, seriously:

TABLE 1

Summary of the Eleven Pre-Contest Pages

—A description of the ravine. (Page 1.)

—A description of the innkeeper, Nikolai Ivanych. (Pages 1–2.)

—A description of Nikolai's (not-named) wife. (Page 3.)

—A description of some birds. (Middle of page 3.)

—A description of the town of Kolotovka. (Bottom of page 3.)

—Descriptions of Booby and Blinker. (Top half of page 4.)

—*An active sequence of dialogue between Booby and Blinker, the gist of which is: there's going to be a singing contest.* (Pages 4–5.)

—A description of the pub. (Page 5.)

—*An active sequence (two lines) in which the narrator enters the pub.* (Bottom of page 5.)

—A description of Yashka. (Bottom of page 5, top of page 6.)

—A description of the Wild Gentleman. (Page 6.)

—A description of the contractor. (Page 6.)

—A description of a peasant. (Bottom of page 6.)

—*An active sequence in which the narrator notices that he, a gentleman, is being noticed by this room of peasants and then his presence is sanctioned by the innkeeper.* (Top of page 7.)

—*An active sequence, as they figure out the details of the contest and it (nearly) begins* (pages 7–8) *but is interrupted by:*

—A (second, more backstory-heavy) description of Booby. (Page 9.)

—A (second, more backstory-heavy) description of Blinker. (Pages 9–10.)

—A description of Yashka and a second pass at the contractor that are not so much descriptions but explanations for why no descriptions can be offered. (Bottom of page 10.)

—A description of the Wild Gentleman. (Pages 11–12.)

—*And the contest finally begins.* (Page 12.)

Examining the table, we notice, to put it mildly, that the story, in its first eleven pages, is front-loaded with static, descriptive passages. (All that really *happens* in these pages is: the narrator approaches the pub, meets Booby and Blinker, goes into the pub, and overhears a discussion of the details of the contest.) Once the contest starts (on page 12), the descriptions recede and the text stays (mostly) in continuous, real-time action, in and around the pub.

(If you want a visual representation of how strange this is, get some markers and go through a photocopy of the story, using the above table as a guide, highlighting the descriptive sequences in one color and the active sections in another.)

There in our TICHN cart we find something like "Noticed: Lots of digressions and static descriptions." And we wonder: Has the story noticed this excess? Is it going to convert it into a virtue?

So, here, let's try to make the case that all of Turgenev's digressions and static descriptions are going to turn out to be "on purpose"—i.e., that he "meant to do that."

Referring again to Table 1, we see that most of the static descriptions are of people.

Here, a word about the way in which Turgenev describes people, because I think this is part of what has irritated my students so much over the years.

At the bottom of page 5, we meet Yashka: "a lean, slender man of twenty-three . . . like a dashing factory hand . . . his health was nothing to boast about . . . sunken cheeks, large, restless gray eyes, straight nose with thin, mobile nostrils, his white receding forehead with light brown curls thrust back from it . . . large but handsome and expressive lips." Can you make a person out of that? I can't. I may be inept at visualization, but this incantation of facial features doesn't add up to anything I can actually see. The parts just do this kind of Picassoesque pileup in my mind. This method of description (all-inclusive, consisting mostly of face-and-body-part listings) pervades the story. The Wild Gentleman has "broad cheekbones, a low forehead, narrow Tartar eyes, a short, flat nose, a square chin, and black, shiny hair, hard as bristles." When we meet the contractor, he's described as "a short, thickset man of about thirty, pock-marked and curly-headed, with a blunt, tipped-up nose, lively brown eyes, and a scanty beard." Nikolai Ivanych has "a bloated face, a pair of sly, genial little eyes, and a fleshy forehead with deep furrows running right across it."

The contemporary reader feels this method of description as old-fashioned. Per our current understanding of fiction, people are to be described selectively—in the sense that not everyone is described and that not everything about them needs to be described. We expect description to be somewhat minimal and serve a thematic purpose, whereas Turgenev seems to be describing things just because they're there.

This method seems to date from a time when stories were understood to serve a more documentary function. Turgenev was a member of the nobility and, like the narrator, would go on hikes into the countryside, to hunt. The book in which "The Singers" first appeared, *A Sportsman's Sketches,* was a groundbreaking work of literary anthropology that afforded the literati a look at how "these people," i.e., rural peasants, lived. Turgenev was praised at the time for the sensitivity and compassion of his portrayals and for their realism. (The narrator's aristocratic positioning explains the earlier-mentioned moment on page 7: "My arrival—I could see it—at first disconcerted Nikolai Ivanych's guests a little; but, observing that he bowed to me as to an old acquaintance, they set their minds at rest and paid no more attention to me.")

So, this description of the Cozy Corner was intended for people who'd maybe never been inside such a place. ("I don't expect many of my readers have had occasion to look into a country pub.") This might also explain the lengthy descriptions we're about to endure, of Nikolai Ivanych and his wife, and of Blinker and Booby. Part of Turgenev's self-understood function here is *reportage;* he's a kind of adventure journalist, giving his readers a glimpse into an exotic world, a world located beneath them.

But this method of description also came out of the way Turgenev worked.

Of Turgenev, Henry James wrote:

> The germ of a story, with him, was never an affair of plot—that was the last thing he thought of: it was the representation of certain persons. The first form in which a tale appeared to him was as the figure of an individual, or a combination of individuals. . . . They stood before him definite, vivid, and he wished to know, and to show, as much as possible of their nature. The first thing was to make clear to himself what he did know, to begin with; and to this end, he wrote out a sort of biography of each of his characters, and everything that they had done and that had happened to them up to the opening of the story. He had their dossier, as the French say. . . . With this material in his hand he was able to proceed; the story lay all in the question, What shall I make them do? . . . But, as he said, the defect of his manner and the reproach that was made him was his want of "architecture"—in other words, of composition. . . . If one reads Turgenev's stories with the knowledge that they were composed—or rather that they came into being—in this way, one can trace the process in every line.

Nabokov put it more grouchily: "[Turgenev's] literary genius falls short on the score of literary imagination, that is, of naturally discovering ways of telling the story which would equal the originality of his descriptive art."

Our current aesthetic understanding says that physical description should come at speed, naturally, presented organically within the action. (We believe in showing, not telling.) We have a low tolerance for the long-winded, endlessly explaining narrator. As one of my students once put it: in Turgenev, action and description seem to take turns stepping up to the microphone, one falling silent while the other speaks. The effect is static, awkward, occasionally maddening. A character's backstory comes in the form of a sort of data dump, while the other characters all stand frozen in place like animatrons in a diorama called *Russian Country Tavern, Circa 1850*.

And so, let's face it, at times the story is rough going. We resist Turgenev's habit of forcing everyone to stop moving and talking so that he can go around collecting data on their brows and hairlines and jackets and so on. The awkward quality of the stagecraft gets almost comical in places. My students always call out one line in particular (toward the bottom of page 8, as the singing is supposedly about to begin) for special derision. The contractor is nervous, stalling. The Wild Gentleman orders him to begin. The contractor steps forward. The tension is high. We've been waiting so very long for some singing to start.

Then we get this:

"But before proceeding with the description of the contest itself, it may be as well to say a few words about each of the characters of my story."

We feel: "Ivan, come on, haven't you already been *doing* that, like, for all of the eight preceding pages?"

Let's say a friend shows up at your house with a bulky, crazy-looking item of clothing—a diving suit made of asbestos, for example—and asks you to put it on. You do so. But it's uncomfortable, itchy, hot. The minutes begin to tick by. At some point, you're going to ask, "Wait, what is this *for*?"

So let's ask that now: What are these laborious character descriptions *for*? Once we know, we might be more willing to put on the itchy clothes contraption that is Turgenev's character-description method.

Or less.

But first, honoring and channeling the spirit of Turgenevian digression, let's take a step back and ask: Why do we even need descriptions of characters in the first place? What purpose do character descriptions serve?

For that matter, why do we need characters?

Well, we need characters, to paraphrase David Mamet on actors, so that they can fulfill the purpose required of them by the story. Why do we need Jacob Marley, in *A Christmas Carol*? To convince Scrooge that he is doomed if he doesn't change. What, then, do we need to know about Marley? Whatever will help him fulfill that purpose. What gives Marley authority is the fact that he and Scrooge were business partners and that if Scrooge ever had a trusted friend, Marley was it. Marley lived exactly the same life that Scrooge is living and committed the same sins. We need to know this (and not much more) so that when Marley tells Scrooge that he'd better change his ways, Scrooge believes it, and we do too. (We don't need to know if Marley was married, or what his childhood was like, or the size of his nose, or how he first met Scrooge.)

So: Do the various side characters in "The Singers" (Booby, Blinker, Nikolai and his wife, the Wild Gentleman) do anything to make the heart of the story (the singing contest) more potent?

Well, yes, we might argue: they function as a panel of judges.

Go back to the contractor's performance (pages 12–13) and read it again, tracking the reactions of the side characters. The heart of the story is a singing performance that we can't actually hear. These side characters tell us what to think about it. We watch them to see how the contractor and Yashka are doing. And we value their assessments *differently*, according to what we've been told about them.

Booby, for example: we know him as a negligible person, a local drunk whose judgment is not to be trusted. ("He had never been known to utter an intelligent, let alone sensible, word: he just babbled and talked a lot of nonsense—a regular booby!") So, he serves as a sort of Idiot Judge—a personification of undiscriminating judgment, mob mentality, the first to react, strongly but, usually, incorrectly. When he pronounces the contractor the winner, it serves as a broad indicator that the contractor has sung well, but it comes too early, and this verdict is then subtly suspended/overturned by Nikolai, the innkeeper, "an excellent judge of what a true Russian considers to be either interesting or important." Or consider the Wild Gentleman; he's been portrayed, via that long description just before the contest begins, as having "enormous influence in all the district." He's "passionately fond of singing." Not only that: "tremendous forces were sullenly hidden within him." When we look to this "Hercules," who was "obeyed instantly and eagerly" by everyone, for help in interpreting the contractor's performance, he first smiles (at a certain transition) and then, toward the end of the song, his gaze softens "a little," though "his lips kept their contemptuous expression." But he doesn't pass any final judgment; he only orders Yashka to stop stalling and "sing as God tells you."

Now let's look at Yashka's performance again (starting on page 15) in this light:

Moved by Yashka's singing, Nikolai's wife, that hardened case, earlier described as a "brisk, sharp-nosed, and quick-eyed tradeswoman" (read: no pushover) starts crying. Nikolai looks down (possibly hiding tears). Blinker turns away (ditto); Booby is stunned into an uncharacteristic silence. The little peasant (who showed his enthusiasm for the contractor earlier by spitting "with conviction") now whimpers, which we read as a more intense reaction. And we find ourselves looking up the judgment chain of command for some authoritative verdict. Who, per the story, has been situated to serve as the ultimate arbiter? The Wild Gentleman, who did not pass definitive judgment after the contractor's performance, now weighs in: a "heavy tear," and then the single word "Yashka" finalizes it: Yashka has won.

We can't go to the opera, but we send four friends and ask them to text us during the performance to let us know how things are going. As long as they don't all have identical tastes, their texts are going to represent a multisourced, real-time review of the opera. To the extent that we know them well, we can weight their responses accordingly.

So (our defense continues): Turgenev has made a panel of judges with different personalities and degrees of susceptibility and authority, which allows him to provide a precise picture of the two performances as they unfold in real time, via a precise hierarchy of response. That is why these side characters must be described: so that when they react, we'll know what those reactions mean, which to credit and which to discount; through them, he creates a sort of ascending ladder of credibility.

But still, we may find ourselves asking, even imploring: Do the descriptions have to be so *long*? Do we need all of those words, to do the job? Say Blinker is going to function as a slightly less wacky foil to Booby—do we need to know so much about his life story, there on pages 9 and 10? (We already know he's a goofball from the scene when he enters the pub.) Do we have to know about his one-sleeved coat, his pointed hat, the shape of his lips and nose? Do these details help tell us what sort of judge we should take him for? There is so *much* information given that we struggle to know what to retain as relevant.

Might there be a more efficient, less description-heavy, less taxing version of the story that would work in the same spirit but more briskly?

I always offer my students this optional assignment: photocopy the story and go through it with a red pen, cutting it down to what feels like a more contemporary pace. Give it a faster clip, while trying to preserve the good things about it. Retype it, if you're feeling ambitious. Read it fresh. Is it still working? Working better? Can you trim it by 20 percent more? Then another 10 percent? When do you first start to feel that you're cutting into the bone, i.e., divesting the story of some of the mysterious beauty that, in spite of its wordiness, is there in the original?

If you try this exercise, I think you'll see that it's all about *touch*—your phrase-to-phrase judgment of what's wheat and what's chaff. Since this type of extreme trimming is something a serious writer is going to need to learn to do on his or her own stories, there's an argument to be made for trying to get the hang of it on someone else's work, especially if they've been dead awhile and can't complain about it. (If you can't bear to cut the Turgenev, try the exercise provided in Appendix A, in which I'll ask/allow you to severely cut something I've written for that purpose.)

By page 17, the contest is over. We move out of the heart of the story, into an epilogue of sorts. Yashka is enjoying his victory "like a child." The narrator goes off to take a nap in a hayloft. It's dark when he wakes up and there's an uproar from the pub ("wild bursts of laughter"). The narrator looks in a window and finds that everyone, including Yashka, is drunk. And Yashka is singing again (humming, actually, playing a guitar, "strands of moist hair" falling over his "terribly pale" face). He's come down a long way from the sacred moment of his victory, just a few hours before. As has everyone.

During the contest, we watched the tavern morph into a church. A holy thing happened there: these rough people (peasants, poor men, worked nearly to death in this sweltering, oppressive setting) were uplifted and transformed through art. They recognized beauty when they saw it. Now, the church descends back into tavern.

Did that experience of art provide some sort of lasting change? No. And, in fact, the powerful artistic experience seems to have moved them so much that now they're getting even drunker than usual. An energy transfer has occurred: the power of the singing had to go somewhere, and it's gone into this epic bender. (This might remind us of an incident earlier in the story when, moved by the contractor's performance, Booby attacked that little peasant, with an overflow of art-inspired violent energy.)

And here we feel the story saying something about our need for art. People, even "lowly" people, crave beauty and will go to great lengths to get a taste of it. But, also, beauty is dangerous, and can get into a person so powerfully that it shakes him up and confuses him and incites him, even, to violence. (I've sometimes found myself thinking, at this point in the story, of all that Nazi pageantry, and those agitated and agitating pre-genocidal Rwandan radio broadcasts.)

And yet, it was beautiful, what just happened in that pub, and needed. Something lovely in these people rose to the occasion.

And overflowing with loveliness, they got totally wasted.

Now, in the middle of page 18, we enter a sort of epilogue.

The narrator walks back down the hill, along that ravine that splits the town in two. He hears a distant voice from the valley below: a boy calling out a name, with "obstinate, tearful desperation, drawing out the last syllable a long time." In other words: singing. A boy is calling for someone in a way that is songlike. He calls/sings the name "thirty times at least." Then an answer comes, "as though from a different world," reminding us, maybe, of the beginning of Yashka's song (which came "not from his chest but from somewhere far away"). And this reply ("Wha-a-at?") is also like singing. The first boy calls/sings, "Come here, you little devil. . . . Dad wants to give you a good hiding!" * Understandably, the second boy makes "no further reply." The first boy keeps calling/singing, and the second boy stays silent. As the narrator moves away, the calls gradually get fainter (although even four miles away, he can still hear the first boy calling out).

What does this last scene give us? Well, first, we note that it's a miniature version of the story itself. Or we try that idea on for size. Yes: two males singing back and forth. One "sings" first, and the other responds.

I associate the first boy with the contractor and the second with Yashka. Why? Well, the first boy is pragmatic; he's trying to get the other boy, presumably his brother, to come home, so their father can beat him. Is there a connection between "pragmatic" and the contractor? Yes: we connect pragmatism with technical prowess. We remem-

---

* Or, in a different translation, by Constance Garnett, "Dad wants to thrash you!"

ber that the contractor, "a highly resourceful and smart tradesman," was also an efficient technical singing wizard.

So: the contractor and the first brother are literalists, technicians; they try to get things done; they have a goal in mind. ("Since Dad wants to beat my brother," reasons the first brother, "I'd better get him home, so I don't get beat myself.") They've been reduced by their harsh surroundings—to pragmatism in the first brother's case and (mere, mechanical) technical prowess in the contractor's. Yashka and the second brother, on the other hand, are passive, fragile, more vulnerable to the brutality that prevails here in this provincial dump.

In the pub, we felt singing as a mode of communication, elevating these rough men. The singing made some of them cry, gave them access to a register of emotion mostly denied them in their everyday lives. But singing, here, at the end of the story, is a way of getting some violence arranged, a form of trickery committed by one brother on another. So the story also becomes about *that*—about exalted things being brought low. The men were uplifted and fell; the town was once nice and is now a wreck; singing can be a transcendent form of communication or a way of getting someone home to take a beating. Singing (art) is persuasive but what it will be used to persuade us to do is an open question.

Not wanting to be found and beaten, the second boy falls silent (stops singing). So has Yashka—or anyhow he's stopped singing in that exalted manner in which he sang earlier. And what's impeded his exalted singing is the same thing that's silenced the second boy: this low, tough town, where beauty can't thrive for long.

Note that as the mind tries to perform these sorts of thematic reductions, it also notes the imperfection of the tracking; there's a correspondence, but it's not neat. The story is too lovely and unruly to be reduced in this way: a wild animal that refuses to get into the box we've made, whose opening, shaped too neatly "like" that animal, discounts the fact that the animal is always in motion.

At any rate, I'd say the epilogue has earned its keep: it's a better story with this last scene in it.

Recalling Lynda Barry's notion of the instantaneous, post-reading retro-assessment for efficiency, I find, here at the end of the story, that a few items that have been waiting in my TICHN cart step forward, asking to be taken into account, all from the problematic, meandering first eleven pages: in particular, the description of the ravine on page 1, and the description of those rooks, crows, and sparrows, and of the town itself, on page 3.

In class, we usually go through these one at a time. I recommend this for you, as an exercise. Pause here, hold each of these up against the heart of the story (the singing contest), and see what happens. How does each "earn its keep"?

What do I mean, though, when I ask you to "hold these up against" the singing contest?

Imagine a painting of a tree: a good, tall, healthy oak, standing proud on top of a hill. Now add a second oak to the painting, but . . . sickly: gnarled, bent, with bare branches. As you look at that painting, your mind will understand it to be "about," let's say: vitality vs. weakness. Or: life vs. death. Or: sickness vs. health. It's a realistic painting of two trees, yes, but there is also a metaphorical meaning implied, by the elements contained in it. We "compare" the two trees (or "compare and contrast" them), at first, anyway, without thought or analysis. We just *see* them. The two trees stand there in our minds, juxtaposed, meaning by inference. We experience, rather than articulate, the result. The juxtaposition results in a *feeling:* instantaneous, spontaneous, complex, multitonal, irreducible.

And we're really good at this. Say the painting has in it that healthy tree and a second one that, on first glance, looks identical. The mind immediately starts scanning for differences. Say there's a bird in one of the trees, barely noticeable. Now we read the bird-containing tree as "life-welcoming," the other as "barren."

We're always rationally explaining and articulating things. But we're at our most intelligent in the moment just before we start to explain or articulate. Great art occurs—or doesn't—in that instant. What we turn to art for is precisely this moment, when we "know" something (we feel it) but can't articulate it because it's too complex and multiple. But the "knowing" at such moments, though happening without language, is real. I'd say this is what art is for: to remind us that this other sort of knowing is not only real, it's superior to our usual (conceptual, reductive) way.

Let's go ahead and try this "holding up against" exercise by holding up that ravine against the singing contest.

When I do that, the first feeling that arises is that there *is* a relation, and this relation is not random.

I want to stay there for just a second, to emphasize that this feeling is the one that really matters. We hold the ravine up against the singing contest and . . . something happens in our mind, and it is good. (On the other hand, if an element is random, we get that "failure to engage" feeling, that "Meaningful Relation Not Found" error message.)

Now let's go on and try to articulate the exact nature of the good feeling we get when we juxtapose "ravine" and "singing contest."

One thing that comes to mind is the notion of a binary: there are two singers, and the town is cleft in two. This makes me ask, of the story: Any other binaries in there? Actually, the story is full of them: the doleful, sympathy-seeking rooks and crows vs. the relatively content, chirping, energetic sparrows; the town's former pastoral glory (it had a common, a pond, a mansion) vs. its present state (the common is "scorched" and "dust-laden," the pond "black and almost incandescent," the mansion "grown over with nettles"); Yashka vs. the contractor; technique vs. emotion; Boy #1 vs. Boy #2; the opposition of the beautiful artistic moment Yashka produced vs. the ugly town in which he produced it; the comfortable gentleman who is our narrator vs. the lowly rustics he's dropped in here to observe.

So, yes, I feel that the lines needed to get that ravine into the story were "worth it." It's a lesser story without the ravine. The ravine, we might say, "unlocks" all of the binary references that are, we now see, seeded within the story.

This "holding against" move can be done in all sorts of directions.

For example, let's hold that little burst of birds on page 3 up against our two singers. The rooks and crows gaze "dolefully," their beaks gape, they beg for sympathy (because of the heat). The sparrows are different, spunkier: they don't "seem to mind" the heat and go on "chirping more furiously than ever." Would you say Yashka or the contractor is more likely to go on "chirping more furiously than ever"? Somehow that quality seems associated with the contractor, who's a peppier, more mechanical performer, more of a showboat, less neurotic than

Yashka. Yashka seems more subdued and beaten down and "doleful." But, complicating things (making more beauty), the sparrows are the ones who (like Yashka, sort of) fly up and hover over the town (they, like Yashka, are capable of ascension). Or we might hold the birds up against the other patrons of the Cozy Corner. (Is Booby a sparrow or a rook/crow?) The two singers, like the sparrows, have a temporary way of escaping the squalor, whereas Booby et al. stay on the ground, like the rooks and crows.

In any event, doing this sort of juxtaposition, we feel that the story's elements are highly intentional, that Turgenev spooned those birds and his human characters out of the same artistic soup. These elements are all speaking energetically to one another. The story has, for all of its looseness in other areas, a high level of organization. It may be wordy and awkward in its stagecraft but its controlling sensibility is far from random.

What does it *mean*, that Yashka has won? To answer, we try to distill the essential characteristics of the two performances. Broadly speaking: the contractor was technically wonderful but produced no feeling in his audience except amazement at his proficiency. Yashka, a little wobbly on technique, evoked undeniably deep feelings in his audience and caused a startling, not entirely rational memory to arise in the mind of the narrator. So, we feel the story to be saying something about technical proficiency vs. emotional power, and coming down in favor of the latter. It is saying that the highest aspiration of art is to move the audience and that if the audience is moved, technical deficiencies are immediately forgiven.

And this is where I always fall in love, again, with the story and forgive it all its faults. Here I've been resenting Turgenev's technical bumbling—those piles of noses and brows and hairlines; the stop-and-start action; the digressions inside of digressions—and suddenly I'm moved: by Yashka's performance, which is beautiful though not particularly technically accomplished, and by Turgenev's performance, an analogous performance, also beautiful though technically rickety.

I'm moved by this clumsy work of art that seems to want to make the case that art may be clumsy if only it moves us.

I've sometimes wondered if this effect was intentional: a sort of apologia from Turgenev for his own lack of craft. If we are moved, Turgenev has, via this story that claims that emotional power is the highest aim of art and can be obtained even in the face of clumsy craft, demonstrated that very thing.

Which would be, you know—pretty great craft.

To write a story that works, that moves the reader, is difficult, and most of us can't do it. Even among those who have done it, it mostly can't be done. And it can't be done from a position of total control, of flawless mastery, of simply having an intention and then knowingly executing it. There's intuition involved, and stretching—trying things that are at the limit of our abilities, that may cause mistakes. Like Yashka, the writer has to risk a cracking voice and surrender to his actual power, his doubts notwithstanding.

Let's say there was a wrist-mounted meter that could measure energy output during dancing and the goal was to give off an energy level of 1,000 units. Or someone would (say) kill you. And you had a notion of how you wanted to dance, but when you danced that way, your energy level was down around 50. And when you finally managed to get your energy level above 1,000, you glanced up at a mirror (there's a mirror in there, wherever you're dancing off death) and—wow. Is that *dancing*? Is that *me* dancing? Good God. But your energy level is at 1,200 and climbing.

What would you do?

You'd keep dancing like that.

If people out in the hall were laughing at you, you'd feel: "Okay, sure, laugh away—my dancing is not perfect, but at least I'm not dead."

The writer has to write in whatever way produces the necessary energy. For Turgenev to get his energy level up above 1,000, he had to make those dossiers. He had to admit that he wasn't good at integrating description and action. He had to plunge ahead, doing things his way, or die. He had to look honestly at himself and conclude, "Yep, Mr. Nabokov is right as usual, even though he hasn't even been born yet: my literary genius *does* fall short on the score of naturally discovering ways of telling the story which would equal the originality of my descriptive art. But what am I supposed to do?"

It's hard to get any beauty at all into a story. If and when we do, it might not be the type of beauty we've always dreamed of making. But we have to take whatever beauty we can get, however we can get it.

I teach "The Singers" to suggest to my students how little choice we have about what kind of writer we'll turn out to be. As young writers, we all have romantic dreams of being a writer of a certain kind, of joining a certain lineage. A painstaking realist, maybe; a Nabokovian stylist; a deeply spiritual writer like Marilynne Robinson—whatever. But sometimes the world, via its tepid response to prose written in that mode, tells us that we are not, in fact, that kind of writer. So we have to find another approach, one that will get us up above the required 1,000 units. We have to become whatever writer is capable of producing the necessary level of energy. ("The writer can choose what he writes about," said Flannery O'Connor, "but he cannot choose what he is able to make live.")

This writer may turn out to bear little resemblance to the writer we dreamed of being. She is born, it turns out, for better or worse, out of that which we really are: the tendencies we've been trying, all these years, in our writing and maybe even in our lives, to suppress or deny or correct, the parts of ourselves about which we might even feel a little ashamed.

Whitman was right: we are large, we do contain multitudes. There's more than one "us" in there. When we "find our voice," what's really happening is that we're *choosing* a voice from among the many voices we're able to "do," and we're choosing it because we've found that, of all the voices we contain, it's the one, so far, that has proven itself to be the most energetic.

Imagine that you spent the first twenty years of your life in a room where a TV was constantly showing glamorous footage of Olympic sprinters. (This room is right down the hall from the one where those other writers are dancing for their lives.) You, inspired by all of those years of watching sprinters, have developed a cherished dream of . . . becoming a sprinter. Then, on your twenty-first birthday, you're released from that room and, in the hallway, stumble upon a mirror to find that you are six foot five and thick with muscle and weigh three hundred pounds (not a born sprinter), and when you go outside and run your first hundred-yard dash, you come in last. What a heartbreak! Your dream is ruined. But as you walk away from the track, depressed, you see a group of people built like you: shot-putters, practicing. In that instant, your dream may come back alive, reconfigured. ("When I said I wanted to be a sprinter, what I really meant was that I wanted to be an *athlete*.")

Something like this can happen to writers too.

In my early thirties I saw myself as a Hemingwayesque realist. My material: the time I'd spent working in the oil fields in Asia. I wrote story after story out of that material, and everything I wrote was minimal and strict and efficient and lifeless and humor-free, even though, in real life, I reflexively turned to humor at any difficult or important or awkward or beautiful moment.

I had chosen what to write, but I couldn't seem to make it live.

One day, serving as a note taker on a conference call at the environmental engineering company where I was working, I started, out of boredom, writing these dark little Seussian poems. When I finished one, I'd draw a cartoon to go along with it. By the end of the call, I had around ten of these poem-and-cartoon pairs, and because they weren't my "real" writing, I almost threw them out as I left work that day. But something stopped me. I brought them home, dropped them on the table, went off to see the kids. And then I heard, from back at the table, the sound of genuine laughter, from my wife, as she read those stupid little poems.

This was, I realized with a start, the first time in years that anyone had reacted to my writing with pleasure. I had been getting, from friends and editors, all of those years, the type of reaction writers dread: my stories were "interesting," there was "a lot going in there, for sure," it was clear that I'd "really worked hard on them."

A switch got thrown in my head, and the next day I started writing a story in that new mode—allowing myself to be entertaining, setting aside my idea of what a "classic" story sounded like, and my usual assumption that only things that happened in the real world were allowed to happen in a story. In this new story, which was set in a futuristic theme park, I was using an awkward, slightly overdriven corporate voice that came naturally to me when I thought, "Go ahead, be funny." I wrote it a few lines at a time, not sure where it was going (what its arc was, or its theme, or its "message"), just paying attention to the line-by-line energy and especially to the humor, keeping an eye on my imaginary reader, to see if she was still with me—if she, like my wife, was laughing from the other room and wanted more of the story rather than hoping it would mercifully end soon.

In this mode, I found, I had stronger opinions than when I was trying to be Hemingway. If something wasn't working, I knew what to do about it, immediately and instinctually, in the form of an impulse ("Oh, that might be cool"), whereas before I'd been rationally *deciding,* in stiff obeisance to what I thought a story should, or must, do.

This was a much freer mode—like trying to be funny at a party.

That story ended up becoming "The Wavemaker Falters," the first story I wrote for what would—seven years (!) later—become my first book, *CivilWarLand in Bad Decline.*

When I finished the story, I could see that it was the best thing I'd ever written. There was some essential "me-ness" in it—for better or worse, no one else could have written it. The things that were actually on my mind at that time, because they were in my life, were in the story: class issues, money shortages, work pressures, fear of failure, the odd-ball tonality of the American workplace, the failures of grace my state of overwork was causing me to commit every day. The story was oddly made, slightly embarrassing—it exposed my actual taste, which, it turned out, was kind of working-class and raunchy and attention-seeking. I held that story up against the stories I loved (some of which are in this book) and felt I'd let the form down.

So, this moment of supposed triumph (I'd "found my voice!") was also sad.

It was as if I'd sent the hunting dog that was my talent out across a meadow to fetch a magnificent pheasant and it had brought back, let's say, the lower half of a Barbie doll.

To put it another way: having gone about as high up Hemingway Mountain as I could go, having realized that even at my best I could only ever hope to be an acolyte up there, resolving never again to commit the sin of being imitative, I stumbled back down into the valley and came upon a little shit-hill labeled "Saunders Mountain."

"Hmm," I thought. "It's so *little.* And it's a *shit-hill.*"

Then again, that was my name on it.

This is a big moment for any artist (this moment of combined triumph and disappointment), when we have to decide whether to accept a work of art that we have to admit we weren't in control of as we made it and of which we're not entirely sure we approve. It is *less,* less than we wanted it to be, and yet it's *more,* too—it's small and a bit pathetic, judged against the work of the great masters, but there it is, all ours.

What we have to do at that point, I think, is go over, sheepishly but boldly, and stand on our shit-hill, and hope it will grow.

And—to belabor this already questionable metaphor—what will make that shit-hill grow is our commitment to it, the extent to which we say, "Well, yes, it is a shit-hill, but it's *my* shit-hill, so let me assume that if I continue to work in this mode that is mine, this hill will eventually stop being made of shit, and will grow, and from it, I will eventually be able to see (and encompass in my work) the whole world."

Did Turgenev intend "The Singers" to serve as an apologia for his lack of craft? While he was writing it? After he had written it? I'm pretty sure he didn't "aim" to produce an apologia—didn't *start out* to do that. I doubt he realized what he'd done, and I don't know that he'd necessarily bless our assessment of it. But here's the important thing: I don't think it matters. He did it, and then he let it stand. Which *is* a form (the ultimate form, for an artist) of "meaning to do it" (of taking responsibility). The blessing an artist gives the final product (which he gives by sending it out into the world) is his way of saying that he approves of everything within it, even parts of it that may, in that moment, be hidden from him.

That is to say, final approval isn't given just by one's conscious mind.

My experience is that, late in the game, finishing a story, we're in such deep relation to it that we're making decisions we're not even aware we're making, for reasons too fine to articulate. And we're in too big of a hurry to articulate them anyway. We're operating in an intuitive zone, deciding quickly, without much deliberation.

We've been preparing a hall for a banquet all day, arranging furniture, hanging and rehanging decorations, working so fast and with such intensity that we wouldn't be able to explain the basis on which we've been working. It's late. The guests are coming soon. We've got to race home and get dressed. We pause in the doorway, taking in the whole room at once. We see nothing to change. By not darting back in to adjust even one more thing, we pronounce the room perfect (we approve it)—and that work of art is finished.

AFTERTHOUGHT #2

In this book, we're discussing what the Russians did, but we're not going to be able to say much, I expect, about how exactly they did it. (They weren't as fond of interviews and craft talks and process-related discussions as we are.) In his exhaustive biography of Chekhov, Henri Troyat mentions "In the Cart" exactly once. We learn that Chekhov wrote it in Nice, at a hotel desk, in a room on the second floor, in a period of a few months, during which he also wrote two other stories, "The Pecheneg" and "The Homecoming." But that's all we know about the circumstances of its creation, other than that writing it in a hotel felt to Chekhov, as he put it, "like sewing on someone else's machine." (In Troyat's biography of Turgenev, "The Singers" isn't mentioned at all.)

But really, it doesn't matter. We know that no matter how the Russians did it, we're each going to have to find our own way.

So I thought here I'd talk a little about the only process with which I'm really familiar (mine), just to underscore the idea that discussing a story in technical terms, as we're doing here, doesn't fully unlock the mystery of how a story actually gets written.

We often discuss art this way: the artist had something he wanted to express, and then he just, you know, expressed it. That is, we buy into some version of the intentional fallacy: the notion that art is about having a clear-cut intention and then confidently executing same.

The actual process, in my experience, is much more mysterious and beautiful and more of a pain in the ass to discuss truthfully.

A guy (Stan) constructs a model railroad town in his basement. Stan acquires a small hobo, places him under a plastic railroad bridge, near that fake campfire, then notices that he's arranged his hobo into a certain posture—the hobo seems to be gazing back at the town. Why is he looking over there? At that little blue Victorian house? Stan notes a plastic woman in the window, then turns her a little, so she's gazing out. Over at the railroad bridge, actually. Huh. Suddenly, Stan has made a love story. (Oh, why can't they be together? If only "Little Jack" would just go home. To his wife. To "Linda.")

What did Stan (the artist) just do? Well, first, surveying his little domain, he *noticed* which way his hobo was looking. Then he chose to *change* that little universe, by turning the plastic woman. Now, Stan didn't exactly decide to turn her. It might be more accurate to say that it occurred to him to do so—in a split second, with no accompanying language, except maybe a very quiet internal "Yes."

He just liked it better that way, for reasons he couldn't articulate, and before he'd had the time or inclination to articulate them.

In my view, all art begins in that instant of intuitive preference.

How, then, to proceed? Skipping over, for the moment, the first draft, assuming some existing text to work with, my method is this: I imagine a meter mounted in my forehead, with a *P* on this side ("Positive") and an *N* on that side ("Negative"). I try to read what I've written the way a first-time reader might ("without hope and without despair"). Where's the needle? If it drops into the *N* zone, admit it. And then, instantaneously, a fix might present itself—a cut, a rearrangement, an addition. There's not an intellectual or analytical component to this; it's more of an impulse, one that results in a feeling of "Ah, yes, that's better." It's akin to that hobo adjustment, above: by instinct, in that moment.

And really, that's about it. I go through the draft like that, marking it up, then go back and enter that round of changes, print it out, read it again, for as long as I still feel sharp—usually three or four times in a writing day.

So: a repetitive, obsessive, iterative application of preference: watch the needle, adjust the prose, watch the needle, adjust the prose (lather, rinse, repeat), through (sometimes) hundreds of drafts, over months or even years. Over time, like a cruise ship slowly turning, the story will start to alter course via those thousands of incremental adjustments.

—

Early in a story, I'll have a few discrete blocks (blobs? swaths?) of loose, sloppy text. As I revise, those blocks will start to . . . get better. Soon, a block will start working—I can get all the way through it without a needle drop. The word that sometimes comes to mind is "undeniable," as in "All right, this bit is pretty much undeniable," which means that I feel that any reasonable reader would like it and would still be with me at the end of it.

A block, revised, starts telling me what it's for; sometimes it asks a question ("Who is this Craig of whom they are speaking?") or seems to want to cause something to happen ("Fern has offended Bryce and he's about to blow"). Once I have a few "undeniable" blocks of text, they start telling me what order they'd like to be in, and sometimes one will say that I really ought to cut it out entirely. ("If you get rid of me, Block B, then Blocks A and C will abut, and look at that—that's good, right?") I start asking questions like "Does E cause F or does F cause E? Which feels more natural? Which makes more sense? Which produces a more satisfying click?" Then certain blocks start to adhere (E must precede F) and I know they won't come unstuck.

When something has achieved "undeniability," it feels like something that has actually happened and can't be undone, instead of just words on a page.

As the blocks start to fall into order, the resulting feeling of causation starts to *mean* something (if a man puts his fist through a wall, then joins a street protest, that's one story; if he comes home from a street protest and puts his fist through the wall, that's another) and starts to suggest what the story might want to be "about" (although part of this process is to shake off that feeling as much as possible and keep returning to that P/N meter, trusting that those big thematic decisions are going to be made, naturally, by way of the thousands of accreting microdecisions at the line level).

But all of this, at every step, is more felt than decided.

When I'm writing well, there's almost no intellectual/analytical thinking going on.

When I first found this method, it felt so freeing. I didn't have to worry, didn't have to decide, I just had to be there as I read my story fresh each time, watching that meter, willing to (playfully) make changes at the line level, knowing that if I was wrong, I'd get a chance to change it back on the next read. I once heard someone say that "given infinite time, anything can happen." That's how this way of revising makes me feel. No need for overarching decisions; the story has a will of its own, one it is trying to make me feel, and if I just trust in that, all will be well, and the story will surpass my initial vision of it.

I once heard the great Chicago writer Stuart Dybek say, "A story is always talking to you; you just have to learn to listen to it." Revising like this is a way of listening to the story and of having faith in it: it wants to be its best self, and if you're patient with it, in time, it will be.

Essentially, the whole process is: intuition plus iteration.

Why iteration?

Let's say I gave you an apartment in New York City, one that I'd had decorated. That would be nice of me. But it might feel a little impersonal (since I don't know you). Say that I then allowed you to redecorate it, at my expense, in one day. The result would be much more like you than my initial attempt. But it would still be limited by the fact that I gave you only one day in which to do it. The result would reflect, we might say, only one of the many possible people that you are.

Now let's say that, instead, I let you take out one item a day (today the couch, tomorrow the clock, the next day that ugly little throw rug) and replace it with an item of equal value, of your choice. And I let you do that for, say, the next two years. By the end of that two years, that apartment will have more "you" in it than either one of us could have imagined at the outset. It will have had the benefit of the opinions of literally hundreds of manifestations of you; you happy, you grouchy, you stern, you euphoric, you blurry, you precise, and so on. Your intuition will have been given thousands of chances to do its best work.

That's how I see revision: a chance for the writer's intuition to assert itself over and over.

A piece written and revised in this way, like one of those seed crystals in biology class, starts out small and devoid of intention and begins to expand, organically, reacting to itself, fulfilling its own natural energy.

The beauty of this method is that it doesn't really matter what you start with or how the initial idea gets generated. What makes you *you,* as a writer, is what you do to any old text, by way of this iterative method. This method overturns the tyranny of the first draft. Who cares if the first draft is good? It doesn't need to be good, it just needs *to be,* so you can revise it. You don't need an idea to start a story. You just need a sentence. Where does that sentence come from? Wherever. It doesn't have to be anything special. It will become something special, over time, as you keep reacting to it. Reacting to that sentence, then changing it, hoping to divest it of some of its ordinariness or sloth, is . . . writing. That's all writing is or needs to be. We'll find our voice and ethos and distinguish ourselves from all the other writers in the world without needing to make any big overarching decisions, just by the thousands of small ones we make as we revise.

When our daughters were small, I'd sometimes dump a bunch of building toys on the floor (Legos and wooden blocks and parts of other sets) and we'd sit there for hours, listening to music and talking and absentmindedly making something. There was no plan; we were just putting this with that, because we liked the way it looked. But pretty soon, a structure would start to appear. These ramps were leading to that platform, and there was a cool little space under that platform, an excellent place for that plastic dragon and Lego plumber to live. The final product was complex, and I think you could say it had "meaning," but it wasn't a meaning we'd intentionally put there; no way could we have planned out something so strange or anticipated the exact effect it would have on us later when, having forgotten we'd made it, we walked past it. That is, the thing we would have planned would have been less. The best it could have been was exactly what we intended it to be. But a work of art has to do more than that; it has to surprise its audience, which it can do only if it has legitimately surprised its creator.

What's interesting to me is that revising by this method (trying to make better sentences, per one's taste, over and over) has unintended effects, ones that we might characterize as "moral-ethical."

When I write, "Bob was an asshole" and then, feeling this sentence to be somewhat lacking in specificity, revise it to read, "Bob snapped impatiently at the barista," then ask myself, seeking yet more specificity, why Bob might have done that, and revise to "Bob snapped impatiently at the young barista, who reminded him of his dead wife," then pause to add "who he missed so much, especially now, at Christmas"—in the process, Bob has gone from "pure asshole" to "grieving widower, so overcome with grief that he has behaved ungraciously to a young person to whom, normally, he would have been nice." Bob started out a cartoon on which I could heap some scorn, so that my reader and I could be united in looking down at Bob, but now he's closer to "us, in a different life."

So we might say that the text has become more "alert to Bob." But that didn't happen because I was trying to be a good guy. It happened because I was discontented with the sentence "Bob was an asshole" and tried to make it better.

But the person who wrote, "Bob snapped impatiently at the young barista, who reminded him of his dead wife, Marie, who he missed so much, especially now, at Christmas, which had always been her favorite time of year" feels like a better guy, somehow, than the one who wrote, "Bob was an asshole."

I find this happening all the time. I like the person I am in my stories better than I like the real me. That person is smarter, wittier, more patient, funnier—his view of the world is wiser.

When I stop writing and come back to myself, I feel more limited, opinionated, and petty.

But what a pleasure it was, to have been, on the page, briefly less of a dope than usual.

What does an artist do, mostly? She tweaks that which she's already done. There are those moments when we sit before a blank page, but mostly we're adjusting what's already there. The writer revises, the painter touches up, the director edits, the musician overdubs. I write, "Jane came into the room and sat down on the blue couch," read that, wince, cross out "came into the room" (why does she have to come into the room?) and "down" (can someone sit *up* on a couch?) and "blue" (why do we care if it's blue?) and the sentence now has become: "Jane sat on the couch," and suddenly, it's better (Hemingwayesque, even), although . . . why is it meaningful for Jane to sit on a couch? Do we really need that?

So we cut "sat on the couch."

And are left with, simply: "Jane."

Which at least doesn't suck, and has the virtue of brevity.

This is, of course, a bit of a joke. But it's also deadly serious. By reducing the sentence to "Jane . . . ," we've preserved our hope of being original. We've averted mediocrity. The whole world of excellence (still) lies before us.

But it's interesting—why did we make those cuts?

Well, we might say that we made them out of respect for our reader. By asking that series of questions ("Why is it meaningful for Jane to sit on a couch?" and so on), we were serving as a sort of advance man for a reader we are assuming to be a smart person, of good taste, a person we wouldn't want to bore.

Consider this passage:

> Entering the restaurant, Jim saw his ex-wife, Sara, sitting closely beside a man who looked to be at least twenty years younger than her. Jim couldn't believe it. It was shocking to see Sara with someone so much younger than her, younger than Jim too, since he and Sara were the same age, so shocking that Jim dropped his car keys.
>
> "Sir," the waiter said, "you dropped these," and handed Jim his car keys.

You may have noted your needle dipping into the N zone in there somewhere, maybe a couple of times (a dip and then a subdip?).

Now consider this edited version:

> Entering the restaurant, Jim saw his ex-wife, Sara, sitting beside a man who looked to be at least twenty years younger than her.
>
> "Sir," the waiter said, "you dropped these," and handed Jim his car keys.

So, what just happened? Well, I cut "Jim couldn't believe it. It was shocking to see Sara with someone so much younger than her, younger than Jim too, since he and Sara were the same age, so shocking that Jim dropped his car keys."

The difference in the two versions is that the latter version has more respect for you, the reader, built into it. The ideas "Jim couldn't believe it" and "It was shocking" are contained in the action of Jim dropping his keys. I made the leap of faith that you'd assume Jim and Sara to be about the same age. In the process, I've saved myself (and you) thirty-seven words—about half the total length of the original bit.

How did I go about making that cut? Well, I imagined that I was you and that you read the same way I do, that you would be discontented with the first version at the same places I was, as I read it.

A story is a frank, intimate conversation between equals. We keep reading because we continue to feel respected by the writer. We feel her, over there on the production end of the process, imagining that we are as intelligent and worldly and curious as she is. Because she's paying attention to where we are (to where she's put us), she knows when we are "expecting a change" or "feeling skeptical of this new development" or "getting tired of this episode." (She also knows when she's delighted us and that, in that state, we're slightly more open to whatever she'll do next.)

This idea of a story as an ongoing communication between two minds arises naturally from the activity of one person telling a story to another. This model applies to these Russian stories we're reading, and would have applied the first time some cavepeople gathered around a fire for the first literary reading, and if that early storyteller ignored this notion of story as ongoing communication between performer and audience, he would have found, as today, that some of his audience was dozing off or sneaking out of the cave early, in that crouching posture people adopt when sneaking out of a literary event, as if crouching like that will make them invisible to the author, which, believe me, it doesn't.

The exciting part of all of this, to me, is that we always have a basis on which to proceed. The reader is out there, and she's real. She's interested in life and, by picking up our work, has given us the benefit of the doubt.

All we have to do is engage her.

To engage her, all we have to do is value her.

THE DARLING

Anton Chekhov

(1899)

THE DARLING

———

Olenka Plemyannikova, the daughter of a retired collegiate assessor, was sitting on her porch, which gave on the courtyard; deep in thought. It was hot, the flies were persistent and annoying, and it was pleasant to think that it would soon be evening. Dark rainclouds were gathering in the east and there was a breath of moisture in the wind that occasionally blew from that direction.

Kukin, a theater manager who ran a summer garden known as The Tivoli and lodged in the wing of the house, was standing in the middle of the courtyard, staring at the sky.

"Again!" he was saying in despair. "It's going to rain again! Rain every day, every day, as if to spite me! It will be the death of me! It's ruin! Such a frightful loss every day!"

He struck his hands together and continued, turning to Olenka:

"There, Olga Semyonovna, that's our life. It's enough to make you weep! You work, you try your utmost, you wear yourself out, you lie awake nights, you rack your brains trying to make a better thing of it, and what's the upshot? In the first place, the public is ignorant, barbarous. I give them the very best operetta, an elaborate spectacle, first-rate vaudeville artists. But do you think they want that? It's all above their heads. All they want is slapstick! Give them trash! And then look at the weather! Rain almost every evening. It started raining on the tenth of May, and it has kept it up all May and June. It's simply terrible! The public doesn't come, but don't I have to pay the rent? Don't I have to pay the artists?"

The next day toward evening the sky would again be overcast and Kukin would say, laughing hysterically:

"Well, go on, rain! Flood the garden, drown me! Bad luck to me in this world and the next! Let the artists sue me! Let them send me to prison—to Siberia—to the scaffold! Ha, ha, ha!"

The next day it was the same thing all over again.

Olenka listened to Kukin silently, gravely, and sometimes tears would come to her eyes. In the end his misfortunes moved her and she fell in love with him. He was a short, thin man with a sallow face, and wore his hair combed down over his temples. He had a thin tenor voice and when he spoke, his mouth twisted, and his face perpetually wore an expression of despair. Nevertheless he aroused a genuine, deep feeling in her. She was always enamored of someone and could not live otherwise. At first it had been her papa, who was now ill and sat in an armchair in a darkened room, breathing with [2] difficulty. Then she had devoted her affections to her aunt, who used to come from Bryansk every other year. Still earlier, when she went to school, she had been in love with her French teacher. She was a quiet, kind, soft-hearted girl, with meek, gentle eyes, and she enjoyed very good health. At the sight of her full pink cheeks, her soft white neck with a dark birthmark on it, and the kind artless smile that came into her face when she listened to anything pleasant, men said to themselves, "Yes, not half bad," and smiled too, while the ladies present could not refrain from suddenly seizing her hand in the middle of the conversation and exclaiming delightedly, "You darling!"

The house in which she lived all her life and which was to be hers by her father's will, was situated on the outskirts of the city on what was known as Gypsy Road, not far from The Tivoli. In the evening and at night she could hear the band play and the skyrockets go off, and it seemed to her that it was Kukin fighting his fate and assaulting his chief enemy, the apathetic public. Her heart contracted sweetly, she had no desire to sleep, and when he returned home at dawn, she would tap softly at her bedroom window and, showing him only her face and one shoulder through the curtain, give him a friendly smile.

He proposed to her, and they were married. And when he had a good look at her neck and her plump firm shoulders, he struck his hands together, and exclaimed, "Darling!"

He was happy, but as it rained on their wedding day and the night that followed, the expression of despair did not leave his face.

As a married couple, they got on well together. She presided over the box office, looked after things in the summer garden, kept accounts and paid salaries; and her rosy cheeks, the radiance of her sweet artless smile showed now in the box office window, now in the wings of the theater, now at the buffet. And she was already telling her friends that the theater was the most remarkable, the most important, and the most essential thing in the world, and that it was only the theater that could give true pleasure and make you a cultivated and humane person.

"But do you suppose the public understands that?" she would ask. "What it wants is slapstick! Yesterday we gave 'Faust Inside Out,' and almost all the boxes were empty, and if Vanichka and I had put on something vulgar, I assure you the theater would have been [3] packed. Tomorrow Vanichka and I are giving 'Orpheus in Hell.' Do come."

And what Kukin said about artists and the theater she would repeat. Like him she despised the public for its ignorance and indifference to art; she took a hand in the rehearsals, correcting the actors, kept an eye on the musicians, and when there was an unfavorable notice in the local paper, she wept and went to see the editor about it.

The actors were fond of her and called her "the darling," and "Vanichka-and-I." She was sorry for them and would lend them small sums, and if they cheated her, she cried in private but did not complain to her husband.

The pair got on just as well together when winter came. They leased the municipal theater for the season and sublet it for short periods to a Ukrainian troupe, a magician, or a local dramatic club. Olenka was gaining weight and beamed with happiness, but Kukin was getting thinner and more sallow and complained of terrible losses, although business was fairly good during the winter. He coughed at night, and she would make him drink an infusion of raspberries and linden blossoms, rub him with eau de Cologne and wrap him in her soft shawls.

"What a sweet thing you are!" she would say quite sincerely, smoothing his hair. "My handsome sweet!"

At Lent he left for Moscow to engage a company of actors for the summer season, and she could not sleep with him away. She sat at the window and watched the stars. It occurred to her that she had something in common with the hens: they too stayed awake all night and were disturbed when the cock was absent from the henhouse. Kukin was detained in Moscow, and wrote that he would return by Easter, and in his letters he sent instructions about The Tivoli. But on the Monday of Passion Week, late in the evening, there was a sudden ominous knock at the gate; someone was banging at the wicket as though it were a barrel—boom, boom, boom! The sleepy cook, her bare feet splashing through the puddles, ran to open the gate.

"Open, please!" someone on the other side of the gate was saying in a deep voice. "There's a telegram for you."

[4]   Olenka had received telegrams from her husband before, but this time for some reason she was numb with fright. With trembling hands she opened the telegram and read the following:

"Ivan Petrovich died suddenly today awaiting prot instructions tuneral Tuesday."

That is exactly how the telegram had it: "tuneral," and there was also the incomprehensible word "prot"; the signature was that of the director of the comic opera company.

"My precious!" Olenka sobbed. "Vanichka, my precious, my sweet! Why did we ever meet! Why did I get to know you and to love you! To whom can your poor unhappy Olenka turn?"

Kukin was buried on Tuesday in the Vagankovo Cemetery in Moscow. Olenka returned home on Wednesday, and no sooner did she enter her room than she sank onto the bed and sobbed so loudly that she could be heard in the street and in the neighboring court-yards.

"The darling!" said the neighbors, crossing themselves. "Darling Olga Semyonovna! How the poor soul takes on!"

Three months later Olenka was returning from Mass one day in deep mourning and very sad. It happened that one of her neighbors, Vasily Andreich Pustovalov, the manager of Babakayev's lumber-yard, who was also returning from church, was walking beside her. He was wearing a straw hat and a white waistcoat, with a gold watch-chain, and he looked more like a landowner than a business-man.

"There is order in all things, Olga Semyonovna," he was saying sedately, with a note of sympathy in his voice; "and if one of our dear ones passes on, then it means that this was the will of God, and in that case we must keep ourselves in hand and bear it submissively."

Having seen Olenka to her gate, he took leave of her and went further. All the rest of the day she heard his sedate voice, and as soon as she closed her eyes she had a vision of his dark beard. She liked him very much. And apparently she too had made an impression on him, because a little later a certain elderly lady, whom she scarcely knew, called to have coffee with her, and no sooner was she seated at table than the visitor began to talk about Pustovalov, saying that he was a fine, substantial man, and that any marriageable woman would be glad to go to the altar with him. Three days later Pustovalov himself paid her a visit. He did not stay more than ten minutes and he said little, but Olenka fell in love with him, so deeply that she stayed awake all night burning as with fever, and in the morning she sent for the elderly lady. The match was soon arranged and then came the wedding. [5]

As a married couple Pustovalov and Olenka got on very well together. As a rule he was in the lumberyard till dinnertime, then he went out on business and was replaced by Olenka, who stayed in the office till evening, making out bills and seeing that orders were shipped.

"We pay twenty percent more for lumber every year," she would say to customers and acquaintances. "Why, we used to deal in local timber, and now Vasichka has to travel to the province of Mogilev for timber regularly. And the freight rates!" she would exclaim, putting her hands to her cheeks in horror. "The freight rates!"

It seemed to her that she had been in the lumber business for ages, that lumber was the most important, the most essential thing in the world, and she found something intimate and touching in the very sound of such words as beam, log, batten, plank, box board, lath, scantling, slab . . .

At night she would dream of whole mountains of boards and planks, of endless caravans of carts hauling lumber out of town to distant points. She would dream that a regiment of beams, 28 feet by

8 inches, standing on end, was marching in the lumberyard, that beams, logs, and slabs were crashing against each other with the hollow sound of dry wood, that they kept tumbling down and rising again, piling themselves on each other. Olenka would scream in her sleep and Pustovalov would say to her tenderly: "Olenka, what's the matter, darling? Cross yourself!"

Whatever ideas her husband had, she adopted as her own. If he thought that the room was hot or that business was slow, she thought so too. Her husband did not care for entertainments and on holidays stayed home—so did she.

"You are always at home or in the office," her friends would say. "You ought to go to the theater, darling, or to the circus."

[6]   "Vasichka and I have no time for the theater," she would answer sedately. "We are working people, we're not interested in such foolishness. What good are these theaters?"

On Saturdays the two of them would go to evening service, on holidays they attended early Mass, and returning from the church they walked side by side, their faces wearing a softened expression. There was an agreeable aroma about them, and her silk dress rustled pleasantly. At home they had tea with shortbread, and various kinds of jam, and afterward they ate pie. Every day at noon, in the yard and on the street just outside the gate, there was a delicious smell of *borshch* and roast lamb or duck, and on fast days there was the odor of fish, and one could not pass the Pustovalov gate without one's mouth watering.

In the office the samovar was always boiling and the customers were treated to tea with doughnuts. Once a week the pair went to the baths and returned side by side, both with red faces.

"Yes, everything goes well with us, thank God," Olenka would say to her friends. "I wish everyone were as happy as Vasichka and I."

When Pustovalov went off to the provinces of Mogilev for timber, she missed him badly and lay awake nights, crying. Sometimes, in the evening, a young army veterinary, by the name of Smirnin, who rented the wing of their house, would call on her. He chatted or played cards with her and that diverted her. What interested her most was what he told her about his domestic life. He had been married and had a son, but was separated from his wife because she had been unfaithful to him, and now he hated her; he sent her forty rubles a month for the maintenance of the child. And listening to him, Olenka would sigh and shake her head: she was sorry for him.

"Well, God keep you," she would say to him as she took leave of him, going to the stairs with him, candle in hand. "Thank you for relieving my boredom, and may the Queen of Heaven give you health!"

She always expressed herself in this sedate and reasonable manner, in imitation of her husband. Just as the veterinary would be closing the door behind him, she would recall him and say:

"You know, Vladimir Platonych, you had better make up with your wife. You ought to forgive her, at least for your son's sake! I am [7] sure the little boy understands everything."

And when Pustovalov came back, she would tell him in low tones about the veterinary and his unhappy domestic life, and both of them would sigh and shake their heads and speak of the boy, who was probably missing his father. Then by a strange association of ideas they would both turn to the icons, bow down to the ground before them and pray that the Lord would grant them children.

Thus the Pustovalovs lived in peace and quiet, in love and harmony for six years. But one winter day, right after having hot tea at the office, Vasily Andreich went out without his cap to see about shipping some lumber, caught a chill and was taken sick. He was treated by the best doctors, but the illness had its own way with him, and he died after four months. Olenka was a widow again.

"To whom can I turn now, my darling?" she sobbed when she had buried her husband. "How can I live without you, wretched and unhappy as I am? Pity me, good people, left all alone in the world—"

She wore a black dress with white cuffs and gave up wearing hat and gloves for good. She hardly ever left the house except to go to church or to visit her husband's grave, and at home she lived like a nun. Only at the end of six months did she take off her widow's weeds and open the shutters. Sometimes in the morning she was seen with her cook going to market for provisions, but how she lived now and what went on in her house could only be guessed. People based their guesses on such facts as that they saw her having tea with the veterinary in her little garden, he reading the newspaper aloud to her, and that, meeting an acquaintance at the post office, she would say:

"There is no proper veterinary inspection in our town, and that's why there is so much illness around. So often you hear of people getting ill from the milk or catching infections from horses and cows. When you come down to it, the health of domestic animals must be as well cared for as the health of human beings."

She now repeated the veterinary's words and held the same opinions about everything that he did. It was plain that she could not live even for one year without an attachment and that she had found new happiness in the wing of her house. Another woman would have [*8*] been condemned for this, but of Olenka no one could think ill: everything about her was so unequivocal. Neither she nor the veterinary mentioned to anyone the change that had occurred in their relations; indeed, they tried to conceal it, but they didn't succeed, because Olenka could not keep a secret. When he had visitors, his regimental colleagues, she, pouring the tea or serving the supper, would begin to talk of the cattle plague, of the pearl disease, of the municipal slaughterhouses. He would be terribly embarrassed and when the guests had gone, he would grasp her by the arms and hiss angrily:

"I've asked you before not to talk about things that you don't understand! When veterinaries speak among themselves, please don't butt in! It's really annoying!"

She would look at him amazed and alarmed and ask, "But Volodichka, what shall I talk about?"

And with tears in her eyes she would hug him and beg him not to be angry, and both of them were happy.

Yet this happiness did not last long. The veterinary left, left forever, with his regiment, which was moved to some remote place, it may have been Siberia. And Olenka remained alone.

Now she was quite alone. Her father had died long ago, and his armchair stood in the attic, covered with dust and minus one leg. She got thinner and lost her looks, and passers-by in the street did not glance at her and smile as they used to. Obviously, her best years were over, were behind her, and now a new kind of life was beginning for her, an unfamiliar kind that did not bear thinking of. In the evening Olenka sat on her porch, and heard the band play at The Tivoli and the rockets go off, but this no longer suggested anything to her mind. She looked apathetically at the empty courtyard, thought of nothing, and later, when night came, she would go to bed and dream of the empty courtyard. She ate and drank as though involuntarily.

Above all, and worst of all, she no longer had any opinions whatever. She saw objects about her and understood what was going on, but she could not form an opinion about anything and did not know what to talk about. And how terrible it is not to have any opinions! You see, for instance, a bottle, or the rain, or a peasant driving in a cart, but what is the bottle for, or the rain, or the peasant, what is the [9] meaning of them, you can't tell, and you couldn't, even if they paid you a thousand rubles. When Kukin was about, or Pustovalov or, later, the veterinary, Olenka could explain it all and give her opinions about anything you like, but now there was the same emptiness in her head and in her heart as in her courtyard. It was weird, and she felt as bitter as if she had been eating wormwood.

Little by little the town was extending in all directions. Gypsy Road was now a regular street, and where The Tivoli had been and the lumberyards, houses had sprung up and lanes had multiplied. How swiftly time passes! Olenka's house had taken on a shabby look, the roof was rusty, the shed sloped, and the whole yard was invaded by burdock and stinging nettles. Olenka herself had aged and grown homely. In the summer she sat on the porch, feeling empty and dreary and bitter, as before; in the winter she sat by the window and stared at the snow. Sometimes at the first breath of spring or when the wind brought her the chime of church bells, memories of the past would overwhelm her, her heart would contract sweetly and her eyes would brim over with tears. But this only lasted a moment, and then there was again emptiness and once more she was possessed by a sense of the futility of life; Trot, the black kitten, rubbed against her and purred softly, but Olenka was not affected by these feline caresses. Is that what she needed? She needed an affection that would take possession of her whole being, her soul, her mind, that would give her ideas, a purpose in life, that would warm her aging blood. And she would shake the kitten off her lap, and say irritably: "Scat! Scat! Don't stick to me!"

And so it went, day after day, year after year, and no joy, no opinion! Whatever Mavra the cook would say, was well enough.

One hot July day, toward evening, when the cattle were being driven home and the yard was filled with clouds of dust, suddenly someone knocked at the gate. Olenka herself went to open it and was dumfounded at what she saw: at the gate stood Smirnin, the veterinary, already gray, and wearing civilian clothes. She suddenly recalled everything and, unable to control herself, burst into tears, silently letting her head drop on his breast. She was so agitated that she scarcely noticed how the two of them entered the house and sat [10] down to tea.

"My dear," she murmured, trembling with joy, "Vladimir Platonych, however did you get here?"

"I have come here for good," he explained. "I have retired from the army and want to see what it's like to be on my own and live a settled life. And besides, my son is ready for high school. I have made up with my wife, you know."

"Where is she?"

"She's at the hotel with the boy, and I'm out looking for lodgings."

"Goodness, Vladimir Platonych, take my house! You don't need to look further! Good Lord, and you can have it free," exclaimed Olenka, all in a flutter and beginning to cry again. "You live here in the house, and the wing will do for me. Heavens, I'm so glad!"

The next day they began painting the roof and whitewashing the walls, and Olenka, her arms akimbo, walked about the yard, giving orders. The old smile had come back to her face, and she was lively and spry, as though she had waked from a long sleep. Presently the veterinary's wife arrived, a thin, homely lady with bobbed hair who looked as if she were given to caprices. With her was the little boy, Sasha, small for his age (he was going on ten), chubby, with clear blue eyes and dimples in his cheeks.

No sooner did he walk into the yard than he began chasing the cat, and immediately his eager, joyous laughter rang out.

"Auntie, is that your cat?" he asked Olenka. "When she has little ones, please give us a kitten. Mama is terribly afraid of mice."

Olenka chatted with him, then gave him tea, and her heart suddenly grew warm and contracted sweetly, as if this little boy were her own son. And in the evening, as he sat in the dining-room doing his homework, she looked at him with pity and tenderness and whispered:

"My darling, my pretty one, my little one! How blond you are, and so clever!"

"An island," he was reciting from the book, "is a body of land entirely surrounded by water."

"An island is a body of land . . ." she repeated and this was the first opinion she expressed with conviction after so many years of silence and mental vacuity. [ss]

She now had opinions of her own, and at supper she had a conversation with Sasha's parents, saying that studying in high school was hard on the children, but that nevertheless the classical course was better than the scientific one because a classical education opened all careers to you: you could be either a doctor or an engineer.

Sasha started going to high school. His mother went off to Kharkov to visit her sister and did not come back; every day his father left town to inspect herds and sometimes he stayed away for three days together, and it seemed to Olenka that Sasha was wholly abandoned, that he was unwanted, that he was being starved, and she moved him into the wing with her and settled him in a little room there.

For six months now Sasha has been living in her wing. Every morning Olenka comes into his room; he is fast asleep, his hand under his cheek, breathing quietly. She is sorry to wake him.

"Sashenka," she says sadly, "get up, my sweet! It's time to go to school."

He gets up, dresses, says his prayers, and sits down to his breakfast: he drinks three glasses of tea and eats two large doughnuts, and half a buttered French roll. He is hardly awake and consequently cross.

"You haven't learned the fable, Sashenka," says Olenka, looking at him as though she were seeing him off on a long journey. "You worry me. You must do your best, darling, study. And pay attention to your teachers."

"Please leave me alone!" says Sasha.

Then he walks down the street to school, a small boy in a big cap, with his books in a rucksack. Olenka follows him noiselessly.

"Sashenka!" she calls after him. He turns around and she thrusts a date or a caramel into his hand. When they turn into the school lane, he feels ashamed at being followed by a tall stout woman; he looks round and says: "You'd better go home, auntie; I can go alone now."

[12]   She stands still and stares after him until he disappears at the school entrance. How she loves him! Not one of her former attachments was so deep; never had her soul surrendered itself so unreservedly, so disinterestedly and with such joy as now when her maternal instinct was increasingly asserting itself. For this little boy who was not her own, for the dimples in his cheeks, for his very cap, she would have laid down her life, would have laid it down with joy, with tears of tenderness. Why? But who knows why?

Having seen Sasha off to school, she goes quietly home, contented, tranquil, brimming over with love; her face, grown younger in the last six months, beams with happiness; people meeting her look at her with pleasure and say:

"Good morning, Olga Semyonovna, darling! How are you, darling?"

"They make the children work so hard at high school nowadays," she says, as she does her marketing. "Think of it: yesterday in the first form they had a fable to learn by heart, a Latin translation and a problem for homework. That's entirely too much for a little fellow."

And she talks about the teachers, the lessons, the textbooks— saying just what Sasha says about them.

At three o'clock they have dinner together, in the evening they do the homework together, and cry. When she puts him to bed, she takes a long time making the sign of the cross over him and whispering prayers. Then she goes to bed and thinks of the future, distant and misty, when Sasha, having finished his studies, will become a doctor or an engineer, will have a large house of his own, horses, a carriage, will marry and become a father. She falls asleep and her dreams are of the same thing, and tears flow down her cheeks from her closed eyes. The black kitten lies beside her purring: Purr-purrr-purrr.

Suddenly there is a loud knock at the gate. Olenka wakes up, breathless with fear, her heart palpitating. Half a minute passes, and there is another knock.

"That's a telegram from Kharkov," she thinks, beginning to tremble from head to foot. "Sasha's mother is sending for him from Kharkov— O Lord!"

She is in despair. Her head, her hands, her feet grow chill and it [13] seems to her that she is the most unhappy woman in the whole world. But another minute passes, voices are heard: it's the veterinary returning from the club.

"Well, thank God!" she thinks.

Little by little the load rolls off her heart and she is again at ease; she goes back to bed and thinks of Sasha who is fast asleep in the next room and sometimes shouts in his sleep:

"I'll give it to you! Scram! No fighting!" ✦

A PATTERN STORY

To review: the fundamental unit of storytelling is a two-part move.

First, the writer creates an expectation: "Once upon a time, there was a dog with two heads." In the reader's mind arises a suite of questions ("Do the heads get along?" "What happens at mealtime?" "Are other animals in this world two-headed?") and the first intimations of what the story might be about ("The divided self?" "Partisanship?" "Optimism vs. pessimism?" "Friendship?").

Second, the writer responds to (or "uses" or "exploits" or "honors") that set of expectations. But not too tightly (using those expectations in a way that feels too linear or phoned in) and not too loosely (taking the story off in some random direction that bears no relation to the expectations it has created).

One time-honored way of creating an expectation: enactment of a pattern.

"Once upon a time, there were three sons. The first son went out to seek his fortune and, because he was constantly checking his phone, fell over a cliff and was killed instantly." If the next line begins: "The second son rose early the next day . . ." we're already (1) expecting the second son to die, and (2) wondering about his relationship to his phone. If we extend the sentence to read, "The second son rose early the next day and, leaving his phone behind, walked out the door," our expectations are again modified: death by phone has been ruled out; misfortune is still expected. If we continue with "Noting the cliff on his right, he skillfully avoided it. Then, singing at the top of his lungs, not paying attention to what was going on around him at all, because he was lost in a fantasy of finally asking Hilda to marry him, the second son was hit by a truck and killed instantly"—there is, I'm sorry to say, some satisfaction in this. We now feel the story to be "about," say, *death by distraction*. And we'll be watching the third son as he goes out the door the next morning, to see what form of inattention he will manifest that will get him killed. If he notes the cliff and avoids falling over it, then patiently waits on the shoulder of the road for a speeding truck to pass, the story will still be "about" inattention—we are still waiting for him to do something inattentive and die—because that's what it has been about so far.

A pattern is established and we expect it to recur. When it does recur, slightly altered, we take pleasure in this and infer meaning from the alteration.

"The Darling" is this type of story—what we might call a "pattern story." Its baseline pattern is: a woman falls in love and that love comes to an end. This pattern recurs three times: with the theater owner Kukin, the lumber guy Vasily, and the veterinary surgeon Smirnin. The story ends in the middle of a fourth recurrence: she is in love with the little boy, Sasha, but that love hasn't yet ended.

Kukin shows up on the first page, lamenting his fate. (How could he possibly have predicted that managing a provincial regional theater would be frustrating?) We learn (on the second page) that Olenka "was always enamored of someone and could not live otherwise." A listing follows: her father, her aunt, a teacher. So: she always has to be in love. And now here's Kukin, lodging in her house.

It's a sweet romance, and Olenka's first, it seems. True, Kukin is a bit of a downer ("a short, thin man with a sallow face . . . [which] perpetually wore an expression of despair") but nevertheless "his misfortunes moved her and she fell in love with him."

Among the things Chekhov tells us about Olenka and Kukin's relationship over the course of pages 2–3, as a particular relationship gets made via specific facts: Kukin's job (he runs a failing theater); the flavor of their courtship (they arrange it themselves and she falls for him out of pity); the flavor of the relationship (they get along well, are sad and worried and united in mutual resentment of the lowbrow public; she gains weight, he loses weight); how Kukin refers to/thinks of her ("Darling!"); how she refers to/thinks of him ("What a sweet thing you are!" and "My handsome sweet!"); the duration of the relationship (ten months); the method of their parting (he dies when away from home, and she hears about it via a garbled telegram); and the length of her mourning period (three months).

For ease of reference, I've compiled this data in Table 2.

TABLE 2
Olenka and Kukin

CATEGORY	DESCRIPTION
His job	Theater owner
Flavor of their courtship	They arrange it themselves. She falls "in the end" from pity. ("His misfortunes moved her.")
Flavor of their relationship	Sad and worried. They resent the public. She is gaining weight, he is "more sallow." "They got on well together."
How he refers to Olenka	"Darling!"
How she refers to him	"What a sweet thing you are!" "My handsome sweet!"
Duration of affair, in pages	2.5 pages
Duration of affair, in time	10 months
Method of his death or their parting	Cause of death unknown. She hears about it via (garbled) telegram.
Period of mourning	3 months.
Status of "the wing"	During the affair Kukin is lodging there. (Kukin comes to her from within her house.) When they are married, the wing goes empty.

For now, let's just note the density of information here and how, really, that's all these first few pages are: a matrix of specific facts about Olenka and Kukin's relationship.

We also get a first look at what we will come to understand as Olenka's signature trait: she loves Kukin so much that she becomes him. On page 3, we find out that she's taken on work at the theater. Soon she's telling her friends that the theater is the most remarkable, important, and essential thing in the world, and is sharing Kukin's opinions to such an extent that the actors start affectionately mocking her for it, calling her "Vanichka-and-I."

At this early point in the story, Olenka's mind meld with Kukin doesn't seem strange. It just feels like she's really in love. It's a sweet, heightened version of what happens to any of us when we fall in love. We mold to the beloved and share their interests, and this feels like a once-in-a-lifetime connection, and we're happy.

By the end of page 3, the happy marriage has been established and the story is in stasis. If, as the pages continue to go by, we just get further iterations of the two of them being content in their particular flavor—him getting thinner and more harried, her plumper and more adorable, as the seasons flow happily by—we'll get that special feeling we get in the face of a narrative that doesn't seem to be going anywhere, the one we get when someone tells us about the long dream they had the night before.

We will begin to wonder, again channeling Dr. Seuss: "Why are you bothering telling me this?"

If I write, "Once there was a dog who really liked to eat. One morning, he ate his dog food, then ate the cat's food. He went outside and ate some apples he found under a tree. Then he ate some more apples he found under a nearby tree. Then he found part of a pork sandwich in the park and ate that"—well, you've got it. You've grasped the pattern ("the dog *eats*") and are waiting for something to disrupt the pattern, either by challenging it (the dog tries to eat a living bear) or showing the consequences of it (the dog gets so fat it can't walk). The fact, "this one dog was always hungry and was constantly eating," may be true, but the world is full of incidental truths like that, the sort we can glean by mere observation: "Once a flower pot had a tennis ball in it." "This one girl kept reaching up to touch the top of her head while waiting for a bus."

The story form asks of the merely anecdotal: "Yeah, but so what?"

What transforms an anecdote into a story is escalation. Or, we might say: when escalation is suddenly felt to be occurring, it is a sign that our anecdote is transforming into a story.

—

Figure 1 is a little number called "Freytag's triangle" that purports to explain how stories work. It does, actually, a pretty good job of helping us understand any story that works, works. It's an after-the-fact construction that won't necessarily help us write a story, but it can help us analyze one that's already up and running or diagnose one that isn't.

As long as Olenka's happy marriage to Kukin continues, we sit becalmed in that flat-line zone labeled "Exposition" ("Usually things were like this"). Even as Olenka is singing Kukin's praises toward the bottom of page 3 ("What a sweet thing you are!"), we feel a little restless, sensing that we already have all we need: the baseline state of things has been established and is waiting to be disrupted. We're alert for some complicating thing to happen, to push us into the "rising action."

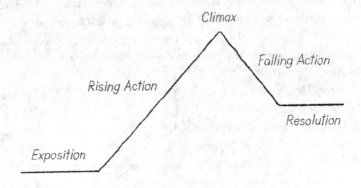

FIGURE 1. Freytag's Triangle

When we read "At Lent he left for Moscow," we go slightly on alert (especially given the mention, two paragraphs above, that he's been ill). This must be why Chekhov is sending Kukin to Moscow: so something can happen to him there to nudge us into the rising action. (I sometimes joke with my students that if they find themselves trapped in exposition, writing pages and pages in which their action doesn't rise, all they need to do is drop this sentence into their story: "Then something happened that changed everything forever." The story has no choice but to respond.)*

---

* In Appendix B, I offer an exercise for the writers among us: a surefire trick to get out of the exposition and into the rising action.

We wait for news from Moscow. Kukin is not coming home as planned ("Kukin was detained in Moscow, and . . . would return by Easter"). We wonder why he's changed his plans. Is he losing interest in Olenka? Having an affair in Moscow? Is it going to become *that* story? If so: Kukin, you pig. But no: he's still sending home instructions about the theater, and we read this as a signal that he must still care about Olenka and their life together. But why would Chekhov send him to Moscow if nothing's going to happen to him there? If things remain unaltered and he just comes home, the same guy he was when he left, we're going to feel that Moscow digression as a little goiter of inefficiency, one that has left us (still) stranded in the exposition.

Then comes the fateful word "But," telling us that the story-changing event we've been waiting for is upon us:

"*But* on the Monday of Passion Week, late in the evening, there was a sudden ominous knock at the gate."

We think: Late-night knock at gate = bad news.

Then, at "telegram": Late-night knock at gate + telegram = death?

The telegram is comically mangled. Which is sad and funny and makes Kukin's death more palatable. We knew, at some level, that Kukin had to be gotten out of the way, and we forgive Chekhov for getting rid of him in such a first-order way (i.e., killing him off), in part because the telegram somehow makes Kukin's death worth it.

So, Kukin has died, there in Moscow. As a new friend of Olenka's, I am sorry for her, the darling.

But as a reader, I am sort of glad.

Goodbye, Kukin, you gave your life for rising action.

Kukin is dead, Olenka is mourning. The story pauses (there just before the last paragraph on page 4). Kukin has been loved, imitated, and died. What now? Will Olenka go crazy, become a drunk, wear black for the rest of her life? Any writer who has ever written a good first few pages of a story knows this neurotic, maddening moment. There are so many possible paths. Which is the best? And how are we supposed to know?

Let's, for a moment, put aside the question "How did Chekhov decide what to do next?" and look at what he *does* next, which is something bold: he skips over the next three months (all ninety-odd of those sad, intervening, post-funeral days) to arrive at: "*Three months later Olenka was returning from Mass.*" What we don't get: "For several days after the funeral, Olenka did nothing at all. One Wednesday she saw some pretty clouds. On Thursday, it was time to do the washing, but she just couldn't bear it. She thought of Kukin, of how nice he had always been to her. Then, on Thursday afternoon, she cleaned the kitchen. There, she found Kukin's spare set of glasses and burst into . . ."

We get none of that daily, calendar-tending, mere accounting. Why not? Because those days don't matter. They aren't meaningful. By whose standard? The story's. The story is telling us, by skipping those days, that nothing meaningful happened during them and that it intends to set us down in front of the next thing it judges meaningful, i.e., relevant to its purpose.

The boldness of this leap teaches us something important about the short story: it is not a documentary or rigorous accounting of the passage of time or a fair-minded attempt to show life as it is really lived; it's a radically shaped, even somewhat cartoonish (when held up against the tedious real world) little machine that thrills us with the extremity of its decisiveness.

As you know, because you've just read it, the story leaps forward to get us to Vasily, the lumberyard manager. Here, I think, is where, on first read, we actually start understanding this as a pattern story—there at the bottom of page 4, literally at the appearance of the (male) name, Vasily. We know that Olenka loved Kukin so much that she basically became him. The story is now about to present her with someone new to love. And we wonder: How *can* she love him (when she loved Kukin so much)? And: How can she love *him* (he who is not Kukin)? And: In *what manner* will she love him? (Will she urge him to go to the theater? Insist that a picture of Kukin hang in the living room? Eventually break things off with Vasily because he doesn't "get" Shakespeare?) We believe we've just seen a woman in love (with Kukin). Now we're going to get a chance to see that woman in love for a second time.

When I was a kid in Chicago, old men used to say, of a good twist in a story, "Oh, that is *rich.*" This introduction of Vasily is *rich.*

Suddenly questions arise about the nature of love.

—

Over the years, our friend develops a certain expression of public intimacy for her husband: whenever they're standing together, she absentmindedly puts a finger through his belt loop.

He dies, our friend remarries, and we see her enacting the same move on her new boyfriend. Who would judge this? Well, everyone. We want to believe that love is singular and exclusive, and it unnerves us to think that it might actually be renewable and somewhat repetitive in its habits. Would your current partner ever call his or her new partner by the same pet name he/she uses for you, once you are dead and buried? Well, why not? There are only so many pet names. Why should that bother you? Well, because you believe it is *you,* in particular, who is loved (that is why dear Ed calls you "honey-bunny"), but no: love just *is,* and you happened to be in the path of it. When, dead and hovering above Ed, you hear him call that rat Beth, your former friend, "honey-bunny," as she absentmindedly puts her traitorous finger into his belt loop, you, in spirit form, are going to think somewhat less of Ed, and of Beth, and maybe of love itself. Or will you?

Maybe you won't.

Because don't we all do some version of this, when in love? When your lover dies or leaves you, there you are, still yourself, with your particular way of loving. And there is the world, still full of people to love.

It happens fast, over three paragraphs on pages 4–5: Olenka is comforted by Vasily on the way home from church, she likes him so much that she has a vision of his "dark beard," they marry—and she starts thinking and talking like him. The full richness is upon us: Olenka is going to love Vasily the same way she loved Kukin, by becoming him.

Should we be happy for Olenka? Think less of her? Do we need to reevaluate her relationship with Kukin?

So, this is all good. This piece of writing is starting to do the work of a story. But if you're a writer, what you're (still) wondering is: Yes, but how did Chekhov *know* to do that leap ahead, to Vasily? That is: How did he, at the time of the writing, "decide" to do that? We want to know this, of course, so as to be instructed in how we might do a similarly clever thing, when the time comes, in one of our stories.

Well, one answer is "How should I know? He was a genius and just, you know, knew, I guess?"

But there might be something for us to learn here about good writerly habit.

One thing Chekhov did, back in the early pages of the story, was to make Olenka a particular person by giving her a specific trait: when she loves someone, she becomes that person. As we saw in our discussion of "In the Cart," once a specific person has been made (via facts), we then know, of all the many things that could happen to her, which would be meaningful.

We might say that in specificity lies nascent plot.

Story: "Once upon a time there was a woman who became whatever she loved."

Chekhov: "Really? How about we test that supposition? Hmm. How to do that? Oh, I know: kill off her first love and present her with a second."

So, "good writerly habit" might consist of continually revising toward specificity, so that specificity can appear and then produce plot (or, as we prefer to call it, "meaningful action").

Consider this sentence, which I'll infuse with increasing specification:

Some guy is sitting in a random room thinking nothing at all and this other guy walks in.

An angry racist is sitting in a room, thinking of how unfairly he's been treated all his life, and a person of another race walks in.

An angry white racist named Mel, who has cancer, is sitting in the examination room, thinking of how unfairly he's been treated all his life, when his doctor, a slightly egotistical Pakistani American, Dr. Bukhari, walks in, bearing bad news for Mel but glowing, in spite of that, with happiness because he's just won a major award.

I don't know what's going to happen next in that last, more specific, room but I'm pretty sure something will.

On pages 5–7, as we move into the second incarnation of the pattern ("Olenka falls in love with Vasily"), the alert reader (or the quasi-alert reader, like me, who taught the story for many years before becoming aware of this) will notice that Chekhov is supplying us with information about the Olenka/Vasily relationship that is *exactly parallel* to what he supplied earlier regarding the Olenka/Kukin relationship. I learned this by starting to make, for Olenka and Vasily, a chart like the one I'd made earlier for Olenka and Kukin (Table 2), then noticing that I didn't have to make a new chart at all: all of the row headings were the same (see Table 3).

And, getting ahead of ourselves a bit, we will find the same parallelism in Chekhov's descriptions of Olenka's forthcoming relationships with Smirnin and Sasha (which I've also included in Table 3).

This is interesting, and even a little bit crazy; it seems to indicate that Chekhov, as he described each of these relationships, essentially carried forward the same set of variables he'd established earlier, in describing the Olenka/Kukin relationship. (Did he do this intentionally? Was he aware that he was doing it? I think not, but let's delay these questions for now.)

So, over pages 5–7, we get: Vasily's job (lumberyard manager); the flavor of their courtship (a chance meeting, then the engagement arranged through an emissary); the flavor of their relationship itself (they are sexually hotter, more sensual: they eat and cook and pray, go to the baths, have an "agreeable aroma" about them; they get along not just well, but "very well"); how Vasily refers to/thinks of her ("Olenka, what's the matter, *darling*?" [emphasis mine]); how she refers to/thinks of him (she is kept awake "burning as with fever" as she thinks of him; she falls in love with him "deeply," "missed him badly"); the duration of the relationship (six years); the method of their parting (he dies, at home, after a chill); and the length of her mourning period (over six months).

It's possible for us to compare—well, I'd say it's impossible for us *not to* compare—the two relationships. The structure forces a comparison. The completed Table 3, with Smirnin and Sasha also accounted for, provides an easy-to-access comparative history of Olenka's relationships.

Table 3 is why I teach "The Darling." It amounts to a brisk little primer on just how much organization the story form can bear and will reward. Pick any row ("How he refers to Olenka," for example), track

TABLE 3
The Various Loves of Olenka

Category	Kukin	Vasily	Smirnin	Sasha
His job	Theater owner	Lumberyard manager	Veterinary Surgeon	Kid
Flavor of their courtship	They arrange it themselves. She falls "in the end" from pity. ("His misfortunes moved her.")	A chance meeting on the way home from church, then arranged through an emissary/matchmaker.	Happens offstage, somewhat illicitly. They never marry. No information on details of the courtship. They, one day, just are a couple.	He is brought to the house and gradually abandoned to her care.
Flavor of their relationship	Sad and worried. They resent the public. She is gaining weight, he is "more sallow." "They got on well together."	They "got on very well together." They eat, cook, pray, there is an "agreeable aroma" about them, they go to the baths together, tea and doughnuts available in the office: health and plenty and enjoyment and, it seems, lust.	He slightly dominates her and is embarrassed by her. After their fights, soon enough, "both of them were happy" (again).	She sees herself as protecting him but he feels her as an oppressive force.
How he refers to Olenka	"Darling!"	"Olenka, what's the matter, darling?" He is attracted to her: "She too had made an impression."	"Don't butt in!" (Never calls her "darling.")	"Leave me alone!" and his dream of a schoolyard fight in the final lines of story.

How she refers to him	"What a sweet thing you are!" "My handsome sweet!"	"She liked him very much" and is kept awake, burning "as with fever." Falls in love with him "deeply" and "missed him badly" when he was away.	She would "beg him not to be angry."	"My darling, my pretty one!" (First time she's called someone "darling.")
Duration of affair, in pages	2.5 pages	3 pages	1 page	3 pages
Duration of affair, in time	10 months	6 years	"did not last long"	Approx. 6 months, by the end of the story
Method of his death or their parting	Cause of death unknown. She hears about it via (garbled) telegram.	On page 6, a feint: Is he about to die? No. Smirnin introduced. An affair? No. Vasily dies at home, of a chill.	He leaves with his regiment. (First man to leave her voluntarily.)	Unknown. She imagines him someday going off to a fine life of his own.
Period of mourning	3 months	Over 6 months	Some number of years, during which she is depressed and her looks fade. She is no longer "darling" to the town.	None required. They are still "together" at the end of the story.
Status of "the wing"	During the affair Kukin is lodging there. (Kukin comes to her from within her house.) When they are married, the wing goes empty.	Empty	Rented to Smirnin but likely mostly empty, as he's living with her.	When Smirnin reappears, Olenka moves into the wing. As he and his wife vanish, Olenka moves Sasha into the wing with her.

across it, and what you will find is . . . variation. The story, seen in this way, is a beautiful system for presenting a pattern of controlled variation. Once Chekhov has introduced an element, he continues to service it mindfully (with variations that are thoughtful, telling, non-robotic) in each of the sequences that follow. What at first appeared to be a life-scaled, pleasurably anecdotal-feeling account of a woman's romantic history turns out to be a near-mathematical fact-conveyance device, a highly organized pattern of similarities and differences tracked across these four sequential relationships. There's variation everywhere we look.

Imagine we're gazing down on a football field full of people. Half of them are wearing red, half are wearing blue. They start to perform some complicated choreography. Just like that, they have begun "to mean." To the extent that the choreography is not random, it is "saying" something by its very patterning. If the red shirts start out in a circle around the blue shirts, then gradually move into the circle, dispersing among the blue shirts, we understand this as, say, "integration." If the blue shirts, en masse, pulse toward the red shirts, who recoil, we understand this as "aggression." And there are some things those people could do, some intricate movements they could perform, the meaning of which, though we might feel it, would prove impossible to articulate—real but irreducible, observable and felt but occurring beyond the reach of language.

So it is with stories. We tend, in discussion, to reduce stories to plot (what happens). We feel, correctly, that something of their meaning resides there. But stories also mean through their internal dynamics—the manner in which they unfold, the way one part interacts with another, the instantaneous, felt, juxtaposition of elements.

Consider the following version of "The Darling," in which the internal dynamics have been neutralized as a source of meaning:

Once upon a time, Olenka had a lover, Kukin, to whom she conformed completely. She loved him at 9 on a scale of 10. They were together six months. Then he died. Then she had another lover, Vasily, to whom she conformed completely. She loved him at 9 on a scale of 10. They were together six months. Then he died. Then she had a third lover, Smirnin, to whom she conformed completely. She loved him at 9 on a scale of 10. They were together six months. Then he died.

That's not a story. It lacks the specificity that creates internal dynamics. (How, exactly, did Kukin die? How long did Olenka mourn? How long, comparatively, did she mourn after Vasily died? Which of her loves was the most physical? The harshest? And so on.) In the above version, nothing is felt to cause anything else. So none of it means anything. The writer has failed to exploit a source of beauty: the internal variation by which things like "progress" and "tragedy" and "reversal" and "redemption" are made to appear to have occurred in a work that is entirely invented.

In an inferior version of that halftime show described above, the people on that football field just drift around, wearing randomly colored street clothes, conveying no meaning. The difference between a master halftime-show choreographer and a hack is the attention paid to the details of internal dynamics.

When we say that "The Darling" is an intensely patterned story and discuss the artful ways in which Chekhov keeps both repeating and subtly varying his pattern, we might seem to be implying something about how it was written, i.e., that Chekhov had it all planned out in advance and sat down every day with his evolving version of Table 3, so he could track the number of pages over which he was keeping each husband alive and remind himself to continue to vary the parameter "Ways in which each lover addresses Olenka," and so on.

So, let me just say: I have no idea how Chekhov wrote "The Darling." Except—no way did he write it like that. My guess is that the story unfolded naturally, organized at speed by his innate sense of story. Having put certain elements into play in the first incarnation of the pattern, he intuitively returned to these in the next, and so on, albeit with a level of exactitude and subtlety that we mortals find astonishing.

I also doubt that Chekhov would have thought of this as "a pattern story."

Because *every* story is a pattern story.

What I mean by this is that every story has patterns within it. ("The Darling" is a daringly purebred "pattern story.")

For example, I have a story called "Pastoralia," set in a failing historical theme park. Our narrator's job is to play a caveman in a diorama. The punch line is that the place has had no visitors for a long time. So the story becomes about the narrator's struggle to maintain discipline under these conditions (he's not supposed to speak English in the cave, and so on).

Early in the story (on the first page) I stumbled onto a convention: our narrator and his faux-cavewoman mate (Janet) get their food every day via something called "the Big Slot." The food just appears there, presumably sent by, you know, management. "Every morning, a new goat, just killed, sits in our Big Slot." The Big Slot appeared as I tried to figure out for myself the details of daily life in the cave. But once I'd blurted out "Big Slot" and let it stand (and I let it stand because I thought it was funny), it became a feature of the world, and an element in the story.

So, on the first page, the baseline condition is established: every morning they get a goat in the Big Slot. Later that morning, the narrator goes to the Big Slot but finds it "goatless." This indicates: "trouble with the theme park." Next morning, again no goat ("continued trouble"). And just like that (voilà!) I'd made "a pattern." Sometimes a goat would appear in the Big Slot (indicating "a temporary improvement in conditions"), sometimes, in apology for the intermittent goat, some supplemental food (a rabbit, for example) would appear in something called the Little Slot; occasionally an explanatory note would accompany whatever was or was not in the Big or Little Slot; and finally, indicating that things had gotten really bad, a plastic goat showed up in the Big Slot, "with a predrilled hole for the spit to go through."

I didn't plan any of this out or think, "Ah, what this story needs is a *pattern*." Trying to have some fun, I found myself typing "Big Slot." Then I accepted that as a reality in the story and kept tending to it, looking over at the Big Slot every now and then to see what was in it.

And that made a pattern, and the pattern, as patterns tend to do, created a series of evolving expectations.

Let's imagine that for three days in a row, just at noon, there's a trumpet blast, and someone wonks you in the head with a hammer.

At 11:59 on the fourth day, you're going to be flinching. If, instead of a trumpet, you hear a flute, you'll think, "Huh, interesting. A variation in the pattern to which I've become accustomed: flute instead of trumpet. Not a complete overthrow of the pattern, but a modification of it that might indicate that today there will be no hammer, but instead—"

Wonk.

Then you think: "Ouch. Okay, so, the pattern now seems to be: sound of *some* musical instrument (in this most recent iteration, a flute), and *then* the wonk."

In other words, the repetition of a pattern makes us anticipate continued repetitions of that pattern, which, in turn, focuses our expectations, and puts us into a tighter relationship with the writer (our sidecar moves closer to his motorcycle).

Because Kukin died on a trip, when Vasily goes on a trip ("off to the provinces of Mogilev," on page 6), we expect him to die. When he doesn't die but comes home safely, only to die six years/one paragraph later, we feel, with pleasure, that the pattern has been both disrupted and honored.

In the interval during which we were expecting Vasily to die, Smirnin shows up. Sensing a possible expansion in the pattern (from "Olenka's lovers die" to "Olenka's lovers get replaced"), we wonder if Smirnin is in the story to become Olenka's lover (this would do the same work as having Kukin die, i.e., would move us on to the next lover and begin the next incarnation of the pattern). Then we see, at the line "What interested her most was what he told her about his domestic life," that an affair is not in the works after all. Adherents of the Ruthless Efficiency Principle that we are, we ask: "Well, then why did Chekhov put Smirnin in the story?" Immediately Chekhov answers: "To give Vasily and Olenka a chance to underscore their domestic bliss by feeling sorry for Smirnin and his neglected son." Noticing us noticing Smirnin, Chekhov pats our hand, so to speak ("Don't worry, I too respect efficiency") by giving Smirnin a purpose that allows for (justifies) his appearance in the story. (But, of course, it's also a feint; Smirnin will become her lover soon enough. And that's pleasurable when it happens too, in part because we expected it earlier and were rebuffed; we were wrong, but not all wrong.)

Likewise: because the deaths of Kukin and Vasily were both preceded by a lover-praising outburst from Olenka ("My handsome sweet!," on page 3, and "I wish everyone were as happy as Vasichka and I," on page 6), once we feel it's time for Smirnin to die (and we expect him to die precisely because the other two lovers have), we expect a parallel joyful outburst from Olenka. But instead, and in place of such an outburst, we get Smirnin's funny-but-cruel line "When veterinaries speak among themselves, please don't butt in! It's really annoying!," which has, we might say, a familial-but-inverted relation to Olenka's outbursts. Instead of praise, coming from her, it's an insult, directed at her.

Again: do we really "notice" these things the first time we read the story? I sure didn't, back when I read it for the first time. But we notice them now, as we analyze the story. These structures are undeniably present. And I'd say we noticed them, on first read, "in our bodies" or "in that deep-reading portion of our minds." The patterning of the story works like a form of Pavlovian conditioning. We react without knowing why. And it's these reactions that make us feel melded to the author, as if we are playing a very important, intimate game of some kind with him.

Vasily dies. Olenka's new lover is Smirnin. Holding this relationship up against her previous relationships, we feel, somehow, that Olenka is in decline. Why do we feel this? Well, look at Table 3, especially the rows "Flavor of their courtship," "Flavor of their relationship," and "How he refers to Olenka." This new relationship is illicit, its inception occurs off-camera (sleazily, somewhere between the bottom of page 7 and the top of page 8), they never marry. When she starts to show her love for him, by talking like him, he rebuffs her. He never once calls her "darling," the ingrate.

In our discussion of "In the Cart," we talked about Chekhov's ability to make a broad statement, then cross-paint it with complications. Here, once we notice that the overall shape of the story seems to be indicating *Olenka in decline,* we do a little instantaneous back-scan, wondering: Wait, has she been in decline all along? Has it been all downhill since Kukin died? Is the story meant to be: "Woman with questionable trait is punished by world, by being made to go steadily downhill?"

The answer is (complicatedly) no. I actually feel the move from

Kukin to Vasily as an improvement of sorts. Kukin is her first love, and it seems like true love, but then, seeing how healthy and horny and devout Olenka and Vasily are, and how much they eat, we think, "Oh wait, maybe *this* is her true love." Or: "Maybe this is *another* true love."

And, although Smirnin is abrupt with her, he's not wrong: he notices, as we've noticed, that she's aping him, and it freaks him out a little. So this could be read as a healthier, franker relationship: finally, Olenka has found a man not fooled by her worshipfulness. This could be good for her. He could teach her to love in a healthier way. (This reading is a stretch but there's a hint of truth in it: a benefit of the crosspainting. When we try to read the story that way, it doesn't entirely refuse us.)

We might also notice that, with each successive partner, she mourns for a longer period (three months for Kukin, more than six months for Vasily, some number of years for Smirnin). These losses seem to be getting harder for her to shake off. Why is this? Is she loving more deeply each time? Getting less resilient with age?

And let's note that we're only asking these questions (which, in turn, are causing the story to ask questions about the nature of love) because the length of each relationship was specified by the story and because Chekhov "remembered" or "took the trouble" to vary this parameter.

On page 8, Smirnin leaves her, and we expect to move into the next (fourth) iteration of the pattern "Olenka falls in love with someone and takes on his opinions and interests."

Because each of the preceding iterations has commenced with the introduction of a new lover, we expect a new lover. And here he comes, in the person of the cat, Trot. Will she fall in love with Trot and start seeing the world through his eyes? "Mice are the worst. They are so small and fast. Also, birds? Weird. Always singing and whatnot?" Well, maybe. Because we expect a lover, Chekhov supplies us with a possible candidate. Because, in the past, anyone would do, we expect that she will love (settle for) Trot. The story has made us expect this, because, so far, we have not seen Olenka consider and then reject someone—whomever Chekhov introduced, she loved. But Chekhov asks (is alert to the value of asking), "Okay, but what if she *doesn't* settle for Trot?" This sort of narrative alertness is one of Chekhov's prime gifts. That is, he's alert to the full potential of an inflection point he's created—the place where he has to (gets to) make an authorial decision. Chekhov pauses and asks: Will it be more meaningful ("richer") for Olenka to love the cat (as the story seems to expect her to do) or reject the cat? (As the optometrists say: "Is this better? Or this?")

The story's higher ground seems to lie in the direction of her rejecting the cat: "No, Trot is not enough." This says that Olenka is not, after all, a robot. The story is not: "She will love any old thing and become it." No. "She needed an affection that would take possession of her whole being, her soul, her mind, that would give her ideas, a purpose in life, that would warm her aging blood." A cat won't do. We feel the story narrowing, making itself more precise, and Olenka becoming more interesting and considerable. "A woman needs something to love" has become "A woman needs something to love *that is worthy of her.*"

And we should note that, again, this lovely emotional gradation was made possible by a simple technical move: the pattern subtly called for a new lover, Chekhov "remembered" that and tried to supply one (Trot), but Olenka rejected that facile solution.

And now, like us, she is waiting for a next, and worthy, lover to appear in the story.

It's Smirnin.

Smirnin returns, at the top of page 10 ("already gray, and wearing civilian clothes"), with his wife and child. We might expect that he and Olenka are going to pick up where they left off and that, in this way, Smirnin will be both Lover #3 and Lover #4. But no, Chekhov has a better idea (an idea that produces another pattern variation): Sasha, Smirnin's little son, will be her next love. (As in "In the Cart," the removal of the first-order option forces the story to supply something better.) As we expect, once Olenka falls for Sasha, she morphs into him ("'An island is a body of land . . .' she repeated") and she is in love again, and happy, maybe the happiest she's ever been.

Why not end the story here? On page 11, like so:

". . . and this was the first opinion she expressed with conviction after so many years of silence and mental vacuity."

THE END.

It's kind of nice, actually: her love (which all her life has been expressed in a romantic/sexual way) has been transformed into maternal love—a surprising and satisfying last incarnation of the pattern. There's also an overtone, from that moment when she and Vasily prayed for children, that motherhood is what she's been seeking all along. She's grown out of mere romantic love into something grander. And so, problem solved: she has someone appropriate to love, someone whose views she can channel, and she is therefore happy, and all is well.

But, looking ahead, we find we still have nearly three pages left.

So: a chance for us, again, to think about how stories end. What allows them to end? When they bypass a place where they might have ended, what must they then go on to accomplish?

Given the extreme efficiency of the form, what will those pages need to do, to not be felt as extraneous?

To our accruing list of universal laws of fiction (Be specific! Honor efficiency!), which, by the way, we should continually remind ourselves to distrust, we might add: Always be escalating. That's all a story is, really: a continual system of escalation. A swath of prose earns its place in the story to the extent that it contributes to our sense that the story is (still) escalating.

At this point in "The Darling," what would constitute an escalation?

Well, let's go back a step. What *is* escalation, anyway? How does a story produce the illusion of escalation? (Or, as a writer might ask it: "How can I get this stupid thing to escalate?") One answer: refuse to repeat beats. Once a story has moved forward, through some fundamental change in the character's condition, we don't get to enact that change again. And we don't get to stay there elaborating on that state—not, as in this case, for two full pages.

On page 11 we are "within" the beat: "Olenka has found a new love (in this case, a little boy) and taken on his opinions and interests and is finally happy again."

Let's read ahead and see what nudges us out of this beat—that is, when we start to feel some escalation.

Toward the bottom of the page, an account of a typical morning: Olenka nags Sasha about his schoolwork, and Sasha says, "Please leave me alone!" As Sasha walks to school, she follows "noiselessly." When he turns around, likely surprised (because she has been so, you know, noiseless), she gives him "a date or a caramel" and "he feels ashamed at being followed by a tall stout woman." We see that Sasha doesn't love her—he barely seems to know her. She is just "auntie."

Just like that, something new has come into the story, something that we haven't thought about (that Chekhov hasn't yet caused us to think about): the effect of Olenka's way of loving on its object. Although it's not entirely new (we might recall Smirnin's earlier, snotty comment to Olenka about "annoying" the veterinaries, on page 8), it's different enough that we feel it as escalatory. That earlier instance of resistance from Smirnin, an adult, represented, let's say, "mildly affronted professional pride," whereas Sasha's resistance here is direct and irritable and comes from a child, who is not a willing participant in this relationship.

Olenka returns home, "contented, tranquil, brimming over with love." (She's unaware of his resistance.) Later, they do homework together (and "cry," which is kind of strange, but suggests that, once again, Olenka is taking on the emotional life of her love interest), and then she dreams of his future as the "black kitten lies beside her purring." She doesn't seem to have noticed Sasha's discomfort, or doesn't credit it. She just *loves* him, and for her, that's all that matters.

And again we might ask: Why not end it there—i.e., with that happily purring kitten? It's good: Olenka is happy, Trot is happy, Sasha . . . is not. He is a mere love object. Olenka's way of loving is seen in a new way: a one-way street, gratifying only to her. (And even the cat has been put—again—into service. Trot is to Olenka as Olenka is to her lovers: if Olenka's happy, so is Trot.)

But there's still half a page left.

Chekhov doesn't stop here because he evidently feels that he can, within that remaining half page, find some further escalation. He's on the hunt for one more expansion in meaning. Let's see what he does next. (I feel like one of those whispering golf announcers: "Anton is approaching the end of the story, Verne. What a moment!")

There comes a knock at the gate, recalling the knock that came when Kukin died, and we (and Olenka) understand this to be a pattern-responsive moment that aligns with earlier moments that signaled, "Olenka's beloved is about to be taken away."

But no. It's only Smirnin, home late from the club.

Five lines left. What's left to do? Can Chekhov find any more escalation?

Of course he can; he's Chekhov.

The story ends like this:

"Little by little the load rolls off her heart and she is again at ease; she goes back to bed and thinks of Sasha who is fast asleep in the next room and sometimes shouts in his sleep:

" 'I'll give it to you! Scram! No fighting!' "

THE END.

What does this give us that's new? (We've already got the beat: "Sasha resists Olenka's love.")

First, Sasha occupies a different rhetorical position now. He is "fast asleep" and dreaming; he is, therefore, entirely honest. We have an access to his inner life that we haven't had before, and this is how he really feels.

Of what is he dreaming?

Well, Olenka, we feel, although it's a little complicated.

"I'll give it to you!" equals "I'll kick your ass." "Scram" equals "You get out of here, person whose ass I will kick if you don't scram." The "No fighting!" (in our translation, by Avrahm Yarmolinsky) makes us think that he's dreaming of breaking up a schoolyard fight. (In the Constance Garnett translation, instead of "No fighting!" he says, "Shut up!"—and we could easily imagine him directing this at a dream version of Olenka.)

In any case, Sasha is dreaming of violence; of angrily interrupting violence; of responding to violence with more violence. Sasha's "I'll give it to you! Scram! No fighting!" also evokes, syntactically, Olenka's earlier rebuke to Trot, back on page 10 ("Scat! Scat! Don't stick to me!"), the sense being: "You are not enough for me! You are not worthy to be the object of my love!"

Again, Olenka doesn't react to this—she doesn't think, "Wow, Sasha is having that unhappy, agitated dream because he feels cramped by me—I'd better lighten up." She didn't react earlier, either, when he said, "Please leave me alone!" or when he was visibly uncomfortable as she followed him to school, but these were "lighter" expressions of the idea: "Sasha is unhappy." So, we feel Sasha's dream as an escalation: back on page 12, Sasha, in public, *mildly* displayed *peevish* unhappiness and she ignored it; here, on the story's last page, Sasha, in an honest and unmediated (private) moment, *angrily* displays *bitter* unhappiness and she (still) ignores it.

And it's interesting: Chekhov, by ending the story where he does, tells us implicitly that Olenka's reaction to Sasha's unhappiness is not going to change anytime soon (otherwise he would have shown us that reaction, because it would have represented another moment of escalation). She's going to keep ignoring Sasha's feelings. She hears what he says in his dream, but she doesn't *hear* it—life between them will go on as it has.

And this is . . . scary. She's modeling the state of every autocrat: happy with her version of things, uninterested in anyone else's. Her trait, her need to be totally absorbed in whatever she loves, charming enough when applied to Kukin et al., now feels narcissistic and oppressive.

"The last words of the story are the child's and a protest," Eudora Welty wrote, "but they are delivered in sleep, as indeed protest to the darlings of this world will always be—out of inward and silent rebellion alone."

It's quite beautiful. The story has increased its meaning into its very last line, and even into the white space afterward. As we've said good endings do, this one creates an entire future world of different, plausible possibilities. Olenka could, eventually, become aware of her oppressive behavior and change her ways, thus learning about real love. Sasha could run away from home or kill her in her sleep. He could continue to submit to her (he has nowhere else to go, after all), getting angrier with every passing year, then spend the rest of his life avoiding anything that looks like smothering affection.

Some readers (Tolstoy among them) have tried to make "The Darling" a story about women—about how a woman should or should not be, a commentary on a certain type of subservient woman who derives her sense of identity from men alone. I think this sells the story short. To me, "The Darling" is about a tendency, present in all of us, to misunderstand love as "complete absorption in," rather than "in full communication with." Could Olenka have been a man? Of course. The notion that "The Darling" is about women—about something innate in women, something unique to women—is contradicted by the story itself, which understands her as an anomaly. That's why the story exists and is about her: because her trait is so unusual. (The other women in the village don't love this way.) It is not a story about women, or "a woman," but about a person, a person with a certain way of loving, and what the story asks is whether this way of loving is positive and exceptional or peculiar and regrettable, a rare, saintly quality or a stunted, obnoxious one.

Chekhov will set some feature of the world in the middle of a room and invite us to walk around it, looking at it from different angles. We see Olenka's mode of loving, from one angle, as a beautiful thing: in that mode, the self disappears and all that remains is affectionate, altruistic regard for the beloved. From another angle, we see it as a terrible thing, the undiscriminating application of her one-note form of love robbing love of its particularity: Olenka, love dullard, vampirically feeding upon whomever she designates as her beloved.

We see this mode of loving as powerful, single-pointed, pure, answering all questions with its unwavering generosity. We see it as weak: her true, autonomous self is nowhere to be found as she molds herself into the image of whatever male happens to be near her (unless he's a cat).

This puts us in an interesting state of mind. We don't exactly know what to think of Olenka. Or, feeling so multiply about her, we don't know how to judge her.

The story seems to be asking, "Is this trait of hers good or bad?"

Chekhov answers: "Yes."

The instant we wake the story begins: "Here I am. In my bed. Hard worker, good dad, decent husband, a guy who always tries his best. Jeez, my back hurts. Probably from the stupid gym."

And just like that, with our thoughts, the world gets made.

Or, anyway, *a* world gets made.

This world-making via thinking is natural, sane, Darwinian: we do it to survive. Is there harm in it? Well, yes, because we think in the same way that we hear or see: within a narrow, survival-enhancing range. We don't see or hear all that might be seen or heard but only that which is helpful for us to see and hear. Our thoughts are similarly restricted and have a similarly narrow purpose: to help the thinker thrive.

All of this limited thinking has an unfortunate by-product: ego. Who is trying to survive? "I" am. The mind takes a vast unitary wholeness (the universe), selects one tiny segment of it (me), and starts narrating from that point of view. Just like that, that entity (George!) becomes real, and he is (surprise, surprise) located at the exact center of the universe, and everything is happening in *his* movie, so to speak; it is all, somehow, both for and about him. In this way, moral judgment arises: what is good for George is . . . good. What is bad for him is bad. (The bear is neither good nor bad until, looking hungry, it starts walking toward George.)

So, in every instant, a delusional gulf gets created between things as we think they are and things as they actually are. Off we go, mistaking the world we've made with our thoughts for the real world. Evil and dysfunction (or at least obnoxiousness) occur in proportion to how solidly a person believes that his projections are correct and energetically acts upon them.

When someone says, "Chicago," a Chicago arises in my mind. But it's an incomplete Chicago—I can only come up with Michigan Avenue and, off to the south, my boyhood home, as it was in 1970. But even if I were standing at the top of the Willis Tower, looking out over the city, using that as a visual aid as I tried to imagine it, I'd still come up short. Chicago's too big. Even if I could be granted magical powers and instantaneously grasp Chicago in its entirety (the smell of every gangway, the contents of every box in every attic, the emotional state of every resident), in the very next instant, time moves on, and that Chicago is no more.

So, that's no problem, and it's even beautiful, but where it gets complicated is in that moment when someone proposes that I *judge* Chicago, so we can do something about it. When someone asks, "Well, what should we do about Chicago?"—Lord help us. A solution *will* arise, and it will likely be dunderheaded, because of how pathetically I've just underimagined good old Chicago.

This is also how we imagine, and then judge, people.

If, in the real world, there was an Olenka, and I knew her, and, on a given day, someone asked me, "What should we do about Olenka?," I'd have an answer. I'd be able to provide a judgment. In fact, I wouldn't be able to help it. (I might not say it out loud, but I'd have it there inside me.)

We have, in fact, been judging her pretty energetically all along. When Olenka was loving Kukin in her way, we judged her and found her sweet. When, later, she began loving Vasily (and then Smirnin) in that same way, we found her strange, a bit robotic. When she was alone and suffering, we felt pity for her, and began to see that her way of loving was not a choice but a feature of who she was. By the time she started inflicting her love on little Sasha, we had a deepened, ambiguous view of the matter; we could see, simultaneously, that this trait was natural to her and felt good to her and yet was oppressive to Sasha.

At the beginning of the story, we love Olenka because we perceive her to be good; in the middle sections we feel distant from her. In the end, we love her again, but in a deeper way: we love her even though we have, by way of Chekhov's guidance, been urged to take her fully into account. We love her even though we see all of her. Maybe we didn't know we could do that, love a person this deeply flawed, someone who is, arguably, doing harm (to a kid, no less), but now we know that we can, at least for a little while.

And maybe "love" isn't quite the right word. We don't approve of her, necessarily, but we *know* her. We've known her in all kinds of weather, we might say. She, like Marya in "In the Cart," has been artificially made into a friend of ours. We feel that her strengths (she loves so fully!) are all tied up with her weaknesses (she loves too fully!) and that none of this is really a choice for her—it's who she is and has always been.

By the end of the story, we feel that her tendency to become that which she loves is innate, a fixed trait of her character that has manifested, naturally, on a series of love objects. The sun that is her way of loving has shone on four different landscapes. That sun is neither good nor bad; it just *is*. Her emotional trait is analogous to, say, the physical trait of being extremely tall. Is it good or bad to be extremely tall? Well, if we need to reach something on a high shelf, it's good. If we have to rush through a low doorway, bad. We don't choose tallness and can't repent of it or resolve to be less tall, and yet the world remains full of tight crawl spaces and basketball hoops and people asking us how the weather is up there and so on.

I feel about Olenka the way I think God might. I know so much about her. Nothing has been hidden from me. It's rare, in the real world, that I get to know someone so completely. I've known her in so many modes: a happy young newlywed and a lonely old lady; a rosy, beloved darling and an overlooked, neglected piece of furniture, nearly a local joke; a nurturing wife and an overbearing false mother.

And look at that: the more I know about her, the less inclined I feel to pass a too-harsh or premature judgment. Some essential mercy in me has been switched on. What God has going for Him that we don't is infinite information. Maybe that's why He's able to, supposedly, love us so much.

AFTERTHOUGHT #3

We ended our last Afterthought with the idea that a story is a frank, intimate conversation between equals.

What could go wrong?

Well, jeez, so many things. (We might pause here to think about unpleasant conversations we've had in the past.)

One of the main symptoms of a bad conversation is this: one of the participants is on autopilot.

Imagine you're on a date. Feeling insecure, you've brought along a set of index cards. You know: "7:00 P.M. Inquire re childhood memories"; "7:15 P.M. Praise her outfit." Now, we can do that, but why would we? Well, anxiety. We really want the date to go well. But every time we glance down at our index cards, this is felt by our date as disengagement. And she's right: we're leaving her out of the process.

Our anxiety has made us crave a method, when what the situation demanded was some moment-to-moment responsiveness to what was actually happening (to the true energy of the conversation).

Those index cards are the conversational equivalent of a plan. A plan is nice. With a plan, we get to stop thinking. We can just execute. But a conversation doesn't work that way, and neither does a work of art. Having an intention and then executing it does not make good art. Artists know this. According to Donald Barthelme, "The writer is one who, embarking upon a task, does not know what to do." Gerald Stern put it this way: "If you start out to write a poem about two dogs fucking, and you write a poem about two dogs fucking—then you wrote a poem about two dogs fucking." And we can add to this my mangling of whatever it was that Einstein actually said, which I rendered earlier as:

"No worthy problem is ever solved in the plane of its original conception."

If we set out to do a thing, and then we (merely) do it, everyone is bummed out. (That's not a work of art, that's a lecture, a data dump.) When we start reading a story, we do so with a built-in expectation that it will surprise us by how far it manages to travel from its humble beginnings; that it will outgrow its early understanding of itself. (Our friend says, "Watch this video of a river." The minute the river starts to overflow its banks, we know why she wanted us to watch it.)

So, why the index cards, on that date? In a word: underconfidence. We prepare those cards and bring them along and keep awkwardly consulting them when we should be looking deeply into our date's eyes because we don't believe that, devoid of a plan, we have enough to offer.

Our whole artistic journey might be understood as the process of convincing ourselves that we *do,* in fact, have enough, figuring out what that is, then refining it.

When I was a kid I had this Hot Wheels set: lengths of plastic tracks, metal cars, a couple of battery-powered plastic "gas stations." Inside each station was a pair of spinning rubber wheels. The little car went in, then got shot out on the other side. If you arranged the gas stations right, you could urge a little car into one as you left for school and come back hours later to find the car still going around the track.

The reader is the little car. The writer's task is to place gas stations around the track so that the reader will keep reading and make it to the end of the story. What are those gas stations? Well, manifestations of writerly charm, basically. Anything that inclines the reader to keep going. Bursts of honesty, wit, powerful language, humor; a pithy description of a thing in the world that makes us really see it, a swath of dialogue that pulls us through it via its internal rhythm—every sentence is a potential little gas station.

The writer spends her whole artistic life trying to figure out what gas stations she is uniquely capable of making. What does she have that will propel the reader around the track? What does she do in real life when seeking a conversational boost of speed? How does she entertain a person, assure him of her affection, show him that she's listening? How does she seduce, persuade, console, distract? What ways has she found of being charming in the world, and what might the writing equivalent of these be? It would be nice if she could just go, "Oh, in real life, I do X," and then do X in her work—but it's trickier than that. She finds out what her unique writerly charms are only by feeling her way toward them through thousands of hours of work (and these may have an oblique relation to her "real" charms or even no relation at all). What she arrives at is not a credo but a set of impulses she gets in the habit of honoring.

Of all the questions an aspiring writer might ask herself, here's the most urgent: What makes a reader keep reading? Or, actually: What makes *my* reader keep reading? (What is it that propels a reader through a swath of *my* prose?)

How would we know? Well, as we've said, the only method by which we *can* know is to read what we've written on the assumption that our reader reads pretty much the way we do. What bores us will bore her. What gives us a little burst of pleasure will light her up too.

This is, on the face of it, a weird assumption. We all know, from book clubs or writing workshops, that people don't read identically.

And yet, in a movie theater, people sometimes do gasp all at once.

And come to think of it, what we're doing (or at least what I'm doing, when I revise) is not so much trying to perfectly imagine another person reading my story, but to imitate myself reading it, if I were reading it for the first time.

In a strange way, that's the whole skill: to be able to lapse into a reasonable impersonation of yourself reading as if the prose in front of you (which you've already read a million times) was entirely new to you. When we go through a section of text like this, monitoring our responses and making changes accordingly, this manifests to the reader as evidence of care. (We might say that a first-time reader is able to intuit the many less-cared-for versions of a sentence behind the one the writer let stand.)

The mystery, to me, is why this immersion in our own, perhaps peculiar, taste should produce prose that speaks more energetically to our reader, prose that she feels respects her more.

To refer back to the conversational model: some conversations feel evasive, ill-considered, agenda-laced, selfish; others feel intense, urgent, generous, truthful. What's the difference? Well, I'd say it's *pres-*

ence. Are we there or not? Is the person across the table there (to us) or not? Writing fiction, we're in conversation with our reader, but with this great advantage: we get to improve the conversation over and over with every pass. We get to "be there" more attentively. When we're reading along and something deflects our needle into the *N* zone, this tells us that, in the instant of the writing, we weren't there. (When I write, "The orange sunset was a beautiful orange color," this indicates that, at the time of the writing, I wasn't there. But now I am. Or at least have a chance to be.)

So we might understand revision as a way of practicing relationship; seeing what, when we do it, improves the relationship between ourselves and the reader. What makes it more intense, direct, and honest? What drives it into the ditch? The exciting thing is that we're not doomed to ask these questions abstractly; we get to ask them locally, by running our meter over the phrases, sentences, sections, etc., that make up our story, while assuming some continuity of reaction between the reader and ourselves.

The difference between a sentence that is pleasing (that feels vivid and truthful and undeniable) and compels the reader to read the next, and one that displeases her and shoots her out of the story is—well, I find I can't complete that sentence, not in any general way. And I don't need to. To be a writer, I only need to read a specific sentence of mine, in its particular context, on a given day, pencil in hand, changing the sentence as it occurs to me to do so.

Then do that again, over and over, until I'm pleased.

MASTER AND MAN

Leo Tolstoy

(1895)

MASTER AND MAN

———

I

It happened in the seventies in winter, on the day after St. Nicholas's Day. There was a fête in the parish and the innkeeper, Vasili Andreevich Brekhunov, a Second Guild merchant, being a church elder, had to go to church, and had also to entertain his relatives and friends at home.

But when the last of them had gone he at once began to prepare to drive over to see a neighboring proprietor about a grove which he had been bargaining over for a long time. He was now in a hurry to start, lest buyers from the town might forestall him in making a profitable purchase.

The youthful landowner was asking ten thousand rubles for the grove simply because Vasili Andreevich was offering seven thousand. Seven thousand was, however, only a third of its real value. Vasili Andreevich might perhaps have got it down to his own price, for the woods were in his district and he had a long-standing agreement with the other village dealers that no one should run up the price in another's district, but he had now learned that some timber-dealers from town meant to bid for the Goryachkin grove, and he resolved to go at once and get the matter settled. So as soon as the feast was over, he took seven hundred rubles from his strong box, added to them two thousand three hundred rubles of church money he had in his keeping, so as to make up the sum to three thousand; carefully counted the notes, and having put them into his pocket-book made haste to start.

Nikita, the only one of Vasili Andreevich's laborers who was not drunk that day, ran to harness the horse. Nikita, though an habitual drunkard, was not drunk that day because since the last day before the fast, when he had drunk his coat and leather boots, he had sworn off drink and had kept his vow for two months, and was still keeping it despite the temptation of the vodka that had been drunk everywhere during the first two days of the feast.

Nikita was a peasant of about fifty from a neighboring village, "not a manager" as the peasants said of him, meaning that he was not the thrifty head of a household but lived most of his time away from home as a laborer. He was valued everywhere for his industry, dexterity, and strength at work, and still more for his kindly and pleasant temper. But he never settled down anywhere for long because about twice a year, or even oftener, he had a drinking bout, [2] and then besides spending all his clothes on drink he became turbulent and quarrelsome. Vasili Andreevich himself had turned him away several times, but had afterward taken him back again—valuing his honesty, his kindness to animals, and especially his cheapness. Vasili Andreevich did not pay Nikita the eighty rubles a year such a man was worth, but only about forty, which he gave him haphazard, in small sums, and even that mostly not in cash but in goods from his own shop and at high prices.

Nikita's wife Martha, who had once been a handsome vigorous woman, managed the homestead with the help of her son and two daughters, and did not urge Nikita to live at home: first because she had been living for some twenty years already with a cooper, a peasant from another village who lodged in their house; and secondly because though she managed her husband as she pleased when he was sober, she feared him like fire when he was drunk. Once when he had got drunk at home, Nikita, probably to make up for his submissiveness when sober, broke open her box, took out her best clothes, snatched up an axe, and chopped all her undergarments and dresses to bits. All the wages Nikita earned went to his wife, and he raised no objection to that. So now, two days before the holiday, Martha had been twice to see Vasili Andreevich and had got from him wheat flour, tea, sugar, and a quart of vodka, the lot costing three rubles, and also five rubles in cash, for which she thanked him as for a special favor, though he owed Nikita at least twenty rubles.

"What agreement did we ever draw up with you?" said Vasili Andreevich to Nikita. "If you need anything, take it; you will work it off. I'm not like others to keep you waiting, and making up accounts and reckoning fines. We deal straightforwardly. You serve me and I don't neglect you."

And when saying this Vasili Andreevich was honestly convinced that he was Nikita's benefactor, and he knew how to put it so plausibly that all those who depended on him for their money, beginning with Nikita, confirmed him in the conviction that he was their benefactor and did not overreach them.

"Yes, I understand, Vasili Andreevich. You know that I serve you and take as much pains as I would for my own father. I understand very well!" Nikita would reply. He was quite aware that Vasili Andreevich was cheating him, but at the same time he felt that it was useless to try to clear up his accounts with him or explain his side of the matter, and that as long as he had nowhere to go he must accept what he could get.

[3]

Now, having heard his master's order to harness, he went as usual cheerfully and willingly to the shed, stepping briskly and easily on his rather turned-in feet; took down from a nail the heavy tasseled leather bridle, and jingling the rings of the bit went to the closed stable where the horse he was to harness was standing by himself.

"What, feeling lonely, feeling lonely, little silly?" said Nikita in answer to the low whinny with which he was greeted by the good-tempered, medium-sized bay stallion, with a rather slanting crupper, who stood alone in the shed. "Now then, now then, there's time enough. Let me water you first," he went on, speaking to the horse just as to someone who understood the words he was using, and having whisked the dusty, grooved back of the well-fed young stallion with the skirt of his coat, he put a bridle on his handsome head, straightened his ears and forelock, and having taken off his halter led him out to water.

Picking his way out of the dung-strewn stable, Mukhorty frisked, and making play with his hind leg pretended that he meant to kick Nikita, who was running at a trot beside him to the pump.

"Now then, now then, you rascal!" Nikita called out, well knowing how carefully Mukhorty threw out his hind leg just to touch his greasy sheepskin coat but not to strike him—a trick Nikita much appreciated.

After a drink of the cold water the horse sighed, moving his strong wet lips, from the hairs of which transparent drops fell into the trough; then standing still as if in thought, he suddenly gave a loud snort.

"If you don't want any more, you needn't. But don't go asking for any later," said Nikita quite seriously and fully explaining his conduct to Mukhorty. Then he ran back to the shed pulling the playful young horse, who wanted to gambol all over the yard, by the rein.

There was no one else in the yard except a stranger, the cook's husband, who had come for the holiday.

[4] "Go and ask which sledge is to be harnessed—the wide one or the small one—there's a good fellow!"

The cook's husband went into the house, which stood on an iron foundation and was iron-roofed, and soon returned saying that the little one was to be harnessed. By that time Nikita had put the collar and brass-studded belly-band on Mukhorty and, carrying a light, painted shaft-bow in one hand, was leading the horse with the other up to two sledges that stood in the shed.

"All right, let it be the little one!" he said, backing the intelligent horse, which all the time kept pretending to bite him, into the shafts, and with the aid of the cook's husband he proceeded to harness. When everything was nearly ready and only the reins had to be adjusted, Nikita sent the other man to the shed for some straw and to the barn for a drugget.

"There, that's all right! Now, now, don't bristle up!" said Nikita, pressing down into the sledge the freshly threshed oat straw the cook's husband had brought. "And now let's spread the sacking like this, and the drugget over it. There, like that it will be comfortable sitting," he went on, suiting the action to the words and tucking the drugget all round over the straw to make a seat.

"Thank you, dear man. Things always go quicker with two working at it!" he added. And gathering up the leather reins fastened together by a brass ring, Nikita took the driver's seat and started the impatient horse over the frozen manure which lay in the yard, toward the gate.

"Uncle Nikita! I say, Uncle, Uncle!" a high-pitched voice shouted, and a seven-year-old boy in a black sheepskin coat, new white felt boots, and a warm cap, ran hurriedly out of the house into the yard. "Take me with you!" he cried, fastening up his coat as he ran.

"All right, come along, darling!" said Nikita, and stopping the sledge he picked up the master's pale thin little son, radiant with joy, and drove out into the road.

It was past two o'clock and the day was windy, dull, and cold, with more than twenty degrees Fahrenheit of frost. Half the sky was hidden by a lowering dark cloud. In the yard it was quiet, but in the street the wind was felt more keenly. The snow swept down from a neighboring shed and whirled about in the corner near the bath-house.

[5]

Hardly had Nikita driven out of the yard and turned the horse's head to the house, before Vasili Andreevich emerged from the high porch in front of the house with a cigarette in his mouth and wearing a cloth-covered sheepskin coat tightly girdled low at his waist, and stepped onto the hard-trodden snow which squeaked under the leather soles of his felt boots, and stopped. Taking a last whiff of his cigarette he threw it down, stepped on it, and letting the smoke escape through his mustache and looking askance at the horse that was coming up, began to tuck in his sheepskin collar on both sides of his ruddy face, clean-shaven except for the mustache, so that his breath should not moisten the collar.

"See now! The young scamp is there already!" he exclaimed when he saw his little son in the sledge. Vasili Andreevich was excited by the vodka he had drunk with his visitors, and so he was even more pleased than usual with everything that was his and all that he did. The sight of his son, whom he always thought of as his heir, now gave him great satisfaction. He looked at him, screwing up his eyes and showing his long teeth.

His wife—pregnant, thin and pale, with her head and shoulders wrapped in a shawl so that nothing of her face could be seen but her eyes—stood behind him in the vestibule to see him off.

"Now really, you ought to take Nikita with you," she said timidly, stepping out from the doorway.

Vasili Andreevich did not answer. Her words evidently annoyed him and he frowned angrily and spat.

"You have money on you," she continued in the same plaintive voice. "What if the weather gets worse! Do take him, for goodness' sake!"

"Why? Don't I know the road that I must needs take a guide?" exclaimed Vasili Andreevich, uttering every word very distinctly and compressing his lips unnaturally, as he usually did when speaking to buyers and sellers.

"Really you ought to take him. I beg you in God's name!" his wife repeated, wrapping her shawl more closely round her head.

"There, she sticks to it like a leech! . . . Where am I to take him?"

[6]   "I'm quite ready to go with you, Vasili Andreevich," said Nikita cheerfully. "But they must feed the horses while I am away," he added, turning to his master's wife.

"I'll look after them, Nikita dear. I'll tell Simon," replied the mistress.

"Well, Vasili Andreevich, am I to come with you?" said Nikita, awaiting a decision.

"It seems I must humor my old woman. But if you're coming you'd better put on a warmer cloak," said Vasili Andreevich, smiling again as he winked at Nikita's short sheepskin coat, which was torn under the arms and at the back, was greasy and out of shape, frayed to a fringe round the skirt, and had endured many things in its lifetime.

"Hey, dear man, come and hold the horse!" shouted Nikita to the cook's husband, who was still in the yard.

"No, I will myself, I will myself!" shrieked the little boy; pulling his hands, red with cold, out of his pockets, and seizing the cold leather reins.

"Only don't be too long dressing yourself up. Look alive!" shouted Vasili Andreevich, grinning at Nikita.

"Only a moment, Father, Vasili Andreevich!" replied Nikita, and running quickly with his inturned toes in his felt boots with their soles patched with felt, he hurried across the yard and into the workmen's hut.

"Arinushka! Get my coat down from the stove. I'm going with

the master," he said, as he ran into the hut and took down his girdle from the nail on which it hung.

The workmen's cook, who had had a sleep after dinner and was now getting the samovar ready for her husband, turned cheerfully to Nikita, and infected by his hurry began to move as quickly as he did, got down his miserable worn-out cloth coat from the stove where it was drying, and began hurriedly shaking it out and smoothing it down.

"There now, you'll have a chance of a holiday with your good man," said Nikita, who from kindhearted politeness always said something to anyone he was alone with.

Then, drawing his worn narrow girdle round him, he drew in his breath, pulling in his lean stomach still more, and girdled himself as tightly as he could over his sheepskin. [7]

"There now," he said addressing himself no longer to the cook but the girdle, as he tucked the ends in at the waist, "now you won't come undone!" And working his shoulders up and down to free his arms, he put the coat over his sheepskin, arched his back more strongly to ease his arms, poked himself under the armpits, and took down his leather-covered mittens from the shelf. "Now we're all right!"

"You ought to wrap your feet up, Nikita. Your boots are very bad."

Nikita stopped as if he had suddenly realized this.

"Yes, I ought to. . . . But they'll do like this. It isn't far!" and he ran out into the yard.

"Won't you be cold, Nikita?" said the mistress as he came up to the sledge.

"Cold? No, I'm quite warm," answered Nikita as he pushed some straw up to the forepart of the sledge so that it should cover his feet, and stowed away the whip, which the good horse would not need, at the bottom of the sledge.

Vasili Andreevich, who was wearing two fur-lined coats one over the other, was already in the sledge, his broad back filling nearly its whole rounded width, and taking the reins he immediately touched the horse. Nikita jumped in just as the sledge started, and seated himself in front on the left side, with one leg hanging over the edge.

II

The good stallion took the sledge along at a brisk pace over the smooth-frozen road through the village, the runners squeaking slightly as they went.

"Look at him hanging on there! Hand me the whip, Nikita!" shouted Vasili Andreevich, evidently enjoying the sight of his "heir," who standing on the runners was hanging on at the back of the sledge. "I'll give it you! Be off to mamma, you dog!"

The boy jumped down. The horse increased his amble and, suddenly changing foot, broke into a fast trot.

The Crosses, the village where Vasili Andreevich lived, consisted of six houses. As soon as they had passed the blacksmith's hut, the last in the village, they realized that the wind was much stronger than they had thought. The road could hardly be seen. The tracks left by the sledge-runners were immediately covered by snow and the road was only distinguished by the fact that it was higher than the rest of the ground. There was a whirl of snow over the fields and the line where sky and earth met could not be seen. The Telyatin forest, usually clearly visible, now only loomed up occasionally and dimly through the driving snowy dust. The wind came from the left, insistently blowing over to one side the mane on Mukhorty's sleek neck and carrying aside even his fluffy tail, which was tied in a simple knot. Nikita's wide coat-collar, as he sat on the windy side, pressed close to his cheek and nose.

"This road doesn't give him a chance—it's too snowy," said Vasili Andreevich, who prided himself on his good horse. "I once drove to Pashutino with him in half an hour."

"What?" asked Nikita, who could not hear on account of his collar.

"I say I once went to Pashutino in half an hour," shouted Vasili Andreevich.

"It goes without saying that he's a good horse," replied Nikita.

They were silent for a while. But Vasili Andreevich wished to talk.

"Well, did you tell your wife not to give the cooper any vodka?" he began in the same loud tone, quite convinced that Nikita must feel flattered to be talking with so clever and important a person as himself, and he was so pleased with his jest that it did not enter his head that the remark might be unpleasant to Nikita.

The wind again prevented Nikita's hearing his master's words.

Vasili Andreevich repeated the jest about the cooper in his loud, clear voice.

"That's their business, Vasili Andreevich. I don't pry into their affairs. As long as she doesn't ill-treat our boy—God be with them."

"That's so," said Vasili Andreevich. "Well, and will you be buying a horse in spring?" he went on, changing the subject.

"Yes, I can't avoid it," answered Nikita, turning down his collar and leaning back toward his master.

The conversation now became interesting to him and he did not wish to lose a word. [9]

"The lad's growing up. He must begin to plow for himself, but till now we've always had to hire someone," he said.

"Well, why not have the lean-cruppered one. I won't charge much for it," shouted Vasili Andreevich, feeling animated, and consequently starting on his favorite occupation—that of horse-dealing—which absorbed all his mental powers.

"Or you might let me have fifteen rubles and I'll buy one at the horse-market," said Nikita, who knew that the horse Vasili Andreevich wanted to sell him would be dear at seven rubles, but that if he took it from him it would be charged at twenty-five, and then he would be unable to draw any money for half a year.

"It's a good horse. I think of your interest as of my own—according to conscience. Brekhunov isn't a man to wrong anyone. Let the loss be mine. I'm not like others. Honestly!" he shouted in the voice in which he hypnotized his customers and dealers. "It's a real good horse."

"Quite so!" said Nikita with a sigh, and convinced that there was nothing more to listen to, he again released his collar, which immediately covered his ear and face.

They drove on in silence for about half an hour. The wind blew sharply onto Nikita's side and arm where his sheepskin was torn.

He huddled up and breathed into the collar which covered his mouth, and was not wholly cold.

"What do you think—shall we go through Karamyshevo or by the straight road?" asked Vasili Andreevich.

The road through Karamyshevo was more frequented and was well marked with a double row of high stakes. The straight road was nearer but little used and had no stakes, or only poor ones covered with snow.

Nikita thought awhile.

"Though Karamyshevo is farther, it is better going," he said.

"But by the straight road, when once we get through the hollow by the forest, it's good going—sheltered," said Vasili Andreevich, who wished to go the nearest way.

"Just as you please," said Nikita, and again let go of his collar.

[10] Vasili Andreevich did as he had said, and having gone about half a verst came to a tall oak stake which had a few dry leaves still dangling on it, and there he turned to the left.

On turning they faced directly against the wind, and snow was beginning to fall. Vasili Andreevich, who was driving, inflated his cheeks, blowing the breath out through his mustache. Nikita dozed.

So they went on in silence for about ten minutes. Suddenly Vasili Andreevich began saying something.

"Eh, what?" asked Nikita, opening his eyes.

Vasili Andreevich did not answer, but bent over, looking behind them and then ahead of the horse. The sweat had curled Mukhorty's coat between his legs and on his neck. He went at a walk.

"What is it?" Nikita asked again.

"What is it? What is it?" Vasili Andreevich mimicked him angrily. "There are no stakes to be seen! We must have got off the road!"

"Well, pull up then, and I'll look for it," said Nikita, and jumping down lightly from the sledge and taking the whip from under the straw, he went off to the left from his own side of the sledge.

The snow was not deep that year, so that it was possible to walk anywhere, but still in places it was knee-deep and got into Nikita's boots. He went about feeling the ground with his feet and the whip, but could not find the road anywhere.

"Well, how is it?" asked Vasili Andreevich when Nikita came back to the sledge.

"There is no road this side. I must go to the other side and try there," said Nikita.

"There's something there in front. Go and have a look."

Nikita went to what had appeared dark, but found that it was earth which the wind had blown from the bare fields of winter oats and had strewn over the snow, coloring it. Having searched to the right also, he returned to the sledge, brushed the snow from his coat, shook it out of his boots, and seated himself once more.

"We must go to the right," he said decidedly. "The wind was blowing on our left before, but now it is straight in my face. Drive to the right," he repeated with decision.

Vasili Andreevich took his advice and turned to the right, but still there was no road. They went on in that direction for some time. [22] The wind was as fierce as ever and it was snowing lightly.

"It seems, Vasili Andreevich, that we have gone quite astray," Nikita suddenly remarked, as if it were a pleasant thing. "What is that?" he added, pointing to some potato vines that showed up from under the snow.

Vasili Andreevich stopped the perspiring horse, whose deep sides were heaving heavily.

"What is it?"

"Why, we are on the Zakharov lands. See where we've got to!"

"Nonsense!" retorted Vasili Andreevich.

"It's not nonsense, Vasili Andreevich. It's the truth," replied Nikita. "You can feel that the sledge is going over a potato-field, and there are the heaps of vines which have been carted here. It's the Zakharov factory land."

"Dear me, how we have gone astray!" said Vasili Andreevich. "What are we to do now?"

"We must go straight on, that's all. We shall come out somewhere—if not at Zakharova, then at the proprietor's farm," said Nikita.

Vasili Andreevich agreed, and drove as Nikita had indicated. So they went on for a considerable time. At times they came onto bare fields and the sledge-runners rattled over frozen lumps of earth. Sometimes they got onto a winter-rye field, or a fallow field on which they could see stalks of wormwood, and straws sticking up through the snow and swaying in the wind; sometimes they came onto deep and even white snow, above which nothing was to be seen.

The snow was falling from above and sometimes rose from below. The horse was evidently exhausted, his hair had all curled up from sweat and was covered with hoarfrost, and he went at a walk. Suddenly he stumbled and sat down in a ditch or water-course. Vasili Andreevich wanted to stop, but Nikita cried to him:

"Why stop? We've got in and must get out. Hey, pet! Hey, darling! Gee up, old fellow!" he shouted in a cheerful tone to the horse, jumping out of the sledge and himself getting stuck in the ditch.

The horse gave a start and quickly climbed out onto the frozen [12] bank. It was evidently a ditch that had been dug there.

"Where are we now?" asked Vasili Andreevich.

"We'll soon find out!" Nikita replied. "Go on, we'll get somewhere."

"Why, this must be the Goryachkin forest!" said Vasili Andreevich, pointing to something dark that appeared amid the snow in front of them.

"We'll see what forest it is when we get there," said Nikita.

He saw that beside the black thing they had noticed, dry, oblong willow-leaves were fluttering, and so he knew it was not a forest but a settlement, but he did not wish to say so. And in fact they had not gone twenty-five yards beyond the ditch before something in front of them, evidently trees, showed up black, and they heard a new and melancholy sound. Nikita had guessed right: it was not a wood, but a row of tall willows with a few leaves still fluttering on them here and there. They had evidently been planted along the ditch round a threshing-floor. Coming up to the willows, which moaned sadly in the wind, the horse suddenly planted his forelegs above the height of the sledge, drew up his hind legs also, pulling the sledge onto higher ground, and turned to the left, no longer sinking up to his knees in snow. They were back on a road.

"Well, here we are, but heaven only knows where!" said Nikita.

The horse kept straight along the road through the drifted snow, and before they had gone another hundred yards the straight line of the dark wattle wall of a barn showed up black before them, its roof heavily covered with snow which poured down from it. After passing the barn the road turned to the wind and they drove into a snow-drift. But ahead of them was a lane with houses on either side, so evidently the snow had been blown across the road and they had to drive through the drift. And so in fact it was. Having driven through the snow they came out into a street. At the end house of the village some frozen clothes hanging on a line—shirts, one red and one white, trousers, leg-bands, and a petticoat—fluttered wildly in the wind. The white shirt in particular struggled desperately, waving its sleeves about.

"There now, either a lazy woman or a dead one has not taken her clothes down before the holiday," remarked Nikita, looking at the fluttering shirts.

[13]

III

At the entrance to the street the wind still raged and the road was thickly covered with snow, but well within the village it was calm, warm, and cheerful. At one house a dog was barking, at another a woman, covering her head with her coat, came running from somewhere and entered the door of a hut, stopping on the threshold to have a look at the passing sledge. In the middle of the village girls could be heard singing.

Here in the village there seemed to be less wind and snow, and the frost was less keen.

"Why, this is Grishkino," said Vasili Andreevich.

"So it is," responded Nikita.

It really was Grishkino, which meant that they had gone too far to the left and had traveled some six miles, not quite in the direction they aimed at, but toward their destination for all that.

From Grishkino to Goryachkin was about another four miles.

In the middle of the village they almost ran into a tall man walking down the middle of the street.

"Who are you?" shouted the man, stopping the horse, and recognizing Vasili Andreevich he immediately took hold of the shaft, went along it hand over hand till he reached the sledge, and placed himself on the driver's seat.

He was Isay, a peasant of Vasili Andreevich's acquaintance, and well known as the principal horse-thief in the district.

"Ah, Vasili Andreevich! Where are you off to?" said Isay, enveloping Nikita in the odor of the vodka he had drunk.

"We were going to Goryachkin."

"And look where you've got to! You should have gone through Molchanovka."

"Should have, but didn't manage it," said Vasili Andreevich, holding in the horse.

"That's a good horse," said Isay, with a shrewd glance at Mukhorty, and with a practiced hand he tightened the loosened knot high in the horse's bushy tail.

[14]   "Are you going to stay the night?"

"No, friend. I must get on."

"Your business must be pressing. And who is this? Ah, Nikita Stepanych!"

"Who else?" replied Nikita. "But I say, good friend, how are we to avoid going astray again?"

"Where can you go astray here? Turn back straight down the street and then when you come out keep straight on. Don't take to the left. You will come out onto the high road, and then turn to the right."

"And where do we turn off the high road? As in summer, or the winter way?" asked Nikita.

"The winter way. As soon as you turn off you'll see some bushes, and opposite them there is a way-mark—a large oak, one with branches—and that's the way."

Vasili Andreevich turned the horse back and drove through the outskirts of the village.

"Why not stay the night?" Isay shouted after them.

But Vasili Andreevich did not answer and touched up the horse. Four miles of good road, two of which lay through the forest, seemed easy to manage, especially as the wind was apparently quieter and the snow had stopped.

Having driven along the trodden village street, darkened here and there by fresh manure, past the yard where the clothes hung out and where the white shirt had broken loose and was now attached only by one frozen sleeve, they again came within sound of the weird moan of the willows, and again emerged on the open fields. The storm, far from ceasing, seemed to have grown yet stronger. The road was completely covered with drifting snow, and only the stakes showed that they had not lost their way. But even the stakes ahead of them were not easy to see, since the wind blew in their faces.

Vasili Andreevich screwed up his eyes, bent down his head, and looked out for the way-marks, but trusted mainly to the horse's sagacity, letting it take its own way. And the horse really did not lose the road but followed its windings, turning now to the right and now to the left and sensing it under his feet, so that though the snow fell thicker and the wind strengthened they still continued to see way-marks now to the left and now to the right of them. [15]

So they traveled on for about ten minutes, when suddenly, through the slanting screen of wind-driven snow, something black showed up which moved in front of the horse.

This was another sledge with fellow-travelers. Mukhorty overtook them, and struck his hoofs against the back of the sledge in front of him.

"Pass on . . . hey there . . . get in front!" cried voices from the sledge.

Vasili Andreevich swerved aside to pass the other sledge. In it sat three men and a woman, evidently visitors returning from a feast. One peasant was whacking the snow-covered croup of their little horse with a long switch, and the other two sitting in front waved their arms and shouted something. The woman, completely wrapped up and covered with snow, sat drowsing and bumping at the back.

"Who are you?" shouted Vasili Andreevich.

"From A-a-a . . ." was all that could be heard.

"I say, where are you from?"

"From A-a-a-a!" one of the peasants shouted with all his might, but still it was impossible to make out who they were.

"Get along! Keep up!" shouted another, ceaselessly beating his horse with the switch.

"So you're from a feast, it seems?"

"Go on, go on! Faster, Simon! Get in front! Faster!"

The wings of the sledges bumped against one another, almost got jammed but managed to separate, and the peasants' sledge began to fall behind.

Their shaggy, big-bellied horse, all covered with snow, breathed heavily under the low shaft-bow and, evidently using the last of its strength, vainly endeavored to escape from the switch, hobbling with its short legs through the deep snow which it threw up under itself.

Its muzzle, young-looking, with the nether lip drawn up like that of a fish, nostrils distended and ears pressed back from fear, kept up for a few seconds near Nikita's shoulder and then began to fall behind.

"Just see what liquor does!" said Nikita. "They've tired that little [16] horse to death. What pagans!"

For a few minutes they heard the panting of the tired little horse and the drunken shouting of the peasants. Then the panting and the shouts died away, and around them nothing could be heard but the whistling of the wind in their ears and now and then the squeak of their sledge-runners over a windswept part of the road.

This encounter cheered and enlivened Vasili Andreevich, and he drove on more boldly without examining the way-marks, urging on the horse and trusting to him.

Nikita had nothing to do, and as usual in such circumstances he drowsed, making up for much sleepless time. Suddenly the horse stopped and Nikita nearly fell forward onto his nose.

"You know we're off the track again!" said Vasili Andreevich.

"How's that?"

"Why, there are no way-marks to be seen. We must have got off the road again."

"Well, if we've lost the road we must find it," said Nikita curtly, and getting out and stepping lightly on his pigeon-toed feet he started once more going about on the snow.

He walked about for a long time, now disappearing and now reappearing, and finally he came back.

"There is no road here. There may be farther on," he said, getting into the sledge.

It was already growing dark. The snowstorm had not increased but had also not subsided.

"If we could only hear those peasants!" said Vasili Andreevich.

"Well they haven't caught us up. We must have gone far astray. Or maybe they have lost their way too."

"Where are we to go then?" asked Vasili Andreevich.

"Why, we must let the horse take its own way," said Nikita. "He will take us right. Let me have the reins."

Vasili Andreevich gave him the reins, the more willingly because his hands were beginning to feel frozen in his thick gloves.

Nikita took the reins, but only held them, trying not to shake them and rejoicing at his favorite's sagacity. And indeed the clever horse, turning first one ear and then the other now to one side and then to the other, began to wheel round.

"The one thing he can't do is to talk," Nikita kept saying. "See what he is doing! Go on, go on! You know best. That's it, that's it!" [17]

The wind was now blowing from behind and it felt warmer.

"Yes, he's clever," Nikita continued, admiring the horse. "A Kirgiz horse is strong but stupid. But this one—just see what he's doing with his ears! He doesn't need any telegraph. He can scent a mile off."

Before another half-hour had passed they saw something dark ahead of them—a wood or a village—and stakes again appeared to the right. They had evidently come out onto the road.

"Why, that's Grishkino again!" Nikita suddenly exclaimed.

And indeed, there on their left was that same barn with the snow flying from it, and farther on the same line with the frozen washing, shirts and trousers, which still fluttered desperately in the wind.

Again they drove into the street and again it grew quiet, warm, and cheerful, and again they could see the manure-stained street and hear voices and songs and the barking of a dog. It was already so dark that there were lights in some of the windows.

Halfway through the village Vasili Andreevich turned the horse toward a large double-fronted brick house and stopped at the porch.

Nikita went to the lighted snow-covered window, in the rays of which flying snowflakes glittered, and knocked at it with his whip.

"Who is there?" a voice replied to his knock.

"From Kresty, the Brekhunovs, dear fellow," answered Nikita. "Just come out for a minute."

Someone moved from the window, and a minute or two later there was the sound of the passage door as it came unstuck, then the latch of the outside door clicked and a tall white-bearded peasant, with a sheepskin coat thrown over his white holiday shirt, pushed his way out holding the door firmly against the wind, followed by a lad in a red shirt and high leather boots.

"Is that you, Andreevich?" asked the old man.

"Yes, friend, we've gone astray," said Vasili Andreevich. "We wanted to get to Goryachkin but found ourselves here. We went a second time but lost our way again."

"Just see how you have gone astray!" said the old man. "Petrushka, go and open the gate!" he added, turning to the lad in the red shirt.

[18]

"All right," said the lad in a cheerful voice, and ran back into the passage.

"But we're not staying the night," said Vasili Andreevich.

"Where will you go in the night? You'd better stay!"

"I'd be glad to, but I must go on. It's business, and it can't be helped."

"Well, warm yourself at least. The samovar is just ready."

"Warm myself? Yes, I'll do that," said Vasili Andreevich. "It won't get darker. The moon will rise and it will be lighter. Let's go in and warm ourselves, Nikita."

"Well, why not? Let us warm ourselves," replied Nikita, who was stiff with cold and anxious to warm his frozen limbs.

Vasili Andreevich went into the room with the old man, and Nikita drove through the gate opened for him by Petrushka, by whose advice he backed the horse under the penthouse. The ground was covered with manure and the tall bow over the horse's head caught against the beam. The hens and the cock had already settled to roost there, and clucked peevishly, clinging to the beam with their claws. The disturbed sheep shied and rushed aside trampling the frozen manure with their hooves. The dog yelped desperately with fright and anger and then burst out barking like a puppy at the stranger.

Nikita talked to them all, excused himself to the fowls and assured them that he would not disturb them again, rebuked the sheep for being frightened without knowing why, and kept soothing the dog, while he tied up the horse.

"Now that will be all right," he said, knocking the snow off his clothes. "Just hear how he barks!" he added, turning to the dog. "Be quiet, stupid! Be quiet. You are only troubling yourself for nothing. We're not thieves, we're friends. . . ."

"And these are, it's said, the three domestic counselors," remarked the lad, and with his strong arms he pushed under the pent-roof the sledge that had remained outside.

"Why counselors?" asked Nikita.

"That's what is printed in Paulson. A thief creeps to a house—the dog barks, that means, 'Be on your guard!' The cock crows, that means, 'Get up!' The cat licks herself—that means, 'A welcome [19] guest is coming. Get ready to receive him!'" said the lad with a smile.

Petrushka could read and write and knew Paulson's primer, his only book, almost by heart, and he was fond of quoting sayings from it that he thought suited the occasion, especially when he had something to drink, as to-day.

"That's so," said Nikita.

"You must be chilled through and through," said Petrushka.

"Yes, I am rather," said Nikita, and they went across the yard and the passage into the house.

IV

The household to which Vasili Andreevich had come was one of the richest in the village. The family had five allotments, besides renting other land. They had six horses, three cows, two calves, and some twenty sheep. There were twenty-two members belonging to the homestead: four married sons, six grandchildren (one of whom, Petrushka, was married), two great-grandchildren, three orphans, and four daughters-in-law with their babies. It was one of the few homesteads that remained still undivided, but even here the dull internal work of disintegration which would inevitably lead to separation had already begun, starting as usual among the women. Two sons were living in Moscow as water-carriers, and one was in the army. At home now were the old man and his wife, their second son who managed the homestead, the eldest who had come from Moscow for the holiday, and all the women and children. Besides these members of the family there was a visitor, a neighbor who was godfather to one of the children.

Over the table in the room hung a lamp with a shade, which brightly lit up the tea-things, a bottle of vodka, and some refreshments, besides illuminating the brick walls, which in the far corner were hung with icons on both sides of which were pictures. At the head of the table sat Vasili Andreevich in a black sheepskin coat, sucking his frozen mustache and observing the room and the people [20] around him with his prominent hawk-like eyes. With him sat the old, bald, white-bearded master of the house in a white homespun shirt, and next him the son home from Moscow for the holiday—a man with a sturdy back and powerful shoulders and clad in a thin print shirt—then the second son, also broad-shouldered, who acted as head of the house, and then a lean red-haired peasant—the neighbor.

Having had a drink of vodka and something to eat, they were about to take tea, and the samovar standing on the floor beside the brick oven was already humming. The children could be seen in the top bunks and on the top of the oven. A woman sat on a lower bunk with a cradle beside her. The old housewife, her face covered with wrinkles which wrinkled even her lips, was waiting on Vasili Andreevich.

As Nikita entered the house she was offering her guest a small tumbler of thick glass which she had just filled with vodka.

"Don't refuse, Vasili Andreevich, you mustn't! Wish us a merry feast. Drink it, dear!" she said.

The sight and smell of vodka, especially now when he was chilled through and tired out, much disturbed Nikita's mind. He frowned, and having shaken the snow off his cap and coat, stopped in front of the icons as if not seeing anyone, crossed himself three times, and bowed to the icons. Then, turning to the old master of the house and bowing first to him, then to all those at table, then to the women who stood by the oven, and muttering: "A merry holiday!" he began taking off his outer things without looking at the table.

"Why, you're all covered with hoar-frost, old fellow!" said the eldest brother, looking at Nikita's snow-covered face, eyes, and beard.

Nikita took off his coat, shook it again, hung it up beside the oven, and came up to the table. He too was offered vodka. He went through a moment of painful hesitation and nearly took up the glass and emptied the clear fragrant liquid down his throat, but he glanced at Vasili Andreevich, remembered his oath and the boots that he had sold for drink, recalled the cooper, remembered his son for whom he had promised to buy a horse by spring, sighed, and declined it.

"I don't drink, thank you kindly," he said frowning, and sat down on a bench near the second window.

"How's that?" asked the eldest brother.

"I just don't drink," replied Nikita without lifting his eyes but looking askance at his scanty beard and mustache and getting the icicles out of them.

[21]

"It's not good for him," said Vasili Andreevich, munching a cracknel after emptying his glass.

"Well, then, have some tea," said the kindly old hostess. "You must be chilled through, good soul. Why are you women dawdling so with the samovar?"

"It is ready," said one of the young women, and after flicking with her apron the top of the samovar which was now boiling over, she carried it with an effort to the table, raised it, and set it down with a thud.

Meanwhile Vasili Andreevich was telling how he had lost his way, how they had come back twice to this same village, and how they had gone astray and had met some drunken peasants. Their hosts were surprised, explained where and why they had missed their way, said who the tipsy people they had met were, and told them how they ought to go.

"A little child could find the way to Molchanovka from here. All you have to do is to take the right turning from the high road. There's a bush you can see just there. But you didn't even get that far!" said the neighbor.

"You'd better stay the night. The women will make up beds for you," said the old woman persuasively.

"You could go on in the morning and it would be pleasanter," said the old man, confirming what his wife had said.

"I can't, friend. Business!" said Vasili Andreevich. "Lose an hour and you can't catch it up in a year," he added, remembering the grove and the dealers who might snatch that deal from him. "We shall get there, shan't we?" he said, turning to Nikita.

Nikita did not answer for some time, apparently still intent on thawing out his beard and mustache.

"If only we don't go astray again," he replied gloomily.

He was gloomy because he passionately longed for some vodka, and the only thing that could assuage that longing was tea and he had not yet been offered any.

[22]   "But we have only to reach the turning and then we shan't go wrong. The road will be through the forest the whole way," said Vasili Andreevich.

"It's just as you please, Vasili Andreevich. If we're to go, let us go," said Nikita, taking the glass of tea he was offered.

"We'll drink our tea and be off."

Nikita said nothing but only shook his head, and carefully pouring some tea into his saucer began warming his hands, the fingers of which were always swollen with hard work, over the steam. Then, biting off a tiny bit of sugar, he bowed to his hosts, said, "Your health!" and drew in the steaming liquid.

"If somebody would see us as far as the turning," said Vasili Andreevich.

"Well, we can do that," said the eldest son. "Petrushka will harness and go that far with you."

"Well, then, put in the horse, lad, and I shall be thankful to you for it."

"Oh, what for, dear man?" said the kindly old woman. "We are heartily glad to do it."

"Petrushka, go and put in the mare," said the eldest brother.

"All right," replied Petrushka with a smile, and promptly snatching his cap down from a nail he ran away to harness.

While the horse was being harnessed the talk returned to the point at which it had stopped when Vasili Andreevich drove up to the window. The old man had been complaining to his neighbor, the village elder, about his third son who had not sent him anything for the holiday though he had sent a French shawl to his wife.

"The young people are getting out of hand," said the old man.

"And how they do!" said the neighbor. "There's no managing them! They know too much. There's Demochkin now, who broke his father's arm. It's all from being too clever, it seems."

Nikita listened, watched their faces, and evidently would have liked to share in the conversation, but he was too busy drinking his tea and only nodded his head approvingly. He emptied one tumbler after another and grew warmer and warmer and more and more comfortable. The talk continued on the same subject for a long time—the harmfulness of a household dividing up—and it was clearly not an abstract discussion but concerned the question of a separation in that house; a separation demanded by the second son who sat there morosely silent. [23]

It was evidently a sore subject and absorbed them all, but out of propriety they did not discuss their private affairs before strangers. At last, however, the old man could not restrain himself, and with tears in his eyes declared that he would not consent to a break-up of the family during his lifetime, that his house was prospering, thank God, but that if they separated they would all have to go begging.

"Just like the Matveevs," said the neighbor. "They used to have a proper house, but now they've split up none of them has anything."

"And that is what you want to happen to us," said the old man, turning to his son.

The son made no reply and there was an awkward pause. The silence was broken by Petrushka, who having harnessed the horse had returned to the hut a few minutes before this and had been listening all the time with a smile.

"There's a fable about that in Paulson," he said. "A father gave his sons a broom to break. At first they could not break it, but when they took it twig by twig they broke it easily. And it's the same here," and he gave a broad smile. "I'm ready!" he added.

"If you're ready, let's go," said Vasili Andreevich. "And as to separating, don't you allow it, Grandfather. You got everything together and you're the master. Go to the Justice of the Peace. He'll say how things should be done."

"He carries on so, carries on so," the old man continued in a whining tone. "There's no doing anything with him. It's as if the devil possessed him."

Nikita having meanwhile finished his fifth tumbler of tea laid it on its side instead of turning it upside down, hoping to be offered a sixth glass. But there was no more water in the samovar, so the hostess did not fill it up for him. Besides, Vasili Andreevich was putting his things on, so there was nothing for it but for Nikita to get up too, put back into the sugar-basin the lump of sugar he had nibbled all round, wipe his perspiring face with the skirt of his sheepskin, and go to put on his overcoat.

[24] Having put it on he sighed deeply, thanked his hosts, said good-bye, and went out of the warm bright room into the cold dark passage, through which the wind was howling and where snow was blowing through the cracks of the shaking door, and from there into the yard.

Petrushka stood in his sheepskin in the middle of the yard by his horse, repeating some lines from Paulson's primer. He said with a smile:

> *"Storms with mist the sky conceal,*
> *Snowy circles wheeling wild.*
> *Now like savage beast 'twill howl,*
> *And now 'tis wailing like a child."*

Nikita nodded approvingly as he arranged the reins.

The old man, seeing Vasili Andreevich off, brought a lantern into the passage to show him a light, but it was blown out at once. And even in the yard it was evident that the snowstorm had become more violent.

"Well, this is weather!" thought Vasili Andreevich. "Perhaps we may not get there after all. But there is nothing to be done. Business! Besides, we have got ready, our host's horse has been harnessed, and we'll get there with God's help!"

Their aged host also thought they ought not to go, but he had already tried to persuade them to stay and had not been listened to.

"It's no use asking them again. Maybe my age makes me timid.

They'll get there all right, and at least we shall get to bed in good time and without any fuss," he thought.

Petrushka did not think of danger. He knew the road and the whole district so well, and the lines about "snowy circles wheeling wild" described what was happening outside so aptly that it cheered him up. Nikita did not wish to go at all, but he had been accustomed not to have his own way and to serve others for so long that there was no one to hinder the departing travelers.

V

Vasili Andreevich went over to his sledge, found it with difficulty in [25] the darkness, climbed in and took the reins.

"Go on in front!" he cried.

Petrushka kneeling in his low sledge started his horse. Mukhorty, who had been neighing for some time past, now scenting a mare ahead of him started after her, and they drove out into the street. They drove again through the outskirts of the village and along the same road, past the yard where the frozen linen had hung (which, however, was no longer to be seen), past the same barn, which was now snowed up almost to the roof and from which the snow was still endlessly pouring, past the same dismally moaning, whistling, and swaying willows, and again entered into the sea of blustering snow raging from above and below. The wind was so strong that when it blew from the side and the travelers steered against it, it tilted the sledges and turned the horses to one side. Petrushka drove his good mare in front at a brisk trot and kept shouting lustily. Mukhorty pressed after her.

After traveling so for about ten minutes, Petrushka turned round and shouted something. Neither Vasili Andreevich nor Nikita could hear anything because of the wind, but they guessed that they had arrived at the turning. In fact Petrushka had turned to the right, and now the wind that had blown from the side blew straight in their faces, and through the snow they saw something dark on their right. It was the bush at the turning.

"Well now, God speed you!"

"Thank you, Petrushka!"

"Storms with mist the sky conceal!" shouted Petrushka as he disappeared.

"There's a poet for you!" muttered Vasili Andreevich, pulling at the reins.

"Yes, a fine lad—a true peasant," said Nikita.

They drove on.

Nikita, wrapping his coat closely about him and pressing his head down so close to his shoulders that his short beard covered his throat, sat silently, trying not to lose the warmth he had obtained while drinking tea in the house. Before him he saw the straight lines of the shafts which constantly deceived him into thinking they were on a well-traveled road, and the horse's swaying crupper with his knotted tail blown to one side, and farther ahead the high shaft-bow and the swaying head and neck of the horse with its waving mane. Now and then he caught sight of a way-sign, so that he knew they were still on a road and that there was nothing for him to be concerned about.

[26]

Vasili Andreevich drove on, leaving it to the horse to keep to the road. But Mukhorty, though he had had a breathing-space in the village, ran reluctantly, and seemed now and then to get off the road, so that Vasili Andreevich had repeatedly to correct him.

"Here's a stake to the right, and another, and here's a third," Vasili Andreevich counted, "and here in front is the forest," thought he, as he looked at something dark in front of him. But what had seemed to him a forest was only a bush. They passed the bush and drove on for another hundred yards but there was no fourth way-mark nor any forest.

"We must reach the forest soon," thought Vasili Andreevich, and animated by the vodka and the tea he did not stop but shook the reins, and the good obedient horse responded, now ambling, now slowly trotting in the direction in which he was sent, though he knew that he was not going the right way. Ten minutes went by, but there was still no forest.

"There now, we must be astray again," said Vasili Andreevich, pulling up.

Nikita silently got out of the sledge and holding his coat, which the wind now wrapped closely about him and now almost tore off, started to feel about in the snow, going first to one side and then to the other. Three or four times he was completely lost to sight. At last he returned and took the reins from Vasili Andreevich's hand.

"We must go to the right," he said sternly and peremptorily, as he turned the horse.

"Well, if it's to the right, go to the right," said Vasili Andreevich, yielding up the reins to Nikita and thrusting his freezing hands into his sleeves.

Nikita did not reply.

"Now then, friend, stir yourself!" he shouted to the horse, but in spite of the shake of the reins Mukhorty moved only at a walk.

The snow in places was up to his knees, and the sledge moved by fits and starts with his every movement. [27]

Nikita took the whip that hung over the front of the sledge and struck him once. The good horse, unused to the whip, sprang forward and moved at a trot, but immediately fell back into an amble and then to a walk. So they went on for five minutes. It was dark and the snow whirled from above and rose from below, so that sometimes the shaft-bow could not be seen. At times the sledge seemed to stand still and the field to run backwards. Suddenly the horse stopped abruptly, evidently aware of something close in front of him. Nikita again sprang lightly out, throwing down the reins, and went ahead to see what had brought him to a standstill, but hardly had he made a step in front of the horse before his feet slipped and he went rolling down an incline.

"Whoa, whoa, whoa!" he said to himself as he fell, and he tried to stop his fall but could not, and only stopped when his feet plunged into a thick layer of snow that had drifted to the bottom of the hollow.

The fringe of a drift of snow that hung on the edge of the hollow, disturbed by Nikita's fall, showered down on him and got inside his collar.

"What a thing to do!" said Nikita reproachfully, addressing the drift and the hollow and shaking the snow from under his collar.

"Nikita! Hey, Nikita!" shouted Vasili Andreevich from above.

But Nikita did not reply. He was too occupied in shaking out the snow and searching for the whip he had dropped when rolling down the incline. Having found the whip he tried to climb straight up the bank where he had rolled down, but it was impossible to do so: he kept rolling down again, and so he had to go along at the foot of the hollow to find a way up. About seven yards farther on he managed with difficulty to crawl up the incline on all fours, then he followed the edge of the hollow back to the place where the horse should have been. He could not see either horse or sledge, but as he walked against the wind he heard Vasili Andreevich's shouts and Mukhorty's neighing, calling him.

"I'm coming! I'm coming! What are you cackling for?" he muttered.

[28]   Only when he had come up to the sledge could he make out the horse, and Vasili Andreevich standing beside it and looking gigantic.

"Where the devil did you vanish to? We must go back, if only to Grishkino," he began reproaching Nikita.

"I'd be glad to get back, Vasili Andreevich, but which way are we to go? There is such a ravine here that if we once get in it we shan't get out again. I got stuck so fast there myself that I could hardly get out."

"What shall we do, then? We can't stay here! We must go somewhere!" said Vasili Andreevich.

Nikita said nothing. He seated himself in the sledge with his back to the wind, took off his boots, shook out the snow that had got into them, and taking some straw from the bottom of the sledge, carefully plugged with it a hole in his left boot.

Vasili Andreevich remained silent, as though now leaving everything to Nikita. Having put his boots on again, Nikita drew his feet into the sledge, put on his mittens and took up the reins, and directed the horse along the side of the ravine. But they had not gone a hundred yards before the horse again stopped short. The ravine was in front of him again.

Nikita again climbed out and again trudged about in the snow. He did this for a considerable time and at last appeared from the opposite side to that from which he had started.

"Vasili Andreevich, are you alive?" he called out.

"Here!" replied Vasili Andreevich. "Well, what now?"

"I can't make anything out. It's too dark. There's nothing but ravines. We must drive against the wind again."

They set off once more. Again Nikita went stumbling through the snow, again he fell in, again climbed out and trudged about, and at last quite out of breath he sat down beside the sledge.

"Well, how now?" asked Vasili Andreevich.

"Why, I am quite worn out and the horse won't go."

"Then what's to be done?"

"Why, wait a minute."

Nikita went away again but soon returned.

"Follow me!" he said, going in front of the horse.   [29]

Vasili Andreevich no longer gave orders but implicitly did what Nikita told him.

"Here, follow me!" Nikita shouted, stepping quickly to the right, and seizing the rein he led Mukhorty down toward a snowdrift.

At first the horse held back, then he jerked forward, hoping to leap the drift, but he had not the strength and sank into it up to his collar.

"Get out!" Nikita called to Vasili Andreevich who still sat in the sledge, and taking hold of one shaft he moved the sledge closer to the horse. "It's hard, brother!" he said to Mukhorty, "but it can't be helped. Make an effort! Now, now, just a little one!" he shouted.

The horse gave a tug, then another, but failed to clear himself and settled down again as if considering something.

"Now, brother, this won't do!" Nikita admonished him. "Now once more!"

Again Nikita tugged at the shaft on his side, and Vasili Andreevich did the same on the other.

Mukhorty lifted his head and then gave a sudden jerk.

"That's it! That's it!" cried Nikita. "Don't be afraid—you won't sink!"

One plunge, another, and a third, and at last Mukhorty was out of the snowdrift, and stood still, breathing heavily and shaking the snow off himself. Nikita wished to lead him farther, but Vasili Andreevich, in his two fur coats, was so out of breath that he could not walk farther and dropped into the sledge.

"Let me get my breath!" he said, unfastening the kerchief with which he had tied the collar of his fur coat at the village.

"It's all right here. You lie there," said Nikita. "I will lead him along." And with Vasili Andreevich in the sledge he led the horse by the bridle about ten paces down and then up a slight rise, and stopped.

The place where Nikita had stopped was not completely in the hollow where the snow sweeping down from the hillocks might have buried them altogether, but still it was partly sheltered from the wind by the side of the ravine. There were moments when the wind [30] seemed to abate a little, but that did not last long and as if to make up for that respite the storm swept down with tenfold vigor and tore and whirled the more fiercely. Such a gust struck them at the moment when Vasili Andreevich, having recovered his breath, got out of the sledge and went up to Nikita to consult him as to what they should do. They both bent down involuntarily and waited till the violence of the squall should have passed. Mukhorty too laid back his ears and shook his head discontentedly. As soon as the violence of the blast had abated a little, Nikita took off his mittens, stuck them into his belt, breathed onto his hands, and began to undo the straps of the shaft-bow.

"What's that you are doing there?" asked Vasili Andreevich.

"Unharnessing. What else is there to do? I have no strength left," said Nikita as though excusing himself.

"Can't we drive somewhere?"

"No, we can't. We shall only kill the horse. Why, the poor beast is not himself now," said Nikita, pointing to the horse, which was standing submissively waiting for what might come, with his steep wet sides heaving heavily. "We shall have to stay the night here," he said, as if preparing to spend the night at an inn, and he proceeded to unfasten the collar-straps. The buckles came undone.

"But shan't we be frozen?" remarked Vasili Andreevich.

"Well, if we are we can't help it," said Nikita.

VI

Although Vasili Andreevich felt quite warm in his two fur coats, especially after struggling in the snowdrift, a cold shiver ran down his back on realizing that he must really spend the night where they were. To calm himself he sat down in the sledge and got out his cigarettes and matches.

Nikita meanwhile unharnessed Mukhorty. He unstrapped the belly-band and the back-band, took away the reins, loosened the collar-strap, and removed the shaft-bow, talking to him all the time to encourage him.

"Now come out! come out!" he said, leading him clear of the shafts. "Now we'll tie you up here and I'll put down some straw and take off your bridle. When you've had a bite you'll feel more cheerful." [31]

But Mukhorty was restless and evidently not comforted by Nikita's remarks. He stepped now on one foot and now on another, and pressed close against the sledge, turning his back to the wind and rubbing his head on Nikita's sleeve. Then, as if not to pain Nikita by refusing his offer of the straw he put before him, he hurriedly snatched a wisp out of the sledge, but immediately decided that it was now no time to think of straw and threw it down, and the wind instantly scattered it, carried it away, and covered it with snow.

"Now we will set up a signal," said Nikita, and turning the front of the sledge to the wind he tied the shafts together with a strap and set them up on end in front of the sledge. "There now, when the snow covers us up, good folk will see the shafts and dig us out," he said, slapping his mittens together and putting them on. "That's what the old folk taught us!"

Vasili Andreevich meanwhile had unfastened his coat, and holding its skirts up for shelter, struck one sulphur match after another on the steel box. But his hands trembled, and one match after another either did not kindle or was blown out by the wind just as he was lifting it to the cigarette. At last a match did burn up, and its flame lit up for a moment the fur of his coat, his hand with the gold ring on the bent forefinger, and the snow-sprinkled oat-straw that stuck out from under the drugget. The cigarette lighted, he eagerly took a whiff or two, inhaled the smoke, let it out through his mustache, and would have inhaled again, but the wind tore off the burning tobacco and whirled it away as it had done the straw.

But even these few puffs had cheered him.

"If we must spend the night here, we must!" he said with decision. "Wait a bit, I'll arrange a flag as well," he added, picking up the kerchief which he had thrown down in the sledge after taking it from round his collar, and drawing off his gloves and standing up on the front of the sledge and stretching himself to reach the strap, he tied the handkerchief to it with a tight knot.

The kerchief immediately began to flutter wildly, now clinging round the shaft, now suddenly streaming out, stretching and flapping.

[32]

"Just see what a fine flag!" said Vasili Andreevich, admiring his handiwork and letting himself down into the sledge. "We should be warmer together, but there's not room enough for two," he added.

"I'll find a place," said Nikita. "But I must cover up the horse first—he sweated so, poor thing. Let go!" he added, drawing the drugget from under Vasili Andreevich.

Having got the drugget he folded it in two, and after taking off the breechband and pad, covered Mukhorty with it.

"Anyhow it will be warmer, silly!" he said, putting back the breechband and the pad on the horse over the drugget. Then having finished that business he returned to the sledge, and addressing Vasili Andreevich, said: "You won't need the sackcloth, will you? And let me have some straw."

And having taken these things from under Vasili Andreevich, Nikita went behind the sledge, dug out a hole for himself in the snow, put straw into it, wrapped his coat well round him, covered himself with the sackcloth, and pulling his cap well down seated himself on the straw he had spread, and leaned against the wooden back of the sledge to shelter himself from the wind and the snow.

Vasili Andreevich shook his head disapprovingly at what Nikita was doing, as in general he disapproved of the peasant's stupidity and lack of education, and he began to settle himself down for the night.

He smoothed the remaining straw over the bottom of the sledge, putting more of it under his side. Then he thrust his hands into his sleeves and settled down, sheltering his head in the corner of the sledge from the wind in front.

He did not wish to sleep. He lay and thought: thought ever of the one thing that constituted the sole aim, meaning, pleasure, and pride of his life—of how much money he had made and might still make, of how much other people he knew had made and possessed, and of how those others had made and were making it, and how he, like them, might still make much more. The purchase of the Goryachkin grove was a matter of immense importance to him. By that one deal he hoped to make perhaps ten thousand rubles. He began mentally to reckon the value of the wood he had inspected in autumn, and on five acres of which he had counted all the trees. [33]

"The oaks will go for sledge-runners. The undergrowth will take care of itself, and there'll still be some thirty sazheens of firewood left on each desyatin," said he to himself. "That means there will be at least two hundred and twenty-five rubles' worth left on each desyatin. Fifty-six desyatins means fifty-six hundreds, and fifty-six hundreds, and fifty-six tens, and another fifty-six tens, and then fifty-six fives. . . ." He saw that it came out to more than twelve thousand rubles, but could not reckon it up exactly without a counting-frame. "But I won't give ten thousand, anyhow. I'll give about eight thousand with a deduction on account of the glades. I'll grease the surveyor's palm—give him a hundred rubles, or a hundred and fifty, and he'll reckon that there are some five desyatins of glade to be deducted. And he'll let it go for eight thousand. Three thousand cash down. That'll move him, no fear!" he thought, and he pressed his pocketbook with his forearm.

"God only knows how we missed the turning. The forest ought to be there, and a watchman's hut, and dogs barking. But the damned things don't bark when they're wanted." He turned his collar down from his ear and listened, but as before only the whistling of the wind could be heard, the flapping and fluttering of the kerchief tied to the shafts, and the pelting of the snow against the woodwork of the sledge. He again covered up his ear.

"If I had known I would have stayed the night. Well, no matter, we'll get there tomorrow. It's only one day lost. And the others won't travel in such weather." Then he remembered that on the 9th he had to receive payment from the butcher for his oxen. "He meant to come himself, but he won't find me, and my wife won't know how to receive the money. She doesn't know the right way of doing things," he thought, recalling how at their party the day before she had not known how to treat the police-officer who was their guest. "Of course she's only a woman! Where could she have seen anything? In my father's time what was our house like? Just a rich peasant's house: just an oatmill and an inn—that was the whole property. But what have I done in these fifteen years? A shop, two taverns, a flour-mill, a grain-store, two farms leased out, and a house with an iron-roofed barn," he thought proudly. "Not as it was in Father's time! Who is talked of in the whole district now? Brekhunov! And why? Because I stick to business. I take trouble, not like others who lie abed or waste their time on foolishness while I don't sleep of nights. Blizzard or no blizzard I start out. So business gets done. They think money-making is a joke. No, take pains and rack your brains! You get overtaken out of doors at night, like this, or keep awake night after night till the thoughts whirling in your head make the pillow turn," he meditated with pride. "They think people get on through luck. After all, the Mironovs are now millionaires. And why? Take pains and God gives. If only He grants me health!"

[34]

The thought that he might himself be a millionaire like Mironov, who began with nothing, so excited Vasili Andreevich that he felt the need of talking to somebody. But there was no one to talk to. . . . If only he could have reached Goryachkin he would have talked to the landlord and shown him a thing or two.

"Just see how it blows! It will snow us up so deep that we shan't be able to get out in the morning!" he thought, listening to a gust of wind that blew against the front of the sledge, bending it and lashing the snow against it. He raised himself and looked round. All he could see through the whirling darkness was Mukhorty's dark head, his back covered by the fluttering drugget, and his thick knotted tail; while all round, in front and behind, was the same fluctuating whity darkness, sometimes seeming to get a little lighter and sometimes growing denser still.

"A pity I listened to Nikita," he thought. "We ought to have driven on. We should have come out somewhere, if only back to Grishkino and stayed the night at Taras's. As it is we must sit here all night. But what was I thinking about? Yes, that God gives to those who take trouble, but not to loafers, lie-abeds, or fools. I must have a smoke!"

He sat down again, got out his cigarette-case, and stretched himself flat on his stomach, screening the matches with the skirt of his coat. But the wind found its way in and put out match after match. At last he got one to burn and lit a cigarette. He was very glad that he had managed to do what he wanted, and though the wind smoked more of the cigarette than he did, he still got two or three puffs and felt more cheerful. He again leaned back, wrapped himself up, started reflecting and remembering, and suddenly and quite unexpectedly lost consciousness and fell asleep. [35]

Suddenly something seemed to give him a push and awoke him. Whether it was Mukhorty who had pulled some straw from under him, or whether something within him had startled him, at all events it woke him, and his heart began to beat faster and faster so that the sledge seemed to tremble under him. He opened his eyes. Everything around him was just as before. "It looks lighter," he thought. "I expect it won't be long before dawn." But he at once remembered that it was lighter because the moon had risen. He sat up and looked first at the horse. Mukhorty still stood with his back to the wind, shivering all over. One side of the drugget, which was completely covered with snow, had been blown back, the breeching had slipped down and the snow-covered head with its waving forelock and mane were now more visible. Vasili Andreevich leaned over the back of the sledge and looked behind. Nikita still sat in the same position in which he had settled himself. The sacking with which he was covered, and his legs, were thickly covered with snow.

"If only that peasant doesn't freeze to death! His clothes are so wretched. I may be held responsible for him. What shiftless people they are—such a want of education," thought Vasili Andreevich, and he felt like taking the drugget off the horse and putting it over Nikita, but it would be very cold to get out and move about and, moreover, the horse might freeze to death. "Why did I bring him with me? It was all her stupidity!" he thought, recalling his unloved wife, and he rolled over into his old place at the front part of the sledge. "My uncle once spent a whole night like this," he reflected, "and was all right." But another case came at once to his mind. "But when they dug Sebastian out he was dead—stiff like a frozen carcass. If I'd only stopped the night in Grishkino all this would not have happened!"

And wrapping his coat carefully round him so that none of the warmth of the fur should be wasted but should warm him all over, neck, knees, and feet, he shut his eyes and tried to sleep again. But try as he would he could not get drowsy, on the contrary he felt wide awake and animated. Again he began counting his gains and the debts due to him, again he began bragging to himself and feeling pleased with himself and his position, but all this was continually disturbed by a stealthily approaching fear and by the unpleasant regret that he had not remained in Grishkino.

[36]

"How different it would be to be lying warm on a bench!" He turned over several times in his attempts to get into a more comfortable position more sheltered from the wind, he wrapped up his legs closer, shut his eyes, and lay still. But either his legs in their strong felt boots began to ache from being bent in one position, or the wind blew in somewhere, and after lying still for a short time he again began to recall the disturbing fact that he might now have been lying quietly in the warm hut at Grishkino. He again sat up, turned about, muffled himself up, and settled down once more.

Once he fancied that he heard a distant cock-crow. He felt glad, turned down his coat-collar and listened with strained attention, but in spite of all his efforts nothing could be heard but the wind whistling between the shafts, the flapping of the kerchief, and the snow pelting against the frame of the sledge.

Nikita sat just as he had done all the time, not moving and not even answering Vasili Andreevich who had addressed him a couple of times. "He doesn't care a bit—he's probably asleep!" thought Vasili Andreevich with vexation, looking behind the sledge at Nikita who was covered with a thick layer of snow.

Vasili Andreevich got up and lay down again some twenty times. It seemed to him that the night would never end. "It must be getting near morning," he thought, getting up and looking around. "Let's have a look at my watch. It will be cold to unbutton, but if I only know that it's getting near morning I shall at any rate feel more cheerful. We could begin harnessing."

In the depth of his heart Vasili Andreevich knew that it could not yet be near morning, but he was growing more and more afraid, and wished both to get to know and yet to deceive himself. He carefully undid the fastening of his sheepskin, pushed in his hand, and felt about for a long time before he got to his waistcoat. With great difficulty he managed to draw out his silver watch with its enameled flower design, and tried to make out the time. He could not see anything without a light. Again he went down on his knees and elbows as he had done when he lighted a cigarette, got out his matches, and proceeded to strike one. This time he went to work more carefully, and feeling with his fingers for a match with the largest head and the greatest amount of phosphorus, lit it at the first try. Bringing the face of the watch under the light he could hardly believe his eyes. . . . It was only ten minutes past twelve. Almost the whole night was still before him. [37]

"Oh, how long the night is!" he thought, feeling a cold shudder run down his back, and having fastened his fur coats again and wrapped himself up, he snuggled into a corner of the sledge intending to wait patiently. Suddenly, above the monotonous roar of the wind, he clearly distinguished another new and living sound. It steadily strengthened, and having become quite clear diminished just as gradually. Beyond all doubt it was a wolf, and he was so near that the movement of his jaws as he changed his cry was brought down the wind. Vasili Andreevich turned back the collar of his coat and listened attentively. Mukhorty too strained to listen, moving his ears, and when the wolf had ceased its howling he shifted from foot to foot and gave a warning snort. After this Vasili Andreevich could not fall asleep again or even calm himself. The more he tried to think of his accounts, his business, his reputation, his worth and his wealth, the more and more was he mastered by fear, and regrets that he had not stayed the night at Grishkino dominated and mingled in all his thoughts.

"Devil take the forest! Things were all right without it, thank God. Ah, if we had only put up for the night!" he said to himself.

"They say it's drunkards that freeze," he thought, "and I have had some drink." And observing his sensations he noticed that he was beginning to shiver, without knowing whether it was from cold or from fear. He tried to wrap himself up and lie down as before, but could no longer do so. He could not stay in one position. He wanted to get up, to do something to master the gathering fear that was rising in him and against which he felt himself powerless. He again got out his cigarettes and matches, but only three matches were left and they were bad ones. The phosphorus rubbed off them all without lighting.

[38] "The devil take you! Damned thing! Curse you!" he muttered, not knowing whom or what he was cursing, and he flung away the crushed cigarette. He was about to throw away the matchbox too, but checked the movement of his hand and put the box in his pocket instead. He was seized with such unrest that he could no longer remain in one spot. He climbed out of the sledge and standing with his back to the wind began to shift his belt again, fastening it lower down in the waist and tightening it.

"What's the use of lying and waiting for death? Better mount the horse and get away!" The thought suddenly occurred to him. "The horse will move when he has someone on his back. As for him," he thought of Nikita—"it's all the same to him whether he lives or dies. What is his life worth? He won't grudge his life, but I have something to live for, thank God."

He untied the horse, threw the reins over his neck and tried to mount, but his coats and boots were so heavy that he failed. Then he clambered up in the sledge and tried to mount from there, but the sledge tilted under his weight, and he failed again. At last he drew Mukhorty nearer to the sledge, cautiously balanced on one side of it, and managed to lie on his stomach across the horse's back. After lying like that for a while he shifted forward once and again, threw a leg over, and finally seated himself, supporting his feet on the loose breeching-straps. The shaking of the sledge awoke Nikita. He raised himself, and it seemed to Vasili Andreevich that he said something.

"Listen to such fools as you! Am I to die like this for nothing?" exclaimed Vasili Andreevich. And tucking the loose skirts of his fur coat in under his knees, he turned the horse and rode away from the sledge in the direction in which he thought the forest and the forester's hut must be.

VII

From the time he had covered himself with the sackcloth and seated himself behind the sledge, Nikita had not stirred. Like all those who live in touch with nature and have known want, he was patient and could wait for hours, even days, without growing restless or irritable. He heard his master call him, but did not answer because he did not want to move or talk. Though he still felt some warmth from the tea he had drunk and from his energetic struggle when clambering about in the snowdrift, he knew that this warmth would not last long and that he had no strength left to warm himself again by moving about, for he felt as tired as a horse when it stops and refuses to go further in spite of the whip, and its master sees that it must be fed before it can work again. The foot in the boot with a hole in it had already grown numb, and he could no longer feel his big toe. Besides that, his whole body began to feel colder and colder. [39]

The thought that he might, and very probably would, die that night occurred to him, but did not seem particularly unpleasant or dreadful. It did not seem particularly unpleasant, because his whole life had been not a continual holiday, but on the contrary an unceasing round of toil of which he was beginning to feel weary. And it did not seem particularly dreadful, because besides the masters he had served here, like Vasili Andreevich, he always felt himself dependent on the Chief Master, who had sent him into this life, and he knew that when dying he would still be in that Master's power and would not be ill-used by Him. "It seems a pity to give up what one is used to and accustomed to. But there's nothing to be done, I shall get used to the new things."

"Sins?" he thought, and remembered his drunkenness, the money that had gone on drink, how he had offended his wife, his cursing, his neglect of church and of the fasts, and all the things the priest blamed him for at confession. "Of course they are sins. But then, did

I take them on of myself? That's evidently how God made me. Well, and the sins? Where am I to escape to?"

So at first he thought of what might happen to him that night, and then did not return to such thoughts but gave himself up to whatever recollections came into his head of themselves. Now he thought of Martha's arrival, of the drunkenness among the workers and his own renunciation of drink, then of their present journey and of Taras's house and the talk about the breaking-up of the family, then of his own lad, and of Mukhorty now sheltered under the drugget, and then of his master who made the sledge creak as he tossed about in it. "I expect you're sorry yourself that you started out, dear man," he thought. "It would seem hard to leave a life such as his! It's not like the likes of us."

[40]

Then all these recollections began to grow confused and got mixed in his head, and he fell asleep.

But when Vasili Andreevich, getting on the horse, jerked the sledge, against the back of which Nikita was leaning, and it shifted away and hit him in the back with one of its runners, he awoke and had to change his position whether he liked it or not. Straightening his legs with difficulty and shaking the snow off them he got up, and an agonizing cold immediately penetrated his whole body. On making out what was happening he called to Vasili Andreevich to leave him the drugget which the horse no longer needed, so that he might wrap himself in it.

But Vasili Andreevich did not stop, but disappeared amid the powdery snow.

Left alone, Nikita considered for a moment what he should do. He felt that he had not the strength to go off in search of a house. It was no longer possible to sit down in his old place—it was by now all filled with snow. He felt that he could not get warmer in the sledge either, for there was nothing to cover himself with, and his coat and sheepskin no longer warmed him at all. He felt as cold as though he had nothing on but a shirt. He became frightened. "Lord, heavenly Father!" he muttered, and was comforted by the consciousness that he was not alone but that there was One who heard him and would not abandon him. He gave a deep sigh, and keeping the sackcloth over his head he got inside the sledge and lay down in the place where his master had been.

But he could not get warm in the sledge either. At first he shivered all over, then the shivering ceased and little by little he began to lose consciousness. He did not know whether he was dying or falling asleep, but felt equally prepared for the one as for the other.

VIII

Meanwhile Vasili Andreevich, with his feet and the ends of the reins, urged the horse on in the direction in which for some reason he expected the forest and forester's hut to be. The snow covered his eyes and the wind seemed intent on stopping him, but bending forward and constantly lapping his coat over and pushing it between himself and the cold harness pad which prevented him from sitting properly, he kept urging the horse on. Mukhorty ambled on obediently though with difficulty, in the direction in which he was driven. [41]

Vasili Andreevich rode for about five minutes straight ahead, as he thought, seeing nothing but the horse's head and the white waste, and hearing only the whistle of the wind about the horse's ears and his coat collar.

Suddenly a dark patch showed up in front of him. His heart beat with joy, and he rode toward the object, already seeing in imagination the walls of village houses. But the dark patch was not stationary, it kept moving; and it was not a village but some tall stalks of wormwood sticking up through the snow on the boundary between two fields, and desperately tossing about under the pressure of the wind which beat it all to one side and whistled through it. The sight of that wormwood tormented by the pitiless wind made Vasili Andreevich shudder, he knew not why, and he hurriedly began urging the horse on, not noticing that when riding up to the wormwood he had quite changed his direction and was now heading the opposite way, though still imagining that he was riding toward where the hut should be. But the horse kept making toward the right, and Vasili Andreevich kept guiding it to the left.

Again something dark appeared in front of him. Again he rejoiced, convinced that now it was certainly a village. But once more it was the same boundary line overgrown with wormwood, once more the same wormwood desperately tossed by the wind and carrying unreasoning terror to his heart. But its being the same wormwood was not all, for beside it there was a horse's track partly snowed over. Vasili Andreevich stopped, stooped down and looked carefully. It was a horse-track only partially covered with snow, and could be none but his own horse's hoofprints. He had evidently gone round in a small circle. "I shall perish like that!" he thought, and not to give way to his terror he urged on the horse still more, peering into the snowy darkness in which he saw only flitting and [42] fitful points of light. Once he thought he heard the barking of dogs or the howling of wolves, but the sounds were so faint and indistinct that he did not know whether he heard them or merely imagined them, and he stopped and began to listen intently.

Suddenly some terrible, deafening cry resounded near his ears, and everything shivered and shook under him. He seized Mukhorty's neck, but that too was shaking all over and the terrible cry grew still more frightful. For some seconds Vasili Andreevich could not collect himself or understand what was happening. It was only that Mukhorty, whether to encourage himself or to call for help, had neighed loudly and resonantly. "Ugh, you wretch! How you frightened me, damn you!" thought Vasili Andreevich. But even when he understood the cause of his terror he could not shake it off.

"I must calm myself and think things over," he said to himself, but yet he could not stop, and continued to urge the horse on, without noticing that he was now going with the wind instead of against it. His body, especially between his legs where it touched the pad of the harness and was not covered by his overcoats, was getting painfully cold, especially when the horse walked slowly. His legs and arms trembled and his breathing came fast. He saw himself perishing amid this dreadful snowy waste, and could see no means of escape.

Suddenly the horse under him tumbled into something and, sinking into a snowdrift, began to plunge and fell on his side. Vasili Andreevich jumped off, and in so doing dragged to one side the breechband on which his foot was resting, and twisted round the pad to which he held as he dismounted. As soon as he had jumped off, the horse struggled to his feet, plunged forward, gave one leap and another, neighed again, and dragging the drugget and the breechband after him, disappeared, leaving Vasili Andreevich alone on the snowdrift.

The latter pressed on after the horse, but the snow lay so deep and his coats were so heavy that, sinking above his knees at each step, he stopped breathless after taking not more than twenty steps. "The copse, the oxen, the leasehold, the shop, the tavern, the house with the iron-roofed barn, and my heir," thought he. "How can I leave all that? What does this mean? It cannot be!" These thoughts flashed through his mind. Then he thought of the wormwood tossed by the wind, which he had twice ridden past, and he was seized with such terror that he did not believe in the reality of what was happening to him. "Can this be a dream?" he thought, and tried to wake up but could not. It was real snow that lashed his face and covered him and chilled his right hand from which he had lost the glove, and this was a real desert in which he was now left alone like that wormwood, awaiting an inevitable, speedy, and meaningless death. [43]

"Queen of Heaven! Holy Father Nicholas, teacher of temperance!" he thought, recalling the service of the day before and the holy icon with its black face and gilt frame, and the tapers which he sold to be set before that icon and which were almost immediately brought back to him scarcely burned at all, and which he put away in the storechest. He began to pray to that same Nicholas the Wonder-Worker to save him, promising him a thanksgiving service and some candles. But he clearly and indubitably realized that the icon, its frame, the candles, the priest, and the thanksgiving service, though very important and necessary in church, could do nothing for him here, and that there was and could be no connection between those candles and services and his present disastrous plight. "I must not despair," he thought. "I must follow the horse's track before it is snowed under. He will lead me out, or I may even catch him. Only I must not hurry, or I shall stick fast and be more lost than ever."

But in spite of his resolution to go quietly, he rushed forward and even ran, continually falling, getting up and falling again. The horse's track was already hardly visible in places where the snow did not lie deep. "I am lost!" thought Vasili Andreevich. "I shall lose the track and not catch the horse." But at that moment he saw something black. It was Mukhorty, and not only Mukhorty, but the sledge with the shafts and the kerchief. Mukhorty, with the sacking and the breechband twisted round to one side, was standing not in his former place but nearer to the shafts, shaking his head which the reins he was stepping on drew downward. It turned out that Vasili Andreevich had sunk in the same ravine Nikita had previously fallen into, and that Mukhorty had been bringing him back to the sledge and he had got off his back no more than fifty paces from where the sledge was.

[44]

IX

Having stumbled back to the sledge Vasili Andreevich caught hold of it and for a long time stood motionless, trying to calm himself and recover his breath. Nikita was not in his former place, but something, already covered with snow, was lying in the sledge and Vasili Andreevich concluded that this was Nikita. His terror had now quite left him, and if he felt any fear it was lest the dreadful terror should return that he had experienced when on the horse and especially when he was left alone in the snowdrift. At any cost he had to avoid that terror, and to keep it away he must do something— occupy himself with something. And the first thing he did was to turn his back to the wind and open his fur coat. Then, as soon as he recovered his breath a little, he shook the snow out of his boots and out of his left-hand glove (the right-hand glove was hopelessly lost and by this time probably lying somewhere under a dozen inches of snow); then as was his custom when going out of his shop to buy grain from the peasants, he pulled his girdle low down and tightened it and prepared for action. The first thing that occurred to him was to free Mukhorty's leg from the rein. Having done that, and tethered him to the iron cramp at the front of the sledge where he had been before, he was going round the horse's quarters to put the breech-band and pad straight and cover him with the cloth, but at that moment he noticed that something was moving in the sledge and Nikita's head rose up out of the snow that covered it. Nikita, who was half frozen, rose with great difficulty and sat up, moving his hand before his nose in a strange manner just as if he were driving away flies. He waved his hand and said something, and seemed to Vasili Andreevich to be calling him. Vasili Andreevich left the cloth unadjusted and went up to the sledge.

"What is it?" he asked. "What are you saying?"

"I'm dy . . . ing, that's what," said Nikita brokenly and with difficulty. "Give what is owing to me to my lad, or to my wife, no matter."

"Why, are you really frozen?" asked Vasili Andreevich.

"I feel it's my death. Forgive me for Christ's sake . . ." said Nikita [45] in a tearful voice, continuing to wave his hand before his face as if driving away flies.

Vasili Andreevich stood silent and motionless for half a minute. Then suddenly, with the same resolution with which he used to strike hands when making a good purchase, he took a step back and turning up his sleeves began raking the snow off Nikita and out of the sledge. Having done this he hurriedly undid his girdle, opened out his fur coat, and having pushed Nikita down, lay down on top of him, covering him not only with his fur coat but with the whole of his body, which glowed with warmth. After pushing the skirts of his coat between Nikita and the sides of the sledge, and holding down its hem with his knees, Vasili Andreevich lay like that face down, with his head pressed against the front of the sledge. Here he no longer heard the horse's movements or the whistling of the wind, but only Nikita's breathing. At first and for a long time Nikita lay motionless, then he sighed deeply and moved.

"There, and you say you are dying! Lie still and get warm, that's our way . . ." began Vasili Andreevich.

But to his great surprise he could say no more, for tears came to his eyes and his lower jaw began to quiver rapidly. He stopped speaking and only gulped down the risings in his throat. "Seems I was badly frightened and have gone quite weak," he thought. But this weakness was not only not unpleasant, but gave him a peculiar joy such as he had never felt before.

"That's our way!" he said to himself, experiencing a strange and solemn tenderness. He lay like that for a long time, wiping his eyes on the fur of his coat and tucking under his knee the right skirt, which the wind kept turning up.

But he longed so passionately to tell somebody of his joyful condition that he said: "Nikita!"

"It's comfortable, warm!" came a voice from beneath.

"There, you see, friend, I was going to perish. And you would have been frozen, and I should have . . ."

But again his jaws began to quiver and his eyes to fill with tears, and he could say no more.

"Well, never mind," he thought. "I know about myself what I know."

[46]

He remained silent and lay like that for a long time.

Nikita kept him warm from below and his fur coats from above. Only his hands, with which he kept his coatskirts down round Nikita's sides, and his legs which the wind kept uncovering, began to freeze, especially his right hand which had no glove. But he did not think of his legs or of his hands but only of how to warm the peasant who was lying under him. He looked out several times at Mukhorty and could see that his back was uncovered and the drugget and breeching lying on the snow, and that he ought to get up and cover him, but he could not bring himself to leave Nikita and disturb even for a moment the joyous condition he was in. He no longer felt any kind of terror.

"No fear, we shan't lose him this time!" he said to himself, referring to his getting the peasant warm with the same boastfulness with which he spoke of his buying and selling.

Vasili Andreevich lay in that way for one hour, another, and a third, but he was unconscious of the passage of time. At first impressions of the snowstorm, the sledge-shafts, and the horse with the shaft-bow shaking before his eyes, kept passing through his mind, then he remembered Nikita lying under him, then recollections of the festival, his wife, the police-officer, and the box of candles, began to mingle with these; then again Nikita, this time lying under that box, then the peasants, customers and traders, and the white walls of his house with its iron roof with Nikita lying underneath, presented themselves to his imagination. Afterward all these impressions blended into one nothingness. As the colors of the rainbow unite into one white light, so all these different impressions mingled into one, and he fell asleep.

For a long time he slept without dreaming, but just before dawn the visions recommenced. It seemed to him that he was standing by the box of tapers and that Tikhon's wife was asking for a five-kopek taper for the Church fête. He wished to take one out and give it to her, but his hands would not lift, being held tight in his pockets. He wanted to walk round the box but his feet would not move and his new clean goloshes had grown to the stone floor, and he could neither lift them nor get his feet out of the goloshes. Then the taper-box was no longer a box but a bed, and suddenly Vasili Andreevich saw himself lying in his bed at home. He was lying in his bed and could not get up. Yet it was necessary for him to get up because Ivan Matveich, the police-officer, would soon call for him and he had to go with him—either to bargain for the forest or to put Mukhorty's breeching straight. [47]

He asked his wife: "Nikolaevna, hasn't he come yet?" "No, he hasn't," she replied. He heard someone drive up to the front steps. "It must be him." "No, he's gone past." "Nikolaevna! I say, Nikolaevna, isn't he here yet?" "No." He was still lying on his bed and could not get up, but was always waiting. And this waiting was uncanny and yet joyful. Then suddenly his joy was completed. He whom he was expecting came; not Ivan Matveich the police-officer, but someone else—yet it was he whom he had been waiting for. He came and called him; and it was he who had called him and told him to lie down on Nikita. And Vasili Andreevich was glad that that one had come for him.

"I'm coming!" he cried joyfully, and that cry awoke him, but woke him up not at all the same person he had been when he fell asleep. He tried to get up but could not, tried to move his arm and could not, to move his leg and also could not, to turn his head and could not. He was surprised but not at all disturbed by this. He understood that this was death, and was not at all disturbed by that either. He remembered that Nikita was lying under him and that he had got warm and was alive, and it seemed to him that he was Nikita and Nikita was he, and that his life was not in himself but in Nikita. He strained his ears and heard Nikita breathing and even slightly snoring. "Nikita is alive, so I too am alive!" he said to himself triumphantly.

And he remembered his money, his shop, his house, the buying and selling, and Mironov's millions, and it was hard for him to understand why that man, called Vasili Brekhunov, had troubled himself with all those things with which he had been troubled.

"Well, it was because he did not know what the real thing was," he thought, concerning that Vasili Brekhunov. "He did not know, but now I know and know for sure. Now I know!" And again he heard the voice of the one who had called him before. "I'm coming! Coming!" he responded gladly, and his whole being was filled with joyful emotion. He felt himself free and that nothing could hold him back any longer.

After that Vasili Andreevich neither saw, heard, nor felt anything more in this world.

All around the snow still eddied. The same whirlwinds of snow circled about, covering the dead Vasili Andreevich's fur coat, the shivering Mukhorty, the sledge, now scarcely to be seen, and Nikita lying at the bottom of it, kept warm beneath his dead master.

[48]

X

Nikita awoke before daybreak. He was aroused by the cold that had begun to creep down his back. He had dreamed that he was coming from the mill with a load of his master's flour and when crossing the stream had missed the bridge and let the cart get stuck. And he saw that he had crawled under the cart and was trying to lift it by arching his back. But strange to say the cart did not move, it stuck to his back and he could neither lift it nor get out from under it. It was crushing the whole of his loins. And how cold it felt! Evidently he must crawl out. "Have done!" he exclaimed to whoever was pressing the cart down on him. "Take out the sacks!" But the cart pressed down colder and colder, and then he heard a strange knocking, awoke completely, and remembered everything. The cold cart was his dead and frozen master lying upon him. And the knock was produced by Mukhorty, who had twice struck the sledge with his hoof.

"Andreevich! Eh, Andreevich!" Nikita called cautiously, beginning to realize the truth, and straightening his back. But Vasili Andreevich did not answer and his stomach and legs were stiff and cold and heavy like iron weights.

"He must have died! May the Kingdom of Heaven be his!" thought Nikita.

He turned his head, dug with his hand through the snow about him and opened his eyes. It was daylight; the wind was whistling as before between the shafts, and the snow was falling in the same way, except that it was no longer driving against the frame of the sledge but silently covered both sledge and horse deeper and deeper, and neither the horse's movements nor his breathing were any longer to be heard.

[49]

"He must have frozen too," thought Nikita of Mukhorty, and indeed those hoof knocks against the sledge, which had awakened Nikita, were the last efforts the already numbed Mukhorty had made to keep on his feet before dying.

"O Lord God, it seems Thou art calling me too!" said Nikita. "Thy Holy Will be done. But it's uncanny. . . . Still, a man can't die twice and must die once. If only it would come soon!"

And he again drew in his head, closed his eyes, and became unconscious, fully convinced that now he was certainly and finally dying.

It was not till noon that day that peasants dug Vasili Andreevich and Nikita out of the snow with their shovels, not more than seventy yards from the road and less than half a mile from the village.

The snow had hidden the sledge, but the shafts and the kerchief tied to them were still visible. Mukhorty, buried up to his belly in snow, with the breeching and drugget hanging down, stood all white, his dead head pressed against his frozen throat: icicles hung from his nostrils, his eyes were covered with hoar-frost as though filled with tears, and he had grown so thin in that one night that he was nothing but skin and bone.

Vasili Andreevich was stiff as a frozen carcass, and when they rolled him off Nikita his legs remained apart and his arms stretched out as they had been. His bulging hawk eyes were frozen, and his open mouth under his clipped mustache was full of snow. But Nikita though chilled through was still alive. When he had been brought to, he felt sure that he was already dead and that what was taking place with him was no longer happening in this world but in the next. When he heard the peasants shouting as they dug him out and rolled the frozen body of Vasili Andreevich from off him, he was at first surprised that in the other world peasants should be shouting in the same old way and had the same kind of body, and then when he realized that he was still in this world he was sorry rather than glad, especially when he found that the toes on both his feet were frozen.

[50]   Nikita lay in hospital for two months. They cut off three of his toes, but the others recovered so that he was still able to work and went on living for another twenty years, first as a farm-laborer, then in his old age as a watchman. He died at home as he had wished, only this year, under the icons with a lighted taper in his hands. Before he died he asked his wife's forgiveness and forgave her for the cooper. He also took leave of his son and grandchildren, and died sincerely glad that he was relieving his son and daughter-in-law of the burden of having to feed him, and that he was now really passing from this life of which he was weary into that other life which every year and every hour grew clearer and more desirable to him. Whether he is better or worse off there where he awoke after his death, whether he was disappointed or found there what he expected, we shall all soon learn. ✦

AND YET THEY DROVE ON

Tolstoy: moral-ethical giant, epic novelist, vegetarian, proponent of chastity (which he failed to practice consistently, even as an old man), agricultural theorist, educational reformer, leader of an international Christian-anarchist religious movement described by Nabokov as "a neutral blend between a kind of Hindu Nirvana and the New Testament—Jesus without the church," early nonviolence advocate with devoted disciples all over the world, including the young Gandhi. It's not much of a stretch to say that his fiction changed the way human beings think about themselves.

So, it's interesting to note that his prose consists almost entirely of *facts*. The language isn't particularly elevated or poetic or overtly philosophical. It's mostly just descriptions of people doing things.

Consider this, from early in "Master and Man":

"[Nikita] went as usual cheerfully and willingly to the shed, stepping briskly and easily on his rather turned-in feet; took down from a nail the heavy tasseled leather bridle, and jingling the rings of the bit went to the closed stable where the horse he was to harness was standing by himself."

Or this, as Nikita gets down to work:

"Having whisked the dusty, grooved back of the well-fed young stallion with the skirt of his coat, he put a bridle on his handsome head, straightened his ears and forelock, and having taken off his halter led him out to water."

Or from their stop in Grishkino:

" 'It is ready,' said one of the young women, and after flicking with her apron the top of the samovar which was now boiling over, she carried it with an effort to the table, raised it, and set it down with a thud."

Here's another color-coding challenge: on any page of the story, mark *facts* in one color, *authorial opinions* (philosophical or religious musings or aphoristic observations on human behavior) in another. You'll find that the story is nearly all facts, heavily weighted toward factual descriptions of action. When Tolstoy does offer a subjective opinion on a character, these are rendered as objectively and precisely as Nikita's crossing of the yard or his preparation of the horse. And since they appear, as they do, in a matrix of facts, we're inclined to accept them. (We accept Tolstoy's assertion that Nikita is usually cheerful and willing in the same spirit that we accept his assertion that the bridle is leather and tasseled.)

Likewise, as we'll see in a bit, when Tolstoy recounts the thoughts or feelings of his characters, he does this succinctly and precisely, using simple objective sentences that *seem* factual in their syntax and modesty of assertion.

A fact draws us in. This seems to be one of those "laws of fiction" we've been seeking. "The car was dented and red" makes a car appear in the mind. Even more so if the fact is an action: "The dented red car slowly left the parking lot." Notice how little we doubt that statement, the spontaneous, involuntary buy-in that makes us forget that there is no car and no parking lot.

But to say that the story is nearly all facts doesn't mean that Tolstoy is a minimalist. He has a gift for making sentences that, staying within factuality, convey a bounty of information and make a rich, detailed, almost overfull world.

Consider the difference between "The maid carried the samovar to the table" and Tolstoy's version: "After flicking with her apron the top of the samovar which was now boiling over, she carried it with an effort to the table, raised it, and set it down with a thud."

That apron flick, the woman carrying the samovar "with an effort," the thud as she sets it down, the fact that she's carrying it below the level of the table (she "raised it" before she could "set it down") are all facts embroidered into the basic action "woman carries samovar to table." Although they don't make a more particular person (anyone could find a samovar heavy), they make a more particular action. The samovar is heavier and hotter than if she'd just "carried the samovar to the table," and I see more of her than, by rights, I should: her red cheeks, the sweat-stained underarms of her blouse (and stepping away from the table, she blows a strand of sweat-plastered hair off her forehead).

So, speaking of little gas stations, here's one of Tolstoy's: saying something that strikes the reader as true. (Nabokov called this Tolstoy's "fundamental accuracy of perception.")

We know how things are and how they are not. We know how things tend to work and how they don't. We know how things mostly go and how they never go. And we like it when a story agrees with our sense of how the world works. It gives us a thrill, and this thrill-at-truth keeps us reading. In a story entirely made up, it's actually the main thing that keeps us reading. Since everything is invented, we read in a continual state of light skepticism. Every sentence is a little referendum on truth. "True or not?" we keep asking. If our answer is "Yes, seems true," we get shot out of that little gas station and keep reading.

"Most Russian writers have been tremendously interested in Truth's exact whereabouts and essential properties," wrote Nabokov. "Tolstoy marched straight at it, head bent and fists clenched." Tolstoy sought the truth in two ways: as a fiction writer and as a moral preacher. He was more powerful in the former but kept being drawn back to the latter. And somehow, it's this struggle, between (as Nabokov put it) "the man who gloated over the beauty of black earth, white flesh, blue snow, green fields, purple thunderclouds and the man who maintained that fiction is sinful and art immoral," that makes us feel Tolstoy as a moral-ethical giant. It's as if he resorts to fiction only when he can't help it and, having to make the sinful indulgence really count, uses it to ask only the biggest questions and answer these with supreme, sometimes lacerating honesty.

Tolstoy was not, however, according to the diaries of his wife, Sonya, much of a moral-ethical giant around the house.

"He pushes everything off onto me," she wrote, "everything, without exception: the children, the management of his property, relations with other people, business affairs, the house, the publishers. Then he despises me for soiling my hands with them all, retreats into his selfishness and complains about me incessantly . . . goes for walks, rides his horse, writes a little, goes wherever he pleases, does absolutely nothing for the family. . . . His biographers will tell how he went to draw water for the porter, but no one will know how he never gave his wife one moment's rest or one drop of water to his sick child; how in thirty-five years he never sat for five minutes by a bedside or let me have a rest or sleep the night through or go for a walk or simply pause for a moment to recover my strength."

Tolstoy's biographer Henri Troyat says that Sonya had a tendency, in her diaries, to "plead her cause, no longer to her family and contemporaries, but to posterity."

Well, duly noted, Sonya: the guy sounds like a pain.

Yet his writing is full of compassion. That's what he's known for. He emanates concern for the weak and powerless, sees all sides of every issue, inhabits character after character (low people, lofty people, horses, dogs, you name it), and the resulting fictional world feels nearly as detailed and various as the real one. A person can hardly read even a few lines of Tolstoy without feeling her interest in life renewed.

What do we make of this?

Well, of course, the writer is not the person. The writer is a version of the person who makes a model of the world that may seem to advocate for certain virtues, virtues by which he may not be able to live.

"Not only is the novelist nobody's spokesman," wrote Milan Kundera,

but I would go so far as to say he is not even the spokesman for his own ideas. When Tolstoy sketched the first draft of *Anna Karenina*, Anna was a most unsympathetic woman, and her tragic end was entirely deserved and justified. The final version of the novel is very different, but I do not believe that Tolstoy had revised his moral ideas in the meantime; I would say, rather, that in the course of writing, he was listening to another voice than that of his personal moral conviction. He was listening to what I would like to call the wisdom of the novel. Every true novelist listens for that suprapersonal wisdom, which explains why great novels are always a little more intelligent than their authors. Novelists who are more intelligent than their books should go into another line of work.

As Kundera suggests, the writer opens himself up to that "suprapersonal wisdom" by technical means. That's what "craft" is: a way to open ourselves up to the suprapersonal wisdom within us.

—

With "craft" in mind, let's take a look at a place where Tolstoy seems pretty darn morally-ethically gigantic, a five-part move that starts on the story's second page.

In the paragraph that begins, "Nikita's wife Martha . . . ," an omniscient narrator tells us an objective truth: Vasili routinely cheats Nikita and his wife.

In the next paragraph ("What agreement did we ever draw up with you?"), Tolstoy lets Vasili, in direct speech (to Nikita), comment on this relationship: "We deal straightforwardly. You serve me and I don't neglect you." (We know this isn't true, because that omniscient narrator has just told us so.)

Next, we move into Vasili's thoughts, which allows us to see how he processes the lie he's just told: he is "honestly convinced that he was Nikita's benefactor." This creates a different Vasili than if his thoughts had been of the "bwa-ha-ha" variety. You know: "Vasili did not mind speaking this lie, because Nikita was a peasant, and Vasili had no compunction about lying to his idiotic servants." The Vasili who would knowingly lie to Nikita is a different Vasili than the one who isn't (quite) aware that he's lying. He wants to have it both ways: to cheat, while still seeing himself as benevolent. He's a hypocrite, in other words, and, like all hypocrites, doesn't know it.

Tolstoy next gives Nikita a chance to respond in direct speech to Vasili's assertion of fair dealing: "I serve you and take as much pains as I would for my own father," Nikita claims. (We doubt this. Nikita's doing a little spinning of his own.)

Finally, we go into Nikita's thoughts (a more honest place), where it's confirmed that he's "quite aware" that he's being cheated. But he knows that trying to explain his side of things is useless and "as long as he had nowhere to go he must accept what he could get."

So, five shifts of vantage point in three paragraphs: (1) the objective truth (via our omniscient narrator), (2) Vasili's public stance (via his speech to Nikita), (3) Vasili's private stance (via his thoughts), (4) Nikita's public stance (via his speech to Vasili), and (5) Nikita's private stance (via his thoughts).

Processing this number of shifts normally requires some extra effort on the part of the reader—a sort of fee gets charged in readerly attention. But here we barely notice, charmed by Tolstoy's "fundamental accuracy of perception." When we go into a character's mind, what we find there feels familiar and true. We've had versions of those same thoughts ourselves, and so we accept them, and the result is a view of the situation that feels holographic and godlike.

Another example of this technique, starting at the bottom of page 24, as Vasili and Nikita are about to leave Grishkino that second (final, fatal) time:

At "Well, this is weather!": We start out in Vasili's thoughts.

In the next two paragraphs: We're in the mind of the "aged host."

Final paragraph of the section: First we're in Petrushka's mind. Then we switch to Nikita's. Finally, in the last two lines, in what feels like both logical proof (QED!) and death sentence, Tolstoy/the omniscient narrator asserts that there is therefore "no one to hinder the departing travelers."

So: five perspectives in four paragraphs.

But it's not just the mind-to-mind movement that makes us believe. It's what Tolstoy does once he's in a mind: he makes a direct, factual report of what he finds there. No judgment, no poetry. Just flat observation—which is, of course, a form of *self*-observation (the writer asking, "What would I be thinking if I were that person, in that situation?"). What else could it be? From where, other than his own mind, could Tolstoy find material with which to fill those other minds? These four people are all Tolstoy, and his recounting of what they're thinking is not extraordinarily "compassionate." He's just ascribing to them thoughts he's had in analogous situations, thoughts not particularly unique, psychologically, to them, produced more by their role in the situation (initiator of the trip; host; young man who loves literature; servant who is cold) than by some secret knowledge Tolstoy has of those particular, individuated minds (which, after all, never existed).

In other words, what makes us think of Tolstoy as a moral-ethical giant here is a *technique* (going from mind to mind) coupled with a *confidence*. Of what is Tolstoy confident? That people are more similar to him than different. That he has an inner Vasili, an inner aged host, an inner Petrushka, an inner Nikita. This confidence serves as a gateway to (what reads as) saintly compassion.

The magician doesn't really have to saw the assistant in half; he just has to look like he's doing so, for the short duration of the performance, with the advantage of being observed by an audience located some distance away that, aware that it's an illusion, has agreed to play along.

That audience is us, and we agree to play along because, for some reason, we like to watch one of our fellow human beings doing a passable version of God, telling us in the process how God sees us, if God exists, and what God thinks of the way we behave.

"Master and Man" has virtues we normally associate with popular entertainment—cinematic virtues, we might say. It's harrowing, the stakes are high, we want to know how things turn out. By the end we're reading to see who dies. Some stories—let's admit it—we read from a sense of duty, the way we walk through a middling local museum: noting things we should feel interested in but aren't, really. Reading such stories, we're merely *reading* them. They keep being a series of words we're dutifully decoding. They're a clever dance the writer is doing, which we are politely enduring. Reading "Master and Man," we begin living it; the words disappear and we find ourselves thinking not about word choice but about the decisions the characters are making and decisions we have made, or might have to make someday, in our actual lives.

That's the kind of story I want to write, the kind that stops being writing and starts being life.

But, Lord, it's harder than it looks.

"Master and Man" does this trick, in part, through its structure.

Imagine I'm about to give you a tour of a mansion. I announce the organizing principle of the tour: we're going to start in the attic and work our way down. If, on the next floor, I digress (I lead you into a side room and up three steps into a little secret room), you'll be fine with that and might even enjoy it, because you know we're still generally following our plan ("working our way down").

One way "Master and Man" achieves its cinematic propulsion is that, early on, Tolstoy announces his organizing principle (his equivalent of "We're working our way down"): "We're driving out to buy that land."

Here's the story in outline:

SECTION	ACTION
I	Preparation for the trip to the home of a neighboring landowner. Intro to Vasili and Nikita.
II	They leave the estate and get lost for the first time, then stumble upon the town of Grishkino.
III	They don't stop; they get lost the second time, stumble upon Grishkino again, and stop this time.
IV	They take a break at the family's house, decline to spend the night.
V	They get lost a third time, must spend the night near the ravine.
VI	That night, from Vasili's point of view. Ends with Vasili riding off.
VII	Slight rewind and then: that night, from Nikita's point of view. Ends with Vasili riding off.
VIII	Vasili's wild ride. He gets lost, walks in circles, has his encounter with the wormwood. The horse runs away. Vasili tracks it, finds . . . the sled.
IX	Vasili lies on top of Nikita, dies, saves Nikita.
X	Nikita's postscript.

A baseline pattern gets repeated four times: they set out from somewhere and get lost. The whole story can be seen as a series of getting-losts and coming-homes, ending with the biggest coming-home of all: Vasili "comes home" to moral completion and, we assume, heaven. (And, come to think of it, the story ends with a double coming-home for Nikita: home to his village, then home to God.)

And, as we saw in "The Darling," a pattern creates propulsion. (Every time we feel we are found again, per the above pattern, we anticipate that we will soon be lost again. And then we are. And that's satisfying.)

There's also an embedded second pattern, a sort of "shadow structure": each section begins with a desire/problem/setback and ends with the dangled hope of some improvement:

SCENE	ACTION
I	Vasili wants that land and it's a holiday *but* goes out to get it.
II	They are lost *but* find the town.

III   They are lost *but* (again) find the town.

IV   They set out again *but* this time with a guide.

V   They are lost *but* admit it and resolve to shelter near the ravine.

VI   Vasili despairs *but* takes action (by running away to save himself).

VII   Nikita is dying *but* accepts it.

VIII   Vasili is lost and on foot *but* finds the sled again.

IX   Vasili is dying *but* dies happy.

X   Nikita lives another twenty years, dies, *but* is glad to be going.

This pattern is also present in the story's larger arc: Vasili botches his life *but* is saved (spiritually) in the end.

This shadow structure supplies some propulsion of its own: within each section, our heroes are in trouble *but* get out of it. They, and we, enter the next section revived by the feeling of relief at having just escaped something. (The tightrope walker falters, seems about to fall, recovers: note the associated uptick in your watching energy.)

We're being swept downriver by the strong current of the overall organizing principle, while being caught along the way in a series of small, distracting local eddies. Our moment-to-moment attention is constantly being drawn to surviving the local eddies, and so we don't notice ourselves racing toward the fatal waterfall at river's end.

In the first part of Section II, Tolstoy's job, per the first outline above, is to get Vasili and Nikita to "leave the estate and get lost for the first time."

There are a number of ways in which a writer might accomplish this.

A lesser writer (that poor, proverbial guy we hope we never are) might do it like this: (1) as they leave home, they pass some things and discuss some random topics; (2) they reach a crossroads and, for reasons we can't discern (that aren't provided or aren't clear), Vasili takes the straight road—he just, you know, takes it; (3) Nikita falls asleep, just because; and (4) somehow, they get lost.

Compare this with Tolstoy's version: (1) As they leave home, Vasili pokes at Nikita by bringing up the painful subject of Nikita's wife. Then he asks if Nikita plans to buy a horse, which suggests a pattern familiar to Nikita: Vasili is going to try to cheat him. These two threads in the discussion leave Nikita irritated. (2) They reach a crossroads. Vasili asks Nikita's opinion (and we feel the opinion Nikita offers is wise, given the weather), then ignores it. When he's ignored, Nikita doesn't push back, only passively says, "Just as you please." (3) Nikita falls asleep. We feel this as a reaction to (1) and (2) above. Having been taunted and then ignored, Nikita takes himself out of the game by falling asleep. (4) With Nikita asleep, Vasili steers by his own lights and gets them lost.

So, the big difference in these two versions is the increased causality in Tolstoy's version.

This "lesser writer's" version reads like a sequence of unrelated events. Nothing causes anything else. Some things . . . occur. But we don't know why. The result of the sequence ("they get lost") feels out of relation with what came before. They just get lost randomly, for no reason, and this means nothing.

We move through the sequence with that frustrated, unmoored feeling we get when following a clueless tour guide. "What are we supposed to be noting?" we wonder. Vasili and Nikita don't become more real or particular to us. They're just stick figures, not deciding anything, not reacting to anything. We know them no better coming out of the sequence than we did going in.

I've worked with so many wildly talented young writers over the years that I feel qualified to say that there are two things that separate writers who go on to publish from those who don't.

First, a willingness to revise.

Second, the extent to which the writer has learned to make causality.

Making causality doesn't seem sexy or particularly literary. It's a workmanlike thing, to make A cause B, the stuff of vaudeville, of Hollywood. But it's the hardest thing to learn. It doesn't come naturally, not to most of us. But that's really all a story is: a series of things that happen in sequence, in which we can discern a pattern of causality.

For most of us, the problem is not in making things happen ("A dog barked," "The house exploded," "Darren kicked the tire of his car" are all easy enough to type) but in making one thing seem to cause the next.

This is important, because causation is what creates the appearance of meaning.

"The queen died, and then the king died" (E. M. Forster's famous formulation) describes two unrelated events occurring in sequence. It doesn't mean anything. "The queen died, and the king died *of grief*" puts those events into relation; we understand that one caused the other. The sequence, now infused with causality, means: "That king really loved his queen."

Causality is to the writer what melody is to the songwriter: a superpower that the audience feels as the crux of the matter; the thing the audience actually shows up for; the hardest thing to do; that which distinguishes the competent practitioner from the extraordinary one.

A well-written bit of prose is like a beautifully hand-painted kite, lying there on the grass. It's nice. We admire it. Causality is the wind that then comes along and lifts it up. The kite is then a beautiful thing made even more beautiful by the fact that it's doing what it was made to do.

To poke at this idea of causality a little, let's look at the encounter with that sled of drunk peasants from the town of "A-a-a" that begins on page 15.

What's this scene doing in the story? It's entertaining enough, but (recalling the Cornfeld Principle) how does it "advance the story in a non-trivial way"? Could we just cut that whole episode? Have Nikita and Vasili carry on through the created blank space on the road, saving us nearly a full page?

Vasili and Nikita have just passed through Grishkino for the first time. Prepared by the story's patterning, we're expecting them to get lost again. Then, "through the slanting screen of wind-driven snow," they see something ahead: another sled. As Vasili goes to pass, the drunken peasant driving that sled decides to race Vasili. We get a glimpse of their horse, "nostrils distended and ears pressed back from fear," as it suffers under the drunken whip. Nikita, two months sober, rebukes them to Vasili with the zeal of the converted: "Just see what liquor does! They've tired that little horse to death. What pagans!" This introduces into the story the notion "A horse may be so badly used that it dies" (which, going forward, will make us look differently at poor, loyal Mukhorty). Also: "Pushing things too hard, in order to win, causes problems" (which resonates with Vasili's insistence on this ill-conceived trip). We contrast Vasili's reaction to this incident with Nikita's: Vasili is fired up by the competition; Nikita feels for the suffering horse. Actually, Vasili is fired up by the mere *appearance* of competition, where there actually was none (his sled had been gaining on the peasant sled all along). This reminds us of his monetary dealings with Nikita: Vasili enjoys winning even a rigged race.

So, these are all good, enjoyable, theme-enforcing reasons for the scene's existence. But what we're really waiting for is an answer to the question "How does this scene advance the story in a non-trivial way?"

Returning to the idea of a story as a process for the transfer of energy: in a good story, the writer makes energy in a beat, then transfers this energy cleanly to the next one (the energy is "conserved"). She does this by being aware of the nature of the energy she's made. In a bad story (or an early draft), the writer doesn't fully understand the nature of the energy she's made, and ignores or misuses it, and it dissipates.

The preferred, most efficient, highest-order form of energy transfer (the premier way for a scene to advance the story in a non-trivial way) is for a beat to *cause* the next beat, especially if that next beat is felt as essential, i.e., as an escalation: a meaningful alteration in the terms of the story.

Expecting to get lost again, we enter the beat "We race a sled full of peasants."

What does the race cause to happen?

Well, it fires Vasili up. Of course it does. This man who lives to win has won: "This encounter cheered and enlivened Vasili Andreevich." His elation then causes the next beat ("he drove on more boldly without examining the way-marks, urging on the horse and trusting to him"), which, in turn, causes the next (essential, very nontrivial) beat: they get lost again.

One of the most memorable things about this story is Grishkino, the little town that serves as a recurring indicator of how lost they are and represents their final squandered chance of salvation.

Let's consider that clothesline outside town that Vasili and Nikita pass four times.

Each time, Tolstoy describes the clothes a little differently:

First time: On page 13, as they approach Grishkino for the first time: "shirts, one red and one white, trousers, leg-bands, and a petti-coat—fluttered wildly in the wind. The white shirt in particular struggled desperately, waving its sleeves about."

Second time: At the bottom of page 14, on their way out of town: the white shirt has come loose from the line and is "now attached only by one frozen sleeve."

The juxtaposition of these two images tells a little story ("As you entered this warm, safe town, I, this white shirt, was frantic, worried, trying to signal to you that there was danger afoot. But you dopes ignored my advice and now are heading back into the storm, and, honestly, all of the energy has gone out of me and I am just barely hanging on here") that underscores our understanding of where we are, physically ("Leaving town again, going out the way we came in") and emotionally ("Ignoring a warning, due to our hubris").

Then:

Third time: On page 17, as they come back into Grishkino: "the frozen washing . . . still fluttered desperately in the wind."

We read this addition of "still" as: "Yes, things continue to be desperate. And Vasili still doesn't see it." Tolstoy doesn't overdo it (two shirts are not, you know, hugging one another in terror), but again we take pleasure in the fact that he's remembered this laundry and has used it.

Fourth time: On page 25, as they leave Grishkino for the second (last) time: "They drove again through the outskirts of the village . . . past the yard where the frozen linen had hung (which, however, was no longer to be seen)."

Gulp. This last image is not a desperate waving but a complete disappearance. It's hard to say why this is so good. A clunky reading might be: "Its previous warnings having been ignored, the laundry has stopped signaling." Or: "Like that shirt, somebody [Vasili] is about to be . . . gone."

Earlier, we defined escalation as that which results when we refuse to repeat beats. Each time we pass that clothesline, the laundry has undergone some small change in its condition. We read this as an escalation, or at least a mini-escalation—a "refusal to repeat." (It would be a lesser story if all four descriptions were identical.)

"Always be escalating," then, can be understood as "Be alert, always, to the possibilities you have created for variation." If an element recurs, the second appearance is an opportunity for variation and, potentially, escalation. Let's say that, in a film, we show a place setting (plate, spoon, fork, knife), and then the camera tracks across three other, identical place settings. That's static. But make the right adjustments to each of the four plate/spoon/fork/knife arrangements, show these in sequence, and that more variation-blessed sequence will be felt to have escalation in it and, therefore, meaning. For example: let's say that, as we track over the plates in sequence, we see: (1) correct/full arrangement (plate/spoon/fork/knife), (2) spoon missing, (3) spoon and fork missing, (4) all the silverware missing (only the plate remains); this will be felt to mean, let's say, "evacuation" or "diminishment."

Here, the pattern of variation isn't too neat or directly metaphorical. (The clothes don't, for example, go from unfrozen to frozen, as Nikita and Vasili soon will, but are frozen the first time we see them.) We barely notice the variations at speed but, on closer examination, feel them to be perfectly pitched. Rather than neatly spitting out some predetermined, reductive meaning, they produce a feeling of mystery, the metaphorical world lightly infiltrating the physical.

After that race with the peasants in the sled fires Vasili up, which gets them lost again, Nikita takes the reins from Vasili and, in effect, hands them to wise little Mukhorty, who leads them back to Grishkino, there near the end of Section III.

We understand this as a chance for Vasili to do what he should have done the first time: stop and be saved. And, relieved, we see that he is, in fact, going to stop (at a "large double-fronted brick house").

The question (as with the teahouse in "In the Cart") is: Why *this* house? Of all the houses in Grishkino (and of all the houses he could have invented), why is Tolstoy having them stop at this particular one?

What we're really asking is: How is this part of the story (this structural unit) going to earn its keep?

A structural unit (in this case, all of the text describing what happens during this stop in Grishkino, pages 17–25), like a story, wants to look something like Freytag's triangle. (This is more aspiration than rule.) A structural unit should, that is, be shaped like a miniature version of a story: rising action, building to a climax. (If a structural unit in a story we're writing isn't shaped like that, we might wonder if it wants to be; if it is shaped like that, we might want to make that shape sharper.)

There are many lovely things going on here (Nikita's struggle not to drink, the general feeling of warmth and comfort that pervades the house, that Paulson-quoting grandson, the funny bit in which Nikita responds to Vasili's chirpy "We shall get there, shan't we?" with a gloomy, "If only we don't go astray again"), but none of this moves us out of the "exposition" part of Freytag's triangle (as applied to this structural unit). As we saw with "The Darling," when we're reading along and start to become aware that we're (still) in exposition, we become alert to anything that might signal a transition into the rising action. I find myself in this state as we approach the conversation that begins at the top of page 23, while the horse is being harnessed (let's call it the "young people are getting out of hand" conversation).

What happens during that conversation that might make it feel climactic?

The main points of the conversation are: (1) The young people are getting out of hand; (2) there's no managing them because they're too clever; (3) it's harmful for a household to defy tradition by dividing up; and (4) the family's second son is thinking of dividing this household and this is breaking his father's heart.

My mind does a little calculating, trying to understand why Tolstoy has chosen to put us in front of this particular conversation.

What, in the story, might be felt to align with "young people who can't be managed because they're too clever"? My mind supplies Vasili. He's not young, exactly, but he's younger than his old host, and seemingly of a new generation: self-centered, profit-driven, drawn to power. His reason for not staying the night ("Business! Lose an hour and you can't catch it up in a year!") feels "clever" and out of step with his host's values. The old master has his family gathered cozily around him, as is proper and traditional, whereas, in the name of commerce, Vasili has left his wife and son behind on a holiday. So, we feel a certain kinship between Vasili and this newfangled, upstart son.

But it's interesting. When the old man finishes speaking, Vasili chimes in, not in defense of the son but on the side of the old man. "You got everything together and you're the master," he says. That is: "You're a master, I'm a master, I get you. Don't back down, stay the course."

So, Tolstoy essentially "splits" Vasili. Vasili's values are, roughly speaking, those of the son, but he speaks up in defense of the father. He seems to want to have it both ways: to be regarded as an old-fashioned, traditional, all-powerful master but also to be allowed to indulge in his free-swinging, anti-traditional, capitalist ventures.

We understand the purpose of this second pause in Grishkino to be: "give Vasili a last chance to save himself and Nikita by agreeing to spend the night at this house." And there he meets a master, like him, who advocates for them spending the night.

It should be a slam-dunk: the person he most admires in the household is urging him (giving him permission) to stay.

Only too bad: Vasili has arrived at exactly the wrong moment, to find the old man, whom he should be inclined to emulate, in a newly weakened state: no longer capable of subduing his children, pleading with them and losing. He gets tears in his eyes, turns on his son, bitterly and awkwardly and in front of company. He might have been a powerful master in his day, but he's not seeming very powerful tonight.

Now, the Vasili we've come to know is a blusterer and a bully. To be happy, he has to be in control, correct, victorious, obeyed. We imagine him at home, a petty tyrant, not loved much, not feared much either; avoided when possible, probably; laughed at behind his back for his incompetence and ego.

He's already declared that they're not staying. And what kind of master reverses himself? The weak kind, that's who, like this old guy—the kind whose household is falling apart, the crying kind, the kind Vasili has been trying all his life not to be but secretly knows he is.

Had they stopped at another house, a house where, say, a young and still-powerful master was making the case for the considerate treatment of one's servants, Vasili, wishing to emulate that powerful master, might have been willing to reverse himself, to show how considerate he was of Nikita, his servant.

But instead he meets this old, weak, defeated master and feels an aversion, and that aversion combines with the fact that the horse has already been harnessed (the dictatorship of politeness) to drive him back out into the night, and to his death.

In a sense, Vasili is killed by his fealty to the idea that, to preserve and broadcast his power, a "master" must be firm, strong, and unpersuadable.

Scrooge starts out grouchy and winds up generous and euphoric. Joy/Hulga in "Good Country People" starts out arrogant and smug and winds up humiliated. Gatsby starts out confident and full of hope and winds up deflated (and dead). King Lear starts out a powerful monarch and winds up—well, also deflated and dead.

In Section VI, one of my favorites in all of literature, Vasili starts out his normal, cranky, impatient, superior, pleased-to-have-placed-a-babyish-flag-in-the-snow self and winds up a panic-stricken coward who leaves Nikita behind to die. I believe it, and I believe that if, God forbid, I ever become a coward, this is exactly how I'd go about it.

It's a powerful, virtuosic section, one that fills us lesser writers (this one, anyway) with envy and resentment, but we might take some consolation from the observation that what creates the illusion of a changed human mind here is a simple pattern: what once worked for Vasili stops working.

The section naturally divides into two episodes: one before Vasili goes to sleep (pages 31–35) and one after he wakes up (on page 35).

In the first, Vasili, starting to feel afraid, tries various methods of distracting himself. He has a cigarette, puts up that flag. He turns his mind to "the one thing that constituted the sole aim, meaning, pleasure, and pride of his life" (i.e., money). He runs the numbers on the purchase he's out here to make ("there'll still be some thirty sazheens of firewood left on each desyatin"). He reconsiders how they got lost, inaccurately spreading out the blame ("God only knows how we missed the turning"—note that "we"), then disparages, with pleasure: dogs ("the damned things don't bark when they're wanted"), "the others" (who won't travel in such weather), and his wife (who "doesn't know the right way of doing things"). He again tells himself the story of his victorious upward journey ("Who is talked of in the whole district now?

Brekhunov!"), reflects on what is so special about him ("I take trouble, not like others who lie abed or waste their time on foolishness"), works himself into a happy froth at the thought that he might become a millionaire, wishes there was someone to talk (brag) to. But no: there's only (lowly) Nikita. He thinks longingly of Grishkino, decides to have another cigarette, has trouble lighting it, finally succeeds, and, like all of us who are healthy and materially prosperous and years away from death, is "glad that he had managed to do what he wanted."

He falls asleep but is jolted awake (page 35) by "something" (his fear, working its way honestly up from his subconscious), and we enter the second episode, during which he will cycle through exactly the same methods of distraction that just now gave him comfort.

Only this time they won't.

He tries disparaging others: peasants ("shiftless people") and his ("unloved") wife (it's her fault for making him bring Nikita). But his fear won't stay quiet and, as if in response, some better part of himself blurts out the first moment of frank self-assessment in the story: "If I'd only stopped the night in Grishkino all this would not have happened!"

He tries that old standby, "bragging to himself and feeling pleased with himself," but his growing anxiety has ruined even this pleasure (he is "disturbed by a stealthily approaching fear"). Suddenly, Nikita is worthy of being talked to; Vasili addresses him "a couple of times." (More mindful than Vasili of the fix they're in, Nikita saves his energy by not answering.) Vasili hears that wolf ("so near that the movement of his jaws as he changed his cry was brought down the wind"), and when his thoughts turn to "his accounts, his business, his reputation," he blurts out: "Devil take the forest! Things were all right without it." Finally, he tries and fails to light a cigarette, and we feel this as a closed and locked door: there will be no more comfort for Vasili from smoking (that is, from getting to do what he wants).

So: two earlier-established coping methods (disparaging others and bragging) stop working. His previous dishonesty about who got them lost converts to honesty. He goes from not deigning to talk to Nikita to addressing him. His thoughts of how much money he'll make from the forest become an open repentance of his desire to ever buy it.

The structural core of this section is a simple before-and-after pattern. Which offers us lesser writers a technique: if we want change to appear to happen in our stories, the first order of business is to note specifically how things are *now*. We write: "The table was dusty." If, later, we write, "The newly dusted table gleamed," this implies that someone who had previously neglected it has now dusted it: someone has changed.

This simple before-and-after feature is hidden within a complex matrix of physical details and depictions of fleeting psychological states and glimpses of snowy roofs and blowing manes and offered cups of tea that we mistake for a real blizzard on a real night. But try coloring in the sentences that constitute the elements I've mentioned above, i.e., the elements that change between the first and second halves of the pattern, and you'll be struck by how many lines are dedicated to this pattern, how nearly mathematical the structure is, how naturally concealed it is in all that (steadily degrading, increasingly terrifying) "reality."

As we watch Vasili, the coward, ride off again, on page 40, this time from Nikita's point of view, the story has come to be about one thing: Will Vasili change? (More generally: Can a jerk change?) It's not, really, about whether they'll be saved—if a sled full of doctors suddenly appears on the horizon, with a pile of blankets and some cigarettes and dry matches, the story's principle question will remain unanswered. The story, by constantly underscoring how *wrong* Vasili is—how selfish, how greedy, how dismissive of Nikita—has told us that it wants to ask not whether such a person can survive, but whether he can change.

It's possible that the story will answer, disappointingly: "Nope."

But the more interesting, higher-order answer would be: "Yes, and here's how."

What would our friend that lesser writer do if instructed: "Make a jerk change"? My impulse would be to have the bad person do some thinking, and come to a revelation, and start acting resolutely on that thought.

But that's not what happens.

Vasili rides along for five minutes, then comes upon "a dark patch." He mistakes it for a village, but it's a stand of wormwood (an herb associated with bitterness, the end times, difficulty, confounded hopes). Like that white shirt on the clothesline, it's "desperately tossing about." The sight of it "tormented by the pitiless wind" makes him shudder, "he knew not why."

He urges Mukhorty on but soon finds himself back at the wormwood. Seeing it again carries "unreasoning terror to his heart," as he realizes he's (again) going in circles.

"I shall perish like that!" he thinks.

The horse falls into a snowdrift, gets up, runs off. Vasili trudges after it but, out of breath, has to stop after twenty steps. Panic sets in. He mentally lists all the things he fears he may soon be leaving behind, a list that omits his wife and consists entirely of material possessions, the last item of which (his "heir") he also seems to regard as a possession, not a beloved child. In this story rich with recursion, he returns (in memory) to the wormwood a third time, and is "seized with such terror that he did not believe in the reality of what was happening to him."

What's so scary about this wormwood?

I was once on a plane that lost an engine (seagulls!) and for about fifteen minutes everyone on board believed we were about to crash. After a sound like a minivan ramming the side of the plane, black smoke began pouring out of those overhead air nozzles, a girls' softball team started screaming, I could see the grid of lit streets (Chicago) coming up, way too fast, and the pilot, sounding panicked, came on the PA just long enough to shout, "Stay in your seats with your seatbelts on!" (Not comforting.) I looked at the seat back in front of me and thought: "I'm going to have to get out of this body now and that's what's going to do it to me." The seat back wasn't for me or against me. It didn't care about me at all. It was just what was going to kill me. ("Hi, I'm Death, I come for all?") And I saw that Death had been in the world all along but that until this moment I had failed to notice it. And it was coming for *me,* now, soon. The only thing in my head was a frenzied incantation ("No, no, no") and a deep desire to rewind time and never have gotten on that plane in the first place. (I desperately wanted to return to my Grishkino, i.e., O'Hare.)

But that wasn't happening. We were *miles above the earth,* with no way to get down but the obvious one. The comfortable, happy, confident person I'd always been before that moment (the person used to doing what he wanted)—how dear and stupid and sweet and lazy and cluelessly trusting in the kindness of the universe he seemed now. I'd always imagined that in a situation like this, I'd be the guy who gathered his wits and silently thanked the universe for all of those happy years, then calmly stood up and led the other passengers in "Kumbaya" or something. But no. My mind was stuck in that "No, no, no" loop, and I had no thought of my wife, or my daughters, or my writing (ha!) and came to understand that when people talk about being so scared they nearly piss themselves, they're not being hyperbolic. My panic was overriding everything, including, any minute now, I could feel, if things got even a little worse, my control over my bodily functions.

I remember that terrible, cornered feeling even now.

But dimly, and I can live with it.

Death is coming for Vasili, and it's nothing personal. This is just what Death does. But now, Vasili, of the charmed life, finds himself in its path. Although he knows and accepts that everything must, in time, pass from the earth, he finds himself having trouble accepting that he's included in that "everything." In his novella *The Death of Ivan Ilyich*, Tolstoy writes, of the terminally ill Ivan: "The syllogism . . . 'Caius is a man, men are mortal, therefore Caius is mortal,' had always seemed to him correct as applied to Caius, but certainly not as applied to himself. . . . He was not Caius, not an abstract man, but a creature quite, quite separate from all others. He had been little Vanya, with a mamma and a papa. . . . What did Caius know of the smell of that striped leather ball Vanya had been so fond of?"

The wormwood is a brilliant and crazy "symbol" that represents several things at once. It's a marker of futility (Vasili would like the wormwood to be a village, but it isn't; he'd like to not keep circling back to it, but he does). It's a physical reminder of the chillingly egalitarian nature of death and the impossibility of avoiding it (no matter where he goes, there it is, not hostile, just indifferent). He identifies with it, sees himself and the wormwood as being in similar straits (like him, it is being "tormented by the pitiless wind"; like it, he has been "left alone" and is "awaiting an inevitable, speedy, and meaningless death").

But, of course, it's also *real wormwood*: swaying in the moonlight, the only dark patch in a world of white, being looked at by . . . well, me.

Whenever I read this section I feel the cold and the dead-end panic (there is literally nowhere I can go where I won't freeze to death) and see the black-blue Russian sky overhead and hear the crunching of my pathetic, familiar boots on the snow, boots soon to be full of (horrors!) my frozen, dead feet.

The wormwood also causes something: it causes Vasili to pray.

But "there was and could be no connection between those candles and services and his present disastrous plight." All of his belief to date has been pro forma, based on the contract: "If I go through the motions of belief, you (God) will spare me forever." Now he sees that he is not going to be spared, and that whatever comfort belief might offer would have required a deeper engagement with the spiritual than he's been willing to make, and that such comfort would, anyway, pertain to the next world, and (like me, on that plane) he desperately wants to stay in *this* one, and be allowed to go back to being the same comfortable, happy, confident, correct person he's always been, doing, ceaselessly, perpetually, what he wants to do.

With the failure of his prayer, the wormwood causes something else: it causes Vasili to panic.

Panicking, following the horse, he rushes forward and "even" runs, and soon finds himself . . . back at the sled (another case of futile circling). His terror is gone and "if he felt any fear it was lest the dreadful terror should return." The wormwood has scared the fear of death right out of him and replaced it with a fear of something worse: the fear that he might again be overcome with fear. What he's afraid of, suddenly, is not death but fear, and what he fears, now, is meaninglessness, the meaninglessness he's just glimpsed back at the wormwood.

How does he propose to keep meaninglessness at bay? Well, that's easy; he knows how to do that. He must "do something—occupy himself with something." This is habitual with him. When anxious (about his own competence, say, or his status relative to his peers) he's always "done something." He did something just a few hours ago: bolted away from his family to add to his holdings and assuage the anxiety that he might get beaten to the punch. And he did something just a few minutes ago: feeling anxious, he abandoned Nikita.

As usual, he looks to his own needs first: opens his coat, shakes the snow out of his boots and glove. Then, "as was his custom when going out of his shop to buy grain from the peasants, he pulled his girdle low down and tightened it and prepared for action." He turns his attention to the horse: frees its leg from the rein, re-tethers it.

All of these actions are essentially selfish; they increase his chance of survival.

Then Nikita calls out to Vasili: he's dying. He gives some last instructions about the disposition of his salary and begs forgiveness "for Christ's sake," in a "tearful voice," waving his hand in front of his face "as if driving away flies."

Then Vasili stands "silent and motionless for half a minute."

And we reach the moment to which this story has been building: Vasili is about to be transformed.

Tolstoy has put himself in a tough spot. He's made a convincing stinker and, as we know from real life, stinkers sometimes stay stinkers. We fear a facile transformation. If Tolstoy suggests an implausible method of change (if he makes Vasili do something the Vasili we've come to know would never do), the story will reveal itself as propaganda and fall apart. He needs to pull off a transformation in which we can believe, one that mimics the sort of transformation a real-life stinker might actually undergo.

How does Tolstoy propose that such a transformation might happen?

First, let's note that after that silent half a minute, Vasili does not launch into a soliloquy or internal monologue describing his changed feelings about master/peasant relations or his radical new understanding of Christian virtue as it applies to the treatment of the less fortunate. He doesn't announce (to us or Nikita or himself) that he has "realized" something. The order of operations is not: a change overcomes him, and then he realizes this, tells us about it, then acts. He just *acts* (or, actually, goes back into action). And he goes back into action just like himself, in the same way he always has, "with the same resolution with which he used to strike hands when making a good purchase." He's doing what he's been doing all his life: boldly getting busy, to forestall anxiety.

He rakes the snow off Nikita, undoes his girdle, opens out his coat, pushes Nikita down, lies on top of him, adjusts the skirt of his coat to tent Nikita in.

They lie there, silently, for "a long time."

The main action of the story is now over. Vasili has changed. We know this because of what he's just done. It's kind of a miracle of writing. Without narrating the logic of the transformation, Tolstoy has made Vasili do exactly what the story has made us believe he could never do.

Vasili is as surprised about it as we are, and we watch his reaction to that change: that beautiful, mysterious utterance that follows Nikita's sigh: "There, and you say you are dying! Lie still and get warm, that's our way . . ." Then "tears came to his eyes and his lower jaw began to quiver rapidly."

"That's our way," he says again, to himself, feeling "a strange and solemn tenderness."

What does he mean, "that's our way"? The Russian way, the way of Russian masters, the human way? It's beautiful: it doesn't occur to him that this has *never* been his way, not at all, until this moment right now. This is a first for him.

Or is it? It's certainly the first time he's been willing to sacrifice his comfort, or well-being, or life for someone else (a peasant, no less), but it's not the first time he's felt himself to be doing good for the world through action.

He feels he's been doing that all his life.

Meanwhile, my plane kept dropping. The flight attendants and pilot had gone frighteningly silent. The familiar nighttime grid of Chicago-Land continued to rush up. Then the passenger beside me, a kid of about fourteen, said, in a scared, thin voice, "Sir, is this supposed to be happening?" My heart went out to him. (What a phrase that is: "My heart went out to him." It sounds like something extraordinary but it is what our hearts are trying to do all the time: go out to someone.)

"Yes, it is," I lied.

Reassuring him like that came naturally to me from years of parenting and teaching. Reassuring him, I felt myself coming back to myself. It's hard to explain. As the old Catholic hymn says, "We must diminish, and Christ increase." I spoke to that kid in the voice I'd always used when trying to persuade or cajole or calm someone, because that was my habit. Responding to him in that voice, with the (familiar) intention of calming/reassuring, and watching him respond (he seemed some-what reassured, if skeptical) changed something in my body. Now my energy was going out, toward him, instead of inward, neurotically. I was me again and, as myself, knew how to act.

I was still scared, but had I died in that state it would have been a bet-ter death than had I died in that earlier, panicked condition.

I think something like this is what happens to Vasili. He gets brought back to himself by acting like himself. As himself, he knows what to do. His natural energy, which for so long had been used to benefit only him-self, gets redirected. A defect becomes a superpower. (A bull about to run through a china shop gets turned in the direction of a house slated for demolition.)

And then, observing himself in action, seeing a charitable, selfless person, he is moved and feels "a peculiar joy," a joy I associate with his relief at finally shucking off a way of being that has always impeded him. He recognizes this new version of himself, feels that "strange and sol-emn tenderness," and starts to cry.

And that is "transformation."

The process by which Vasili is transformed puts me in mind of an-other literary transformation, that of Scrooge. Scrooge is led by the ghosts, back in time, through his life. He is shown himself as a lonely little boy left behind on the Christmas holiday; a young man in love; the recipient of his employer's kindness. The ghosts don't change Scrooge into someone else; they remind him that he used to be someone else. He was once someone who felt other than the way he feels now, and those earlier people still exist in him. The ghosts, we might say, switch those former people back on.

Vasili remembers that, in the past, he used to be someone else, someone who, confronted with a problem, solved it with work energy. This best part of himself (the tireless worker) now returns. But Vasili has been educated, back there in the wormwood. Now when Nikita claims to be dying, Vasili can *hear* him and is primed to respond, "Yes, I know, me too." (Vasili, the wormwood, and Nikita are all equally powerless and doomed to die.) In this way, the border of the Nation of Vasili gets moved out just enough to encompass Nikita. Vasili is still acting in his own interest, but now that Nikita has become a colony of Vasili, action on his behalf feels natural (like an action on behalf of

Vasili himself), and so Nikita gets the full benefit of Vasili's (admirable) energy.

Beautifully, post-transformation, Vasili remains . . . Vasili, mostly. He considers retrieving the horse's blanket but can't bring himself to disturb "the joyous condition" he finds himself in. He's still himself, still self-celebratory, still living to feel good about himself, still fundamentally selfish and proud. (He is so good at saving people!) When he says, "No fear, we shan't lose him this time," he speaks, Tolstoy tells us, "with the same boastfulness with which he spoke of his buying and selling."

But something has changed. As he lies there on top of Nikita, we watch him again scroll through the items that, in Section VI, comforted him, then failed to comfort him. Now he transcends or converts them, one by one. He's still doing some victorious thinking (but his triumph is that he is saving Nikita). He's no longer dishonest; quite the contrary ("I know about myself what I know"). In Section VI he went from not speaking to Nikita to speaking to him; now he rejoices at not even being a separate person from Nikita ("he was Nikita and Nikita was he") and reasons that as long as Nikita is alive, he, Vasili, is alive too, since they are now one. He remembers the man he used to be, who troubled himself so much about money. That Vasili did not know "what the real thing was," but this new being he has become does.

He would have been a good man if there'd been someone to freeze him to death every day of his life.

Tolstoy is proposing something radical: moral transformation, when it happens, happens not through the total remaking of the sinner or the replacement of his habitual energy with some pure new energy but by a redirection of his (same old) energy.

What a relief this model of transformation is. What else do we have but what we were born with and have always, thus far, been served (and imprisoned) by? Say you're a world-class worrier. If that worry energy gets directed at extreme personal hygiene, you're "neurotic." If it gets directed at climate change, you're an "intense visionary activist."

We don't have to become an entirely new person to do better; our view just has to be readjusted, our natural energy turned in the right direction. We don't have to swear off our powers or repent of who we are or what we like to do or are good at doing. Those are our horses; we just have to hitch them to the right, uh, sled.

What kept Vasili so small all his life? (What is keeping us so small now?) He wasn't small, actually, as proven by his end. He was infinite. He had access to as much great love as any of our beloved spiritual heroes. Why did he live out his life in that small country of selfishness? What was it that finally jolted him out of it? Well, it was truth. He saw that his idea of himself was untrue. His idea that he *was* himself was untrue. All of those years, he was only part of himself. He had made that part, was always making it and defending it, with his thoughts and his pride and his desire to win, which continually separated him, Vasili, from everything else. As that entity, Vasili, faded away, what was left behind discerned the fallacy and joined (rejoined) the great non-Vasili of it all.

If we could reverse the process (let him come alive again, warm that body up, melt away the snow, cause him to forget all he's learned tonight) what we would see would be a mind gradually reasserting a series of lies: "You are separate" and "You are central" and "You are correct" and "Go forth and prove that you are better, that you are the best."

And then he would be all the way himself again.

AFTERTHOUGHT #4

I didn't want to sully my celebration of "Master and Man," back there in the body of my essay, by raising a slight quibble I've always had with the story.

But let me raise it now.

In Section VI, we watch Vasili work through the fact of his possible coming death. In Section VII, it's Nikita's turn.

Abandoned by Vasili, Nikita briefly becomes frightened, but he prays and is immediately comforted by the notion that "he was not alone but that there was One who heard him and would not abandon him." Beginning to lose consciousness, he feels equally prepared for sleep or death.

Nikita takes the notion of his own possible death in stride because he had "always felt himself dependent on the Chief Master, who had sent him into this life." As for his sins—well, that's how God made him. As for Vasili, Nikita thinks, charitably: "I expect you're sorry yourself that you started out, dear man." And: "It would seem hard to leave a life such as his!"

This section strikes me as . . . less. Less interesting, less detailed. Nikita seems too good to be true. The emotion a real person like Nikita would experience in the face of death feels like it's being suppressed by Tolstoy's desire to make some sort of ideal peasant. Nikita's not afraid of death because he's so simple, selfless, and authentic; his fears are soothed by the mere thought of God. This sets him up in opposition to Vasili, that neurotic, complicated, faithless, terrified landlord.

But surely there were peasants who were not simple, peasants who were neurotic, peasants who, simple or not, were terrified of death, peasants who did not believe in God, because "peasants" were, after all, people, not "peasants." In other words, I feel that Tolstoy may have a touch of that which he accuses Vasili of: a failure to regard Nikita as a full human being.

Fast-forward to the last section of the story (Section X).

Warmed by Vasili, Nikita lives. He's dug out the next day, "surprised that in the other world peasants should be shouting in the same old way." When he realizes he's still alive, he's not happy about it but "sorry," especially when he finds that he has frostbite in both feet.

In the final paragraph, we leap ahead twenty years. And may find ourselves wondering: What did Nikita do with those twenty years, the time Vasili's sacrifice won for him?

Well, it turns out, not much. Or, more of the same.

How did that night change him? It seems it didn't.

Just before Nikita dies, he asks his wife's forgiveness and forgives her relationship with the cooper, which implies that he hasn't done these things previously—he didn't, twenty years ago, hobble home from the hospital, feet bandaged, full of Vasili-inspired compassion, and set things right. Because we aren't told otherwise, we assume that he just went back to his usual ways, being kind to animals and occasionally attacking his wife's clothes with an ax and so on.

We never see Nikita wondering about that crazy night at the sled. He doesn't reflect on Vasili's cowardice or his redemption, never asks, "Why did my master do that?" or "What happened to him, there at the end?" Vasili felt that he and Nikita had merged into one person, but Nikita? Not so much. He doesn't seem grateful to Vasili. He doesn't think of Vasili at all.

Which is . . . strange. If a person gives his life to save another person, and the saved person never thinks about it, doesn't appear grateful, seems unchanged by it, it makes us wonder about the value of the sacrifice. It also makes us wonder about the person saved.

It also makes us wonder about the writer.

As Vasili died, we got to witness his last moments, in a long inner monologue (pages 46–48) that closes Section IX. When Nikita's time comes, we get the bare facts of his death ("He died at home as he had wished . . . under the icons with a lighted taper in his hands") but nothing about what he felt or thought as he died. A scrim gets put up and we're told that we'll have to wait for our own deaths to see whether Nikita "was disappointed or found there what he expected."

Once, I was teaching a flawed but considerable Gogol story called "Nevsky Prospect" and a student said she didn't like it because it was sexist. I responded with a rare bit of teacherly wisdom by asking, "Where?" And she showed us exactly where, by offering two examples of places where a character gets insulted. When a man was insulted, Gogol went into the character's head and we got to hear his response. When a woman was insulted, the third-person narrator stepped in and made a joke at her expense.

Then I asked the class to imagine the story if Gogol had kept things fair, by allowing the woman her own internal monologue. There followed a bit of silence and then a collective sigh/smile, as we all, at once, saw the better story it could have been: just as dark and strange, but funnier and more honest.

So, yes, the story was sexist, but another way of saying this was that it was a story with a technical flaw. That flaw was (or would have been, had Gogol not been dead) correctable. The sexism my student identified was definitely there, and it was manifesting in a particular way in the text, in the form of "inequitable narration."

I'd say there's a general thesis in here somewhere: any story that suffers from what seems like a moral failing (that seems sexist, racist, homophobic, transphobic, pedantic, appropriative, derivative of another writer's work, and so on) will be seen, with sufficient analytical snooping, to be suffering from a technical failing, and if that failing is addressed, it will (always) become a better story.

Here, an accusation we've been dancing around ("Tolstoy seems to be exhibiting class bias")* gets converted (by asking, "Where, exactly?") into a neutral, more workable, technical observation: "In (at least) two places—when Nikita comes home from the hospital and in their respective death scenes—Nikita is denied the interiority that Tolstoy gave Vasili in similar moments."

---

* Tolstoy had a big investment in the idea of the simple, virtuous peasant, which sometimes caused him to make peasants who weren't quite real, who, as Nabokov put it, we might find "doing the most repellent jobs—but performing them with angelic indifference."

Now, a story as wonderful as "Master and Man" should be accepted with gratitude, for all of the beautiful things in it.

But it's kind of fun to poke at it, just in an ornery spirit of technical exploration.

So: Can we imagine a version of Section X in which Nikita is granted narrative resources equal to the ones Tolstoy granted Vasili at parallel moments?

That version might start with a scene of him in the hospital, just after his rescue, thinking. The Nikita we've come to know was wise to Vasili's tricks. He saw Vasili as a fixed quantity: stubborn, self-centered, a lost cause, someone to be worked around and tolerated. What does Nikita think of Vasili now? Is he astonished? Confused? How does he process the fact that Vasili sacrificed his life for him, Nikita, a "mere" peasant? Throughout the story, Vasili has underestimated Nikita but, in truth, Nikita has also been underestimating Vasili. What might this realization cause Nikita to think and feel?

We might also rework the last paragraph of the story, trying to make it as frank and omniscient as the text describing Vasili's death, at the end of Section IX.

That would actually be a good exercise, if you're up for it.

So, yes, an exercise: rewrite Section X.

Write it like Tolstoy. Use, you know, a lot of facts. Ha, ha.

THE NOSE

Nikolai Gogol

(1836)

THE NOSE

I

On March 25th there took place, in Petersburg, an extraordinarily strange occurrence. The barber Ivan Yakovlevich, who lives on Voznesensky Avenue (his family name has been lost and even on his signboard, where a gentleman is depicted with a lathered cheek and the inscription "Also bloodletting," there is nothing else)—the barber Ivan Yakovlevich woke up rather early and smelled fresh bread. Raising himself slightly in bed he saw his spouse, a rather respectable lady who was very fond of drinking coffee, take some newly baked loaves out of the oven.

"I won't have any coffee to-day, Praskovya Osipovna," said Ivan Yakovlevich. "Instead, I would like to eat a bit of hot bread with onion." (That is to say, Ivan Yakovlevich would have liked both the one and the other, but he knew that it was quite impossible to demand two things at once, for Praskovya Osipovna very much disliked such whims.) "Let the fool eat the bread; all the better for me," the wife thought to herself, "there will be an extra cup of coffee left." And she threw a loaf onto the table.

For the sake of propriety Ivan Yakovlevich put a tailcoat on over his shirt and, sitting down at the table, poured out some salt, got two onions ready, picked up a knife and, assuming a meaningful expression, began to slice the bread. Having cut the loaf in two halves, he looked inside and to his astonishment saw something white. Ivan Yakovlevich poked it carefully with the knife and felt it with his finger. "Solid!" he said to himself. "What could it be?"

He stuck in his finger and extracted—a nose! Ivan Yakovlevich was dumbfounded. He rubbed his eyes and felt the object: a nose, a nose indeed, and a familiar one at that. Ivan Yakovlevich's face expressed horror. But this horror was nothing compared to the indignation which seized his spouse.

"You beast, where did you cut off a nose?" she shouted angrily. "Scoundrel! drunkard! I'll report you to the police myself. What a ruffian! I have already heard from three people that you jerk their noses about so much when shaving that it's a wonder they stay in place."

But Ivan Yakovlevich was more dead than alive. He recognized the nose as that of none other than Collegiate Assessor Kovalyov, whom he shaved every Wednesday and Sunday.

"Hold on, Praskovya Osipovna! I shall put it in a corner, after I've wrapped it in a rag: let it lie there for a while, and later I'll take it away."

[2]

"I won't even hear of it. That I should allow a cut-off nose to lie about in my room? You dry stick! All he knows is how to strop his razor, but soon he'll be in no condition to carry out his duty, the rake, the villain! Am I to answer for you to the police? You piece of filth, you blockhead! Away with it! Away! Take it anywhere you like! Out of my sight with it!"

Ivan Yakovlevich stood there as though bereft of senses. He thought and thought—and really did not know what to think. "The devil knows how it happened," he said at last, scratching behind his ear with his hand. "Was I drunk or wasn't I when I came home yesterday, I really can't say. Whichever way you look at it, this is an impossible occurrence. After all, bread is something baked, and a nose is something altogether different. I can't make it out at all."

Ivan Yakovlevich fell silent. The idea that the police might find the nose in his possession and bring a charge against him drove him into a complete frenzy. He was already visualizing the scarlet collar, beautifully embroidered with silver, the saber—and he trembled all over. At last he got out his underwear and boots, pulled on all these tatters and, followed by rather weighty exhortations from Praskovya Osipovna, wrapped the nose in a rag and went out into the street.

He wanted to shove it under something somewhere, either into the hitching-post by the gate—or just drop it as if by accident and then turn off into a side street. But as bad luck would have it, he kept running into people he knew, who at once would ask him, "Where are you going?" or "Whom are you going to shave so early?," so that Ivan Yakovlevich couldn't find the right moment. Once he actually did drop it, but a policeman some distance away pointed to it with his halberd and said: "Pick it up—you've dropped something there," and Ivan Yakovlevich was obliged to pick up the nose and hide it in his pocket. He was seized with despair, all the more so as the number of people in the street constantly increased when the shops began to open.

He decided to go to St. Isaac's Bridge—might he not just manage to toss it into the Neva? But I am somewhat to blame for having so far said nothing about Ivan Yakovlevich, in many ways a respectable man. [3]

Like any self-respecting Russian artisan, Ivan Yakovlevich was a terrible drunkard. And although every day he shaved other people's chins his own was ever unshaven. Ivan Yakovlevich's tailcoat (Ivan Yakovlevich never wore a frockcoat) was piebald, that is to say, it was all black but dappled with brownish-yellow and gray; the collar was shiny, and in place of three of the buttons hung just the ends of thread. Ivan Yakovlevich was a great cynic, and when Collegiate Assessor Kovalyov told him while being shaved, "Your hands, Ivan Yakovlevich, always stink," Ivan Yakovlevich would reply with the question, "Why should they stink?" "I don't know, my dear fellow," the Collegiate Assessor would say, "but they do," and Ivan Yakovlevich, after taking a pinch of snuff, would, in retaliation, lather all over his cheeks and under his nose, and behind his ear, and under his chin—in other words, wherever his fancy took him.

This worthy citizen now found himself on St. Isaac's Bridge. To begin with, he took a good look around, then leaned on the railings as though to look under the bridge to see whether or not there were many fish swimming about, and surreptitiously tossed down the rag containing the nose. He felt as though all of a sudden a ton had been lifted off him: Ivan Yakovlevich even smirked. Instead of going to shave some civil servants' chins he set off for an establishment bearing a sign "Snacks and Tea" to order a glass of punch when he suddenly noticed, at the end of the bridge, a police officer of distinguished appearance, with wide sideburns, wearing a three-cornered hat and with a sword. His heart sank: the officer was wagging his finger at him and saying, "Step this way, my friend."

Knowing the etiquette, Ivan Yakovlevich removed his cap while still some way off, and approaching with alacrity said, "I wish your honor good health."

"No, no, my good fellow, not 'your honor.' Just you tell me, what were you doing over there, standing on the bridge?"

"Honestly, sir, I've been to shave someone and only looked to see if the river were running fast."

"You're lying, you're lying. This won't do. Just be so good as to answer."

[4]   "I am ready to shave your worship twice a week, or even three times, and no complaints," replied Ivan Yakovlevich.

"No, my friend, all that's nonsense. I have three barbers who shave me and deem it a great honor, too. Just be so good as to tell me, what were you doing over there?"

Ivan Yakovlevich turned pale. . . . But here the whole episode becomes shrouded in mist, and of what happened subsequently absolutely nothing is known.

II

Collegiate Assessor Kovalyov woke up rather early and made a "b-rr-rr" sound with his lips as he was wont to do on awakening, although he could not have explained the reason for it. Kovalyov stretched and asked for the small mirror standing on the table. He wanted to have a look at the pimple which had, the evening before, appeared on his nose. But to his extreme amazement he saw that he had, in the place of his nose, a perfectly smooth surface. Frightened, Kovalyov called for some water and rubbed his eyes with a towel: indeed, no nose! He ran his hand over himself to see whether or not he was asleep. No, he didn't think so. The Collegiate Assessor jumped out of bed and shook himself—no nose! He at once ordered his clothes to be brought to him, and flew off straight to the chief of police.

In the meantime something must be said about Kovalyov, to let the reader see what sort of man this collegiate assessor was. Collegiate assessors who receive their rank on the strength of scholarly diplomas can by no means be equated with those who make the rank in the Caucasus. They are two entirely different breeds. Learned collegiate assessors . . . But Russia is such a wondrous land that if you say something about one collegiate assessor all the collegiate assessors from Riga to Kamchatka will not fail to take it as applying to them, too. The same is true of all our ranks and titles. Kovalyov belonged to the Caucasus variety of collegiate assessors. He had only held that rank for two years and therefore could not forget it for a moment; and in order to lend himself added dignity and weight he never referred to himself as collegiate assessor but always as major. "Listen, my dear woman," he would usually say on meeting in the street a woman selling shirt fronts, "come to my place, my apartment is on Sadovaya; just ask where Major Kovalyov lives, anyone will show you." And if the woman he met happened to be a pretty one, he would also give some confidential instructions, adding, "You just ask, lovey, for Major Kovalyov's apartment."—That is why we, too, will henceforth refer to this collegiate assessor as Major.

[5]

Major Kovalyov was in the habit of taking a daily stroll along Nevsky Avenue. The collar of his dress shirt was always exceedingly clean and starched. His sidewhiskers were of the kind you can still see on provincial and district surveyors, or architects (provided they are Russians), as well as on those individuals who perform various police duties, and in general on all those men who have full rosy cheeks and are very good at boston; these sidewhiskers run along the middle of the cheek straight up to the nose. Major Kovalyov wore a great many cornelian seals, some with crests and others with Wednesday, Thursday, Monday, etc., engraved on them. Major Kovalyov had come to Petersburg on business, to wit, to look for a post befitting his rank; if he could arrange it, that of a vice-governor; otherwise, that of a procurement officer in some important government department. Major Kovalyov was not averse to getting married, but only in the event that the bride had a fortune of two hundred thousand. And therefore the reader can now judge for himself what this major's state was when he saw, in the place of a fairly present-able and moderate-sized nose, a most ridiculous flat and smooth surface.

As bad luck would have it, not a single cab showed up in the street, and he was forced to walk, wrapped up in his cloak, his face covered with a handkerchief, pretending that his nose was bleeding. "But perhaps I just imagined all this—a nose cannot disappear in this idiotic way." He stepped into a coffee-house just in order to look at himself in a mirror. Fortunately, there was no one there. Serving boys were sweeping the rooms and arranging the chairs; some of them, sleepy-eyed, were bringing out trays of hot turn-overs; yesterday's papers, coffee-stained, lay about on tables and [6] chairs. "Well, thank God, there is no one here," said the Major. "Now I can have a look." Timidly he approached the mirror and glanced at it. "Damnation! How disgusting!" he exclaimed after spitting. "If at least there were something in place of the nose, but there's nothing!"

Biting his lips with annoyance, he left the coffee-house and de-cided, contrary to his habit, not to look or to smile at anyone. Sud-denly he stopped dead in his tracks before the door of a house. An inexplicable phenomenon took place before his very eyes: a carriage drew up to the entrance; the doors opened; a gentleman in uniform jumped out, slightly stooping, and ran up the stairs. Imagine the horror and at the same time the amazement of Kovalyov when he recognized that it was his own nose! At this extraordinary sight ev-erything seemed to whirl before his eyes; he felt that he could hardly keep on his feet. Trembling all over as though with fever, he made up his mind, come what may, to await the gentleman's return to the carriage. Two minutes later the Nose indeed came out. He was wearing a gold-embroidered uniform with a big stand-up collar and doeskin breeches; there was a sword at his side. From his plumed hat one could infer that he held the rank of a state councillor. Every-thing pointed to his being on the way to pay a call. He looked right and left, shouted to his driver, "Bring the carriage round," got in and was driven off.

Poor Kovalyov almost went out of his mind. He did not even know what to think of this strange occurrence. Indeed, how could a nose which as recently as yesterday had been on his face and could neither ride nor walk—how could it be in uniform? He ran after the carriage, which fortunately had not gone far but had stopped before the Kazan Cathedral.

He hurried into the cathedral, made his way past the ranks of old beggarwomen with bandaged faces and two slits for their eyes, whom he used to make such fun of, and went inside. There were but few worshippers there: they all stood by the entrance. Kovalyov felt so upset that he was in no condition to pray and searched with his eyes for the gentleman in all the church corners. At last he saw him standing to one side. The Nose had completely hidden his face in his big stand-up collar and was praying in an attitude of utmost piety.

"How am I to approach him?" thought Kovalyov. "From every- [7] thing, from his uniform, from his hat, one can see that he is a state councillor. I'll be damned if I know how to do it."

He started clearing his throat, but the Nose never changed his devout attitude and continued his genuflections.

"My dear sir," said Kovalyov, forcing himself to take courage, "my dear sir . . ."

"What is it you desire?" said the Nose turning around.

"It is strange, my dear sir . . . I think . . . you ought to know your place. And all of a sudden I find you—and where? In church. You'll admit . . ."

"Excuse me, I cannot understand what you are talking about. . . . Make yourself clear."

"How shall I explain to him?" thought Kovalyov and, embold-ened, began: "Of course, I . . . however, I am a major. For me to go about without my nose, you'll admit, is unbecoming. It's all right for a peddler woman who sells peeled oranges on Voskresensky Bridge, to sit without a nose. But since I'm expecting—and besides, having many acquaintances among the ladies—Mrs. Chekhtaryova, a state councillor's wife, and others . . . Judge for yourself . . . I don't know, my dear sir . . ." (Here Major Kovalyov shrugged his shoul-ders.) "Forgive me, if one were to look at this in accordance with rules of duty and honor . . . you yourself can understand. . . ."

"I understand absolutely nothing," replied the Nose. "Make yourself more clear."

"My dear sir," said Kovalyov with a sense of his own dignity, "I don't know how to interpret your words . . . The whole thing seems to me quite obvious . . . Or do you wish . . . After all, you are my own nose!"—

The Nose looked at the major and slightly knitted his brows.

"You are mistaken, my dear sir, I exist in my own right. Besides, there can be no close relation between us. Judging by the buttons on your uniform, you must be employed in the Senate or at least in the Ministry of Justice. As for me, I am in the scholarly line."

Having said this, the Nose turned away and went back to his prayers.

Kovalyov was utterly flabbergasted. He knew not what to do or [8] even what to think. Just then he heard the pleasant rustle of a lady's dress: an elderly lady, all in lace, had come up near him and with her, a slim one, in a white frock which agreeably outlined her slender figure, and in a straw-colored hat, light as a cream-puff. Behind them, a tall footman with huge sidewhiskers and a whole dozen collars, stopped and opened a snuff-box.

Kovalyov stepped closer, pulled out the cambric collar of his dress shirt, adjusted his seals hanging on a golden chain and, smiling in all directions, turned his attention to the ethereal young lady who, like a spring flower, bowed her head slightly and put her little white hand with its translucent fingers to her forehead. The smile on Kovalyov's face grew even wider when from under her hat he caught a glimpse of her little round dazzling-white chin and part of her cheek glowing with the color of the first rose of spring. But suddenly he sprang back as though scalded. He remembered that there was absolutely nothing in the place of his nose, and tears came to his eyes. He turned round, intending without further ado to tell the gentleman in uniform that he was merely pretending to be a state councillor, that he was a rogue and a cad and nothing more than his, the major's, own nose. . . . But the Nose was no longer there; he had managed to dash off, probably to pay another call.

This plunged Kovalyov into despair. He went back, stopped for a moment under the colonnade and looked carefully, this way and that, for the Nose to turn up somewhere. He remembered quite well that the latter had a plumed hat and a gold-embroidered uniform, but he had not noticed his overcoat, or the color of his carriage or of his horses, not even whether he had a footman at the back, and if so in what livery. Moreover, there was such a multitude of carriages dashing back and forth and at such speed that it was difficult to tell them apart; but even if he did pick one of them out, he would have no means of stopping it. The day was fine and sunny. There were crowds of people on Nevsky Avenue. A whole flowery cascade of ladies poured over the sidewalk, all the way down from Police Bridge to Anichkin Bridge. Here came a court councillor he knew, and was used to addressing as lieutenant-colonel, especially in the presence of strangers. Here, too, was Yarygin, a head clerk in the Senate, a great friend of his, who invariably lost at boston when he went up eight. Here was another major who had won his assessorship in the Caucasus, waving to Kovalyov to join him. . . . [9]

"O hell!" said Kovalyov. "Hey, cabby, take me straight to the chief of police!"

Kovalyov got into the cab and kept shouting to the cabman, "Get going as fast as you can."

"Is the chief of police at home?" he called out as he entered the hall.

"No, sir," answered the doorman, "he has just left."

"You don't say."

"Yes," added the doorman, "he has not been gone long, but he's gone. Had you come a minute sooner perhaps you might have found him in."

Without removing the handkerchief from his face, Kovalyov got back into the cab and in a voice of despair shouted, "Drive on!"

"Where to?" asked the cabman.

"Drive straight ahead!"

"What do you mean straight ahead? There is a turn here. Right or left?"

This question nonplussed Kovalyov and made him think again. In his plight the first thing for him to do was to apply to the Police Department, not because his case had anything to do directly with the police, but because they could act much more quickly than any other institution; while to seek satisfaction from the superiors of the department by which the Nose claimed to be employed would be pointless because from the Nose's own replies it was obvious that this fellow held nothing sacred, and that he was capable of lying in this case, too, as he had done when he had assured Kovalyov that they had never met. Thus Kovalyov was on the point of telling the cabman to take him to the Police Department when the thought again occurred to him that this rogue and swindler, who had already treated him so shamelessly during their first encounter, might again seize his first chance to slip out of town somewhere, and then all search would be futile or might drag on, God forbid, a whole month. Finally, it seemed, heaven itself brought him to his senses. He decided to go straight to the newspaper office and, before it was too late, place an advertisement with a detailed description of the Nose's [10] particulars, so that anyone coming across him could immediately deliver him or at least give information about his whereabouts. And so, his mind made up, he told the cabby to drive to the newspaper office, and all the way down to it kept whacking him in the back with his fist, saying, "Faster, you villain! faster, you rogue!"—"Ugh, mister!" the cabman would say, shaking his head and flicking his reins at the horse whose coat was as long as a lapdog's. At last the cab drew up to a stop, and Kovalyov, panting, ran into a small reception room where a gray-haired clerk in an old tailcoat and glasses sat at a table and, pen in his teeth, counted newly brought in coppers.

"Who accepts advertisements here?" cried Kovalyov. "Ah, good morning!"

"How do you do," said the gray-haired clerk, raising his eyes for a moment and lowering them again to look at the neat stacks of money.

"I should like to insert—"

"Excuse me. Will you wait a moment," said the clerk as he wrote down a figure on a piece of paper with one hand and moved two beads on the abacus with the fingers of his left hand. A liveried footman, whose appearance suggested his sojourn in an aristocratic house, and who stood by the table with a note in his hand, deemed it appropriate to demonstrate his savoir-faire: "Would you believe it, sir, this little mutt is not worth eighty kopecks, that is, I wouldn't even give eight kopecks for it; but the countess loves it, honestly she does—and so whoever finds it will get one hundred rubles! To put it politely, just as you and I are talking, people's tastes differ: if you're a hunter, keep a pointer or a poodle; don't grudge five hundred, give a thousand, but then let it be a good dog."

The worthy clerk listened to this with a grave expression while at the same time trying to count the number of letters in the note brought to him. All around stood a great many old women, salespeople and house porters with notes. One of them offered for sale a coachman of sober conduct; another, a little-used carriage brought from Paris in 1814; still others, a nineteen-year-old serf girl experienced in laundering work and suitable for other kinds of work; a sound droshky with one spring missing; a young and fiery dappled-gray horse seventeen years old; turnip and radish seed newly received from London; a summer residence with all the appurtenances—to wit, two stalls for horses and a place for planting a grove of birches or firs; there was also an appeal to those wishing to buy old boot soles, inviting them to appear for final bidding every day between eight and three o'clock. The room in which this entire company was crowded was small, and the air in it was extremely thick; but Collegiate Assessor Kovalyov was not in a position to notice the smell, because he kept his handkerchief pressed to his face and because his nose itself was goodness knows where.

"My dear sir, may I ask you . . . It is very urgent," he said at last with impatience.

"Presently, presently! Two rubles forty-three kopecks! Just a moment! One ruble sixty-four kopecks," recited the gray-haired gentleman, tossing the notes into the faces of the old women and the house porters. "What can I do for you?" he said at last, turning to Kovalyov.

"I wish . . . ," said Kovalyov. "There has been a swindle or a fraud . . . I still can't find out. I just wish to advertise that whoever hands this scoundrel over to me will receive an adequate reward."

"Allow me to inquire, what is your name?"

"What do you want my name for? I can't give it to you. I have many acquaintances: Mrs. Chekhtaryova, the wife of a state councillor; Pelageya Grigoryevna Podtochina, the wife of a field officer . . . What if they suddenly were to find out? Heaven forbid! You

[22]

can simply write down: a collegiate assessor or, still better, a person holding the rank of major."

"And was the runaway your household serf?"

"What do you mean, household serf? That wouldn't be such a bad swindle! The runaway was . . . my nose. . . ."

"Hmm! what a strange name! And did this Mr. Nosov rob you of a big sum?"

"My nose, I mean to say—You've misunderstood me. My nose, my very own nose has disappeared goodness knows where. The devil must have wished to play a trick on me!"

"But how did it disappear? I don't quite understand it."

"Well, I can't tell you how; but the main thing is that it is now [12] gallivanting about town and calling itself a state councillor. And that is why I am asking you to advertise that whoever apprehends it should deliver it to me immediately and without delay. Judge for yourself. How, indeed, can I do without such a conspicuous part of my body? It isn't like some little toe which I put into my boot, and no one can see whether it is there or not. On Thursdays I call at the house of Mrs. Chekhtaryova, a state councillor's wife. Mrs. Podtochina, Pelageya Grigoryevna, a field officer's wife, and her very pretty daughter, are also very good friends of mine, and you can judge for yourself how can I now . . . I can't appear at their house now."

The clerk thought hard, his lips pursed tightly in witness thereof.

"No, I can't insert such an advertisement in the papers," he said at last after a long silence.

"How so? Why?"

"Well, the paper might lose its reputation. If everyone were to write that his nose had run away, why . . . As it is, people say that too many absurd stories and false rumors are printed."

"But why is this business absurd? I don't think it is anything of the sort."

"That's what you think. But take last week, there was another such case. A civil servant came in, just as you have, bringing a note, was billed two rubles seventy-three kopecks, and all the advertisement consisted of was that a black-coated poodle had run away.

Doesn't seem to amount to much, does it now? But it turned out to be a libel. This so-called poodle was the treasurer of I don't recall what institution."

"But I am not putting in an advertisement about a poodle—it's about my very own nose; that is, practically the same as about myself."

"No, I can't possibly insert such an advertisement."

"But when my nose actually has disappeared!"

"If it has disappeared, then it's a doctor's business. They say there are people who can fix you up with any nose you like. However, I observe that you must be a man of gay disposition and fond of kidding in company."

"I swear to you by all that is holy! Perhaps, if it comes to that, [43] why I'll show you."

"Why trouble yourself?" continued the clerk, taking a pinch of snuff. "However, if it isn't too much trouble," he added, moved by curiosity, "I'd like to have a look."

The collegiate assessor removed the handkerchief from his face.

"Very strange indeed!" said the clerk. "It's absolutely flat, like a pancake fresh off the griddle. Yes, incredibly smooth."

"Well, will you go on arguing after this? You see yourself that you can't refuse to print my advertisement. I'll be particularly grateful and am very glad that this opportunity has given me the pleasure of making your acquaintance. . . ." The major, as we can see, decided this time to use a little flattery.

"To insert it would be easy enough, of course," said the clerk, "but I don't see any advantage to you in it. If you really must, give it to someone who wields a skillful pen and let him describe this as a rare phenomenon of nature and publish this little item in *The Northern Bee*" (here he took another pinch of snuff) "for the benefit of the young" (here he wiped his nose), "or just so, as a matter of general interest."

The collegiate assessor felt completely discouraged. He dropped his eyes to the lower part of the paper where theatrical performances were announced. His face was about to break out into a smile as he came across the name of a pretty actress, and his hand went to his pocket to check whether he had a blue note, because in his opinion field officers ought to sit in the stalls—but the thought of his nose spoiled it all.

The clerk himself seemed to be moved by Kovalyov's embarrassing situation. Wishing at least to ease his distress he deemed it appropriate to express his sympathy in a few words: "I really am grieved that such a thing happened to you. Wouldn't you care for a pinch of snuff? It dispels headaches and melancholy; it's even good for hemorrhoids." With those words the clerk offered Kovalyov his snuffbox, rather deftly snapping open the lid which pictured a lady in a hat.

This unpremeditated action made Kovalyov lose all patience. "I can't understand how you find this a time for jokes," he said angrily. "Can't you see that I lack the very thing one needs to take snuff? To hell with your snuff! I can't bear the sight of it now, even if you offered me some *râpé* itself, let alone your wretched Berezin's." After saying this he left the newspaper office, deeply vexed, and went to visit the district police inspector, a man with a passion for sugar. In his house the entire parlor, which served also as the dining room, was stacked with sugar loaves which local tradesmen brought to him out of friendship. At the moment his cook was pulling off the inspector's regulation topboots; his sword and all his military trappings were already hanging peacefully in the corners, and his three-year-old son was reaching for his redoubtable three-cornered hat, while the inspector himself was preparing to taste the fruits of peace after his day of warlike, martial pursuits.

Kovalyov came in at the moment when the inspector had just stretched, grunted and said, "Oh, for a couple of hours' good snooze!" It was therefore easy to see that the collegiate assessor had come at quite the wrong time. And I wonder whether he would have been welcome even if he had brought several pounds of tea or a piece of cloth. The police inspector was a great patron of all arts and manufactures, but he preferred a banknote to everything else. "This is the thing," he would usually say. "There can be nothing better than it—it doesn't ask for food, it doesn't take much space, it'll always fit into a pocket, and if you drop it it won't break."

The inspector received Kovalyov rather coolly and said that after dinner was hardly the time to conduct investigations, that nature it-

[14]

self intended that man should rest a little after a good meal (from this the collegiate assessor could see that the aphorisms of the ancient sages were not unknown to the police inspector), that no real gentleman would allow his nose to be pulled off, and that there were many majors in this world who hadn't even decent underwear and hung about in all sorts of disreputable places.

This last was too close for comfort. It must be observed that Kovalyov was extremely quick to take offense. He could forgive whatever was said about himself, but never anything that referred to rank or title. He was even of the opinion that in plays one could allow references to junior officers, but that there should be no criticism of field officers. His reception by the inspector so disconcerted him that he tossed his head and said with an air of dignity, spreading his arms slightly: "I confess that after such offensive remarks on your part, I've nothing more to add. . . ." and left the room. [15]

He came home hardly able to stand on his feet. It was already dusk. After all this fruitless search his apartment appeared to him melancholy or extraordinarily squalid. Coming into the entrance hall he caught sight of his valet Ivan who, lying on his back on the soiled leather sofa, was spitting at the ceiling and rather successfully hitting one and the same spot. Such indifference on the man's part infuriated him; he struck him on the forehead with his hat, saying, "You pig, always doing something stupid!"

Ivan jumped up abruptly and rushed to take off his cloak.

Entering his room the major, tired and sad, sank into an armchair and at last, after several sighs, said:

"O Lord, O Lord! What have I done to deserve such misery? Had I lost an arm or a leg, it would not have been so bad; had I lost my ears, it would have been bad enough but nevertheless bearable; but without a nose a man is goodness knows what; he's not a bird, he's not a human being; in fact, just take him and throw him out the window! And if at least it had been chopped off in battle or in a duel, or if I myself had been to blame; but it disappeared just like that, with nothing, nothing at all to show for it. But no, it can't be," he added after some thought. "It's unbelievable that a nose should disappear; absolutely unbelievable. I must be either dreaming or just imagining it. Maybe, somehow, by mistake instead of water I drank the vodka which I rub on my chin after shaving. That fool Ivan didn't take it away and I probably gulped it down."—To satisfy himself that he was not drunk the major pinched himself so hard that he cried out. The pain he felt fully convinced him that he was wide awake. He stealthily approached the mirror and at first half-closed his eyes, thinking that perhaps the nose would appear in its proper place; but the same moment he sprang back exclaiming, "What a caricature of a face!"

It was indeed incomprehensible. If a button, a silver spoon, a watch, or some such thing had disappeared—but to disappear, and for whom to disappear? and besides in his own apartment, too! . . . After considering all the circumstances, Major Kovalyov was in-clined to think that most likely it was the fault of none other than the field officer's wife, Mrs. Podtochina, who wanted him to marry her daughter. He, too, liked to flirt with her but avoided a final show-down. And when the field officer's wife told him point-blank that she wanted to marry her daughter off to him, he eased off on his at-tentions, saying that he was still young, that he had to serve another five years when he would be exactly forty-two. And so the field of-ficer's wife, presumably in revenge, had decided to put a curse on him and hired for this purpose some old witchwomen, because it was impossible even to suppose that the nose had been simply cut off: no one had entered his room; the barber, Ivan Yakovlevich, had shaved him as recently as Wednesday and throughout that whole day and even on Thursday his nose was all there—he remembered and knew it very well. Besides, he would have felt the pain and no doubt the wound could not have healed so soon and be as smooth as a pancake. Different plans of action occurred to him: should he for-mally summons Mrs. Podtochina to court or go to her himself and expose her in person? His reflections were interrupted by light breaking through all the cracks in the door, which told him that Ivan had lit the candle in the hall. Soon Ivan himself appeared, carrying it before him and brightly illuminating the whole room. Kovalyov's first gesture was to snatch his handkerchief and cover the place where his nose had been only the day before, so that indeed the silly fellow would not stand there gaping at such an oddity in his master's strange appearance.

[16]

Barely had Ivan gone into his cubbyhole when an unfamiliar voice was heard in the hall saying, "Does Collegiate Assessor Kovalyov live here?"

"Come in. Major Kovalyov is here," said Kovalyov, jumping up quickly and opening the door.

In came a police officer of handsome appearance with sidewhiskers that were neither too light nor too dark, and rather full cheeks, the very same who at the beginning of this story was standing at the end of St. Isaac's Bridge.

"Did you happen to mislay your nose?"

"That's right."

"It has been recovered."

"What are you saying!" exclaimed Major Kovalyov. He was tongue-tied with joy. He stared at the police officer standing in front of him, on whose full lips and cheeks the trembling light of the candle flickered. "How?" [17]

"By an odd piece of luck—he was intercepted on the point of leaving town. He was about to board a stagecoach and leave for Riga. He even had a passport made out a long time ago in the name of a certain civil servant. Strangely enough, I also at first took him for a gentleman. But fortunately I had my glasses with me and I saw at once that it was a nose. You see, I am nearsighted and when you stand before me all I can see is that you have a face, but I can't make out if you have a nose or a beard or anything. My mother-in-law, that is, my wife's mother, can't see anything, either."

Kovalyov was beside himself. "Where is it? Where? I'll run there at once."

"Don't trouble yourself. Knowing that you need it I have brought it with me. And the strange thing is that the chief villain in this business is that rascally barber from Voznesensky Street who is now in a lockup. I have long suspected him of drunkenness and theft, and as recently as the day before yesterday he stole a dozen buttons from a certain shop. Your nose is quite in order."—With these words the police officer reached into his pocket and pulled out a nose wrapped up in a piece of paper.

"That's it!" shouted Kovalyov. "That's it, all right! Do join me in a little cup of tea today."

"I would consider it a great pleasure, but I simply can't: I have to drop in at a mental asylum. . . . All food prices have gone up enormously. . . . I have my mother-in-law, that's my wife's mother, living with me, and my children; the eldest is particularly promising, a very clever lad, but we haven't the means to educate him."

Kovalyov grasped his meaning and, snatching up a red banknote from the table, thrust it into the hands of the inspector who, clicking his heels, went out the door. Almost the very same instant Kovalyov heard his voice out in the street where he was admonishing with his fist a stupid peasant who had driven his cart onto the boulevard.

After the police officer had left, the collegiate assessor remained for a few minutes in a sort of indefinable state and only after several [18] minutes recovered the capacity to see and feel: his unexpected joy had made him lose his senses. He carefully took the newly found nose in both his cupped hands and once again examined it thoroughly.

"That's it, that's it, all right," said Major Kovalyov. "Here on the left side is the pimple which swelled up yesterday." The major very nearly laughed with joy.

But there is nothing enduring in this world, and that is why even joy is not as keen in the moment that follows the first; and a moment later it grows weaker still and finally merges imperceptibly into one's usual state of mind, just as a ring on the water, made by the fall of a pebble, merges finally into the smooth surface. Kovalyov began to reflect and realized that the whole business was not yet over: the nose was found but it still had to be affixed, put in its proper place.

"And what if it doesn't stick?"

At this question, addressed to himself, the major turned pale.

Seized by unaccountable fear, he rushed to the table and drew the looking-glass closer, to avoid affixing the nose crookedly. His hands trembled. Carefully and deliberately, he put it in its former place. O horror! the nose wouldn't stick. . . . He carried it to his mouth, warmed it slightly with his breath, and again brought it to the smooth place between his two cheeks; but the nose just wouldn't stay on.

"Well, come on, come on, you fool!" he kept saying to it. But the nose was as though made of wood and plopped back on the table with a strange corklike sound. The major's face was twisted in convulsion. "Won't it really grow on?" he said fearfully. But no matter how many times he tried to fit it in its proper place, his efforts were unsuccessful as before.

He called Ivan and sent him for the doctor who occupied the best apartment on the first floor of the same house. The doctor was a fine figure of a man; he had beautiful pitch-black sidewhiskers, a fresh, healthy wife, ate raw apples first thing in the morning, and kept his mouth extraordinarily clean, rinsing it every morning for nearly three quarters of an hour and polishing his teeth with five different kinds of little brushes. The doctor came at once. After asking him how long ago the mishap had occurred, he lifted Major Kovalyov's face by the chin and flicked him with his thumb on the very spot where the nose used to be, so that the major had to throw his head back with such force that he hit the back of it against the wall. The doctor said this didn't matter and, suggesting that he move a little away from the wall, told him first to bend his head to the right, and, after feeling the spot where the nose had been, said "Hmm!" Then he told him to bend his head to the left and said "Hmm!"; and in conclusion he again flicked him with his thumb so that Major Kovalyov jerked his head like a horse whose teeth are being examined. Having carried out this test, the doctor shook his head and said: "No, can't be done. You'd better stay like this, or we might make things even worse. Of course, it can be stuck on. I daresay, I could do it right now for you, but I assure you it'll be worse for you."

"I like that! How am I to remain without a nose?" said Kovalyov. "It couldn't possibly be worse than now. This is simply a hell of a thing! How can I show myself anywhere in such a scandalous state? I have acquaintances in good society; why, this evening, now, I am expected at parties in two houses. I know many people: Mrs. Chekhtaryova, a state councillor's wife, Mrs. Podtochina, a field officer's wife . . . although after what she's done now I'll have nothing more to do with her except through the police. I appeal to you," pleaded Kovalyov, "is there no way at all? Fix it on somehow, even if not very well, just so it stays on; in an emergency, I could even prop it up with my hand. And besides, I don't dance, so I can't do any harm

[19]

by some careless movement. As regards my grateful acknowledgment of your visits, be assured that as far as my means allow. . . ."

"Would you believe it," said the doctor in a voice that was neither loud nor soft but extremely persuasive and magnetic, "I never treat people out of self-interest. This is against my principles and my calling. It is true that I charge for my visits, but solely in order not to offend by my refusal. Of course I could affix your nose; but I assure you on my honor, if you won't take my word for it, that it will be much worse. Rather, let nature take its course. Wash the place more often with cold water, and I assure you that without a nose you'll be as healthy as if you had one. As for the nose itself, I advise you to put the nose in a jar with alcohol, or, better still, pour into the jar two tablespoonfuls of aqua fortis and warmed-up vinegar—and then you can get good money for it. I'll buy it myself, if you don't ask too much."

[20]

"No, no! I won't sell it for anything!" exclaimed Major Kovalyov in desperation. "Let it rather go to blazes!"

"Excuse me!" said the doctor, bowing himself out, "I wanted to be of some use to you. . . . Never mind! At least you saw my good will." Having said this the doctor left the room with a dignified air. Kovalyov didn't even notice his face and in his benumbed state saw nothing but the cuffs of his snow-white shirt peeping out of the sleeves of his black tailcoat.

The very next day he decided, before lodging a complaint, to write to Mrs. Podtochina requesting her to restore him his due without a fight. The letter ran as follows:

Dear Madam Alexandra* Grigoryevna,
    I fail to understand your strange behavior. Be assured that, acting in this way, you gain nothing and certainly will not force me to marry your daughter. Believe me that the incident with my nose is fully known to me, just as is the fact that you—and no one else—are the principal person involved. Its sudden detachment from its place, its flight and its disguise, first as a certain civil servant, then at last in its own shape, is nothing other than the result of a spell cast by you or by those

---

* [Earlier in the story her first name is Pelageya.—EDITOR, 1992.]

who engage like you in such noble pursuits. I for my part deem it my duty to forewarn you that if the abovementioned nose is not back in its place this very day I shall be forced to resort to the defense and protection of the law.

Whereupon I have the honor to remain, with my full respect,

Your obedient servant

Platon Kovalyov

Dear Sir

Platon Kuzmich,

Your letter came as a complete surprise to me. I frankly confess that I never expected it, especially as regards your unjust reproaches. I beg to inform you that I never received in my house the civil servant you mention, neither in disguise nor in his actual shape. It is true that Filipp Ivanovich Potanchikov had been visiting me. And though he did indeed seek my daughter's hand, being himself of good sober conduct and great learning, I never held out any hopes to him. You also mention your nose. If by this you mean that I wanted to put your nose out of joint, that is, to give you a formal refusal, then I am surprised to hear you mention it, for I, as you know, was of the exactly opposite opinion, and if you now seek my daughter in marriage in the lawful way, I am ready to give you immediate satisfaction, for this has always been the object of my keenest desire, in the hope of which I remain always at your service,

Alexandra Podtochina

"No," said Kovalyov, after he had read the letter. "She certainly isn't guilty. Impossible! The letter is written in a way no person guilty of a crime can write."—The collegiate assessor was an expert in this matter, having been sent several times to take part in a judicial investigation while still serving in the Caucasus.—"How then, how on earth could this have happened? The devil alone can make it out," he said at last in utter dejection.

In the meantime rumors about this extraordinary occurrence had spread all over the capital and, as is usual in such cases, not without some special accretions. In those days the minds of everybody were particularly inclined toward things extraordinary: not long before, the whole town had shown an interest in experiments with the effects of hypnotism. Moreover, the story of the dancing chairs in Konyushennaya Street was still fresh in memory, and one should not be surprised therefore that soon people began saying that Collegiate Assessor Kovalyov's nose went strolling along Nevsky Avenue at precisely three o'clock. Throngs of curious people came there every day. Someone said that the Nose was in Junker's store: and such a crowd and jam was created outside Junker's that the police had to intervene. One profit-seeker of respectable appearance, with side-whiskers, who sold a variety of dry pastries at the entrance to a theater, had specially constructed excellent, sturdy wooden benches, on which he invited the curious to mount for eighty kopecks apiece. One veteran colonel made a point of leaving his house earlier than usual and with much difficulty made his way through the crowd, but to his great indignation saw in the window of the shop instead of the nose an ordinary woollen undershirt and a lithograph showing a young girl straightening her stocking and a dandy, with a lapeled waistcoat and a small beard, peeping at her from behind a tree—a picture which had been hanging in the same place for more than ten years. Moving away he said with annoyance, "How can they confound the people by such silly and unlikely rumors?"—Then a rumor went round that Major Kovalyov's nose was out for a stroll, not on Nevsky Avenue but in Taurida Gardens, that it had been there for ages; that when Khosrev-Mirza lived there he marveled greatly at this strange freak of nature. Some students from the Surgical Academy went there. One aristocratic, respectable lady, in a special letter to the Superintendent of the Gardens, asked him to show her children this rare phenomenon, accompanied, if possible, with an explanation edifying and instructive for the young.

All the men about town, the *habitués* of society parties, who liked to amuse ladies and whose resources had by that time been exhausted, were extremely glad of all these goings-on. A small percentage of respectable and well-meaning people were extremely displeased. One gentleman said indignantly that he could not un-

[22]

derstand how in this enlightened age such senseless stories could spread and that he was surprised at the government's failure to take heed of it. This gentleman apparently was one of those gentlemen who would like to embroil the government in everything, even in their daily quarrels with their wives. After that . . . but here again the whole incident is shrouded in fog, and what happened afterwards is absolutely unknown.

III

Utterly nonsensical things happen in this world. Sometimes there is absolutely no rhyme or reason in them: suddenly the very nose which had been going around with the rank of a state councillor and created such a stir in the city, found itself again, as though nothing were the matter, in its proper place, that is to say, between the two cheeks of Major Kovalyov. This happened on April 7th. Waking up and chancing to look in the mirror, he sees—his nose! He grabbed it with his hand—his nose indeed! "Aha!" said Kovalyov, and in his joy he very nearly broke into a barefooted dance round the room, but Ivan's entry stopped him. He told Ivan to bring him some water to wash in and, while washing, glanced again at the mirror—his nose! Drying himself with his towel, he again glanced at the mirror—his nose! [23]

"Take a look, Ivan, I think there's a pimple on my nose," he said, and in the meantime thought, "How awful if Ivan says: 'Why, no sir, not only there is no pimple but also the nose itself is gone!'"

But Ivan said: "Nothing, sir, no pimple—your nose is fine!"

"That's great, damn it!" the major said to himself, snapping his fingers. At that moment the barber Ivan Yakovlevich peeped in at the door but as timidly as a cat which had just been whipped for stealing lard.

"First you tell me—are your hands clean?" Kovalyov shouted to him before he had approached.

"They are."

"You're lying."

"I swear they are, sir."

"Well, we'll see."

Kovalyov sat down. Ivan Yakovlevich draped him with a napkin and instantly, with the help of a shaving brush, transformed his chin and part of his cheek into the whipped cream served at merchants' namesday parties. "Well, I never!" Ivan Yakovlevich said to himself, glancing at his nose, and then cocked his head on the other side and looked at it sideways: "Look at that! Just you try and figure that out," he continued and took a good look at his nose. At last, gently, with the greatest care imaginable, he raised two fingers to grasp it by the tip. Such was Ivan Yakovlevich's method.

"Now, now, now, look out there!" cried Kovalyov. Dumbfounded and confused as never before in his life, Ivan Yakovlevich let his hands drop. At last he began cautiously tickling him with the razor under the chin, and although it wasn't at all handy for him and difficult to shave without holding on to the olfactory portion of the face, nevertheless, somehow bracing his gnarled thumb against the cheek and the lower jaw, he finally overcame all obstacles and finished shaving him.

When everything was ready, Kovalyov hastened to dress, hired a cab and went straight to the coffee-house. Before he was properly inside the door he shouted, "Boy, a cup of chocolate!" and immediately made for the mirror: the nose was there. He turned round cheerfully and looked ironically, slightly screwing up one eye, at two military gentlemen one of whom had a nose no bigger than a waistcoat button. After that he set off for the office of the department where he was trying to obtain the post of a vice-governor or, failing that, of a procurement officer. Passing through the reception room, he glanced in the mirror: the nose was there. Then he went to visit another collegiate assessor or major, a great wag, to whom he often said in reply to various derisive remarks: "Oh, come off it, I know you, you're a kidder." On the way there he thought: "If the major doesn't explode with laughter on seeing me, it's a sure sign that everything is in its proper place." The collegiate assessor did not explode. "That's great, that's great, damn it!" Kovalyov thought to himself. On the street he met Mrs. Podtochina, the field officer's wife, together with her daughter, bowed to them and was hailed with joyful exclamations, and so everything was all right, no part of

[24]

him was missing. He talked with them a very long time and, deliberately taking out his snuff-box, right in front of them kept stuffing his nose with snuff at both entrances for a very long time, saying to himself: "So much for you, you women, you stupid hens! I won't marry the daughter all the same. Anything else, *par amour*—by all means." And from that time on, Major Kovalyov went strolling about as though nothing had happened, both on Nevsky Avenue, and in the theaters, and everywhere. And his nose too, as though nothing had happened, stayed on his face, betraying no sign of having played truant. And thereafter Major Kovalyov was always seen in good humor, smiling, running after absolutely all the pretty ladies, and once even stopping in front of a little shop in Gostinny Dvor and buying himself the ribbon of some order, goodness knows [25] why, for he hadn't been decorated with any order.

That is the kind of affair that happened in the northern capital of our vast empire. Only now, on second thoughts, can we see that there is much that is improbable in it. Without speaking of the fact that the supernatural detachment of the nose and its appearance in various places in the guise of a state councillor is indeed strange, how is it that Kovalyov did not realize that one does not advertise for one's nose through the newspaper office? I do not mean to say that advertising rates appear to me too high: that's nonsense, and I am not at all one of those mercenary people. But it's improper, embarrassing, not nice! And then again—how did the nose come to be in a newly baked loaf, and how about Ivan Yakovlevich? . . . No, this is something I can't understand, positively can't understand. But the strangest, the most incomprehensible thing of all, is how authors can choose such subjects. I confess that this is quite inconceivable; it is indeed . . . no, no, I just can't understand it at all! In the first place, there is absolutely no benefit in it for the fatherland; in the second place . . . but in the second place, there is no benefit either. I simply don't know what to make of it. . . .

And yet, in spite of it all, though, of course, we may assume this and that and the other, perhaps even . . . And after all, where aren't there incongruities?—But all the same, when you think about it, there really is something in all this. Whatever anyone says, such things happen in this world; rarely, but they do. ✦

THE DOOR TO THE TRUTH MIGHT BE STRANGENESS

THOUGHTS ON "THE NOSE"

We've been talking about the role of truth, of "the actual," in fiction. We've said that when a story references the world in a way that rings true, this draws the reader in.

In "Master and Man," when Tolstoy tells me, "The wind came from the left, insistently blowing over to one side the mane on Mukhorty's sleek neck and carrying aside even his fluffy tail, which was tied in a simple knot," I see that horse and feel the bitter wind on my neck and maybe even the cold, hard wood of the bench through my thin, hand-sewn Russian pants.

So that's one way a story can be true.

Here's another: the *sequence of events* in it can strike us as truthful. An arrogant landowner insists on taking over the reins on a sled ride through a snowstorm, gets lost, then blames the peasant. I feel, "Yep, that's how it is in the world sometimes." The "fundamental accuracy of observation" at work makes me trust the writer and feel engaged.

This is, roughly speaking, the essence of "realism": there's a world out there and the writer makes his story resemble it.

But as we're seeing, realism isn't all that real. The Chekhov, Turgenev, and Tolstoy stories we've read so far are compressed and exaggerated, with crazy levels of selection and omission and shaping going on in them. (Was there ever a woman as self-abnegating as Olenka? Ever a master as one-noted as Vasili? Do your trips home from town contain as much compressed drama as Marya's?)

I once heard the term "consensus reality" used to describe the set of things about the world that we all pretty much agree to be true. Water is blue, birds sing, and so on. And although water is not simply blue and not all birds sing, and to call what some birds do "singing" approximates and undersells what they actually do, agreeing on this consensus view is natural and useful. When I say, "Singing birds were skimming low over an expanse of blue water," that image is useful if you want to know, roughly, what's going on down at the lake. When I say, "Look out, a piano is about to fall on your head from above," the fact that we've agreed to call that collection of wood, ivory, and metal a "piano," and that thing at the end of your neck a "head," and that direction up there "above" enables you to step out of the way in time, I hope.

"Realism" exploits this fondness of ours for consensus reality. Things happen roughly as they do in the real world; the mode limits itself to what usually happens, to what's physically possible.

But a story can also be truthful if it declines consensus reality—if things happen in it that don't and could never happen in the real world.

If I assign you to write a story in which the characters are a cellphone, a pair of gloves, and a fallen leaf, chatting away in a wheelbarrow in a suburban driveway, could that story be truthful? Yes. It could be truthful in the way it reacts to itself, in the way it responds to its premise, in the way it proceeds—by how things change within it, the contours of its internal logic, the relationships between its elements.

With sufficient care, that wheelbarrow full of things could become an entire system of meaning, saying truthful things about our world, some of which might have been impossible to say via a more conventionally realistic approach. That system would mean, not by the plausibility or acuity of its initial premise, but by the way it *reacts to* that premise—by what it does with it.

If a writer introduces a strange event, then lets the fictive world respond to that event, what we're really learning about is what we might call the fictive world's psychological physics. What are the rules there? How do things proceed? A story like that will feel truthful and essential to the extent that the psychological physics of the fictive world are felt to be similar to the psychological physics of our own.

Which brings us to "The Nose."

—

Ivan Yakovlevich finds a nose in his morning loaf of bread. ("Solid!" he exclaims in our translation; "Firm!" in another, by Richard Pevear and Larissa Volokhonsky.) He's "dumbfounded," as we would be.

The nose in the bread is the initial strange event. Now we wait to see how the fictive world (in this case, Ivan and his wife, Praskovya Osipovna) will react to it. That's where the story's meaning is going to be made—not in the fact of the nose in the bread but in what the couple does about it in response. This world, where a nose can appear in a loaf of bread, is not our world, but it is *a* world, and there are going to be rules in that world, and we wait to see what they are.

Praskovya Osipovna, not dumbfounded, knows exactly how that nose got in there: Ivan, a barber, cut it off the face of a client.

For an instant, we accept this accusation. A nose is there, one that's been separated from its face; it's a "familiar" nose; Ivan is a barber; it's his own dear wife leveling this charge.

But it doesn't quite hold together.

If I were Ivan, my response would be something like "Sweetie, hang on, think about it. Why would I cut off a client's nose? And if I did, why would I bring it home? And if I brought it home, why would I put it in the dough, which, come to think of it, wasn't even made yet last night, when I got here? Also, why didn't you notice that nose in there, earlier this morning, while you were kneading the dough?"

Ivan doesn't say any of this, and in the distance between his reaction and what ours would have been the Gogolian world begins to be made. What Ivan does is immediately accept her (skewed) logic. (If something disastrous has happened, he must be the one who did it.) Then he recognizes the nose as belonging to one of his clients, Kovalyov. (Would I be able to recognize a freestanding nose belonging to someone I see twice a week? The nose of the guy who sits at the front desk of my gym, say? I doubt it. Well, depends on the nose, I guess.)

So, as I sit there with Ivan and Praskovya on a crude wooden chair I've pulled up to that rickety nineteenth-century Russian table, nose-in-a-loaf there in front of us, barely a page into the story, I'm already departing from them. They're reacting differently to this than I would, jumping to conclusions I can't endorse, failing to ask questions I'd feel inclined to ask, such as: Wouldn't Kovalyov have noticed his nose being cut off and have had some feelings about that? What has Kovalyov been doing in the hours since his nose went missing? If Ivan didn't cut off the nose and bring it home with him, which it seems he didn't, how did it get here?

What should they do? What would you do? I'd take a breath and try to figure out how this crazy thing happened. ("Praskovya, was I drunk when I came home? What did I do when I first came in? Let's go see if my razor's bloody.") Concluding that I was innocent, I'd find Kovalyov, return his nose, explain that I had nothing to do with its disappearance.

But Ivan's impulse is to "put it in a corner . . . let it lie there for a while." He'll "take it away" later. But Praskovya wants it out of here now. So, they're not quarreling over whether to do the irrational, evasive thing (get rid of the nose) but when.

Praskovya assumes that Ivan is guilty, and he agrees. But what's he guilty of? He's afraid that the "police might find the nose in his possession and bring a charge against him." What charge? We know, and he should, that he hasn't done anything wrong. And anyway, how would it happen that the police would "find" the nose, there in the house? So, they're concerned, we feel, about the wrong thing: not that a man has lost his nose but that they might get blamed for it.

Ivan then does approximately what I would do, I guess, if "get rid of the evidence" was my goal. He wraps the nose in a rag, plans to "shove it under something somewhere . . . or just drop it as if by accident and then turn off into a side street." But he keeps running into people he knows and can't find the right moment. There's something . . . *off* about this. If I imagine myself in, say, New York City, with my gym guy's nose wrapped in a rag, it seems to me that no matter how many acquaintances I run into, I'm still going to be able to find a way to get rid of it—give it the old drop-and-kick, say, or find a garbage can outside a Starbucks or something. It's wrapped in a rag, after all, and looks like garbage. There's something too strict about the conditions Ivan needs to have in place in order to discard the nose; he's a little paranoid.

Finally, he succeeds in dropping it, but a policeman immediately sees him and orders him to pick it up. (So, Ivan's paranoia is justified: this world really is that watchful.)

Then he takes the nose to St. Isaac's Bridge and tosses it into the river. There he's accosted by a second policeman, not for tossing a nose into the river but for the crime of standing on a bridge in a story by Gogol.

This scene, like the entire story, is infused with what we might call Multiple Superimposed Weirdness Syndrome. Initial weirdness: a nose appears in a loaf of bread. Second-level weirdness: the couple reacts irrationally to the nose's presence in the bread. Third-level weirdness: because they've reacted irrationally, they make an odd plan in response (ditch the nose). Fourth-level weirdness: Ivan executes the plan badly; he can't get the job done because he approaches it with too much apprehension and because the world he finds out there is inflected with a slight, ornery hostility toward him: a constant flow of acquaintances and a street thick with policemen, or at least two of them in as many pages.

And there's one more level of weirdness, one that has to do with how the story's being told.

While Ivan's standing on the bridge there on page 3, we pause for a digression. The narrator has, he confesses, "said nothing about Ivan," who is "in many ways a respectable man." But the digression doesn't do much to convince us of Ivan's respectability. He's a drunk, we're told, and dresses badly, and his hands stink. We're also told that he's a "cynic" and, as proof, are offered the fact that when Kovalyov claims that Ivan's hands stink, Ivan replies with a reasonable question ("Why should they stink?"). In retaliation, Ivan lathers Kovalyov "all over his cheeks and under his nose, and behind his ear, and under his chin"— that is, all the places, approximately, a barber should lather.

So, the digression is executed with a straight face and a semblance of authority but (like Ivan) seems unable to do what it sets out to do; we come out of it having learned nothing much about Ivan as a person, and what we have learned undercuts the narrator's claim that Ivan is respectable. It's as if the narrator had misheard his own thesis statement, then set out to prove it using an inverted, goofy system of logic.

And we begin to suspect that not only is Gogol's universe off, his narrator is too.

Gogol's prose, compared to Chekhov's or Tolstoy's, feels a little clunky, graceless, rambling. It's strangely inexact and, like Ivan and Praskovya, reaches odd conclusions. In the first paragraph of the story, the narrator states that Ivan's family name has "been lost"—i.e., he, the narrator, doesn't know it. He then points out that the family name is missing "even" on the signboard outside. But these are not connected facts: the narrator has been unable to document Ivan's family name, but Ivan presumably *knows* his family name; he didn't leave it off the signboard because he didn't know it. Praskovya Osipovna is described as "rather respectable," but what does it mean to say that a person is "rather" respectable? (What's the difference between *rather* respectable and, you know, *full-blown* respectable?) When we feel that the conversation between the couple has veered off into illogic, the narrator never steps in to reassure us that he feels that way too. (" 'You beast, where did you cut off a nose?' she shouted angrily, *neglecting the fact that this was an impossibility, since, had Ivan done that, his client would, no doubt, have objected.*")

The narration in "The Nose," it turns out, is a particular Russian form of unreliable first-person narration called *skaz*. Imagine an actor telling a story in character. And that character is . . . not right. He is, per the literary critic Viktor Vinogradov, "sharply characterized by his substandard speech." According to another critic, Robert Maguire, the Gogolian *skaz* narrator "has little formal education and little idea of how to develop an argument, let alone talk in an eloquent and persuasive way about his feelings, although he wishes to be considered informed and observant; he tends to ramble and digress and cannot distinguish the trivial from the important." The writer and translator Val Vinokur adds (and this we've already begun to notice) that the resulting story is distorted by "improper narrative emphasis" and "misplaced assumption." As Maguire puts it, the narrator's "enthusiasms outrun common sense."

So, this isn't graceless writing; this is a great writer writing a graceless writer writing. (And not only that: it's a great writer writing a graceless writer writing *about a world in which a severed nose winds up in a loaf of bread.*)

Our narrator is touched with a stiff but imprecise literary formality. He's pedantic and superior and overestimates his intelligence and charm. He has one arm over our shoulders and something strange on his breath as he (clumsily, grandiosely, making basic errors) invites us, his fellow sophisticates, to join him in looking down at his (lowly) characters. ("Observe, my friend, those stupid mortals down there, so unlike you and me.") The effect is that we start looking askance at the narrator ("Who *is* this guy?") and distrusting his narration. The narrator's aspiration to literary moves he's seen in other stories but can't quite execute (like that botched digression) and his failure to register adequate amazement at the strange things he's narrating implicate him in the odd system he's describing, although he sees himself as located above it, judging it. The purpose of this attempt at elevation is to keep himself above the Ivans and Praskovyas of the world. But because he's no good at it, he gets placed, by us, down there beside, or even below, them. He's decidedly not Gogol but a creation of Gogol's, another character in the story—a functionary who, through his prose style, unconsciously reveals that he's not as important or smart as he thinks he is.

So, Ivan is off and Praskovya is off and now, it seems, our narrator is off too.

But, you know—who isn't?

The *skaz* tradition (American variants of which we see in Twain, and John Kennedy Toole, and the comedian Sarah Cannon doing Minnie Pearl, and Sacha Baron Cohen doing Borat, and Rainn Wilson doing Dwight Schrute) challenges the notion that a disinterested, objective, third-person-omniscient narrator exists anywhere in the real world. It's fun to pretend that such a person exists, and writers have made beautiful use of that notion (Chekhov, Turgenev, and Tolstoy among them), but, suggests Gogol, they have done so at a certain cost to the truth. Every story is narrated by someone, and since everyone has a viewpoint, every story is misnarrated (is narrated subjectively).

Since all narration is misnarration, Gogol says, let us misnarrate joyfully.

It's like a prose version of the theory of relativity: no fixed, objective, "correct" viewpoint exists; an unbalanced narrator describes, in an unbalanced voice, the doings of a cast of unbalanced characters.

In other words, like life.

Douglas Unger, one of my professors at Syracuse years ago, offered a model for how people communicate in the world.

When two people are talking, Doug suggested, each has a cartoon bubble overhead, full of his or her private hopes and projections and fears and preexisting worries and so on. Person A talks, Person B listens, waiting to respond, but as what Person A is saying passes into Person B's cartoon bubble, it gets mangled.

Say Person B's bubble is full of guilt because, after she forgot to call her mother on her birthday, her brother chidingly texted her about it. When Person A says, "I have to give a speech next week," Person B, thinking of the rude things her brother just texted, replies (out of her bubble), "People can be so harsh." Person A, his bubble full of anxiety about this forthcoming speech, hears: "It's true, you'll probably blow it," and frowns. Person B thinks, "Oh, great, Person A is frowning at me because he sees that I'm the kind of jerk who forgets her mother's birthday."*

There is no world save the one we make with our minds, and the mind's predisposition determines the type of world we see.

A woman who lives in a tiny ranch house, obsessed with the fact that her grass is dying, goes to Versailles and is impressed, mostly, by the lawns.

A dominated guy in a bad marriage goes to a play and can't get over how much his wife is like Lady Macbeth.

Such is life.

No, really, says Gogol, such *is* life.

I'm reminded of a story: A rich Hollywood agent's Ferrari breaks down in the desert outside Los Angeles. This is terrible; he's got the biggest meeting of his life scheduled for later that day. His phone is dead, and there's nobody in sight. But wait: off in the distance, a vehicle approaches. As it gets closer, he sees that it's a pickup truck. An old, beat-up pickup truck. Of the kind driven by farmers. Oh, God. Conservative farmers, who see a guy like him (Ferrari, beautiful suit, tons of hair product) and assume he must be rolling in money and does no real work, like, you know, farm work, out in the broiling sun, wrestling cows or whatnot. A punk rich kid, making all that money for what? Talking people into things! What a faker! Jeez, just his luck, the agent thinks, of all the people in the world who might have come along to help, he

---

* The exchange of letters between Kovalyov and Madam Grigoryevna, toward the end of Section II, is a good example of this kind of miscommunication.

gets *this* guy? What does that stupid hick know about his life, about how hard he's worked all these years? Zeke or Clem or whoever's probably got a nice stable marriage, to some old farmer lady, whereas Jeannine left him last month because of all the long hours he spends agenting and now he hardly ever sees little Rex and—

The truck pulls up.

"Need a lift?" asks the kindly farmer.

"Fuck you!" shouts the agent.

I think, therefore I am wrong, after which I speak, and my wrongness falls on someone also thinking wrongly, and then there are two of us thinking wrongly, and, being human, we can't bear to think without taking action, which, having been taken, makes things worse.

If you've ever wondered, as I have, "Given how generally sweet people are, why is the world so fucked up?," Gogol has an answer: we each have an energetic and unique *skaz* loop running in our heads, one we believe in fully, not as "merely my opinion" but "the way things actually are, for sure."

The entire drama of life on earth is: *Skaz*-Headed Person #1 steps outside, where he encounters *Skaz*-Headed Person #2. Both, seeing themselves as the center of the universe, thinking highly of themselves, immediately slightly misunderstand everything. They try to communicate but aren't any good at it.

Hilarity ensues.

Ivan finds a nose in his bread, reasons badly about this, and leaps into (ineffective, misdirected) action. Kovalyov, across town, wakes up without his nose, reacts strangely to it (more miffed than terrified, objecting to the "idiotic way" in which it disappeared, wishing there were, at least, "something in place of" it), then leaps into action himself and runs into his own nose, which, although it was small enough to fit into a loaf of bread the last time we saw it, is now the size of a man.

That was a fun sentence to type. Why was it?

In the answer lies an important aspect of Gogol's genius.

When Kovalyov sees his rebellious nose for the first time, our translation (by Mary Struve) has it this way: "Imagine the horror and at the same time the amazement of Kovalyov when he recognized that it was his own nose!" The Pevear and Volokhonsky translation has: "What was Kovalyov's horror as well as amazement when he recognized him as his own nose!" What's the "it"? Who's the "him"? What, exactly, does Kovalyov *see*? Does the Nose have . . . a nose? Does the Nose have a face? If so, its face is not described. But the confident statement that "he recognized that it was his own nose" causes our mind to insert, here, a Nose, a Platonic Nose, one that we couldn't, if pressed, draw.

Yet there it is, rushing into a house.

When, a few minutes later, the Nose comes out again, there's no additional attempt to answer the question of why Kovalyov thinks this (man? nose?) is his nose. We learn only that "he" is "wearing a gold-embroidered uniform with a big stand-up collar and doeskin breeches" and that "from his plumed hat one could infer that he held the rank of a state councillor." (The focus is on the nose's change in status, not its new form or size.)

This is "improper narrative emphasis" being used to sidestep a question that, had these events really happened, and had we been there, we would have been able to answer. The Nose either has a face or it doesn't. It's sometimes depicted as a human-sized nose wearing a hat, with arms and legs, but elsewhere in the text we learn that the Nose "slightly knitted his brows," i.e., it has a face. If the Nose has a face, where did that face get its eyes and mouth and so on? Whose are they? Who does it resemble? Or is it just a big nose, with brows?

We're left to conclude that the Nose is both a nose without a face and a nose with a face, at once. Or neither, exactly, or both, as needed by the syntactic moment.

The fun here is spending a few moments in the land where language goes to admit what it really is: a system of communication with limitations, suitable for use in everyday life but wonky in its higher registers. Language can appear to say more than it has a right to say; we can form it into sentences that are not in relationship with what actually is or even what could be.

If I type, "The desk thought to scratch its arm but, recalling that it was armless and that one of its legs was shorter than the others, blushed slightly," the personification of the desk is one level of nonsense. But that's not all: the desk, its blush receding, can return to the emblem it was ratifying, or the freedom-dimple it was juxtaposing, or the Canada it couldn't help but upholstering with implacable small fate-muffins.

Does any of that arise in your mind? It does in mine, sort of. How many fate-muffins are there? Just how "small" are they, and where have you located them? Near those juxtaposed freedom-dimples? The fate-muffins, though only partially made by the mind, can now be eaten, or thrown out the Empathy Port, or repurposed into cylindrical Newark documents, for Judy to loose-ascertain as she rips the flight-superior cat mandate.

What does it mean that all of this now, sort of, *is*? It means that language can make worlds that don't and could never exist. Reading Gogol, it may occur to us that this is what our mind is doing all the time: making, with words, a world that doesn't, quite, exist. Language is a meaning approximator that sometimes gets too big for its britches and deceives us, intentionally (someone with an agenda twists language to urge us into action) or unintentionally (with an idea in mind, we build an earnest case, seeking the language to make our idea seem true, unaware that, too fond of our idea, we're stretching the thin fabric of language over untrue places in our argument).

Language, like algebra, operates usefully only within certain limits. It's a tool for making representations of the world, which, unfortunately, we then go on to mistake for the world itself. Gogol is not making a ridiculous world; he's showing us that we ourselves make a ridiculous world in every instant, by our thinking.

Like someone who watches a friend freak out during an emergency, we may, after reading Gogol, never look at our old pal language the same way again.

Which is a good thing. We wouldn't want to mistake a truth-approximating tool for the truth itself.

It's kind of problematic to be talking about the language of a piece we can read only in translation.

To read Gogol in English is one thing; to read him in Russian is, apparently, quite another. He's funnier in Russian; there are aural jokes and assonances and puns that can't be rendered in English, and that's that. Early in my teaching career, I had a colleague at Syracuse come in and talk to my class about the challenges of translation. It was wonderful and nearly sunk the whole course. When she was done, we realized what pale imitations of the originals we were reading. She talked us through a section of another Gogol short story masterpiece, "The Overcoat," showing us all of the sound-related jokes we were missing. For example, early in that story, a mother needing to name her new-born works through a series of names and finally decides to call him after his father, so that he becomes Akakii Akakievich. In Russian, my colleague told us, the language in that section contains a series of feces-evoking sounds that culminate in the announcement of the baby's name. The "ka-ka" sound having the same associations in Russian as in English, "Akakii Akakievich" sounds, to the Russian ear, especially after this shit-related buildup, something like, you know, "Shit O'Shitvich." (Or "Crap P. Poopton." Or "Dumpy Dumperton." I could go on.) A Russian audience, she told us, would have been giggling throughout and would have exploded in laughter at the reveal of the name.

That, to say the least, was not our reaction. To us, it just seemed like a slightly off-balance account of how babies were traditionally named, we assumed, back there in nineteenth-century Russia.

But even in translation, one of the pleasures of Gogol's prose is the way a genuine emotion, passed through the distortive *skaz* filter, comes out the other side, still genuine but twisted.

I heard a version of this growing up. Late at some neighborhood party, cornered by some pal of my parents' who'd had too much to drink and longed to convey to someone, anyone, how the world seemed to him (beautiful, unfair, full of hidden messages he'd missed), a sort of Chicago *skaz* got performed: "You got moxie but, trust me, the fucks are gonna fuck with you, and you gotta give 'em *this*"—*insert raised middle finger*—first time they try that shit!"

Every soul is vast and wants to express itself fully. If it's denied an adequate instrument (and we're all denied that, at birth, some more than others), out comes . . . poetry, i.e., truth forced out through a re-stricted opening.

That's all poetry is, really: something odd, coming out. Normal speech, overflowed. A failed attempt to do justice to the world. The poet proves that language is inadequate by throwing herself at the fence of language and being bound by it. Poetry is the resultant bulging of the fence. Gogol's contribution was to perform this throwing of him-self against the fence in the part of town where the little men live, the sputtering, inarticulate men whose language can't rise to the occasion but who still feel everything the big men (articulate, educated, at ease) feel.

The result is awkward, funny, and true, touched with the spirit of the (odd) person doing the telling.

One model of writing is that we strive upward to express ourselves precisely, at the highest levels of language (think Henry James). Another is that we surrender to our natural mode of expression, flawed though it may be, and, by way of concentrated work within that mode, raise it up, so to speak, creating a poetic rarefication of that (inefficient) form of expression.

When a corporate person says, "The stress being felt by some is, in terms of how we might view it is, we did not meet or exceed our goals that we all will remember Mark from Corporate communicated so clear last month in his critical missive," that is a poem, because it is not right. There's a true statement inside it ("We failed and are fucked"), but there's also something true about its not-rightness, the flavor of which tells us things about the speaker and his culture that aren't conveyed by "We failed and are fucked."

So, it's a poem: a machine for conveying bonus meaning.

We might also notice that, in places, the clumsiness of Gogol's *skaz* narration suddenly falls away and the prose becomes beautifully articulate: "But there is nothing enduring in this world," the narrator tells us after Kovalyov recovers his nose, only to find that it won't reattach, "and that is why even joy is not as keen in the moment that follows the first; and a moment later it grows weaker still and finally merges imperceptibly into one's usual state of mind, just as a ring on the water, made by the fall of a pebble, merges finally into the smooth surface."

Nothing "substandard" about that speech.

So, the form of *skaz* Gogol is using here has real range. Sometimes this is a great writer writing a graceless writer writing and sometimes it's . . . a great writer, writing.

"Gogol was a strange creature," Nabokov wrote, "but genius is always strange; it is only your healthy second-rater who seems to the grateful reader to be a wise old friend, nicely developing the reader's own notions of life." Tolstoy and Chekhov, Nabokov said, also had their "moments of irrational insight" that produced an abrupt moment of "focal shift," but in Gogol "this shifting is the very basis of his art."

Gogol was obsessed with noses, afraid of leeches and worms; he could, apparently, touch the top of his (lengthy) nose with the tip of his tongue. His school nickname? "The mysterious dwarf." "He was a weakling," Nabokov tells us, "a trembling mouse of a boy with dirty hands and greasy locks, and pus trickling out of his ear. He gorged himself on sticky sweets. His schoolmates avoided touching the books he had been using." His aristocratic classmates looked down on him, according to one of them with the Gogolian name of V. I. Liubich Romanovich, who said that the young Gogol "seldom washed his face and hands in the morning, was always wearing dirty linen and stained clothes." Gogol would sit in the last row of the classroom, "so as not to be subjected to ridicule."

Gogol was a provincial from Ukraine, a bit of a mama's boy (and the feeling seemed to be mutual: his mother fondly credited him with the invention of the railroad and the steamship) who moved to St. Petersburg and found himself outclassed by the more aristocratic writers he met there.

"Russian prose had attained perfect ease and clarity in the works of Pushkin and Mikhail Lermontov," Richard Pevear writes in his wonderful introduction to Gogol's novel *Dead Souls*. "Gogol admired them greatly and did not try to match them. He set about creating another sort of medium, not imitative of the natural speech of educated men, not graced with the 'prose virtues' of concision and accuracy, but apparently quite the opposite."

According to Andrei Sinyavsky,* to do this, Gogol resorted "not to the speech in which we talk, but rather—to the inability to speak in an ordinary way."

Here was Gogol's self-assessment: "Pushkin . . . told me that no other writer before has had this gift of presenting the banality of life so vividly, of being able to describe the banality of the banal man with such force that all the little details that escape notice flash large in everyone's eyes. That is my main quality, which belongs to me alone, and which indeed no other writer possesses."

---

* As translated by Pevear in that same introduction.

How does someone write in a way "not imitative of the natural speech of educated men," how might he exploit our "inability to speak in an ordinary way"? How does he get so good at describing "the banality of the banal man"?

Well, we might suspect an inside job. Maybe Gogol was not observing some banal man out in the world and writing up his observations but observing the banal man that existed within him and writing *that* up.

In his best work, I'd say, Gogol is two people at once: the inarticulate, bombastic, stiff, provincial narrator and the writer of acute taste looking over at that provincial, using him by channeling him, fine-tuning that voice into a thing of sublime comic beauty.

In the last ten years of his life, Gogol lost this gift of splitting himself. Or, we might say, the banal man took over entirely. Frustrated as he tried to write the second volume of his novel *Dead Souls,* Gogol veered off into mysticism and grandiosity and started sending, from Italy, condescending letters full of spiritual advice to his sophisticated, astonished, occasionally insulted friends back in Russia. (In one letter, Gogol counseled a man grieving the recent death of his wife as follows: "Jesus Christ will help you to become a gentleman, which you are neither by education or inclination—she is speaking through me.") These were compiled in *Selected Passages from Correspondence with Friends,* described by Donald Fanger as "a deeply, often embarrassingly personal book" that entirely lacked "that ironic, critical stance which had marked the best of Gogol's earlier writing."

"Abandoning (or abandoned by) the comic sense that had produced his best works," Fanger writes, "he comes increasingly to resemble one of his own caricatures."

"O believe my words," Gogol urged one of his correspondents. "I myself do not dare disbelieve them."

That's a line that could have come out of the mouth of one of Gogol's *skaz* narrators, but it was written by the man himself, and in earnest.

There's something familiar and terrifying about "The Nose." *A man loses something valuable and goes in search of it.* Who hasn't had that nightmare? We're seeking something and can't find it. The dreamworld rises up, intent on frustrating us. The meaning of the dream lies in the flavor of that particular dreamworld's unhelpfulness.

Here, in outline, is the part of the story we might call "Kovalyov, having just met his own nose, goes off in search of help" (starting on page 9):

—He goes to the home of the chief of police, who isn't there.

—He goes to the newspaper office, where he is misunderstood and frustrated.

—He goes to the home of the district police inspector (not the chief of police), and is offended.

—He goes home, reasons that this whole thing is the fault of Mrs. Podtochina, who, he feels, is a witch.

—A policeman arrives with the nose.

—The nose will not reattach.

—Kovalyov is visited by a doctor, who could fix the nose but advises against it and instead tries to buy it.

—Kovalyov writes an accusatory letter to Mrs. Podtochina, who, in her letter back, indicates that she has entirely misunderstood him.

The pattern here is, roughly: Kovalyov tries something reasonable and gets an unsatisfactory response.

He just misses the police chief, is misunderstood by the newspaper clerk, offended by the inspector, misadvised by the doctor. He goes to all the right places, petitions all the right people (he proceeds approximately as we would), and everyone is perfectly polite (except the district police inspector, who is rude within acceptable limits, given that he outranks Kovalyov). These people say all the right things (they express concern and sympathy, they're cordial and curious, they want to help, or at least be seen as helpful), but they can't help, because they are not (not yet) living the nightmare he's living, that nightmare that can take many forms: the loss of one's nose, sure, but also the loss of an arm or one's health or livelihood or wife or child or sanity. The world is full of nightmares waiting to happen to us but the people to whom Kovalyov turns don't believe this, or don't believe it *yet,* just as we don't; they understand this nightmare to be uniquely Kovalyov's (exceptional, freakish, embarrassing) rather than a preview of the (pending, inevitable) nightmare that will eventually come for all of us.

Also, it's not their job. Each of them stays strictly within the bounds of what they're allowed to do and expected to do by the system of which they are part. That system (their society) has been engineered for normal operation; it can't help someone in such extraordinary need as Kovalyov. (Their reactions are strangely mild, as if Kovalyov has lost not his nose but a suitcase.)

So, everything goes on normally, though a man has lost his nose and crippled beggars are mocked in front of a cathedral and innocent prisoners rot in filthy czarist prisons and children starve while the rich dance at elaborate balls, and here we might list hundreds of other outrages that would have been occurring in that fictional St. Petersburg, on that March 25, 1835, or on any day, in any real city, outrages that, it is tacitly agreed by all of us, must continue, because solving them would be beyond the scope of that which might be reasonably expected.

Let's focus on just one of Kovalyov's interactions (with the newspaper clerk, pages 10–14) to discern the precise flavor of the Gogolian dreamworld's unhelpfulness.

Kovalyov (hiding his missing nose with a handkerchief) says he'd like to place an ad. He does not say, "My nose is missing" but, rather coyly/shyly, "There has been a swindle." He is not, really, looking for the nose that was formerly on his face but for the "scoundrel" the nose has now become (that is, a nose with a mind of its own). His emphasis is not "My nose has gone missing" but "My nose has offended me by leaving my face to become someone else, someone above me who is not treating me with respect and needs to be caught and brought into line."

The clerk asks his name. Kovalyov declines to give it. This is fine with the clerk. (Then why did he ask?) The clerk misunderstands Kovalyov, thinks he's looking for a runaway serf. (As in that nightmare, we keep getting further away from the actual business at hand.) But the clerk has got it partly right—or, anyway, Kovalyov accepts the error, with a slight modification: there *was* a runaway involved, yes, but the runaway is his nose. The clerk mishears this, modifies his misunderstanding of the situation: "And did this Mr. Nosov rob you of a big sum?" Kovalyov corrects him again: "My nose, my very own nose has disappeared." The clerk is not shocked. He would, however, like a little more information. "I don't quite understand it," he says mildly.

Kovalyov needs to find his nose not for the obvious reason (it's his nose and it's gone) but because it's a part of the body whose absence is impossible to hide, and . . . well, you know, he calls on many prominent people, and so . . .

He assumes that this clerk, notches below him on the social ladder, will accept this as a reasonable motivation. The clerk considers running the ad but then demurs, protecting, he says, the reputation of the paper; he can't publish something so outrageous. Also, the clerk says, if his nose is missing, Kovalyov should go to a doctor. But . . . it's not *really* missing, is it? Kovalyov seems, he says, like "a man of gay disposition . . . fond of kidding in company." (There's something distinctly Gogolian about this clerk's notion that "kidding," done by "a man of gay disposition" might consist of coming into a crowded room of strangers and claiming not to have a nose.)

Goaded, Kovalyov takes the handkerchief away from his face (the big reveal, the first time we've had outside proof that Kovalyov's nose really is gone, that he's not just a crazy person imagining his nose is gone). "It's absolutely flat," the clerk confirms, "like a pancake fresh off the griddle." He isn't horrified, however. He isn't even surprised. Or all that interested. (It's not *his* nose that's missing.) He says he doesn't see "any advantage" to Kovalyov in running the ad. Is this true? If, in fact, the nose is still riding around town in the carriage, such an ad might cause someone, seeing a human-sized nose, to put two and two together and get in contact with Kovalyov, and some progress might get made: quite a potential "advantage" to Kovalyov. (And here we see how far Gogol has taken us. We're now arguing earnestly for the ad to be run, having accepted not only the reality of a nose's conversion into a person but the idea that a notice in a newspaper might help us find it, even though we—still—don't exactly know what it is that we're looking for or, you know, whom. The limits of what we find outrageous keep being expanded.)

Does Kovalyov object to the clerk's illogic? No. He feels "completely discouraged" and then sees the name of a pretty actress and thinks about going to the theater. And just like that, via the one-two punch of discouragement plus distraction, Kovalyov's quest, or at least this part of it, is thwarted.

Why is Kovalyov thwarted? What thwarts him? Not lack of sympathy. ("I really am grieved that such a thing happened to you," the clerk says, before offering him a pinch of exactly what he most wants but can't have.) There's something thwarting in the very mechanics of Gogol-world, an essential miscommunication at work, one that saturates everything, even the structure of the story, even its internal logic.

It's sadder, the saddest, that the clerk, not at all malevolent, is still utterly unhelpful.

And we learn something about Kovalyov that rings true for all of us: he adapts quickly (too quickly) to insane new conditions. He has access to limited outrage. Sooner than we expect him to, he accepts his terrifying new state and goes on living, sad, peeved, but not rebellious; that would be impolite.

Everywhere we go, people are (mostly) kind and earnest and seem to believe in approximately the same things we do: responsibility, truth, neighborliness. And yet every night, on the news, etc., etc. And also, every era, in the history books, etc., etc. There is no cruel thing someone hasn't done somewhere, no story of degradation and hopelessness that hasn't been lived by someone (isn't being lived by someone right now).

Personally, I've never met a person who was evil in the classic Hollywood mode, who throws down happily on the side of evil while cackling, the sworn enemy of all that is good because of some early disillusionment. Most of the evil I've seen in the world—most of the nastiness I've been on the receiving end of (and, for that matter, the nastiness I, myself, have inflicted on others)—was done by people who intended good, who thought they were doing good, by reasonable people, staying polite, making accommodations, laboring under slight misperceptions, who haven't had the inclination or taken the time to think things through, who've been sheltered from or were blind to the negative consequences of the belief system of which they were part, bowing to expedience and/or "commonsense" notions that have come to them via their culture and that they have failed to interrogate. In other words, they're like the people in Gogol. (I'm leaving aside here the big offenders, the monstrous egos, the grandiose-idea-possessors, those cut off from reality by too much wealth, fame, or success, the hyperarrogant, the power-hungry-from-birth, the socio- and/or psychopathic.)

But on the mundane side of things, if we want to understand evil (nastiness, oppression, neglect) we should recognize that the people who commit these sins don't always cackle while committing them; often they smile, because they're feeling so useful and virtuous.

In *I Will Bear Witness,* Victor Klemperer's memoir about Holocaust Germany, the people who, because he's a Jew, take away his office at the university, his right to shop at certain shops, his job, his home, do so politely, even apologetically. (It's not their idea; it's coming down from those boneheads in Berlin. But what's a person to do?) They seem to like Klemperer, they aren't anti-Semites, but they're also not, in those moments, *anti*-anti-Semites. They're well-mannered, abashed-but-willing parts of the Nazi machine.

The Germany in Klemperer's book has something in common with Gogol's printing office. In both, something troubling (a missing nose, a hateful political agenda) is met with polite, well-intended civility—a civility that wants things to go on as usual.

Writing about Gregor von Rezzori's classic *Memoirs of an Anti-Semite,* Deborah Eisenberg pointed out the great harm that can be done by a handful of evil people, as long as they have the "passive assistance of many, many other people who glance out of the windows of their secure homes and see a cloudless sky." She goes on to list the sins of such passive people: "carelessness, poor logic, casual snobbery—either social or intellectual—inattentiveness."

What prevents Gogol's clerk from being truly helpful? The clerk's firm location in himself, his extreme preference for, and protection of, all that is his: his viewpoint, his habits, his interests, his understanding of the limits of his responsibilities. How can what is happening to Kovalyov really matter to him, when it happened to . . . not-him?

None of the writers we're reading here, including Gogol, could have imagined the horrors of the Holocaust (or the Russian Revolution or the Stalinist purges), but Gogol, I think, could have *narrated* these; his style could have accommodated them. When I look at those Technicolor films of the Nazi leaders on vacation, I find them utterly Gogolian. Mass murderers looking bad in swimsuits, dancing, cutting up, appearing occasionally self-conscious before the camera, their bad ideas seeming good to them, a twisted *skaz* loop (technocratic, racist, ideologically agitated) playing in their heads.

Let me underscore something here: the story doesn't add up.

There are impossible events in it, yes. Can a story have an impossible event in it? Sure. Say we're at a dinner party in a story and the host's head suddenly pops off, hits the ceiling, then lands in his soup. Allowed? Of course. What readerly expectations does it raise? That the writer noticed it and will now cause the story to notice it. (If no one else at the table notices, we feel this lack of acknowledgment as an oversight on the writer's part, i.e., bad writing.) There is also the assumption that the rest of the story will take the event into account (someone else's head will pop off, or the host will be shown sobbing in his bed that night, full of shame, obsessively checking his head/neck juncture). That is, as we've said, the meaning of a story in which something impossible happens is not that the thing happened (it's only language, after all, with somebody at the other end of it, making it up) but in the way the story reacts to the impossibility. That is how the story tells us what it believes.

In a Gogol story, when something impossible happens, either: (1) no one notices, or (2) they notice but misunderstand it and then proceed to miscommunicate about it. This includes the narrator, who keeps failing to comment on oddnesses we notice, and misinterpreting things and providing explanations we don't buy, and failing to provide reasonable methods by which the things he is narrating could have occurred.

Procedural questions pile up behind us as we read.

Ivan drops the nose in the river and a few hours later it's seen by Kovalyov near the coffee shop, getting out of a carriage, wearing a dress uniform. How did it get out of the river? Did it become human-sized before or after getting out of the river? How did it, in those few hours, get rich enough to afford a carriage? And learn to talk? Who's driving that carriage? How was he hired? Did the driver notice, while being interviewed for the job, that his prospective employer was a nose?

The Nose tries to leave town by using a passport "made out a long time ago in the name of a certain civil servant" (that "long time ago" is weird, since the nose has only been away from Kovalyov for a few hours) and boarding a stagecoach bound for Riga. Why does the Nose feel a need to leave town? Has it heard that Kovalyov is looking for it? How would it have heard this? Does the Nose have ears? Who has it been talking to? Who would talk to it? Do other people recognize it as a nose? A policeman mistakes the Nose for a gentleman, realizes he is a nose, and arrests it. How does he "realize" this? What tips him off? For what does he arrest the Nose? How does he arrive at the conclusion that the Nose belongs to Kovalyov? Does the Nose confess? Presumably, the Nose is, at the time of its apprehension, still human-sized, but somehow, before it gets returned to Kovalyov, in that piece of paper, it has shrunk down again and lost its clothes and its mobility and its ability to speak. Did it shrink when the handcuffs went on? Or before? What caused its reversion to nosehood? Why does the policeman still suspect that Ivan is "the chief villain in this business," given that he never saw Ivan throw the nose into the river and that, even if he had, he would have had no way of knowing it was a nose that had been thrown, since the nose would have immediately started swimming downriver, while transforming, underwater, into a state councillor, later to climb out somewhere downstream?

And so on.

It's not just that these questions aren't answered; it's that most of them *couldn't* be answered, not in a way consistent with the spatial and temporal facts laid out in other places in the story.

Kovalyov summarizes all of this quite concisely: "How could a nose which as recently as yesterday had been on his face and could neither ride nor walk—how could it be in uniform?" And, like the story, he can't come up with an answer (in part, because there is no answer that could satisfy the "facts" of the story as presented).

In workshop, one of the first critiques that will be made about a story is that it doesn't make sense. "You've said it's winter; why is Gertrude in a bathing suit, out by the pool? It doesn't make sense." "I don't think it makes sense that Larry would be so calm, having just been castrated by a space alien." We understand a story's meaning, in part, by tracking its causality, and a story's power stems from our sense that its causality is truthful, which is to say, that its internal logic is solid.

So, why don't we just dismiss "The Nose" as bad writing?

Well, one reason is . . . we just don't. This elaborate joke—a story that seems to make a certain logical sense but doesn't—is done so well that it tricks our reading mind into assuming coherence in the same way that the eye, perceiving a series of snapshots, sells it to us as continuous motion.

"The Nose" might be thought of as a pile of ceramic shards, all imprinted with the same pattern, lying in a certain arrangement on the floor that makes us think: "vase, broken." But when we try to reassemble it, the pieces don't fit, because it was never a coherent vase to begin with. The potter didn't make a vase and break it; he made a bunch of shards and laid them out in a shattered-vase arrangement.

But the higher-order reason is this: we come to feel that the story's strange logic is not the result of error, is not perverse or facile or random, but is the universe's true logic—that it is the way things actually work, if only we could see it all clearly.

Sometimes life feels a certain way that we call "absurd": nothing matters, all efforts are for naught, everything seems random and perverse, positive intention is perpetually thwarted. This stance communicates darkness and edginess, which can feel like wisdom. But we don't live as if life is absurd; we live as if it has meaning and makes sense. We live (or try to) by kindness, loyalty, friendship, aspiration to improvement, believing the best of other people. We assume causality and continuity of logic. And we find, through living, that our actions do matter, very much. We can be a good parent or a bad parent, we can drive safely or like a maniac. Our minds can feel clean and positive and clear or polluted and negative. To have an ambition and pursue it feels healthy. A life without earnest striving is a nightmare. (When desire vanishes from a normal life, that is called depression.) We live by the assumption that some modes of existence are preferable to others and that we are capable of determining what those better ways are and moving toward them.

And yet, as incorrect as it seems to say that life is entirely absurd, it seems equally incorrect to say that life is entirely rational. Well-made plans are confounded. We do everything right and get punished. Someone we love dies early; our mind goes bad; we are unfairly misunderstood; the world suddenly seems to have turned against us. We set a glass on a shelf and it falls right off. Our dog stops to poop on the nicest-looking lawn on the block, and from out of the house steps our boss. Power is held by shitheads; virtuous people suffer unfairly. Happy, fortunate people, to whom everything has been given, preach positivity to sad, unlucky people, who were given nothing. We push the button labeled "I Need Help" and one of those boxing gloves comes out and hits us in the face as the machine lets out a comic farting noise.

So, life is mostly rational, with occasional bursts of absurdity.

Or, maybe: an assumption of rationality holds under normal conditions but frays under duress.

Some stories show us the process of rationality fraying under duress (*Kolyma Tales,* set in a Siberian work camp; *The Handmaid's Tale,* set in a dystopian, misogynist future). "The Nose" suggests that rationality is frayed in *every moment,* in the most normal of moments. But distracted by the temporary blessings of stability and bounty and sanity and health, we don't notice.

Gogol is sometimes referred to as an absurdist, his work meant to communicate that we live in a world without meaning. But to me, Gogol is a supreme realist, looking past the way things seem to how they really are.

Gogol says that we are, in our everyday perceptions, deceived. We feel, mostly, that our actions matter, and that earnest communication is happening, that we are real and permanent and in control of our fate. And under normal circumstances, these things are (mostly) true: we are sane sailors on a sturdy ship in a calm harbor. But every now and then the scrim drops (there's a scrim in this metaphorical harbor) and out there: the open ocean, huge waves, fierce winds. And we find ourselves heading out. Soon it becomes clear that we are not, after all, in control, not a high-functioning sailor standing stably on a nice calm deck, a deck that we have created through our virtue. The ship is pitching, and the deck is covered in ice, and we're wearing special headphones that distort what our crewmates are shouting and special mouthpieces that distort what we're shouting back in return. And now the ship is going down and some action is required, some cooperation, some compassion. And we intend to be compassionate, we really do, but the intended compassion, passing out through those distorting mouthpieces and being received through those distorting headphones, is *off*; it doesn't help, and may even hurt, or, worst of all, may make no difference at all.

Gogol hears, in everyday life, the first hints of the small miscommunications that, under duress, become catastrophic. It's funny enough when Kovalyov, in the cathedral, can't seem to get a straight answer from his own nose, but this same species of miscommunication, writ large, causes revolutions and genocides and political upheavals and family disasters that never get healed (divorces, estrangements, bitter grudges) and is, Gogol implies, at the heart of all human suffering— that is, at the heart of that constant nagging feeling of unrest and dissatisfaction that attends every human interaction.

There is something eternal about Gogol. He is true in all times and places. When the end of the world comes, he seems to say, it will (it can only) come out of *this* moment, out of the way we are thinking in this (and every) moment. The misunderstanding operative in the larger world is operative within us, right now, even if we're sitting alone in a quiet room.

But we'd be remiss if we didn't acknowledge that Gogol's main currency is joy. My favorite part of the story—a part that feels neither old or new but timeless—comes toward the beginning of the scene in the newspaper office when somehow, magically, a group of people waiting to place ads get transformed into that for which they are advertising, and suddenly that little office is full of "a coachman of sober conduct . . . a nineteen-year-old serf girl . . . a sound droshky with one spring missing . . . a young and fiery dappled-gray horse . . . a summer residence with all the appurtenances."

That is what makes Gogol great—that he somehow felt inclined to do that, and then did it, with such strange, happy confidence. The inexplicable uptick in fondness for the world I feel, moving through that section, which is not essential to the action of the story but seems to have been done just for the fun of it, is, for me, what Gogol is all about.

So, what does the story "mean"? What change does its main character undergo? How do the events of the story "change everything forever"?

Well, hmm: Kovalyov's nose leaves him, then comes back. It refuses to reattach and then, seemingly on a whim, reattaches. What does Kovalyov learn from this terrible trial? Nothing. What is his hero's journey? "A momentous, miraculous thing happened to me, and I stayed the same throughout, although, at times, I did become rather vexed."

Who is Kovalyov before he loses his nose? A player, an egotist, an unreflective social climber, a name-dropper. How does the nose's absence and its miraculous recovery change him? It doesn't. Who is he once his nose goes back on his face? Same guy. "And from that time on"—as soon as his nose was restored—"Major Kovalyov went strolling about as though nothing had happened," we are told. "And his nose too, as though nothing had happened, stayed on his face." "Everything was all right, no part of him was missing." (Or, in the Pevear and Volokhonsky translation, "he was in no way damaged.") The last time we see Kovalyov, he's doing the same thing he was doing when we first met him: pretending to a rank he hasn't earned, by "buying himself the ribbon of some order, goodness knows why, for he hadn't been decorated with any order."

We might detect an echo here of "Master and Man." Like Vasili, Kovalyov gets a foretaste of death: a warning from the universe that those periods during which one gets to do what one wants (smoke a cigarette, have a nose) are brief and rescindable.

But unlike Vasili, Kovalyov doesn't take the hint. It never occurs to him that his ways need changing. He just wants to get *back* to them, as soon as possible.

So, Kovalyov is a fool. But he's also any one of us. There are some issues with a medical test. Could this be it? Our life suddenly seems precious, our habits stupid. Why do we golf so much? Why are we always on email, when our precious wife is sitting right there? The results come back: all is well. The mind relaxes into its previous torpor, and we're happy again, and hop on email to see about booking a tee time, as our wife sits there watching.

What does the nose represent? What does it want? Why does the nose leave Kovalyov's face in the first place? We never find out. Early on, we might feel the nose's disappearance as a sort of, uh, walkout, in protest of Kovalyov's superficiality and ambition and arrogance. But this doesn't hold up: the nose doesn't leave in response to anything Kovalyov does and doesn't come back in response to anything he stops doing; it doesn't return once it's satisfied that Kovalyov has taken the correction, because Kovalyov doesn't change at all in response to its absence. The nose comes back only because it's *brought* back, by that policeman, and goes back on Kovalyov's face only because . . . well, for no reason at all, narratively, except that it, like Gogol, may feel it's time to wrap things up.

On the other hand, Kovalyov may not be that much of a fool. "I lost my nose for no reason and it came back for no reason," he seems to say. "Disasters like these are going to happen no matter how I live. So, I guess I'll keep being aggressively myself, doing what I do, collecting medals I never earned and *chasing* the *ladies.*" The world is full of such people, and we are such people ourselves: sticking to hobbies and sweet daily habits, getting up early to write, frequenting a certain café, collecting ceramic ducks, going to Packers games with our faces painted green and yellow, and so on, trying to get in a few moments of celebration before that earlier-mentioned sinking ship goes down.

The nose (or the Nose) does well in its (or *his*? Does this Nose have a penis?) brief time wandering the world—better than Kovalyov has done. It has got, in one morning, things that we imagine Kovalyov must crave: a promotion, panache, authority, a carriage with a driver. It's happier and freer than he is, more proactive and dashing. (Like the hero in a romance novel, it's apprehended as it is "about to board a stagecoach and leave for Riga.")

The nose is the best part of Kovalyov, the non-toadying part, the confident part, the part capable of shucking off the habit of convention to which Kovalyov is addicted, and thinking and living anew, and, you know, lighting out for the continent. The nose is his wild inner spirit, chafing against the constraints of modern life, the nose is even (speaking of penises) a penis, to some critics (with its loss, Kovalyov is unmanned, unable to resume his life of romantic avarice), but the beauty of the story is that, through all of this, or in spite of all of this, or all of this notwithstanding, the nose is still . . . a nose. A nose of sorts. A real nose and a metaphorical one. A nose that keeps changing in response to what the story needs of it. The nose is a tool to get us looking at the ways in which we go in search of that which is essential and which we have lost. The nose is the means by which Gogol does his crazy dance of joy. But also, it's a nose. It even has a pimple.

How does a writer get out of a story like this?

At the beginning of Section III, the nose appears back on Kovalyov's face. To celebrate, Kovalyov goes out to Nevsky Avenue and, to top off a great day, with nose, on the town, buys himself that unearned ribbon. This has the feeling of an ending. (We could end it right after "for he hadn't been decorated with any order.") That story would seem to be saying something like "Once a man lost his nose and got it back and it didn't change him." But there would be something unsatisfying about the story ending there that has to do, I think, with a little item that's been sitting in our TICHN cart all this time, that we touched upon earlier: the irrationality we've been patiently enduring over the course of the story—all of those loose ends and accumulating implausibilities, that trail of unexplained and inexplicable events the narrator's left littered behind him, his *skaz*-related quirks (his rambling and digressions and failures to "distinguish the trivial from the important" and his "improper narrative emphasis" and his "misplaced assumption"). We feel that we've been conned, somehow. All along we've been trusting this narrator and now, here at the very end, he still hasn't come clean. He hasn't (the story hasn't) justified (accounted for) these excesses in his mode of narration.

We feel that all of this needs to be *explained,* somehow, and our friend the lesser writer might be tempted to do just that ("Actually, it turns out, what had really happened was . . ."), but if the story's crazy logic gets explained away, then so does that revelatory feeling it has produced in us, the sense that the story's logic is actually the logic of the universe—that the story is an artificial occasion to show us how things really are, whereas normally those workings are hidden, until a moment of loss or disaster brings them into the open.

So what does Gogol do?

He confesses.

"Only now, on second thoughts," the narrator says, "can we see that there is much that is improbable in it."

"Uh, *yeah,*" we think.

But what a relief, to hear this admission.

We're having dinner with a friend. It's going badly. Something has been off since the moment we sat down and now dinner's almost over. What to do? Well: admit it. Blurt out the truth. "This has been such a stilted conversation. I feel we've been avoiding the topic of your fiancé, Ken, who, as you know, I loathe." Suddenly, just like that, the conversation is no longer stilted. You just de-stultified it. There was falsity and you eliminated it, by facing your friend and speaking the truth.

Or: we're on a bus that for many miles now has been making a strange clunking sound from below, which the driver's been ignoring. Finally, he turns around and says it: "Jeez, that's one ominous clunk, folks, isn't it?"

We instantly think better of the driver and feel part of a saner system.

As the narrator (in the last two paragraphs) looks askance at his own story with increasing perplexity, expressing the same reservations we've been feeling but suppressing ("the supernatural detachment of the nose and its appearance in various places in the guise of a state councillor is indeed strange"), I feel my residual reservations falling away. (The car dealer, in mid-transaction, wonders aloud how he can stand here telling me all of these lies, and I respond to his honesty with a renewed burst of trust and end up buying the car.)

Even in the midst of this self-denunciation, the narrator stays his usual *skaz* self. He criticizes the wrong things (Kovalyov has used an improper method to "advertise for one's nose," for example), then goes off on a digression that fizzles out ("it's improper, embarrassing, not nice!"), gets momentarily back on topic ("how did the nose come to be in a newly baked loaf?"), then veers off again, to wonder how an author (i.e., himself) can even choose such a subject. He addresses exactly none of the concerns he's raised ("I simply don't know what to make of it"), but the flailing gestures he's making in that direction have the effect of emptying out my TICHN cart.

I make a protest about the story's failure to cohere logically.

"I know, right?" the narrator says. "It's a train wreck, isn't it?"

Somehow that's enough.

And just like that—like one of those Tibetan monks who spend weeks fastidiously creating a sand mandala—Gogol happily destroys his magnificent creation and sweeps it into the river.

AFTERTHOUGHT #5

Once, grading some student papers on Kafka's *Metamorphosis,* I came across this line: "Upon perusing this story, I felt myself at a distinct tilt."

Hmm, wow, I thought. Pretty bad. But also: kind of great.

I started trying to imitate that voice, feeling around inside myself for a corollary. Pretty soon I had a few pages of my version of that voice, and in there was this: "Back in the time of which I am speaking, due to our Coordinators had mandated us, we had all seen that educational video of *It's Yours to Do With What You Like!* in which teens like ourselfs speak on the healthy benefits of getting off by oneself and doing what one feels like in terms of self-touching."

Just like that, a roomful of teenagers appeared, apparently horny, and their horniness was so problematic that someone had felt the need to subject them to a masturbation-encouraging short film.

Needless to say, I had not thought to myself, "I'd like to do a little something on the topic of how a group of confined teens deal with their powerful dawning sexuality." I was just riffing on that sentence in the student paper, trying to sound "like" that sentence.

A few lines later, guided by the content of my first sentence, I wrote, "And then nightfall would fall and our facility would fill with the sounds of quiet fast breathing from within our Privacy Tarps, as we all experimented per the techniques taught us in *It's Yours to Do With What You Like!* and what do you suspect, you had better make sure that that little gap between the main wall and the wall that slides out to make our Gender Areas is like really really small."

Suddenly there were Privacy Tarps and Gender Areas, which raised the question of whether, since both boys and girls seemed to be present (wherever this was), some of those Boys and Girls might want to leave their respective Gender Areas and have sex. And, it turned out, they did, they did want to, and two of them (Ruthie and Josh) did so, on the very next page, and I found, to invoke a phrase we used earlier, that "the path the story was on had narrowed."

We might imagine a story as a room-sized black box. The writer's goal is to have the reader go into that box in one state of mind and come out in another. What happens in there has to be thrilling and non-trivial.

That's it.

What is the exact flavor of the thrill? The writer doesn't have to know. That's what he's writing to find out.

How is the thrill accomplished?

To use an archery metaphor (and how often does a person get to do that?), one way to produce the thrill is to stop aiming at the target and concentrate on the feeling of the arrow leaving the bow. In this alternate version of archery, the arrow then sails off in a certain direction and keeps adjusting course, and wherever it lands . . . that's the target.

When I was a kid in Chicago, you could get a certain kind of pathetic power by being good at imitating a teacher, or another kid (the same size as you or smaller), or "doing" a certain type of person (a "grouchy neighbor" or a "hippie" or a "used-car salesman"). I had a couple of uncles who were really good at this. They would create these funny personas and stay in character, sometimes for a strangely long time. I was fascinated by what they did to a room just by walking in—people were always so happy to see them. What they were doing, I can see now, was improv: reading the room, adjusting their performances accordingly, trying to entertain the audience by imitating a person, and sometimes that person was imaginary. And when they stopped doing it, or if they showed up not in a mood to do it—that was sad.

That is the approach I discovered, or rediscovered, that day at the engineering company as, supposedly transcribing a conference call, I wrote those little Seussian poems.

This approach might be called "following the voice."

An idea for a voice appears, and off you go. You just "feel like" doing that voice. (And you find that you can.) Sometimes the inspiration for that voice might be a real person. Sometimes it's a tendency in myself that I'll exaggerate (in a story called "The Falls," for example, I gave my main character, Morse, a ratcheted-up version of my own neurotic, worry-prone monkey mind). Sometimes it's a fragment of language that came from elsewhere (like that line from the student paper).

The main thing I'd like to say about this mode of writing is that it's fun. When I do it, I'm giving almost no thought to anything but sustaining the voice—not thinking of the story's themes or what needs to happen next or any of that. In the early stages, I might not even be clear about why the person is talking the way he is. My only goal is to keep the energy of the voice high, to keep the character sounding like himself, which means, I've found, that the voice has to keep expanding. Having grasped the approximate "rules" of the voice, the reader will get restless if subjected to a series of sentences that (merely) abide by those rules. So I have to keep finding new ways to make the person sound like himself. The best way to do this is to keep putting new events in front of him, events that are escalatory (new to him), so that he has to find new registers in his voice with which to respond. (If a character, talking along in a certain voice, has never seen a horse before, and I show him one, his voice has to expand, to accommodate the horse.)

In the story mentioned above ("Jon"), what I found myself doing as I sat down to write every day, approximately, was giving myself permission to turn up a certain dial in my head labeled "Level of Inarticulateness." That is, letting myself be (even) more inarticulate than usual, easing up on the self-correction-before-speech we all normally do. I was just, you know, letting it rip, telling myself something like "Okay, do part surfer, part corporate wonk." I was aiming to make sentences that would be funny because of their defective syntax but that would also feel oddly efficient. ("Then came the final straw that broke the back of me saying no to my gonads.")

I'd also recently become aware of a trend: corporations were employing "typical" teenagers to give feedback about their products, so as to more effectively exploit that market (i.e., of "typical teens"), and I was struck by how cynical and yet sensible this was, and by how sad it was that a kid solicited on the basis of how very average he was would respond, "Sure, love to!"

That seemed to say something interesting about our culture.

So, really, two things were happening at once: the voice was leading me, and I was leading the voice. It's a chicken-or-egg thing that's a little hard to explain. But the point is that the voice-creation was an ongoing way of beating back any conceptions that might arise about the "outcome" or the "message" of the story—of making sure that I didn't end up (just) "writing a poem about two dogs fucking."

"Jon" eventually came to be "about" a lot of things—corporate capitalism, the dangers of materialism, the way commerce deforms language, love, marriage, loyalty—but none of that was intended at the beginning. Throughout, the main driver was the pleasure and fun of finding that voice within myself—of letting the voice teach me how to do it, and finding myself blurting out things like "And then she kissed me with a kiss I can only describe as melting," of looking up one day to find that a whole facility had appeared, one that had a system of drugging these kids into bliss, and that each kid in there had a chip in his or her neck, loaded with every TV commercial ever made, and that those commercials, indexed by something called an LI (Location Indicator), were part of why my narrator was talking the way he was.

A whole world came into being from the DNA of the voice in that student paper, which, in trying to imitate, I altered.

So, one way to get a story out of "the plane of its original conception" is to try not to *have* an original conception. To do this, we need a method. For me (and, I like to imagine, for Gogol, when he was in *skaz* mode) that method is to "follow the voice." But there are many methods. Each involves the writer proceeding in a way that honors or helps her pursue something *about which she has strong opinions.* It could be that she has strong opinions (is delighted by) patterns of recurring imagery. She might have strong opinions about the way the words look on the page. She might be a sound poet, guided by some obscure aural principle even she can't articulate. She might be obsessed with the minutiae of structure. It can be anything. The idea is that with her attention focused on that thing that delights her, about which she has strong opinions, she's less likely to know too well what she's doing and indulge in that knowing-in-advance that, as we've said, has a tendency to deaden a work and turn it into a lecture or a one-sided performance and drive the reader away.

—

When Jon finally succeeds in having sex with Carolyn, a girl he's crazy about, he describes it like this:

"And though I had many times seen LI 34321 for Honey Grahams, where the stream of milk and the stream of honey enjoin to make that river of sweet-tasting goodness, I did not know that, upon making love, one person may become like the milk and the other like the honey, and soon they cannot even remember who started out the milk and who the honey, they just become one fluid, this like honey/milk combo."

What he means is "I really enjoyed that and I think I'm in love."

But he's feeling more than just *that*.

And his voice is required, to tell us what else (what all) he's feeling.

In the sentence above, I feel his happiness, and I feel *his* happiness. That is, in that sentence, love has fallen on a particular, goofy person. Which is what love always falls on: a particular, goofy person. That's all there is for love *to* fall on.

Any of us who's ever walked out of their house on a lovely summer morning knows that the truth of that moment is more than just "I walked out of my house one morning in June." In that sentence, there's something missing, which is the "I" walking out of the house. That morning has to fall on a certain mind for it to feel like any kind of real morning.

In other words, voice is not just an embellishment; it's an essential part of the truth. In "The Nose," we feel the narrator to be from that world of functionaries and petty officials and we hear that in his voice, and the story benefits from this; told in this way, the story has an extra dimension of truth, and of joy.

It may be possible that, when all is said and done, that's what we're really looking for—in a sentence, in a story, in a book: joy (overflow, ecstasy, intensity). An acknowledgment, in the prose, that all of this is too big to be spoken of, but also that death begins the moment we give up on trying to speak of it.

Which brings us back to that black box.

If I think of a story as something that has to convey a certain message, as a train that has to pull into a certain station at a certain time, and myself as the stressed-out engineer trying to make that happen— it's too much. I freeze up and no fun is had.

But if I imagine myself as a sort of genial carnival barker, trying to usher you into my magical black box, the workings of which even I don't fully understand—that, I can do.

"What's going to happen to me in there?" you ask.

"I really don't know," I say, "but I promise I've done my best to make it thrilling and non-trivial."

"Will there be any joy in there?" you ask.

"Well, I hope so," I say. "I mean, that's what I was trying to feel as I made it, so . . ."

The kind of intuitive, line-by-line attention to editing we've been talking about—that's what makes it more likely that what happens in there will be thrilling and non-trivial, that whatever happens in there will happen more crisply and definitively. And since, in every decision, I'm proceeding by the question "Does this delight me?" there should be some delight for you in there too.

In this way, that black box (speaking of carnivals) is like a roller coaster. The roller-coaster designer focuses her attention on particular curves and drops. She knows, technically, how to maximize the intensity at those places. She doesn't know or care much about the exact flavor of your reaction. What she really wants is for you to get your ass kicked at those places, then step out of that little car at the end so dazed and changed and happy that, for a few seconds, you've got nothing much to say.

GOOSEBERRIES

Anton Chekhov

(1898)

GOOSEBERRIES

The sky had been overcast since early morning; it was a still day, not hot, but tedious, as it usually is when the weather is gray and dull, when clouds have been hanging over the fields for a long time, and you wait for the rain that does not come. Ivan Ivanych, a veterinary, and Burkin, a high school teacher, were already tired with walking, and the plain seemed endless to them. Far ahead were the scarcely visible windmills of the village of Mironositzkoe; to the right lay a range of hills that disappeared in the distance beyond the village, and both of them knew that over there were the river, and fields, green willows, homesteads, and if you stood on one of the hills, you could see from there another vast plain, telegraph poles, and a train that from afar looked like a caterpillar crawling, and in clear weather you could even see the town. Now, when it was still and when nature seemed mild and pensive, Ivan Ivanych and Burkin were filled with love for this plain, and both of them thought what a beautiful land it was.

"Last time when we were in Elder Prokofy's barn," said Burkin, "you were going to tell me a story."

"Yes; I wanted to tell you about my brother."

Ivan Ivanych heaved a slow sigh and lit his pipe before beginning his story, but just then it began to rain. And five minutes later there was a downpour, and it was hard to tell when it would be over. The two men halted, at a loss; the dogs, already wet, stood with their tails between their legs and looked at them feelingly.

"We must find shelter somewhere," said Burkin. "Let's go to Alyohin's; it's quite near."

"Let's."

They turned aside and walked across a mown meadow, now going straight ahead, now bearing to the right, until they reached the road. Soon poplars came into view, a garden, then the red roofs of barns; the river gleamed, and the view opened on a broad expanse of water with a mill and a white bathing-cabin. That was Sofyino, Alyohin's place.

The mill was going, drowning out the sound of the rain; the dam was shaking. Wet horses stood near the carts, their heads drooping, and men were walking about, their heads covered with sacks. It was damp, muddy, dreary; and the water looked cold and unkind. Ivan Ivanych and Burkin felt cold and messy and uncomfortable through and through; their feet were heavy with mud and when, having crossed the dam, they climbed up to the barns, they were silent as though they were cross with each other.

[2]

The noise of a winnowing-machine came from one of the barns, the door was open, and clouds of dust were pouring from within. On the threshold stood Alyohin himself, a man of forty, tall and rotund, with long hair, looking more like a professor or an artist than a gentleman farmer. He was wearing a white blouse, badly in need of washing, that was belted with a rope, and drawers, and his high boots were plastered with mud and straw. His eyes and nose were black with dust. He recognized Ivan Ivanych and Burkin and was apparently very glad to see them.

"Please go up to the house, gentlemen," he said, smiling; "I'll be there directly, in a moment."

It was a large structure of two stories. Alyohin lived downstairs in what was formerly the stewards' quarters: two rooms that had arched ceilings and small windows; the furniture was plain, and the place smelled of rye bread, cheap vodka, and harness. He went into the showy rooms upstairs only rarely, when he had guests. Once in the house, the two visitors were met by a chambermaid, a young woman so beautiful that both of them stood still at the same moment and glanced at each other.

"You can't imagine how glad I am to see you, gentlemen," said Alyohin, joining them in the hall. "What a surprise! Pelageya," he said, turning to the chambermaid, "give the guests a change of clothes. And, come to think of it, I will change, too. But I must go and bathe first, I don't think I've had a wash since spring. Don't you want to go into the bathing-cabin? In the meanwhile things will be got ready here."

The beautiful Pelageya, with her soft, delicate air, brought them bath towels and soap, and Alyohin went to the bathing-cabin with his guests.

"Yes, it's a long time since I've bathed," he said, as he undressed. "I've an excellent bathing-cabin, as you see—it was put up by my father—but somehow I never find time to use it." He sat down on the steps and lathered his long hair and neck, and the water around him turned brown.

"I say—" observed Ivan Ivanych significantly, looking at his [3] head.

"I haven't had a good wash for a long time," repeated Alyohin, embarrassed, and soaped himself once more; the water about him turned dark-blue, the color of ink.

Ivan Ivanych came out of the cabin, plunged into the water with a splash and swam in the rain, thrusting his arms out wide; he raised waves on which white lilies swayed. He swam out to the middle of the river and dived and a minute later came up in another spot and swam on and kept diving, trying to touch bottom. "By God!" he kept repeating delightedly, "by God!" He swam to the mill, spoke to the peasants there, and turned back and in the middle of the river lay floating, exposing his face to the rain. Burkin and Alyohin were already dressed and ready to leave, but he kept on swimming and diving. "By God!" he kept exclaiming. "Lord, have mercy on me."

"You've had enough!" Burkin shouted to him.

They returned to the house. And only when the lamp was lit in the big drawing room upstairs, and the two guests, in silk dressing-gowns and warm slippers, were lounging in armchairs, and Alyohin himself, washed and combed, wearing a new jacket, was walking about the room, evidently savoring the warmth, the cleanliness, the dry clothes and light footwear, and when pretty Pelageya, stepping noiselessly across the carpet and smiling softly, brought in a tray with tea and jam, only then did Ivan Ivanych begin his story, and it was as though not only Burkin and Alyohin were listening, but also the ladies, old and young, and the military men who looked down upon them, calmly and severely, from their gold frames.

"We are two brothers," he began, "I, Ivan Ivanych, and my brother, Nikolay Ivanych, who is two years my junior. I went in for a learned profession and became a veterinary; Nikolay at nineteen began to clerk in a provincial branch of the Treasury. Our father was a *kantonist*,* but he rose to be an officer and so a nobleman, a rank that he bequeathed to us together with a small estate. After his death there was a lawsuit and we lost the estate to creditors, but be that as it may, we spent our childhood in the country. Just like peasant children we passed days and nights in the fields and the woods, herded horses, stripped bast from the trees, fished, and so on. And, you know, whoever even once in his life has caught a perch or seen thrushes migrate in the autumn, when on clear, cool days they sweep in flocks over the village, will never really be a townsman and to the day of his death will have a longing for the open. My brother was unhappy in the government office. Years passed, but he went on warming the same seat, scratching away at the same papers, and thinking of one and the same thing: how to get away to the country. And little by little this vague longing turned into a definite desire, into a dream of buying a little property somewhere on the banks of a river or a lake.

[4]

"He was a kind and gentle soul and I loved him, but I never sympathized with his desire to shut himself up for the rest of his life on a little property of his own. It is a common saying that a man needs only six feet of earth. But six feet is what a corpse needs, not a man. It is also asserted that if our educated class is drawn to the land and seeks to settle on farms, that's a good thing. But these farms amount to the same six feet of earth. To retire from the city, from the struggle, from the hubbub, to go off and hide on one's own farm—that's not life, it is selfishness, sloth, it is a kind of monasticism, but monasticism without works. Man needs not six feet of earth, not a farm,

---

* The son of a private, registered at birth in the army and trained in a military school.

but the whole globe, all of Nature, where unhindered he can display all the capacities and peculiarities of his free spirit.

"My brother Nikolay, sitting in his office, dreamed of eating his own *shchi*, which would fill the whole farmyard with a delicious aroma, of picnicking on the green grass, of sleeping in the sun, of sitting for hours on the seat by the gate gazing at field and forest. Books on agriculture and the farming items in almanacs were his joy, the delight of his soul. He liked newspapers too, but the only things he read in them were advertisements of land for sale, so many acres of tillable land and pasture, with house, garden, river, mill, and millpond. And he pictured to himself garden paths, flowers, fruit, birdhouses with starlings in them, crucians in the pond, and all that sort of thing, you know. These imaginary pictures varied with the [*5*] advertisements he came upon, but somehow gooseberry bushes figured in every one of them. He could not picture to himself a single country-house, a single rustic nook, without gooseberries.

"'Country life has its advantages,' he used to say. 'You sit on the veranda having tea, and your ducks swim in the pond, and everything smells delicious and—the gooseberries are ripening.'

"He would draw a plan of his estate and invariably it would contain the following features: a) the master's house; b) servants' quarters; c) kitchen-garden; d) a gooseberry patch. He lived meagerly: he deprived himself of food and drink; he dressed God knows how, like a beggar, but he kept on saving and salting money away in the bank. He was terribly stingy. It was painful for me to see it, and I used to give him small sums and send him something on holidays, but he would put that away too. Once a man is possessed by an idea, there is no doing anything with him.

"Years passed. He was transferred to another province, he was already past forty, yet he was still reading newspaper advertisements and saving up money. Then I heard that he was married. Still for the sake of buying a property with a gooseberry patch he married an elderly, homely widow, without a trace of affection for her, but simply because she had money. After marrying her, he went on living parsimoniously, keeping her half-starved, and he put her money in the bank in his own name. She had previously been the wife of a postmaster, who had got her used to pies and cordials. This second husband did not even give her enough black bread. She began to sicken, and some three years later gave up the ghost. And, of course, it never for a moment occurred to my brother that he was to blame for her death. Money, like vodka, can do queer things to a man. Once in our town a merchant lay on his deathbed; before he died, he ordered a plateful of honey and he ate up all his money and lottery tickets with the honey, so that no one should get it. One day when I was inspecting a drove of cattle at a railway station, a cattle dealer fell under a locomotive and it sliced off his leg. We carried him in to the infirmary, the blood was gushing from the wound—a terrible business, but he kept begging us to find his leg and was very anxious about it: he had twenty rubles in the boot that was on that leg, and he was afraid they would be lost."

[6]

"That's a tune from another opera," said Burkin.

Ivan Ivanych paused a moment and then continued:

"After his wife's death, my brother began to look around for a property. Of course, you may scout about for five years and in the end make a mistake, and buy something quite different from what you have been dreaming of. Through an agent my brother bought a mortgaged estate of three hundred acres with a house, servants' quarters, a park, but with no orchard, no gooseberry patch, no duck-pond. There was a stream, but the water in it was the color of coffee, for on one of its banks there was a brickyard and on the other a glue factory. But my brother was not at all disconcerted: he ordered a score of gooseberry bushes, planted them, and settled down to the life of a country gentleman.

"Last year I paid him a visit. I thought I would go and see how things were with him. In his letter to me my brother called his estate 'Chumbaroklov Waste, or Himalaiskoe' (our surname was Chimsha-Himalaisky). I reached the place in the afternoon. It was hot. Everywhere there were ditches, fences, hedges, rows of fir trees, and I was at a loss as to how to get to the yard and where to leave my horse. I made my way to the house and was met by a fat dog with reddish hair that looked like a pig. It wanted to bark, but was too lazy. The cook, a fat, barelegged woman, who also looked like a pig, came out of the kitchen and said that the master was resting after dinner. I went in to see my brother, and found him sitting up in bed, with a quilt over his knees. He had grown older, stouter, flabby; his cheeks, his nose, his lips jutted out: it looked as though he might grunt into the quilt at any moment.

"We embraced and dropped tears of joy and also of sadness at the thought that the two of us had once been young, but were now gray and nearing death. He got dressed and took me out to show me his estate.

" 'Well, how are you getting on here?' I asked.

" 'Oh, all right, thank God. I am doing very well.'

"He was no longer the poor, timid clerk he used to be but a real landowner, a gentleman. He had already grown used to his new manner of living and developed a taste for it. He ate a great deal, steamed himself in the bathhouse, was growing stout, was already having a lawsuit with the village commune and the two factories and was very much offended when the peasants failed to address him as 'Your Honor.' And he concerned himself with his soul's welfare too in a substantial, upper-class manner, and performed good deeds not simply, but pompously. And what good works! He dosed the peasants with bicarbonate and castor oil for all their ailments and on his name day he had a thanksgiving service celebrated in the center of the village, and then treated the villagers to a gallon of vodka, which he thought was the thing to do. Oh, those horrible gallons of vodka! One day a fat landowner hauls the peasants up before the rural police officer for trespassing, and the next, to mark a feast day, treats them to a gallon of vodka, and they drink and shout 'Hurrah' and when they are drunk bow down at his feet. A higher standard of living, overeating and idleness develop the most insolent self-conceit in a Russian. Nikolay Ivanych, who when he was a petty official was afraid to have opinions of his own even if he kept them to himself, now uttered nothing but incontrovertible truths and did so in the tone of a minister of state: 'Education is necessary, but the masses are not ready for it; corporal punishment is generally harmful, but in some cases it is useful and nothing else will serve.'

" 'I know the common people, and I know how to deal with them,' he would say. 'They love me. I only have to raise my little finger, and they will do anything I want.'

[7]

"And all this, mark you, would be said with a smile that bespoke kindness and intelligence. Twenty times over he repeated: 'We, of the gentry,' 'I, as a member of the gentry.' Apparently he no longer remembered that our grandfather had been a peasant and our father just a private. Even our surname, 'Chimsha-Himalaisky,' which in reality is grotesque, seemed to him sonorous, distinguished, and delightful.

"But I am concerned now not with him, but with me. I want to tell you about the change that took place in me during the few hours that I spent on his estate. In the evening when we were having tea, the cook served a plateful of gooseberries. They were not bought, they were his own gooseberries, the first ones picked since the bushes were planted. My brother gave a laugh and for a minute looked at the gooseberries in silence, with tears in his eyes—he could not speak for excitement. Then he put one berry in his mouth, glanced at me with the triumph of a child who has at last been given a toy he was longing for and said: 'How tasty!' And he ate the gooseberries greedily, and kept repeating: 'Ah, how delicious! Do taste them!'

"They were hard and sour, but as Pushkin has it,

[8]

> *The falsehood that exalts we cherish more*
> *Than meaner truths that are a thousand strong.*

I saw a happy man, one whose cherished dream had so obviously come true, who had attained his goal in life, who had got what he wanted, who was satisfied with his lot and with himself. For some reason an element of sadness had always mingled with my thoughts of human happiness, and now at the sight of a happy man I was assailed by an oppressive feeling bordering on despair. It weighed on me particularly at night. A bed was made up for me in a room next to my brother's bedroom, and I could hear that he was wakeful, and that he would get up again and again, go to the plate of gooseberries and eat one after another. I said to myself: how many contented, happy people there really are! What an overwhelming force they are! Look at life: the insolence and idleness of the strong, the ignorance and brutishness of the weak, horrible poverty everywhere, overcrowding, degeneration, drunkenness, hypocrisy, lying— Yet in all the houses and on all the streets there is peace and quiet; of the fifty thousand people who live in our town there is not one who would cry out, who would vent his indignation aloud. We see the people who go to market, eat by day, sleep by night, who babble nonsense, marry, grow old, good-naturedly drag their dead to the cemetery, but we do not see or hear those who suffer, and what is terrible in life goes on somewhere behind the scenes. Everything is peaceful and quiet and only mute statistics protest: so many people gone out of their minds, so many gallons of vodka drunk, so many children dead from malnutrition— And such a state of things is evidently necessary; obviously the happy man is at ease only because the unhappy ones bear their burdens in silence, and if there were not this silence, happiness would be impossible. It is a general hypnosis. Behind the door of every contented, happy man there ought to be someone standing with a little hammer and continually reminding him with a knock that there are unhappy people, that however happy he may be, life will sooner or later show him its claws, and trouble will come to him—illness, poverty, losses, and then no one will see or hear him, just as now he neither sees nor hears others. But there is no man with a hammer. The happy man lives at his ease, faintly fluttered by small daily cares, like an aspen in the wind—and all is well. [9]

"That night I came to understand that I too had been contented and happy," Ivan Ivanych continued, getting up. "I too over the dinner table or out hunting would hold forth on how to live, what to believe, the right way to govern the people. I too would say that learning was the enemy of darkness, that education was necessary but that for the common people the three R's were sufficient for the time being. Freedom is a boon, I used to say, it is as essential as air, but we must wait awhile. Yes, that's what I used to say, and now I ask: Why must we wait?" said Ivan Ivanych, looking wrathfully at Burkin. "Why must we wait, I ask you? For what reason? I am told that nothing can be done all at once, that every idea is realized gradually, in its own time. But who is it that says so? Where is the proof that it is just? You cite the natural order of things, the law governing all phenomena, but is there law, is there order in the fact that I, a living, thinking man, stand beside a ditch and wait for it to close up of itself or fill up with silt, when I could jump over it or throw a bridge across it? And again, why must we wait? Wait, until we have no strength to live, and yet we have to live and are eager to live!

"I left my brother's place early in the morning, and ever since then it has become intolerable for me to stay in town. I am oppressed by the peace and the quiet, I am afraid to look at the windows, for there is nothing that pains me more than the spectacle of a happy family sitting at table having tea. I am an old man now and unfit for combat, I am not even capable of hating. I can only grieve inwardly, get irritated, worked up, and at night my head is ablaze with the rush of ideas and I cannot sleep. Oh, if I were young!"

[10]   Ivan Ivanych paced up and down the room excitedly and repeated, "If I were young!"

He suddenly walked up to Alyohin and began to press now one of his hands, now the other.

"Pavel Konstantinych," he said imploringly, "don't quiet down, don't let yourself be lulled to sleep! As long as you are young, strong, alert, do not cease to do good! There is no happiness and there should be none, and if life has a meaning and a purpose, that meaning and purpose is not our happiness but something greater and more rational. Do good!"

All this Ivan Ivanych said with a pitiful, imploring smile, as though he were asking a personal favor.

Afterwards all three of them sat in armchairs in different corners of the drawing room and were silent. Ivan Ivanych's story satisfied neither Burkin nor Alyohin. With the ladies and generals looking down from the golden frames, seeming alive in the dim light, it was tedious to listen to the story of the poor devil of a clerk who ate gooseberries. One felt like talking about elegant people, about women. And the fact that they were sitting in a drawing room where everything—the chandelier under its cover, the armchairs, the carpets underfoot—testified that the very people who were now looking down from the frames had once moved about here, sat and had tea, and the fact that lovely Pelageya was noiselessly moving about—that was better than any story.

Alyohin was very sleepy; he had gotten up early, before three o'clock in the morning, to get some work done, and now he could hardly keep his eyes open, but he was afraid his visitors might tell an interesting story in his absence, and he would not leave. He did not trouble to ask himself if what Ivan Ivanych had just said was intelligent or right. The guests were not talking about groats, or hay, or tar, but about something that had no direct bearing on his life, and he was glad of it and wanted them to go on.

"However, it's bedtime," said Burkin, rising. "Allow me to wish you good night."

Alyohin took leave of his guests and went downstairs to his own quarters, while they remained upstairs. They were installed for the night in a big room in which stood two old wooden beds decorated with carvings and in the corner was an ivory crucifix. The wide cool beds which had been made by the lovely Pelageya gave off a pleasant smell of clean linen. [11]

Ivan Ivanych undressed silently and got into bed.

"Lord forgive us sinners!" he murmured, and drew the bed-clothes over his head.

His pipe, which lay on the table, smelled strongly of burnt tobacco, and Burkin, who could not sleep for a long time, kept wondering where the unpleasant odor came from.

The rain beat against the window panes all night. ✦

A SWIM IN A POND IN THE RAIN

THOUGHTS ON "GOOSEBERRIES"

My first semester as a grad student at Syracuse, one of our professors, the great short story writer Tobias Wolff, gave a reading, one of the first I'd ever been to. Rather than reading from his own work, he read us some Chekhov. He started out with a story called "The Man in a Shell," followed that with "Gooseberries," and closed with "About Love." (These three stories make up what is sometimes called the "Little Trilogy" or the "About Love Trilogy.")

I didn't know much about Chekhov at that point. What I'd read had struck me (lunkhead that I was) as mild and voiceless and swagger-free—a fatal diagnosis at that point in my development.

But in Toby's reading, we could hear how funny Chekhov was, how personable and bright, how closely he was in communication with his audience. It was like being in that earlier-mentioned motorcycle sidecar—wherever the story went, there we went too. We could feel, channeled through Toby, Chekhov's humor and tenderness and slightly cynical (loving) heart. It was like having Chekhov himself there in the room with us: a charming, beloved person who thought highly of us and wanted, in his quiet way, to engage us.

The podium was set up in front of some big windows, and as Toby read, what I remember as the first snow of the year started to fall softly behind him. I felt part of a literary community, finally, a community that included everyone in the room and all the other writers who'd come through the program and Raymond Carver, who'd recently taught there, and Chekhov too; all of us acolytes together in the short story priesthood.

It was, honestly, a bit of a life changer.

At the time I was struggling with all sorts of young-writer questions:

Was writing supposed to be smart or entertaining? Philosophical or performative? Enlightening or fun? Toby's reading of Chekhov answered: Yes, of course, all of those. Suddenly, the potential for fiction as a vital force in the world felt unlimited. It could be *everything:* the most effective mode of mind-to-mind communication ever devised, a powerful form of entertainment, in the highest sense of that word. I suppose part of me had been wondering if the short story was going to be enough—enough for my grandiose ambitions, enough to accommodate my (youthful) ideas about art (that it should speak to everybody, to the best part of everybody, and make life better).

After Toby's reading, I wasn't wondering about the power of the short story anymore. I was just desperate to figure out how to start writing better ones.

All of that to say, "Gooseberries" has a special place in my heart.

On its surface, it's not a story you'd expect to change anybody's life. Nothing much happens in it, really. There's no big culminating action, no active conflict. Nobody's trajectory gets altered forever. Nobody dies or fights or falls in love. It's basically just: two friends, caught in a rainstorm while hunting, shelter at the home of a third friend, where one of them tells a story unsatisfying to the others.

Here's "Gooseberries" in outline:

—Ivan and Burkin, out hunting, walk across a Russian plain.

—Burkin reminds Ivan that Ivan owes him a story.

—It starts to rain.

—They head for the home of Alyohin, a friend who lives nearby.

—There we meet Alyohin and Pelageya, his maid.

—The men go to the bathing cabin.

—Alyohin blackens the water.

—Ivan enjoys his swim (too much, according to Burkin).

—Back at the house, in a cozy drawing room, Ivan tells the promised story, in which:

Ivan's brother, Nikolay, longing for the country life, lives fru-
gally in an effort to obtain it.
Nikolay marries a widow for her money and basically kills her
with his frugality.
Nikolay gets his farm.
Ivan visits the farm.

—There in the drawing room, the memory of that visit causes Ivan
to make a speech:

The happy are an overwhelming force, enabled by the (silent)
unhappy.
The happy need to be reminded that not everyone is happy.
It is now a torment for Ivan to see happiness.
He urges Burkin and Alyohin: Live not for happiness but for
something greater. "Do not cease to do good!"

—Back in the drawing room, Ivan's story is judged a big drag.

—Burkin pronounces it bedtime.

—They go to bed.

Now, one thing we might notice: there's a (rain-caused) digression
that begins toward the bottom of the first page, as Ivan's about to tell
his story, and ends at the top of page 4, two pages later, once he starts to
tell it. Not only is it a digression, it can be popped right out of the story.
Watch—if we cut those pages, the result reads like this:

Ivan Ivanych heaved a slow sigh and lit his pipe before beginning his
story. [TWO-PAGE CUT HERE.] "We are two brothers," he began,
"I, Ivan Ivanych, and my brother, Nikolay Ivanych, who is two years
my junior."

(The seam is invisible.)
This digression is one of those "Things We Couldn't Help Noticing," albeit one that, in fact, we probably actually didn't notice on our
first read. It feels completely natural. It rains, so, of course, Ivan has
to wait to tell his story until they find shelter. We tag along, not real-

izing we're in a digression, just trying, like them, to get somewhere dry.

And yet, there it is: an 82-line digression in a story of 342 lines, representing nearly a fourth of the story's length.

As we've been discussing, the story form makes a de facto case for efficiency. Its limited length suggests that all of its parts must be there for a purpose. We assume that everything, down to the level of punctuation, is intended by the writer.

For now, let's just log that digression as a structural feature of the story (a quirk, a goiter). It's in our TICHN cart, and when we get to the end, we're going to find ourselves looking over at it, asking, "Okay, so what were you *for*?"

You'll recall the technique we applied to Turgenev, useful when trying to get to the bottom of a piece of fiction, of turning our minds to the question "What is the heart of the story?"

Here, because it gets delayed, and because the whole mechanism of the story seems designed to get us to it, we feel Ivan's anecdote about his brother (pages 4–10) to be the heart of "Gooseberries" (its raison d'être, the answer to the Seussian question "Why are you bothering telling me this?").

At the heart of that anecdote (i.e., the heart of the heart of the story) is Ivan's impassioned speech about the nature of happiness, which runs from approximately the bottom of page 8 to the middle of page 10.

It's a radical, startling speech. I'm moved and convinced anew by it every time. "Behind the door of every contented, happy man there ought to be someone standing with a little hammer and continually reminding him with a knock that there are unhappy people, that however happy he may be, life will sooner or later show him its claws, and trouble will come to him." I believe it. And I bet Chekhov believed it, too; the speech feels like it could have come right out of his journal. And because that speech (the heart of the heart of the story) is "about" the question of whether our urge to be happy is to be indulged or resisted, we feel the story to be a sort of meditation on that question. Ivan's conclusion that "there is no happiness and there should be none" hangs, retroactively, over the whole story.

Suddenly, we feel that the story is, or wants to be, "about" happiness.

—

There's a small, surprising moment toward the middle of page 10 when, charmed and convinced by Ivan's story, we find out that Burkin and Alyohin . . . aren't. They've found it boring, this "story of the poor devil of a clerk who ate gooseberries." In that setting (warm, well-fed, drinking tea under portraits of Alyohin's dead relatives), "one felt like talking about elegant people, about women." Why? Because "the very people who were now looking down from the frames had once moved about here, sat and had tea."

Well, of course Burkin and Alyohin wouldn't like it. They're examples of exactly what Ivan's been talking about: concerned only with their own pleasure, all bourgeoisie-clean, having recently stuffed themselves with food someone else cooked. Their reaction proves Ivan's point. The contented and happy just don't *listen*. They don't want to hear anything depressing that might impede their enjoyment.

The men go off to bed ("the wide cool beds which had been made by the lovely Pelageya"). Ivan murmurs one last depressing thing ("Lord forgive us sinners!"), draws the covers over his head, and, presumably, goes off to sleep.

And that's the story.

But, actually, there are two paragraphs left, the first of which, it turns out, changes everything.

That paragraph is this: "His pipe, which lay on the table, smelled strongly of burnt tobacco, and Burkin, who could not sleep for a long time, kept wondering where the unpleasant odor came from."

So, Ivan, that great moral thinker with whom we've been siding, has done a thoughtless thing with a consequence for his friend: Burkin can't sleep because of the stink. Or, more correctly, he can't sleep because of the agitation caused by Ivan's speech and, wide awake, notices the stink.

Ivan's thoughtlessness complicates our feelings about him. "Do not cease to do good!" exhorted the guy so worked up by the sound of his voice that he neglected to enact common courtesy. ("Do not cease to do good"? Clean your pipe, Mr. Big Shot.) Is Ivan's speech still true? Well, yes. And yet, we feel, suddenly, that it isn't, quite. Or it's somehow suspect, coming from a source unable to take its own advice—a speech about leading a thoughtful life from someone who's just acted thought-lessly.

In what we felt as the conclusion of the heart of the heart of the story, Ivan pronounced that "there is no happiness and there should be none."

How do we feel about that now?

I find myself scanning back through the story, looking for: "Happiness, Things About." That is, looking for places that might shed light on the question "Happiness: Pro or con?"

Like, for example, that outbreak of swimming on page 3.

That was *Ivan,* we now remember with a touch of pleasant incredulity, bursting out of the bathing cabin, plunging, during a rainstorm, into a river* described as looking "cold and unkind," Ivan who, with the energy of his swimming, "raised waves on which white lilies swayed," who, like a kid, kept diving to touch the bottom, then swam joyfully across to have a friendly chat with some peasants—the same Ivan who just gave us the big irate lecture on the evils of happiness.

So, is he for happiness or against it?

His speech notwithstanding, it seems that Ivan is still susceptible to happiness and, in fact, seems to crave it more, and be more in touch with it, than either of his friends.

Maybe he's so against it because he's so for it?

Does this revised reading ("Ivan is actually, sometimes, energetically *for* happiness") override the earlier one ("Ivan is against happiness")? No. The two readings coexist, making a truth bigger than either would have alone.

The story just got enlarged. It is, yes, still about the possible deca-

---

* The Russian word here is *plyos*. A Russian friend tells me this is an archaic word, not much used anymore, a noun related to the verb *pleskat'ya,* which means "to produce the sounds of splashing or lapping." *Plyos* can refer to a stretch of open water, the region of a river between bends, or the part of a reservoir where the water is the deepest. This word is rendered as "pool" or "the reach" in other translations I have at hand, and I seem to remember it being expressed as "pond" somewhere or other (maybe in the translation Toby read from all those years ago). At any rate, it's always been a pond in my mind: no current, cold, calm, reed-lined, peaceful, deep, surrounded by pine trees.

dence of happiness, but it's also now about how trivial it is to hold a one-dimensional opinion. Or how impossible it is. Ivan doesn't really believe that happiness is bad, or, if he does, he also, at the same time, believes that it's essential.

So, in light of the smelly pipe reveal, Ivan's speech now reads a little differently.

What seemed on first read a virtuous cry on behalf of the oppressed ("Look at life: the insolence and idleness of the strong") now seems kind of . . . grumpy. He doesn't like the strong but isn't all that crazy about the weak either: "Look at . . . the ignorance and brutishness of the weak." The whole place (the earth) is, per Ivan, a mess: "horrible poverty everywhere, overcrowding, degeneration, drunkenness, hypocrisy, lying." His speech now seems not just anti-happiness but sort of anti-*everything* (anti-*life*). He says (on page 9) that he, too, used to "hold forth on how to live." But he's doing that right now: telling Burkin and Alyohin (and us) how to live. His virtuous takedown of happiness seems touched with a bit of emotional bolshevism: thou shalt not be happy, as I have deemed it sinful. Or: you may be as happy as I consider it healthy for you to be.

He gets heated (looks "wrathfully" at his friend Burkin), makes a forced, not-quite-logical leap to the idea of the futility of waiting for progress ("Why must we wait?"), and then there's a slight bump at the pronoun "you," at the bottom of page 9, with "You cite the natural order of things." Ivan is addressing an objection made not by Burkin or Alyohin but by some imaginary critic in his head.

Rather than an insightful moral thinker, moved by the intimacy of the evening to share a hard-won insight with two dear friends, Ivan now sounds (sounds *also*) like a frustrated old man: fed up and venting, unaware of the fact that he's boring his (captive) audience.

To the extent that we're still wondering about the mild structural goiter that is the digression, we may now be feeling that the digression was, in a sense, necessary; it "allowed" that swimming scene, which, in turn, produced these complications in our understanding of Ivan.

But the swimming scene isn't the only thing enabled by the digression.

In there we also meet the maid, Pelageya, and the landowner, Alyohin.

—

Whenever Pelageya appears in the story, she's described through the same narrow, appearance-emphasizing lens (as "beautiful," "soft," "delicate," "pretty"; as "stepping noiselessly" while "smiling softly"; as "lovely" and then "lovely" again); her purpose seems to be to represent undeniable beauty. Or: to serve as an embodiment of pointless loveliness. Ivan and Burkin's reaction to her proves that no one is immune to an outburst of startling loveliness; they are made instantly more alive just by seeing her. Pelageya is a human version of that refreshing pond. She is unexpectedly beautiful, in that household—more beautiful than we expect her to be, more beautiful than she needs to be. She is, in short, a source of gratuitous delight, a reminder that beauty is an unavoidable, essential part of life; it keeps showing up and we keep responding to it, our theoretical positions notwithstanding, and if we ever stop responding to it, we have become more corpse than person.

The moment when Pelageya stops Ivan and Burkin in their tracks with her good looks is, for my money, the best proof of a character's beauty in all of literature. ("Once in the house, the two visitors were met by a chambermaid, a young woman so beautiful that both of them stood still at the same moment and glanced at each other.") Chekhov tells us nothing about her (no hair length, no height, nothing about her body, or her perfume, or the color of her eyes, or the shape of her nose) and yet the fact that she stuns these two presumably well-mannered old farts into borderline rudeness causes me to see her, or create her, in my mind.

"Yes, happiness can be self-indulgent, and our pursuit of it can oppress others," she seems to say, "but, on the other hand, none of us can live a moment without joy and beauty and pleasure, as proven, gentlemen, by your reaction, just now, to me." She makes us feel, viscerally, how joyless and pedantic and brittle it would be to deny that beauty is real or claim that happiness is best avoided.

Her presence causes the story to issue a caution, even as it sincerely asks whether happiness is morally justifiable: "Careful not to neglect the reality of positive emotions in your quest for moral purity."

Ivan and Burkin's reaction to her seems so involuntary as to be beyond critique—the equivalent of an audible gasp at a fireworks show. What kind of person suppresses that gasp?

Can we really live without happiness?

Do we want to?

But she has another, complicating purpose: she's the one doing all the dang work. She runs inside to fetch the towels and soap and then, while the men are bathing, lays out the gowns and slippers, dashes back and makes the tea and puts the jam on a plate and carries it out, then runs back and presumably makes up the beds in the guest room, and so on. Her presence supports Ivan's position that "the happy man is at ease only because the unhappy ones bear their burdens in silence, and if there were not this silence, happiness would be impossible." Why does she have to work so hard to get these men comfortable so they can sit around discussing the extent to which the pursuit of happiness is valid?

What about Alyohin? He seems to have withdrawn from the world, seeks no pleasure. And yet he's happy, or happy enough. He has a quiet integrity, is a sort of anti-Ivan: alert to what pleasures there are (an evening of stories with friends), free of the need to pontificate or philosophize. He's also a sort of anti-Nikolay: he farms, we feel, for the "right" reasons (not to satisfy some petty, gooseberry-related ambition or be exalted by his peasants but to do some honest work in the world). He doesn't talk down to his peasants like Nikolay but works alongside them. A form of honorable happiness is possible, his presence says, if one dedicates oneself quietly to a task—no bliss, just quiet satisfaction.

On the other hand, his life is . . . sad. It has a tragic, resigned quality. His dirtiness and the fact that he lives in the (lowly) stewards' quarters suggest that something has shut down in him, that he has lost some of his vitality by forgoing aspiration. He's what happens to a person who gives up on happiness: he becomes lost and badly tended and lives, somehow, beneath his potential.

Another item enabled by the digression: Burkin's grumpy reaction to Ivan's swimming.

Burkin functions as a sort of anti-joy, stolidity-enforcing referee, putting the brakes on Ivan whenever Ivan gets too enthusiastic. In addition to yanking Ivan out of the water, he interrupts his giddy story about the cattle dealer whose leg got cut off ("That's a tune from another opera") and ends the night prematurely ("However, it's bedtime") when it seems that Ivan and Alyohin would be happy to stay up and keep talking.

Nobody likes a killjoy. Then again, Ivan's joy could use some killing. He makes Burkin and Alyohin wait on the shore while he swims for too long, takes up the whole evening giving a lecture that nobody wants to hear (and fails to notice their boredom), and that smelly pipe is the (selfish) residue of another narcissistic indulgence: he's happily smoking it even as he inveighs against pleasure and happiness.

On the other hand, Burkin is (also) a (different kind of) bummer. We feel him resisting the truth at the core of Ivan's speech: happiness oppresses. It's the Burkins of the world (those stolid, unimaginative reactionaries, who swim for exactly the right length of time and enjoy it exactly the correct amount) who keep the big, evil machine rolling. What's keeping Burkin awake there at the end is *the bitter truth,* which, like that smelly pipe, is not always pleasant. The Burkins of the world prefer their truth to be flattering and palatable so they can sleep right through it. A smelly pipe is sometimes necessary to get their attention—a by-product of the passion required to proclaim difficult truths, a sort of necessary collateral damage.

On the other, other hand: Burkin is not, actually, kept awake by the pipe but by the aftereffects of Ivan's speech. And this, maybe, speaks well of him. Though he at first tries to deny Ivan's truth, it gets inside him and agitates him and won't let him sleep. So maybe he's heard Ivan after all.

There's one more thing the digression allows into the story: the rainstorm itself.

Before the storm, Ivan and Burkin, observing the landscape, are happy ("both of them thought what a beautiful land it was"). Then the rain comes and, soon enough, they're "silent as though they were cross with each other."

Let's first just notice this as a structural module, a pair of before-and-after photographs.

Before: The weather is great, the world is beautiful, they're happy.

After: The weather goes bad, the world goes ugly, they're mad.

The storm introduces into the story the notion that happiness exists in relation to material conditions, conditions beyond our control. It's not always within our power to choose to be happy. Happiness is a gift, a conditional gift. We'd best accept it when it comes. Feeling happy can be a valuable tool, a necessary condition for doing good. (It's hard to "Do good!" or even "Feel okay!" when you're "cold and messy and uncomfortable through and through.") And isn't it nice (doesn't it refresh us and increase the possibility that we might be able to do good in the world, wouldn't we be foolish to refuse the empowering uplift) when we come in from the rain to find the beautiful Pelageya bringing us towels and soap and dressing gowns and slippers and tea?

The rain functions in the story like a side character: it continues to fall as the men bathe, then disappears until the story's last line, when it makes a final appearance: "The rain beat against the window panes all night." Rain has been a source of unhappiness (as they hiked), a source of happiness (falling on them as they swam in the pond), and now provides a persistent, low-level, nagging reminder of . . . well, something. To be in touch with the complex beauty of the story, try writing out what it is that the rain is "reminding" you of (or "saying" to you or "representing") as it taps on the window there at the end. It's not just one thing. It's many things at once. And it's personal; even if I could articulate my answer (I've tried several times and each time have deleted the result, finding it reductive and insufficient), my answer would not be yours, precisely.

Luckily, we don't have to say.

That's part of why the story was written: to produce that irreducible final moment, about which nothing more needs to be said.

Here's a version of what the story would look like without the digression:

In the bright sunlight, Ivan tells the story of his brother to (just) Burkin as they cross some non-rain-dampened fields. Ivan's final supplication ("There is no happiness and there should be none, and if life has a meaning and a purpose, that meaning and purpose is not our happiness but something greater and more rational. Do good!") is addressed to just Burkin. Night falls, the slightly disappointed Russian stars twinkling down, wishing, like Burkin, that Ivan's story had been better.

What's lost?

Well, as we've said (and in order this time): the rainstorm, Alyohin, Pelageya, the swimming, Burkin's reaction to the swimming.

In this digression-free version, Ivan lays out his case against happiness and there's nothing in counterweight. The result is an unchallenged lecture from Ivan with a simple takeaway: "Happiness—not as great as you think."

A lecture worth hearing, but not the complex experience that is "Gooseberries."

If we understand the story to be asking, "Is it right to seek happiness?" the material contained within the digression splinters that question into others: "If we choose to disavow happiness, what do we lose?" "Is life to be lived for pleasure or duty?" "How much belief is too much?" "Is life a burden or a joy?" And many more that I'm sure your mind supplied as you read or is supplying now, as we work through the story.

The digression, which all this time has been sitting there in our TICHN cart, has now, we might say, fully justified itself.

The story turns to us and says, "See why I had to indulge in that digression? To give myself some space in which to self-complicate, and thus avoid being merely a one-dimensional position paper against happiness, and become something mysterious and beautiful that, no matter how many times you read it, will keep revealing new dimensions to you, many of which George is entirely missing in this essay." *

Now, my claim that the digression justifies itself by yielding complicating elements might be said to be tautological, since the digression is pretty much all the story *is*, save Ivan's speech about his brother and the short post-speech epilogue on the last two pages. (Where else could

---

* Let's decide, for example, that the story isn't about happiness but *extremism*—guess what? It is. Look at how many extremists are in it: Ivan is extreme in his condemnation of happiness and in his enthusiasm for swimming. He has to be called out of the water by Burkin, that extremist for moderation. Nikolay is, of course, a gooseberry extremist, and Alyohin an extreme ascetic. Is Pelageya an extremist? Well, she's extremely pretty and an extremely hard worker. Is the story for extremism or against it? Yes. And we can do the same trick with other notions. (Try "duty," try "passion," try "suppression.")

the story find that stuff, but in the digression that constitutes so much of its length?) Also, I might seem to be implying something (that I have no way of knowing) about how the story was written: that Chekhov first wrote Ivan's speech and then purposely framed it with the pre- and post-speech material, to complicate it.

But regardless of how the story came to be, part of the pleasure of reading it lies in this: what we first felt as waste or indirectness (the digression) turns out to be exactly what elevates the story "out of the plane of its original conception" and makes it so complex and mysterious. What at first seemed like a digression is understood to be beautifully efficient.

A story means, at the highest level, not by what it concludes but by how it proceeds.

"Gooseberries," as we're seeing, proceeds by a method of persistent self-contradiction. If one aspect of it seems to be expressing a certain view, a new aspect of it will appear and challenge that view.

The story is not there to tell us what to think about happiness. It is there to help us think about it. It is, we might say, a structure to help us think.

In what way does that structure want us to think?

Well, how does *it* think?

It thinks via a series of "on the other hand" statements. "Ivan is against happiness; on the other hand, he sure does enjoy swimming." "Alyohin is living such an admirably calm and excess-free life; on the other hand, he darkened the water with self-neglect." "Ivan's passion is selfish; on the other hand, Burkin's continual efforts to moderate Ivan are annoying." "Having a passion for something as trivial as gooseberries is weird; on the other hand, at least Ivan's brother loves something, even if it's just a type of berry, although, on the other, other hand, at least Alyohin never frugalitied anyone to death." And so on.

Another way of saying this: the story seems to want its reader to stay off autopilot, to stay alert to the possibility that it (and the reader) might be solidifying around some too-simple concept and in the process becoming false. So, it keeps qualifying itself until it qualifies itself right out of the business of judgment. We keep trying to get to a place of stability, to understand the story as being "for" or "against" something, so we can be for or against that thing too. But the story keeps insisting that it would rather not judge.

It's hard to be alive. The anxiety of living makes us *want* to judge, be sure, have a stance, definitively decide. Having a fixed, rigid system of belief can be a great relief.

Wouldn't it be nice to just decide to live as an anti-happiness zealot? Disallow yourself all pond swimming, frown whenever you meet a Pelageya. Completely consistent, you'll never need to be confused again. You can just stalk around, having sold your bathing suit, looking down your nose at everything.

For that matter, wouldn't it be nice to just throw down on the side of being happy? To decide to live life as an ardent pro-happiness advocate, always striving to celebrate, dance, have fun, maximize your joy? But then, before you know it, you're an obnoxious turd on Instagram, standing in a waterfall with a garland of flowers, thanking God for blessing you with this wonderful life you must have somehow earned via your immaculate mindfulness.

As long as we don't decide, we allow further information to keep coming in. Reading a story like "Gooseberries" might be seen as a way of practicing this. It reminds us that any question in the form "Is X right or wrong?" could benefit from another round of clarifying questions.

Question: "Is X good or bad?"

Story: "For whom? On what day, under what conditions? Might there be some unintended consequences associated with X? Some good hidden in the bad that is X? Some bad hidden in the good that is X? Tell me more."

Every human position has a problem with it. Believed in too much, it slides into error. It's not that no position is correct; it's that no position is correct for long. We're perpetually slipping out of absolute virtue and failing to notice, blinded by our desire to *settle in*—to finally stop fretting about things and relax forever and just be correct; to find an agenda and stick with it.

What I admire most about Chekhov is how free of agenda he seems on the page—interested in everything but not wedded to any fixed system of belief, willing to go wherever the data takes him. He was a doctor, and his approach to fiction feels lovingly diagnostic. Walking into the examination room, finding Life sitting there, he seems to say, "Wonderful, let's see what's going on!" It's not that he didn't have strong opinions (his letters are proof that he did). But in his best stories (and here I'd include, in addition to the three in this book, "The Lady with the Pet Dog," "In the Ravine," "Enemies," "About Love," and "The Bishop") he seems to be using the form to move *beyond* opinions, to destabilize the usual ways we go about formulating them.

If he has a program, it's being wary of having a program.

"My holy of holies," he wrote, "is the human body, health, intelligence, talent, inspiration, love, and absolute freedom—freedom from violence and falsehood, no matter how the last two manifest themselves."

He was criticized for this perceived lack of a political or moral stance. Tolstoy's early assessment: "He is full of talent, he undoubtedly has a very good heart, but thus far he does not seem to have any very definite attitude toward life."

But this quality is what we love him for now. In a world full of people who seem to know everything, passionately, based on little (often slanted) information, where certainty is often mistaken for power, what a relief it is to be in the company of someone confident enough to stay unsure (that is, perpetually curious).

His health was bad (he died at forty-four, of tuberculosis), his family was affectionate but needy, he became famous young and people were constantly bothering him with requests. But through it all, he stayed gentle, seemed glad to be alive, tried to be kind. "He felt discretion," Troyat wrote, "to be a sign of breeding; decent people did not make a display of their misfortunes." He lived a short, frenetic life full of offhand generosity. He read and commented on any and all manuscripts sent to him, gave free medical treatment to anyone who needed it, and financed hospitals and schools all over Russia, many of which still exist today.

This feeling of fondness for the world takes the form, in his stories, of a constant state of reexamination. ("Am I sure? Is it really so? Is my preexisting opinion causing me to omit anything?") He has a gift for reconsideration. Reconsideration is hard; it takes courage. We have to deny ourselves the comfort of always being the same person, one who arrived at an answer some time ago and has never had any reason to doubt it. In other words, we have to stay open (easy to say, in that confident, New Age way, but so hard to actually do, in the face of actual, grinding, terrifying life). As we watch Chekhov continually, ritually doubt all conclusions, we're comforted. It's all right to reconsider. It's noble—holy, even. It can be done. We can do it. We know this because of the example he leaves in his stories, which are, we might say, splendid, brief reconsideration machines.

One more thought on Ivan's speech.

Many young writers start out with the idea that a story is a place to express their views—to tell the world what they believe. That is, they understand the story as a delivery system for their ideas. I know I felt that way. A story was where I got to set the world straight and achieve glory via the sheer originality of my advanced moral positions.

But, as a technical matter, fiction doesn't support polemic very well. Because the writer invents all the elements, a story isn't really in a position to "prove" anything. (If I make a dollhouse out of ice cream and put it in the sun, it doesn't prove the notion "Houses melt.")

In a "young" story we feel the writer in there, witty, superior, entirely correct, often in the guise of some tormented but attractive character returned from an enlightening overseas trip, looking over, eyebrow raised, at all these other dopes who make up his culture. This has led to a general (and, I think, correct) notion that a writer's beliefs should be kept out of his or her story.

Though maybe it's a question not of *if* a belief is represented in a story but of *how*—of what use is made of it.

Ivan's speech is the stuff of an excellent essay: articulate, earnest, precisely expressed, supported with examples, infused with sincere intent. That's why we believe it and why we're moved by it. But then Chekhov makes double use of the speech by *attributing it* to Ivan. When Ivan, speaking through Chekhov, diverges from Chekhov (when, on page 9, he gets heated and cranky and inexact), Chekhov lets this be ("It's not me, it's him") and allows the story to react to that new Ivan. Noticing this new aspect of Ivan he's just discovered, Chekhov tracks him into that "big room in which stood two old wooden beds," asking,

"What might a person in such a state (agitated, frustrated, just having delivered a passionate speech that fell flat) do next?" And discovers an answer: "He might thoughtlessly forget to clean his pipe, then, spent, fall asleep."

This allays our suspicion that the story is merely the occasion for an authorial lecture. Chekhov has it both ways: he gets the power of his heartfelt opinion (the truth of which we feel), destabilized by its attribution to Ivan (whose flaws we note).

If I'm writing in a character's voice and he or she suddenly blurts something out, is that "me"? Well, sort of. That blurt came out of me, after all. But is it really "me"? Do I "believe" it? Well, who cares? There it is. Is it good? Any power in it? If so, it would be crazy not to use it. That's how characters get made: we export fragments of ourselves, then give those fragments pants and a hairstyle and a hometown and all of that.

Having made a character in this way, we can take a step back, look a little askance at "him." Any consequences to believing that way? Any suspicious overtones in what "he" just said? Any collateral damage anticipated? Latent unforeseen consequences? (Any smelly pipes?)

I was once writing a scene in a story ("Victory Lap") in which a teen-aged girl was waiting for her mother to pick her up and take her to dance class. I'd gotten tired of writing violent, hyperdramatic stories and had decided to write something nice, like Chekhov's "After the Theatre," in which nothing much happens except a sweet sixteen-year-old sits around thinking giddily about love in a way so much like a real sixteen-year-old might think that it makes the reader sixteen and happy by association. But somehow, her whole future life is in there too; the reader feels the forty-year-old woman she'll someday become.

So I decided to do something . . . like that. Only, when I tried it, it was no good. It was a chatty inner monologue, anecdotal, static, nothing at stake. But in there was something interesting. At one point, channeling my arrogant sixteen-year-old self, who regarded all adult dysfunction (addiction, divorce, adultery—all those late-seventies maladies, you know) as mistakes that could be easily rectified if only adults would decide to be *better,* I'd blurted out the following, in her voice: "To do good, you just have to decide to do good. You have to be brave. You have to stand up for what's right."

Did I believe that? Well, I *had* believed it, once upon a time. I didn't believe it as I wrote it, as a fifty-one-year-old. But as soon as she said it, it was *her* saying it, not me, and an opportunity for plot appeared.

Her: "To do good, you just have to decide to do good."

Story: "Oh, really?"

The story was now going to have to challenge her current (my former) facile belief.

I won't ruin the story for you if you haven't read it, but suffice to say, my desire to write a sweet, nonviolent story got upended by my stronger desire to write a story that a reader might finish.

Any idea we express is just one of many we have within us. In daily life, of course, we choose to identify with, and endorse, and live by, and fight for certain of those ideas and dampen others that, nevertheless, we're capable of imagining: vestigial traces of philosophies we embraced when young but have since rejected (hello, Ayn Rand), the strange voices in which we used to speak, ideas that we disagree with politically and that make us uncomfortable when we find traces of them within us.

If you're a pro-immigration person, are there anti-immigrant feelings down there inside you? Of course: that's why you get so emotional when arguing for immigrants' rights. You're arguing against that latent part of yourself. When you get mad at a political opponent, it's because he's reminding you of a part of yourself with which you're uncomfortable. You could, if forced, do a decent imitation of an anti-immigrant person. (Similarly, that angry anti-immigration advocate is railing against his inner leftist.)

Mostly we walk around identifying with one set of opinions and assessing the world from that position. Our inner orchestra has been instructed that certain instruments are to dominate, others to play softly or not at all. Writing, we get a chance to change the mix. Quieter instruments are allowed to come to the fore; our usual blaring beliefs are asked to sit quietly, horns in their laps. This is good; it reminds us that those other, quieter instruments were there all the time. And that, by extrapolation, every person in the world has his or her inner orchestra, and the instruments present in their orchestras are, roughly speaking, the same as the ones in ours.

And this is why literature works.

—

There's a lovely moment in Henri Troyat's biography of Chekhov, describing the first time Chekhov and Tolstoy met. Chekhov had put off the meeting, feeling "reticent about bowing before the redoubtable prophet, the Tolstoy who insisted on denying scientific progress to promote progress of a spiritual nature."

But on August 8, 1895, Chekhov traveled to Tolstoy's home, Yasnaya Polyana, to meet the great man.

"They met on a beech-lined path leading to the house," Troyat writes. "Tolstoy was wearing a white smock and had a towel over his shoulder; he was on his way to bathe in the river. He invited Chekhov to join him. The two men undressed and jumped in, and they had their first conversation in a state of nature, paddling neck-deep through the water. Tolstoy's simplicity won him over to the point that he all but forgot he was face to face with a monument of Russian literature."

We might imagine the whole of "Gooseberries" contained in that swim: Tolstoy playing a kind of condensed Ivan, making grand, strict, moral pronouncements while also delightedly paddling around naked; Chekhov playing Burkin (resisting Tolstoy's passionate generalizing); both of them playing Alyohin (hard workers taking a break). And come to think of it, Chekhov was also playing a version of Ivan, embodying both his sanctimonious and his celebratory sides: he came to judge Tolstoy but found himself loving him, and later would write, "I am afraid of Tolstoy's death. If he were to die, there would be a big, empty place in my life. To begin with, because I have never loved any man as much as him." Chekhov died first, however, in 1904, and when he did, Tolstoy wrote, "I never knew he loved me so much."

Three years after their swim, in 1898, Chekhov wrote "Gooseberries."

AFTERTHOUGHT #6

The stories we're reading here are among the best their authors ever wrote. But these authors also wrote lesser ones, and it's important to read those too, if only to remind ourselves that nobody hits it out of the park every time, and that a masterpiece might have three or four test runs behind it, in which the artist was working some things out.

Allow me to offer two exercises to explore this idea, one from Russian literature and one from film.

When he was young, Tolstoy was a passenger in a sled that got lost in a snowstorm. The party drove for twenty straight hours, through the night, before finding shelter. Not long after, he wrote a story based on this experience, called "The Snowstorm." Forty years later, he used that same material to write "Master and Man." To read those two stories in sequence is to get a glimpse of what Tolstoy had learned about narrative in the intervening forty years.

Second, there's a boxing sequence in an early Charlie Chaplin short called *The Champion*. Sixteen years later, Chaplin put a very similar sequence in *City Lights*.

So, the exercise is:

Having recently read "Master and Man," now read "The Snowstorm."

Watch, in either order, the boxing sequence in *City Lights* and the corresponding sequence in *The Champion*.

Let the later work resonate against the earlier one.

What I think you'll find is that the later works feel like more highly organized systems.

In "The Snowstorm," Tolstoy's aim seems to be to document the actual event. The point is that the getting lost in the storm *happened.* None of the characters stand for anything or do anything that indicates character. They get saved by chance. There are some fine things in it (the main character, afraid that he's freezing to death, dozes off and has a dream of summertime, for example, and the descriptions of the storm and the horses are dazzling), but the story has none of the drama of "Master and Man," and it doesn't seem to be saying anything in particular about human beings, except that, this one time, some of them got lost.

Compared to the corresponding sequence in *City Lights,* the fight in *The Champion* feels saggy and static. It's working hard—there's lots of jumping around that seems improvised. The younger Chaplin is using early versions of the same gags that will later show up in *City Lights,* but they keep getting repeated and it doesn't seem to have occurred to him yet to arrange these into a tight, escalatory pattern, as he'll later do wonderfully in *City Lights*.

So, to generalize a bit here: in a highly organized system, the causation is more pronounced and intentional. The elements seem to have been more precisely selected. Things escalate decisively; everything is to purpose.

A more highly organized system is just, you know, better.

The obvious question for the artist, then, is: How do I get my system to be more highly organized?

If you gather ten writers in a room, ranging from the great to the bad, and ask them to put together a list of the prime virtues of fiction, you won't get much disagreement. It turns out, there *is* such a list of prime virtues, one we've been casually compiling as we've worked our way through these Russian stories: Be specific and efficient. Use a lot of details. Always be escalating. Show, don't tell. And so on. The respective craft talks of those ten writers will all involve some restatement/personalization of those prime virtues, plus or minus a few, with some likable variation in the anecdotes they use to sing the praises of those virtues and claim that they always faithfully work by them.

But anyone can google "how to hit a curveball" and be informed that a hitter must "identify the spin" and "hit the bad ones but let the good ones go by" and so on, and we can all be yapping about that on our way to the batting cage, but once we get there, we'll find that, nevertheless, some of us can hit a curveball and some of us can't.

The difference between a great writer and a good one (or a good one and a bad one) is in the quality of the instantaneous decisions she makes as she works. A line pops into her head. She deletes a phrase. She cuts this section. She inverts the order of two words that have been sitting there in her text for months.

Five writers might be sitting in a row at a long table in the same café, all believers in specificity, but at the moment of truth, some of them will find a charming way of being specific and others won't.

So, that's harsh.

But it's also freeing. It narrows the number of things we have to worry about down to just one: the moment when, reading a line of our work, we decide whether to change it.

We can reduce all of writing to this: we read a line, have a reaction to it, trust (accept) that reaction, and do something in response, instantaneously, by intuition.

That's it.

Over and over.

It's kind of crazy but, in my experience, that's the whole game: (1) becoming convinced that there is a voice inside you that really, really knows what it likes, and (2) getting better at hearing that voice and acting on its behalf.

"There is something essentially ridiculous about critics, anyway," said Randall Jarrell, a pretty good critic himself. "What is good is good without our saying so, and beneath all our majesty we know this."

Right.

We *do* know.

Or: we know for us, *for now.* Tomorrow it may be different. And so, today, we boldly make the change (or don't). And the beauty of it is, we get to pass this way again tomorrow, and the next day, and the day after that, and read that sentence again, and leave it alone or change it again, and we can even change it back again to what it was at the very beginning.

We do this repetitively until a decision has been reached, and the way we know a decision has been reached is that that place stops changing.

—

So, what we're calling a "more highly organized system" is the cumulative result of all of this repetitive choosing on the line level, those thousands of editing microdecisions. (That apartment I gave you in New York, once you've done those two years of discretionary shopping, during which you kept replacing what was there with what you preferred? That's going to be one highly organized system.)

Let's say this passage shows up to open your story: "The sun fell into Ann's window with a force that, lying in bed, she keenly felt on her wrist as she went to answer the phone. It was so early. Who could be calling so early? Outside there was a truck or bus going by."

Well, there's work to be done, but what work? What offends you about that passage? What do you like? Let's fancily call your system of preferences your "editing basis." Well, get to it. Apply your editing basis. You'll find out everything there is to know about yourself as a writer by what you feel like doing to that swath of prose.

What I feel like doing is cutting to the chase: "Jesus. Who could be calling so early?" my story might begin. Per my editing basis, the sun coming in and the truck/bus going by aren't important, because the sun causes a problem with the sentence it's in (by falling "with a force") and the truck or bus is a cliché feature of every city street scene (which makes me feel, "Blah, get out of my story"). So, my editing basis tells me to run away from the whole idea of the sun coming in, and cut the truck/bus. But another writer might like the way that "sun coming in a window" and "person in bed" combine in her mind. She might feel like straightening that phrase out, so it lands better: "The sun fell into Marie's window and across her arm, with a warmth just short of burning." Another person might feel like doing this: "Outside, truck or bus. Dreaming, Marie knew the truck or bus to be Greg, but as the ringing phone woke her, she came out of her dream to realize, no: Greg, neither truck nor bus, was still in Dallas . . ." Or whatever. The point is: if you start with that sad little swath of prose and then begin (to use another fancy technical term) "energetically messing with it," per exactly your taste (no defense or rationalization needed), it will start to become a more highly organized system. It just will. And it will have something of you in it. It will, potentially, have a lot of you in it, nothing *but* you in it. It's being organized per your taste, after all. Maybe you value speed or clarity; maybe you resist speed and like to slow things down. Maybe "clarity" feels, to you, like oversimplification. My point is that it's not the flavor of your taste that matters; it's the intensity with which you apply your taste that will cause the resulting work of art to feel highly organized.

Maybe you've seen a mixing board in a recording studio, with rows of fader switches. A story can be thought of as a version of that mixing board, only with thousands of fader switches on it—thousands of decision points.

Let's say that, in a story, Mike has to borrow money for his son's operation and goes to ask his father for it. A fader switch appears, labeled "Mike's Relationship with His Father." If they're very close, that's one story; if they haven't spoken in twenty years, that's another. The writer has to choose where to set that fader switch. "Mike's Father Himself" is another fader switch. He might be wealthy and generous, say, or wealthy and frugal (or poor and frugal, or poor and generous).

Within this model, we might say that a writer has to do two things: create the fader switch in the first place (stumble on the moment when Mike thinks of appealing to his father and leave that moment in) and then *set* that switch. He has to decide which of the myriad versions of Mike's father is the one he wants in his story.

And here, let me slightly adjust my metaphor. That mixing board is designed not to record music but to flood a room with beautiful, high-intensity light. Every adjustment of any one of those thousands of fader switches will subtly change the quality and intensity of light in that room. In a perfect story, every switch is set just right, and the light in there couldn't get any brighter or more beautiful.

In this model, revision is the process of going through a story again and again, microtuning the adjustment of the existing fader switches and introducing new ones as needed (maybe Mike's mom has a role?). Every time you move one of those switches even a fraction of an inch, the system gets slightly more highly organized, and has more of you in it, and the light in the room gets more beautiful. (Well, that's actually true only for the *good* decisions. But since we're going to be deciding over and over again, we assume that, eventually, all our decisions will be good ones.)

I like what I like, and you like what you like, and art is the place where liking what we like, over and over, is not only allowed but is the essential skill. How emphatically can you like what you like? How long are you willing to work on something, to ensure that every bit of it gets infused with some trace of your radical preference?

The choosing, the choosing, that's all we've got.

ALYOSHA THE POT

Leo Tolstoy

(1905)

ALYOSHA THE POT

———

Alyosha was the younger brother. He was called "Pot" because one time his mother sent him to take a pot of milk to the deacon's wife and he tripped and broke the pot. His mother gave him a beating and the boys began to tease him with the name "Pot." Alyosha the Pot—that was his nickname from then on.

Alyosha was a skinny, lop-eared boy (his ears stuck out like wings) with a big nose. The boys used to tease him: "Alyosha has a nose like a dog on a hill!" There was a school in the village, but writing didn't come easy for Alyosha and, besides, there wasn't that much time for study. The older brother worked for a merchant in town, so Alyosha had to help his father from the time he could walk. Six years old and he was already watching after the sheep and the cow in the pasture with his baby sister, and a little older he was looking after the horses day and night. By the time he was twelve he was plowing and driving the wagon. He wasn't strong but he knew how to do things. He was always in a good mood. The boys would laugh at him and either he would keep quiet or he would laugh, too. When his father yelled at him he kept quiet and listened. And the minute the yelling stopped he smiled and went on with whatever it was he had to do.

Alyosha was nineteen when his brother got drafted. So his father fixed it for Alyosha to get his brother's old job as hired man with the merchant. They gave Alyosha his brother's old boots and his father's cap and jacket and took him to town. Alyosha was tickled pink with his new clothes, but the merchant didn't like the way Alyosha looked.

"I thought I was going to get a man to take Simon's place," said the merchant, looking Alyosha up and down, "and what's this snot-nose supposed to be? What good is he to me?"

"He can do anything—he can hitch up a team and go get stuff and he works like crazy. He just looks puny but you can't wear him out."

"Well, looks like I'll have to find out."

"And the main thing is, he'll never give you any back talk. He'd rather work than eat."

"Oh, what the hell. Leave him here."

So Alyosha began to live at the merchant's.

[2] The merchant didn't have a big family. There was his wife, his old mother, and his oldest son, married, who didn't finish school, was in the business with his father; and the other boy had a good education, finished school and went to college before they threw him out, and he lived at home; and then there was a daughter, a high-school girl.

At first they didn't like Alyosha. He was just too much of a peas-ant. His clothes were terrible and he didn't know how to behave and didn't even know what Russian to use for people above his level. But before long they got used to him. He was an even better worker than his brother. It was the truth that he never talked back, because they sent him to do everything, and he did everything right that minute, very willingly, never even rested between one job and the next. And at the merchant's it was just like at home—they piled everything on Alyosha. The more he did the more they all piled things on him. The merchant's wife, and his mother, and his daughter, and his son, and the steward, and the cook, all sent him here, there, and yonder; do this and do that. All you could hear was, "Run, get this," or "Aly-osha, take care of this," or "Alyosha, don't tell me you forgot!" or "Alyosha, make sure you don't forget!" And Alyosha was forever running and taking care of things and looking after things and he never forgot and managed it all and kept on smiling.

It wasn't long before he wore out his brother's boots and the boss let him have it for walking around with his boots falling apart and his toes sticking out, and he ordered some new boots for him in the market. The boots were new and Alyosha was thrilled to have them, but he had the same old feet, and toward evening they were killing him and he was mad at the boots. Alyosha was afraid that when his father came to collect his week's pay he'd be mad about the merchant taking the boots out of the pay.

In the wintertime Alyosha would get up before dawn, chop the firewood, sweep the yard, and feed and water the cow and the horse. Then he would light the stoves, shine the shoes, brush the boss's clothes, set the samovars going after he'd cleaned them, and then the steward would call him to move some merchandise or else the cook would set him to kneading dough and cleaning pans. Then they'd send him to town with a note for somebody, or to fetch the daughter at her school, or to get some lamp oil for the old lady. And there'd always be somebody to say "Where the hell have you been so long?!" Or, "Why should you bother? Alyosha will run get it. [3] Alyosha! Oh, Alyosha!" And Alyosha ran to get it.

He would grab a bite to eat when he could, and it was a rare thing for him to be back in time to eat with the rest of them at night. The cook would yell at him for not being on time, but she still felt sorry for him and put aside something hot for him to have at dinner and supper. There was really a lot of work to get ready for the holidays and during the holidays. And Alyosha really loved the holidays, because during the holidays he would get tips—not a whole lot, about sixty kopecks, but still it was his own money. He could spend it however he wanted to. As for his week's pay, he never laid eyes on that. His father would come in and pick that up and all Alyosha heard from him was complaining about how fast he was wearing out boots.

When he'd saved up two rubles from his tips, he took the cook's advice and bought himself a red knitted jacket, which when he put on he couldn't keep a straight face he was so happy.

Alyosha never said much and when he did say something it always came out in short, broken pieces. And if ever they told him to do something or asked him *could* he do so and so, why, he'd say "Sure" before they were hardly finished and he'd start doing it and do it.

He didn't know a single prayer. His mother had taught him some but he'd forgotten them all, but he still prayed, mornings and evenings, prayed with his hands, and crossed himself.

That's how Alyosha lived for a year and a half, and then sud-

denly, in the second half of the second year, something happened to
him that had never happened before in his life. This something was
that he found out, to his amazement, that besides those connections
between people based on someone needing something from somebody else, there are also very special connections: not a person having to clean boots or take a parcel somewhere or harness up a horse,
but a person who was in no real way necessary to another person
could still be needed by that person, and caressed, and that he, Alyosha, was just such a person. This he learned from the cook, Ustinya.
Ustinya was an orphan, young, who worked just like Alyosha. She
started feeling sorry for Alyosha and Alyosha felt for the first time
that he—he himself, not his work—but he himself was needed by
[4] another person. When his mother felt sorry for him he didn't even
notice because it seemed to him that was the way it was supposed to
be—it was just the same as him feeling sorry for himself. But here
all of a sudden he saw that this Ustinya, no kin to him at all, felt
sorry for him anyway, and would leave him some buttered cereal in
the pot and then prop her chin on her bare arm and watch him while
he was eating it. And he would glance at her and she would start
laughing and then he would start laughing.

This was so new and strange that at first Alyosha was afraid. He
felt like this might stop him working the way he used to work. But
he was happy anyway, and when he looked at his pants that Ustinya
had mended he'd shake his head and smile. Often when he was
working or on the way somewhere he'd remember Ustinya and say,
"Oh, yes, Ustinya!" Ustinya helped him out whenever she could
and he helped her. She told him about herself, how she'd lost both
her parents, how an aunt had taken her in, how she'd got this job in
town, how the boss's son had tried to talk her into doing something
stupid and how she'd cut him dead. She loved to talk and he liked
listening to her. He heard that in cities it often happened that peasants who'd been hired as workers got married to cooks. And one
time she asked him if they were going to marry him any time soon.
He said he didn't know but that he didn't feel like being married to
a country girl.

"Oh? You have your eye on somebody?" said she.

"Well, I'd marry you. Would you?"

"Well, listen to Pot! Pot comes right out with the question," said Ustinya, and gave him a little poke in the back with her hand. "Why wouldn't I?"

At Shrovetide his old man came to town to pick up his wages. The merchant's wife had learned that Alyosha had taken it into his head to marry Ustinya, and she didn't like it. "She'll get pregnant and what good will she be with a kid?" she told her husband.

The boss turned over Alyosha's money to his father.

"How's my boy doing? All right?" said the peasant. "I told you he wouldn't talk back."

"Well as far as back talk goes I don't get any back talk, but he's up to some foolishness. Got the idea he's going to marry the cook. But I won't have the help marrying. That doesn't suit us."

[5]

"Why that fool . . ." said his father. "Don't you give it another thought. I'll tell him to forget the whole thing."

His father went into the kitchen and sat down at the table to wait for his son. Alyosha was out running errands and came back all out of breath.

"I thought you had some sense, and now what are you thinking of?" said his father.

"Nothing . . . I . . ."

"What, nothing? You were thinking of getting married. I'll marry you off when the time comes, and I'll marry you to a fit woman, not one of these town sluts."

His father talked for a long time and Alyosha stood there and sighed. When his father was finished Alyosha smiled.

"Well, we can just forget it."

"That's right."

When his father had gone and left Alyosha alone with Ustinya (who had been standing behind the door and heard everything the father said to the son), he told her:

"Looks like our plan won't work. You hear? He got mad, won't let me."

She began to weep quietly into her apron.

Alyosha said, "Tch. Tch."

"Have to mind him. Looks like we have to forget about it."

That night when the boss's wife called him to close the shutters, she said, "Well, you going to obey your father and forget that nonsense?"

"Looks like I have to," said Alyosha with a laugh, and then he began to cry.

From that time on Alyosha never mentioned marriage to Ustinya again and went on living the way he had before.

One day during Lent the steward sent him to clean the snow off the roof. He climbed up on the roof, cleaned it all off, and had started clearing the frozen snow out of the gutters when his foot slipped and he fell with his shovel. Unfortunately he did not fall in the snow but onto an iron roof over a door. Ustinya and the boss's daughter ran up to him.

[6]

"Alyosha, are you hurt?"

"A little. It's all right."

He tried to stand up but he couldn't and began to smile. They carried him into the yardkeeper's lodge. The doctor's orderly came. He examined him and asked him where it hurt.

"It hurts all over, but it's all right. Just so the boss don't get mad. Better send tell Daddy about it."

Alyosha lay in bed for two days and on the third day they sent for the priest.

"You aren't going to die, are you?" Ustinya asked.

"What do you think—we live forever? Have to die sometime . . ." said Alyosha, speaking quickly as always. "Thanks, Ustinya, for being nice to me. See—it's better they wouldn't let us get married, it'd all be for nothing. Now everything's fine."

He prayed with the priest but only with his hands and his heart. In his heart was the thought that if it's good down here when you do what they tell you and don't hurt anybody, then it'll be good up there too.

He didn't talk much. He just kept asking for water and looked like he was amazed at something.

Then something seemed to startle him and he stretched his legs and died. ✦

THE WISDOM OF OMISSION

THOUGHTS ON "ALYOSHA THE POT"

A character starts out a proper noun—a stick figure we load with attributes. With the first word of this story, we know there's a person named Alyosha. Then he trips and falls, breaking a pot. For this, he gets beaten by his mother and teased by the other boys and given a nickname, "Alyosha the Pot."

A kid has started to appear.

Furthermore, he's "skinny" and "lop-eared," with a big nose ("a nose like a dog on a hill" or, in another translation, by A. S. Carmack, "a nose like a gourd on a pole"). In either case, not the nose one would choose—but we like him for that nose, poor little guy. He's not a natural student, and anyway there isn't time for school. He's a worker, one of the hardest workers in all of literature: helping his father "from the time he could walk," a shepherd at six, plowing by twelve.

In the second paragraph, our stick figure gets fleshed out: skinny kid, big nose, hard worker, slight outcast. We could imagine someone, also the object of abuse and a funny-looking hard worker, who's mean as hell. But that's not Alyosha: "He was always in a good mood." Then Tolstoy tells us the exact flavor of that "good mood" (of all the good moods in the world, which type of good mood is he always in?): when the other boys laugh at Alyosha, he either goes silent or laughs along with them; when his father yells at him, he goes silent and listens. This is a very specific kid, different from the one who, say, fights back when the other boys make fun of him or who, after being yelled at by his father, makes faces behind his back. What Alyosha does after his father is done yelling, is: smiles, then gets back to work.

Like Olenka in "The Darling," Alyosha may at first strike us as a sort of cartoon, if we apply that word without pejorative overtones. Alyosha is presented with the complicating frequencies filtered out, winnowed down to just one trait. In this story, simple as a fairy tale, that trait is cheerful obedience.

And we like him for this. Already the story is saying something like "There are, in this world, people whose lives, from beginning to end, are sheer drudgery. How should such a person live?" Alyosha represents a position we've all taken from time to time. "Since I have to get through this, I'll try my best to do it happily." It's a valid position. Imagine yourself at some school function, but no chairs have been put out. Here comes a little guy with a big nose. "I can help!" he says, and gets to work, and is energetic and smiling and efficient. Over in the corner is his little Goth pal, moping, pretending to be on his cellphone. Who do you like more? Who's lived that moment better?

Once our stick figure has been fitted with a defining attribute, the story goes about putting that attribute to the test. "Once upon a time, a cheerfully obedient boy went out into the world." And that's what Alyosha does, there at the bottom of the first page, as the rising action begins: he goes to the home of a merchant, to whom his father has basically rented him out.

There, more abuse. He's not a man but a "snot-nose," per his new boss. Does his father defend him? Well, sort of, but in the same way he might defend a horse he's trying to sell: "He just looks puny but you can't wear him out." And the merchant's family doesn't like Alyosha either—he's uncouth, a real peasant.

In a story, attribute must meet adversity. (Olenka, in "The Darling," is an extreme one-man woman; then that man dies. Vasili, in "Master and Man," is arrogant; a blizzard appears, to humble him.) Here, the family's reception of Alyosha is a minor, introductory adversity. How will Alyosha respond? By doing what he's always done: cheerfully working hard. He doesn't talk back, does everything immediately and "willingly," never rests. Does this approach work? Yes. He becomes indispensable to the household. Are they grateful? Not really. They just pile on more work. He is "forever running and taking care of things and looking after things and he never forgot and managed it all and kept on smiling." So, this is a repetition of the first beat of the story but in a slightly higher-risk setting. Even here, on this larger stage, at this merchant's fancy house, his approach works. At home, he worked hard and smiled and was "rewarded," with this job. Now he applies the same work-and-smile approach. Will he again be rewarded?

He will, in a bit, with Ustinya's love.

But first, at the bottom of page 2, another adversity: his boots fall apart.

And we find out something new about him. (Notice that, in its quiet way, the story has been steadily telling us new things about him with every paragraph.) When his boots wear out and he gets a new pair, he worries that his father will be angry that the merchant has deducted the cost of the boots from his pay. The first hint of a question appears over the story: "Might there be a downside to Alyosha's cheerful obedience? Is he, maybe, *too* obedient?" That is, our sense of fairness tells us that he is being ill-used but his sense of fairness doesn't. We diverge a bit from him. What we felt as a positive trait is now being called slightly into question.

He has no desires, or only very meek ones. He loves the holidays, because he gets tips (his father collects his salary). With his tips he buys "a red knitted jacket" that makes him happy—so happy he can't "keep a straight face" (or, in the Carmack translation: "so surprised and delighted that he just stood in the kitchen gaping and gulping").

So, Alyosha, though humble, has a capacity for happiness and a need for it and, this being a masterpiece of extreme economy, this capacity, once introduced, must be used.

Soon, "something happened to him that had never before happened in his life." What is this thing?

> This something was that he found out, to his amazement, that besides those connections between people based on someone needing something from somebody else, there are also very special connections: not a person having to clean boots or take a parcel somewhere or harness up a horse, but a person who was in no real way necessary to another person could still be needed by that person, and caressed, and that he, Alyosha, was just such a person.

Compare that (by Clarence Brown) to Carmack's version:

This experience was his sudden discovery, to his complete amaze-ment, that besides those relationships between people that arise from the need that one may have for another, there also exist other relationships that are completely different: not a relationship that a person has with another because that other is needed to clean boots, or run errands or to harness horses; but a relationship that a person has with another who is in no way necessary to him, simply because that other one wants to serve him and to be loving to him. And he discovered that he, Alyosha, was just such a person.

Pevear and Volokhonsky have it like this:

This event consisted in his learning, to his own amazement, that be-sides the relations between people that come from their need of each other, there are also quite special relations: not that a person needs to have his boots polished, or a purchase delivered, or a horse har-nessed, but that a person just needs another person for no reason, so as to do something for him, to be nice to him, and that he, Alyosha, was that very person.

You might take a few minutes here to compare these three versions, just to give yourself a sense of the distance that can exist between good translations, and the extent to which choices on the level of the phrase create the world of the story. (Three different Ustinyas are made in these translations: one who causes Alyosha to feel that he could be "needed . . . and caressed," another who "wants to serve him and to be loving to him," and a third who needs Alyosha around "so as to do something for him, to be nice to him.")

But this may be a particularly challenging passage. Brown had this to say about translating it: "When Alyosha first awakens to the no-tion of disinterested sympathy, of plain human fondness, the thought is so astonishing that Tolstoy's syntax collapses into a kind of hash; this is an image of Alyosha's almost languageless mentality groping toward a new idea. Most translators thwart Tolstoy by rendering this story in a style suitable for the drawing rooms of *War and Peace*. I have tried to be as low, simple, and even ungrammatical as the original."*

The story is written in the indirect third person, and this is still the Tolstoyan narrator telling the story, but Alyosha's consciousness is seeping in around the edges. Why did Tolstoy write it like this? To be more truthful. Alyosha is stumbling toward a new truth and the only tool he has to use is his own limited language.

It's not much of a stretch from what Tolstoy does with Alyosha's voice here to what Woolf would soon do in *To The Lighthouse* (and Joyce in *Ulysses* and Faulkner in *The Sound and the Fury*). Tolstoy has reached an understanding that would pervade modernism: a person and her language can't be separated. (If you want to know my truth, let me tell it to you in my words, in the diction and syntax natural to me.)

So, Alyosha falls for Ustinya, who gives him the gift of realizing that he is more than just the value he provides; even if a person doesn't need you to perform a task, she might still need *you*. She might like you and enjoy your company and want to be good to you. This is a radical idea to him—no one, other than his mother, has ever made him feel this way before. Is he happy about this? Well, yes, but also: "This was so new and strange that at first Alyosha was afraid." Through the dialogue passage at the bottom of page 4, Alyosha proposes to Ustinya. To mark the occasion, she either (1) gives him "a little poke in the back with her hand" or (2) performs (per Carmack) the ritual Russian proposal-acceptance ceremony of "cuffing him playfully on the back with her ladle." (A Russian friend assures me that there is no ladle involved; instead, as in the Pevear and Volokhonsky version, she accepts the proposal while "slapping him in the back with a towel.")

Their joy is short-lived; his father shoots the idea down immediately, and one of the most painful things in the story is the reveal that, as the

---

* A translator is a stylist. And a stylist is a translator, translating a mental image into the perfectly evocative phrase. Those of us who aspire to be stylists can learn something about what we value stylistically by making efforts at translation, even if we don't speak the language in question. See Appendix C for an exercise.

father is calling Ustinya a "town slut," Ustinya is standing right there behind the door, hearing the whole thing, including Alyosha's failure to stand up for her.

"Looks like our plan won't work," Alyosha meekly tells her. "You hear? He got mad, won't let me."

Ustinya starts to cry. Alyosha doesn't comfort her or vow to go back to his father and plead their case but only clucks his tongue at her (in the Pevear and Volokhonsky translation), which Brown renders as "Tch. Tch." That is, he urges her not to make too much of it.

They will, he says, "have to mind" his father.

At this moment, a contemporary reader looks over at Alyosha, disappointed. He seems weak and deficient. His supposedly positive trait seems like a character flaw. Is his cheerful obedience actually habitual passivity? Evidence not of humility but of a limited imagination? A knee-jerk response to authority? A sort of working-class flinch?

That night, the merchant's wife checks in. Is Alyosha going to "forget that nonsense?"

"Looks like I have to," he says in the Brown translation.

"Yes. Of course, I've forgot it," he says in the Carmack.

"Seems I have," he says in the Pevear and Volokhonsky.

Then he tries to do what he always tries to do (stay cheerful). In two translations, he "laughed." In one he "smiled." But then, in all three, he departs from his usual peppiness and bursts into tears.

That is, he "began to cry" (Brown)," "immediately began weeping" (Carmack)," or "all at once wept" (Pevear and Volokhonsky).

Had Alyosha responded to the merchant's wife in his usual style (" 'Looks like I have to,' Alyosha said with a smile, then bounded out of the room because there was work yet to be done") we would have felt this as a repeated beat, a failure of escalation: Alyosha continuing to be what he's always been.

But this bursting into tears narrows the path of the story. Alyosha does, in fact, feel the unfairness of what his father has done, is aware that he's failed to defend Ustinya. It's not the case that Alyosha is a simpleton, with no feelings, not the case that he has no desires or ego. He *does* want things, and *can* love, and *can* be hurt.

We're in new territory now. So is he. For the first time in his life, his obedient cheerfulness has cost him something, and he knows it.

We wait to see what this is going to cause him to do.

Well, the story says, nothing: "From that time on Alyosha . . . went on living the way he had before." We doubt this is true. We hope it isn't. Actually, we know it isn't. If something causes a lowly servant to burst into tears in front of the lady of the house, that thing is not going to just go away. It might be denied or suppressed, but it doesn't vanish. Even if he continues living the same life outwardly, inside something has changed.

Injustice has caused something to coil up in the story, and now we long for the uncoiling.

We're less than a page away from the ending. As it rushes up, look how attentively we're scanning the text for an answer to the question the story has made us ask: "What is Alyosha going to do about that injustice?" (Or "How is the injustice Alyosha has experienced going to come home to roost?")

Let's pause and consider the possibilities. There's a version of the story in which Alyosha returns to his life and outwardly lives "the way he had before" but is inwardly bitter. Then that bitterness begins to take a toll: he talks back to the merchant's daughter, say, gets fired, turns to drink. There's a variant of that in which his bitterness causes him, finally, to confront his father. There's a variant in which the bitterness never causes anything, and finally dissipates to a manageable level. Not the most dramatic variant, admittedly, but it's possible, and it happens to real people all the time, and this seems the variant Alyosha is fated to live.

But then Tolstoy does something smart: he knocks Alyosha off that roof. This has the effect of forcing all of the psychic consequences of the broken engagement to play out within a compressed time frame. If Alyosha is going to act on that disappointed energy, he's only got the remainder of this last page in which to do it.

"Alyosha the Pot" is in the lineage of Gogol's masterpiece "The Overcoat," in which a poor and humble clerk aspires to a new coat for the winter. In both stories, a nonentity springs briefly to life: Alyosha through his feelings for Ustinya, Akakii Akakievich by acquiring the new overcoat and then, showing uncharacteristic brio, wearing it out to a party. Both men are punished severely for the hubris of presuming to be fully human. Alyosha falls off that roof. Akakii's coat is stolen as he makes his way home from the party, and while trying to recover it, he is shouted at so harshly by a bureaucrat to whom he's turned for help (an "important personage") that he essentially dies from the shock of it.

Akakii's fatal dressing-down is understood as a natural continuation of a lifetime of petty abuse. Alyosha's tumble off the roof is not *caused by* anything, really. "His foot slipped and he fell with his shovel." He just dies by chance, in a manner equivalent to, say, being hit by a falling tree. (Or does he? I always feel his fall as a kind of suicide-by-agitation—not intentional, but somehow in response to the incident with his father, the sort of thing the body unconsciously does when, for example, we're distracted and become clumsy. His father has mastered him, locked him into a state of perpetual adolescence, and so Alyosha, regarding the frozen plain that is about to be the rest of his life, subconsciously opts out.)

In any case, the fall speeds up the time frame in which our question ("What is Alyosha going to do about that injustice?") will be answered.

Alyosha dies not because he falls off a roof but because Tolstoy, at this late point in his art, knows what it is that we want to know and aims to give it to us as quickly as possible.

As Alyosha lies there in the snow, Ustinya asks if he's hurt. Obviously, he is: he's fallen hard enough to make it impossible for him to stand. He's going to die within a few days, likely of internal bleeding. He is hurt, he admits, "A little," but adds, "It's all right." He tries to stand, can't. His response? He smiles. Or, actually, he "began to smile" (or, in Carmack, "just smiled"). Why does he smile? Is this a meaningless, automatic response to hardship that he learned to perform years ago? An act of suppression? An attempt to comfort Ustinya? Or is he so good, so simple, that even now he still feels actually happy and is smiling genuinely?

In "The Overcoat," Akakii's coiled rage finds an outlet: he becomes a ghost, stalking the bureaucrat who disrespected him. At this late moment in "Alyosha the Pot," we may find ourselves wondering: Does Alyosha even *have* any coiled rage?

Kurt Vonnegut used to say that part of what makes *Hamlet* so powerful is the fact that we don't know how to understand the ghost of Hamlet's father: Is it real or only in Hamlet's mind? This infuses every moment of the play with ambiguity. If the ghost is imaginary, it's wrong for Hamlet to kill his uncle. If real, it's necessary that he do so. That ambiguity is part of the play's power.

Here, something similar is happening. We observe Alyosha maintaining cheerful obedience in all situations, even now, as he lies mortally wounded in the snow. What we don't know is *how* he's doing that. Is he feeling all the things we would feel in that situation but forcibly suppressing them? In the past, when Alyosha was tired and his feet hurt and he'd just completed a difficult task and gotten no gratitude for it and then another task was heaped on him, did he notice? Was there ever an instant of internal complaint? Or was there not? These are two different people (one who sometimes internally complains, one who never does).

Which is Alyosha?

He lies in bed for two days and on the third day the priest is called.

"You aren't going to die, are you?" asks Ustinya. (Another Russian friend translates this as "What now, are you gonna die or something?")

Nobody lives forever, Alyosha says, we all have to go eventually. It's as if he can't allow himself to be sad or frightened. Or, if he is sad or frightened, he can't allow himself to be honest about it. He thanks Ustinya for "being nice" to him ("feeling sorry" for him in Carmack, "pitying" him in Pevear and Volokhonsky) and concludes that it was better they didn't get married after all; nothing would have come of it and now "everything's fine."

Wait, *is* it? we wonder. Is everything really "fine"? Might the fact of the marriage have altered all that came afterward? Isn't Alyosha sort of rushing to this positive assessment?

Here, with three short paragraphs left, we're waiting for Alyosha to acknowledge the injustice he's just suffered (the crowning glory of a life full of such injustices). (Personally, I'd like to see him sit up in bed and chew out his father and apologize to Ustinya and call for the priest to marry them right then and there, in front of the merchant and that whole crappy, demanding family.) Each unit of text still lying there in front of us represents a place where Alyosha might protest or push back.

We're allowed one last glance into Alyosha's mind before he dies.

Is the protest in there?

No.

Brown: "In his heart was the thought that if it's good down here when you do what they tell you and don't hurt anybody, then it'll be good up there too."

Carmack: "And in his heart he felt that if he was good here, if he obeyed and did not offend, then there all would be well."

Pevear and Volokhonsky: "And in his heart was this: that, as it is good here, provided you obey and do not hurt anyone, so it will be good there."

(Another Russian friend offered this literal translation: "And in his heart he had that, like it is good here if you obey and don't offend, it will be good there as well.")

He still, apparently, sees nothing wrong with the way he's lived. Just as he brought his meek way of doing things from his house to the merchant's house, he plans to bring his meek way of doing things to wherever he's headed next—that is, he hopes, the afterlife.

And off he goes.

He didn't talk much. He just kept asking for water and looked like he was amazed at something.

Then something seemed to startle him and he stretched his legs and died.

Anything in there that might indicate some last-minute recognition on Alyosha's part? My eye goes to the phrases "looked like he was *amazed* at something" and "something seemed to *startle* him."

What is it that amazes/startles him?

The Brown translation we're using (quoted above) seems to say that while looking amazed at something, he is then startled; that is, he is startled out of an ongoing state of amazement. This is echoed in other translations.

Carmack:

He said little. He only asked for something to drink and smiled won-deringly. Then he seemed surprised at something, and stretched out and died.

Pevear and Volokhonsky:

He spoke little. Only asked to drink and kept being surprised at something.

He got surprised at something, stretched out, and died.

That is, in those translations, he's surprised by two different things, in sequence.

A former student of mine, fluent in Russian, and his wife, a native speaker, and a Russian poet they consulted, and my former student's tutor in Russian, who is a linguist, all agree that this is a tricky bit of translation. The "asking for a drink" and the "being surprised" that occur in the penultimate line, they tell me, should be understood to be happening repetitively over a period of time; Alyosha doesn't ask for a drink just once, and he is being surprised, over that same period of time, by a number of things, not just one. Then, in the final line, one of those things leaps out and surprises him most of all. (As my former student put it, he is "surprised, not once, not even twice, it seems, but multiple times, and then one last time.")

My former student, his wife, the poet, and the linguist offered me the following collective version of those last two lines:

He was only asking for something to drink and was being periodi-cally surprised by things.

One of those things surprised him, he stretched out and died.

We've been waiting, we're still waiting, for Alyosha to be dislodged from his position of total passivity.

Now, we feel, it may have happened.

So, the question is: What is that one last thing that surprises him there at the end?

—

For many years, I taught the story this way: "What surprises Alyosha in his last moments is the sudden realization that he has lived too submissively. He should have stood up for himself and for Ustinya. Tolstoy doesn't say this, exactly, but the story is a masterpiece of understatement, and (impelled by the strong emotion generated by the breaking off of the engagement, which is still fresh in our minds, since it happened just one page ago) we put two and two together and feel that, as he leaves the world, Alyosha sees things as we do: he could have been loved, he could have been a full human being."

These days, I'm not so sure.

At one point, another student of mine challenged this view by pointing out that it contradicts Tolstoy's aesthetic and moral position at the time of the story's writing (1905). And there's something to this. Toward the end of his life, according to the Slavic studies scholar Ewa Thompson, Tolstoy was "determined to forswear the 'nonsense' of his former style and to make all of his fictional works conveyances for the message of the Christian teaching as he understood it." He valued simplicity in style ("Look how wonderfully the peasants tell a story," he said to Gorky. "Everything is simple. Few words, but much feeling. True wisdom needs few words—like 'God have mercy'") and believed the teaching of morality to be the true function of art.

So, is it possible that Tolstoy intended us to read the story as a simple praise of Alyosha, who, even in the face of death, and over the course of his whole life, enacted radical Christian humility—a sad story, on the human level, but ultimately a story of the triumph of simplicity and faith?

One way to read Alyosha is as an example of what is called, in Russia, a "holy fool." A person, in the words of (yet another) Russian friend,* "utterly ruled, or led, by God." Someone who, as described by Richard Pevear, "lives and dies with a purity and inner peace that forever eluded

---

* It may seem like I have a lot of Russian friends, but really there are just three, each lovely, helpful, and generous. I am very grateful to Luba Lapina and Yana Tyulpanova (both of the Moscow English Literature Club) and Valeriy Minukhin, for their insights and for their patience with my many inquiries about this story.

Tolstoy and most of his characters." For such a person, the state of "being cheerful" is, in itself, a valid spiritual aim. To keep one's heart full of love, no matter what, is a profound spiritual accomplishment, a form of active faith in God's essential goodness.

Since so much can happen that is beyond our control, let us control our minds, and let the roiling world do its thing, as we stay above it, full of love, love for things just as they are, subjugating the self, the self that is a temporary fiction anyway.

"I have decided to stick with love," Martin Luther King, Jr., said. "Hate is too great a burden to bear." And we feel that this is the conclusion Alyosha's life has brought him to as well. (Or maybe he was born with this conclusion already in his heart.)

In his last novel, *Resurrection,* Tolstoy wrote, "If once we admit—be it only for an hour or in some exceptional case—that anything can be more important than a feeling of love for our fellows, then there is no crime which we may not commit with easy minds. . . . Men think there are circumstances when one may deal with human beings without love. But there are no such circumstances. . . . If you feel no love, sit still. Occupy yourself with things, with yourself, with anything you like, only not with men. . . . Only let yourself deal with a man without love . . . and there are no limits to the suffering you will bring on yourself."

The aspiration, then, is to never fail in love, and if this requires that we sacrifice the normal, protective concerns of the ego, so be it.

In this, Alyosha succeeds. We might see him as a sort of simple genius of love. He doesn't speak or think a hateful word in the whole story or, as far as we're told, his whole life.

So that's good, right?

Per this reading, then, what is it that surprises Alyosha as he dies?

Let's try a quick scan back over the story, asking, "Has the concept of 'amazement/being startled' occurred anywhere else?" Well, it has: back in the scene on page 4 where Alyosha had his life-changing realization about Ustinya. There we find the word "amazement." (That moment with Ustinya and this one on his deathbed represent the two major surprises of Alyosha's short life, as far as we know.)*

---

* A third, smaller surprise occurs on page 3, when he first puts on that new red jacket.

So, we associate the two incidents: whatever surprised him here at the end may be (ought to be) a species of whatever it is that surprised him back on page 4.

What surprised him there?

Alyosha was startled to find that there was such a thing as love, and that he could be the object of it; that someone could care about him, just as he is—not expecting any work from him, just loving him unconditionally.

Our minds try this out: Might he, on his deathbed, be startled to find that there exists an even greater form of this sort of love (that is, God's love) and that he is the object of it? That is, might he be feeling the universal form of that which he received earlier from Ustinya? (That would make a person smile "wonderingly.")

Seen this way, it's a radical, slightly troubling story: "Once a man was meek and no matter what happened to him or who ran roughshod over him he just stayed meek and in the end that was just the right way to live and because of this he was welcomed into God's love."

It's troubling, but it makes a kind of sense as a possible solution to a timeless dilemma, the dilemma of how to deal with evil in the world: Don't let it mess with your love.

The problem with this reading is that it lets assholes stay assholes. Alyosha's father, for example. Alyosha's passivity enables his father to continue to regard Alyosha as a beast of burden. Wouldn't it have been better, for Alyosha, to assert himself? Wouldn't it have been better *for his father*? Might this have been seen as an act of compassion, by Alyosha, one that might have caused the scales to fall from his father's eyes? ("Ah, my son is a human being, deserving of my respect. I never would've realized this, had he not corrected me. I will henceforth live differently.") It might not have had this effect, of course, but if Tolstoy wants us to understand Alyosha as a superstar of selfless love, then Alyosha should have at least tried pushing back against his father; to have not done so, we feel, was a failure of love.

Alyosha also fails in love, to my way of thinking, by allowing Ustinya to stand, undefended, behind that door, and then by consigning her, through his meek acquiescence, to a life without him, a man she apparently loves. And he leaves her unconsoled at the end, offering her, as he dies, only dishonest bromides.

Alyosha, then, takes the eternal advice of the powerful to the powerless: Suck it up, be cheerful. Don't worry, be happy.

And Tolstoy seems to approve of that message.

So, this "Alyosha is admirably passive" reading lands a little uncomfortably on a contemporary reader.

Is it possible that Tolstoy wrote the story to mean one thing ("Hail, Alyosha, you humble saint!") but that we understand it now to mean another ("Too bad, Alyosha, you excessively passive victim"), because we have, in the years since the story was written, become more attuned to the suffering of the unfortunate and less susceptible to religious traditions that ask suffering people to suffer silently?

Well, maybe, but according to my friend the writer Mikhail Iossel, the discomfort we feel with the "Hail, Alyosha!" ending may be exactly what Tolstoy intended; he meant to surprise/rankle/discomfit a secular reader, to make him see how conventional and reflexive and ultimately ineffective our habitual way of reacting to a tormentor (i.e., fighting back) is—in other words, he meant it as a provocation.

Fighting back is the way we humans have always responded to perceived enemies. To do otherwise is considered weak.

But how has that worked out for us?

A few great hearts have urged a different way. Tolstoy is saying, maybe, that Alyosha is just such a (rare, spiritual) person.

Was Jesus not serious when he said, "Love your enemies, bless those who curse you, do good to those who hate you, and pray for those who mistreat you and persecute you"? Did Gandhi not mean it when he said, "Forgiveness is the attribute of the strong"? Was the Buddha being facetious when he said, "Hatred does not cease by hatred, but only by love; this is the eternal rule"?

Well, I *am* provoked, but not satisfied.

If Tolstoy really means for me to accept Alyosha as a moral role model, I feel he's designed the guy badly. That is, the position of passive resistance—or, as it happens, nonresistance—that Alyosha occupies, he occupies too willingly, too early, and toward too trivial an object: he could easily push back against his father and still remain well within Christian principles. Christ did not, on finding that there were money-lenders in the temple, meekly walk out, full of love. What he did was trash the joint, full of love. And later, to establish the principle of un-conditional love at the highest level, he said, of his murderers, as he was dying, "Father, forgive them, for they know not what they do." He did not say, "It's fine, all is well, nobody has done anything to offend me." To forgive them, Christ had to know and admit that they were killing him. Alyosha doesn't seem, even now, to feel that any wrong has been done to him. Maybe he sincerely hasn't noticed? But I remember that bursting into tears. He noticed *that* injustice, for sure. And his failure to acknowledge it feels more evasive than saintly. He seems not like a moral avatar but like someone incapable of self-assertion—depressed, maybe, or simple.

In fact, Richard Pevear, in his introduction to *The Death of Ivan Ily-ich and Other Stories,* tells us that there was an actual Alyosha, em-ployed on Tolstoy's estate, a young man Tolstoy's sister-in-law thought of as "an ugly halfwit."* One of my Russian friends tells me that, read-ing the story in Russian, the reader feels that Alyosha is "mentally dis-abled." We can imagine Tolstoy anthropologically regarding such a person and projecting onto him certain virtues dear to Tolstoy himself; we can also imagine Tolstoy omitting, or perhaps not considering, some of the hardships such a person might have experienced, mistak-ing a cheerful aspect for a peaceful interior.

But let's say that the fictive Alyosha (Alyosha the character) is a per-son of limited mental capacity. His humble approach to life, then, may be the best he can manage. Since it's beyond his capacity to imagine

---

* In a different translation, by a group imposingly calling itself "The Russian Translation Project of the American Council of Learned Societies," this sister-in-law, Tatyana Kuzminskaya (the model for Natasha in *War and Peace*) wrote: "The assistant cook and porter was a semiidiot . . . who, for some reason or other, was ro-manticized in such a way that reading about him I didn't recognize our own inno-cent and malformed Alyosha the Pot. As far as I remember him, he was a quiet, harmless man, who uncomplainingly carried out everything that was required of him."

sticking up for himself or defying authority, he has decided or has learned to obey cheerfully, and to assume that there's wisdom in authority, and in this way has been able to find his place in the world. His simple moral program (do what they tell you and don't hurt anybody) could be worse; there are mentally limited people with far more ambitious and nastier agendas.

So maybe Tolstoy isn't telling us all to live like Alyosha; maybe he's just observing this one person, Alyosha, with tenderness and admiration?

But I don't buy it. The story seems to be holding Alyosha up as a moral exemplar. Regardless of why he does what he does (whether he's a saint because he's simple or simple because he's a saint), it feels like we're meant to admire him.

Except I don't.

I feel sorry for him, and wish he'd had the guts to stand up for himself.

Although, actually, I do sort of admire him.

He could have been just another pissed-off, bitter victim of a cruel system, but somehow he's avoided that trap and become something better: a patient, happy, (still-)loving victim of it.

But then I think: Wait, *is* that better?

So, I can't quite find a way to accept the conclusion Tolstoy seems to want me to reach: that Alyosha was right to live and die so uncomplainingly. Maybe it's just an outdated story, ruined by the writer's desire to push a polemical agenda we've outgrown?

But I love this story and am moved every time I read it.

So, I wonder: Is it possible that Tolstoy intended to praise Alyosha but inadvertently did something else, something more complicated, something that is still speaking to me all of these years later? Well, yes, and in fact Tolstoy describes this very possibility in an essay he wrote about Chekhov's "The Darling," in which he proposes that in writing that story, Chekhov started out to mock a certain sort of woman (subservient, man-pleasing), that is, to "show what woman ought not to be." Like Balaam in the Book of Numbers, Tolstoy suggests, Chekhov went up the mountain to curse Olenka, "but when he began to speak, the poet blessed what he had come to curse." That is, Chekhov set out to parody Olenka, only the Holy Spirit of "suprapersonal wisdom" came upon him, and he came to love her, and now, so do we.

In "Alyosha the Pot," we might say that Tolstoy did the inverse: he unintentionally cursed what he set out to bless. That is, though he admires Alyosha in theory, and wrote the story to praise his acquiescence and cheerful obedience, the story itself, touched by Tolstoy's honest artistry, can't quite bring itself to deliver that message unambiguously.

Let's take a closer look at Alyosha's death scene:

> He didn't talk much. He just kept asking for water and looked like he was amazed at something.
> Then something seemed to startle him and he stretched his legs and died.

Here's a playful attempt at an alternate version, in accord with the "Alyosha was a cheerful, obedient saint we should admire" reading of the story (i.e., the version we think Tolstoy intended):

> He didn't talk much. He just kept asking for water and looked like he was amazed at something. He saw that God loved him and approved of his obedient cheerfulness, and that God had been pleased when Alyosha unquestioningly obeyed his father. Feeling himself drawn to that eternal reward he had earned, and to which we should all aspire, he stretched his legs and died.

What's the difference between these versions?
I'll show you:

> He didn't talk much. He just kept asking for water and looked like he was amazed at something. ~~He saw that God loved him and approved of his obedient cheerfulness, and that God had been pleased when Alyosha unquestioningly obeyed his father. Feeling himself drawn to that eternal reward he had earned, and to which we should all aspire~~ [A]nd he stretched his legs and died.

That cut stuff is all interior monologue I made up. As you can see, unlike me, Tolstoy declined to go into Alyosha's head. Or, actually, he decided to *get out of* Alyosha's head (he was in there during the preceding sentence: "In his heart was the thought that if it's good down here when you do what they tell you and don't hurt anybody, then it'll be good up there too"). In other stories (including "Master and Man") Tolstoy has shown himself perfectly willing to stay in a character's head as that character dies. But here he comes out (at the sentence "He didn't talk much"), and then we watch Alyosha die from there beside his bed. Whatever happens inside him in those last seconds, we have to deduce by observation. *

Except we can't.

If Tolstoy's intention was to praise Alyosha's cheerful obedience, even unto the end, why not just write it that way? Why not just *say* it?

Or if his intention was to criticize Alyosha's cheerful obedience (as in "my" reading of the story), why not write it this way:

He didn't talk much. He just kept asking for water and looked like he was amazed at something. He suddenly saw that he had lived incorrectly, been too passive. He should have stood up for himself and for Ustinya. And now it was too late. And he stretched his legs and died.

He might even have had it both ways:

He didn't talk much. He just kept asking for water and looked like he was amazed at something. He suddenly saw that he had lived incorrectly, been too passive. He should have stood up for himself and for Ustinya. And now it was too late. But it was all right. None of that mattered, he realized, as, amazed, he suddenly felt God's love washing over him. And he stretched his legs and died.

In any case, why omit those final thoughts, thoughts that would have told us exactly how to read the story?

---

* As was the case in "Master and Man," the person whose head Tolstoy declines to be in at the moment of death is a peasant.

Well, maybe that's it: he didn't *want* to tell us exactly how to read the story.

Or part of him didn't.

Tolstoy had a dual nature; he advocated sexual abstinence yet kept getting Sonya pregnant even into their later years (their thirteenth and last child, Ivan Lvovich, was born in 1888, when Tolstoy was sixty and Sonya forty-four). He preached universal love but fought bitterly with Sonya; he sanctimoniously praised a young peasant man for not having "sinned with" his fiancée before marriage but gleefully quizzed Chekhov on whether he'd "whored a great deal" when young. Once, in conversation with Gorky (as recounted in Gorky's *Reminiscences of Leo Nikolaevich Tolstoy*), Tolstoy categorically rejected a certain idea having to do with the way some families seem to degenerate over successive generations. But then when Gorky presented him with a real-life example of the phenomenon, Tolstoy grew excited: "Now, that's true. I know it; there are two families like that in Tula. It ought to be written. . . . You must do it."

Gorky records Tolstoy expressing the following opinion about drinking: "I do not like people when they are drunk, but I know some who become interesting when they are tipsy, who acquire what is not natural to them in their sober state; wit, beauty of thought, alertness, and richness of language. In such cases I am ready to bless wine."

Once, walking down the street with the theater director Leopold Sulerzhitsky, Tolstoy saw a couple of soldiers approaching, full of obnoxious youthful confidence. (Gorky wrote, "The metal of their accoutrements shone in the sun; their spurs jingled; they kept step like one man; their faces, too, shone with the self-assurance of strength and youth.") Tolstoy launched into a mumbled diatribe against them, their arrogance, their faith in their own physical prowess, their mindless obedience. ("What pompous stupidity! Like animals trained by the whip. . . .") But then they passed and, following them "caressingly with his eyes," Tolstoy changed his tune. On the other hand: how strong and beautiful they were. "O Lord!" he said. "How charming it is when man is handsome, how very charming!"

"So-called great men are always terribly contradictory," Tolstoy told Gorky. "That is forgiven them with all their other follies. Though contradictoriness is not folly: a fool is stubborn, but does not know how to contradict himself."

Tolstoy knew how to contradict himself.

"Novels and short stories," he wrote in his diary in 1896, "describe the revolting manner in which two creatures become infatuated with each other . . . and all the while life, all of life, is beating at us with urgent questions—food, the distribution of property, labor, religion, human relations! It's a shame! It is ignoble!" He also wrote this, thirty years earlier, in 1865: "The aim of the artist is not to solve a problem irrefutably but to make people love life in all its countless inexhaustible manifestations." It wasn't just age that produced the contradiction; the artist and the prude seemed to flicker on and off in him at every stage of his life.

He could even be contradictory about the Christ by whose principles he claimed to live. "I think he regards Christ as simple and deserving of pity," Gorky wrote, "and, although at times he admires him, he hardly loves him. It is as though he were uneasy: if Christ came to a Russian village, the girls might laugh at him." (This dorky Christ bears a resemblance to Alyosha.) Gorky also noted a strange joylessness in Tolstoy whenever he spoke of God. "On this subject," Gorky said, "he spoke coldly and wearily."

So, we can read the story in two contradictory and equally viable ways:

The story makes a beautiful case for cheerful obedience.

The story makes a beautiful case for the argument that making a beautiful case for cheerful obedience is a gift to tyrants.

Which is it?

The wonder of the story is that it fails to answer that question; or, rather, that it answers—it succeeds in answering—in favor of both views, simultaneously.

Technically speaking, the reason we can't "decide" on one reading or the other is that we're denied Alyosha's thoughts at the critical moment. (That "startle" meant something, and only one thing, to Alyosha, but the story seems intent on not telling us what that was.) We want to privilege one reading over the other, but the story won't let us. The two readings keep moving forward and then receding, as in the optical illusion called Rubin's vase:

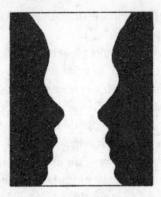

"The story" is really these two coexistent interpretations, eternally struggling for prominence. If we decide that the story supports cheerful obedience, it does. If we decide that it opposes cheerful obedience, it does. Both readings feel radical; both pose the question of how to deal with oppression, then and now, in a world divided into haves and have-nots, the most urgent one of all.

But the story, in declining to answer (in obscuring the place where it might have answered), feels like it's not avoiding the question but irradiating it with increased intensity.

How did Tolstoy manage this feat?

One possible answer: by accident.

According to Pevear, Tolstoy wrote the story in one day. When he was done, he didn't like it. "Wrote Alyosha, very bad," he recorded in his diary. "Gave it up."

What didn't he like about it? Why did he quit?

Let's speculate.

In the death scene, presented with a chance to go into Alyosha's head, Tolstoy . . . declined. What did that decision look like? That is, if we could get inside Tolstoy's seventy-seven-year-old head, as he bent low over the page, coming up on that final paragraph, what would we find going on in there? My guess is: the approach, then a split-second swerve. The (mere) scribbling man, guided by that "suprapersonal wisdom" (that is, by a lifetime of artistic practice), didn't *decide* not to go into Alyosha's head; he just didn't *feel like it*. He had, in that moment, let's say, some discomfort (not overt, intellectual discomfort but buried, subconscious discomfort) about his desire to advocate for cheerful obedience. In that swerve we feel him resisting his own didacticism. A form of what we might call artistic reserve kicked in. Like Bartleby, Tolstoy "preferred not to."

So he didn't.

He wrote around that moment when he might have specified what Alyosha was feeling (what, precisely, he was surprised about) because—well, because he didn't know. Or didn't know yet. Or didn't like the answer he was about to come up with. That swerve represents a sort of interim decision to not, at that moment, decide—to defer deciding.

The most artful and truthful thing is sometimes simply that which allows us to avoid being false: the swerving away, the deletion, the declining to decide, the falling silent, the waiting to see, the knowing when to quit.

Omission is sometimes a defect and leads to unclearness. But other times it's a virtue and leads to ambiguity and an increase in narrative tension.

"The secret of boring people," Chekhov said, "lies in telling them everything."

Once Gorky asked Tolstoy whether he agreed with an opinion Tolstoy had assigned to one of his characters.

"Are you very anxious to know?" Tolstoy asked.

"Very," said Gorky.

"Then I shan't tell you," said Tolstoy.

After that one day of writing, Tolstoy apparently never went back to "Alyosha the Pot." We don't know why. He was sick during this period, was spending much of his time and energy collecting aphorisms from the world's great religions and philosophies and compiling them into books like *The Cycle of Readings* and *The Way of Life* (which are kind of wonderful). Maybe, now and then, his mind turned to Alyosha and he felt he still didn't have a satisfactory solution.

In any event, he never went back to it, and "Alyosha the Pot" comes to us as he left it.

And I'd say it's perfect.

Had he come back to it, he might have "improved" it by making the meaning of Alyosha's last moments clearer or, in some other way, being more forthcoming about his, Tolstoy's, opinion of Alyosha's way of living.

But would that have been an improvement?

"Alyosha's pathetic fate moves us to pity," Clarence Brown said, "but most readers will wonder what exactly we are to do or refrain from doing as a result of reading about it."

Right. We do wonder. We've seen such a cruel thing happen: a small life, with no pleasure in it, blossomed momentarily (a red jacket! a girlfriend!), and it seemed that Alyosha might have a chance to be loved, a chance even the humblest person deserves, but no, that possibility gets yanked away, for no good reason, and no one apologizes, because no one sees anything wrong with it.

In the scale of things, this is a small injustice, but imagine the number of such injustices that have occurred since the beginning of time. All of those people who were wronged in life and remained unavenged or unsatisfied or bitter or longing for love on their deathbeds (all of those people who found this life a frustration, a disappointment, a torment), what, for them, is the real end of the story of this life?

Well, aren't we all, at some level, one of those people? Has it all gone perfectly for us down here? At this very moment, are you (am I) at total peace, completely satisfied? When the end comes, will you feel, "If only I could go back and do it over, I'd do it better, fighting boldly and fearlessly against all that would reduce me" or "All is well, I was the way I was, for better or worse, and now I'm leaving happily, to rejoin something bigger"?

Every time I read "Alyosha the Pot," it puts me in that state of wondering.

And it never gives me an answer but only says: "Keep wondering."

And that, I think, is its real accomplishment.

AFTERTHOUGHT #7

The writer and the reader stand at either end of a pond. The writer drops a pebble in and the ripples reach the reader. The writer stands there, imagining the way the reader is receiving those ripples, by way of deciding which pebble to drop in next.

Meanwhile, the reader receives those ripples and, somehow, they speak to her.

In other words, they're in connection.

These days, it's easy to feel that we've fallen out of connection with one another and with the earth and with reason and with love. I mean: we have. But to read, to write, is to say that we still believe in, at least, the *possibility* of connection. When reading and writing, we feel connection happening (or not). That's the essence of these activities: ascertaining whether connection is happening, and where, and why.

Those two people, in those postures, across that pond, are doing essential work. This is not a hobby, pastime, or indulgence. By their mutual belief in connection, they're making the world better, by making it (at least between the two of them, in that small moment) more friendly. We might even say they're preparing for future disaster; when disaster comes, they'll enter it with a less panicky, reactive vision of the Other, because they've spent so much time in connection with an imaginary Other, while reading or writing.

That's the idea, anyway, and speaking of craft talks, if you've ever been to a literary event or read an interview with a writer, you've likely heard some version of this "fiction is essential" argument.

But it's interesting.

These stories we've just read were written during an incredible seventy-year artistic renaissance in Russia (the time of, yes, Gogol, Turgenev, Chekhov, and Tolstoy, but also of Pushkin, Dostoyevsky, Ostrovsky, Tyutchev, Tchaikovsky, Mussorgsky, Rimsky-Korsakov, and many more) that was followed by one of the bloodiest, most irrational periods in human history. Twenty million or more killed by Stalin, the torture and imprisonment of countless others; widespread starvation, even, in places, cannibalism; kids turning their own parents in, husbands ratting out their wives; the systematic and deliberate overthrow of the humanist values by which our four writers lived.

In *The Gulag Archipelago,* Solzhenitsyn wrote: "If the intellectuals in the plays of Chekhov who spent all their time guessing what would happen in twenty, thirty, or forty years had been told that in forty years interrogation by torture would be practiced in Russia; that prisoners would have their skulls squeezed within iron rings; that a human being would be lowered into an acid bath [and here he goes on to compile a long and terrible list of other Stalinist tortures that I'll spare you from], not one of Chekhov's plays would have gotten to its end because all the heroes would have gone off to insane asylums." *

So, the artistic bounty of this period wasn't enough to avert that disaster, and I suppose, in some ways, it might have (must have, actually) even contributed to it. Did it soften up the reading classes for the Bolsheviks? Cause an impatience for change that led to a too-convulsive revolution? Was all of this excellent art made by, and for, the bourgeoisie enabling and cloaking czarist excesses all along, and was this part of the reason the Stalinists turned so violently against humanist virtues?

These questions are above my pay grade. (Even asking them has made me a little anxious.)

I raise them just to say that whatever fiction does to or for us, it's not simple.

There's a certain way of talking about stories that treats them as a kind of salvation, the answer to every problem; they are "what we live by," and so on. And, to an extent, as you can see by this book, I agree. But I also believe, especially as I get older, that we should keep our expectations humble. We shouldn't overestimate or unduly glorify what

---

* I first became aware of this quote in an eye-opening essay on the nature of Soviet cruelty by Gary Saul Morson, "How the Great Truth Dawned," *New Criterion,* September 2019.

fiction does. And actually, we should be wary of insisting that it do any-thing in particular. The critic Dave Hickey has written about this, the notion that saying what art *should* do might enable a reactionary estab-lishment to start saying what it *must* do, and then to begin silencing those artists whose works aren't doing that. In other words, whenever we get up on the soapbox and sing fiction's praises, explaining how good it is for everyone, we're actually limiting its freedom to be . . . whatever it wants to be (perverse, contrary, frivolous, objectionable, useless, too difficult for any but a few to read, and so on).

And let's be even more honest: those of us who read and write do it because we love it and because doing it makes us feel more alive and we would likely keep doing it even if it could be demonstrated that its over-all net effect was zero, and I, for one, have a feeling that I would keep doing it even if it could be demonstrated that its overall net effect was negative. (I once got an email from a guy who'd (mis)read one of my stories and, on that basis, prematurely consigned his elderly mother to a nursing home. Thanks, literature! Nevertheless, I was up and writing the next day.)

Still, I often find myself constructing rationales for the beneficial ef-fects of fiction, trying, in essence, to justify the work I've been doing all these years.

So, trying to stay perfectly honest, let's go ahead and ask, diagnosti-cally: What is it, exactly, that fiction does?

Well, that's the question we've been asking all along, as we've been watching our minds read these Russian stories. We've been comparing the pre-reading state of our minds to the post-reading state. And *that's* what fiction does: it causes an incremental change in the state of a mind. That's it. But, you know—it really does it. That change is finite but real.

And that's not nothing.

It's not everything, but it's not nothing.

We End

I hope you've enjoyed this walk through these Russian stories as much as I have, or even half as much, which, given how much I've enjoyed it, would still be a lot.

A few closing thoughts.

At its best, in my experience, artistic mentoring works something like this: the mentor strongly expresses his view as if it is the only and entirely correct view. The student pretends to accept that position: takes the teacher on faith (tries on his aesthetic principles for size, surrenders to his approach), to see if there might be something in it. At the end of the mentoring period (now), the student snaps out of it, disavows the teacher's view, which is starting to feel like a set of bad-fitting clothes anyway, and goes back to her own way of thinking. But maybe along the way she's picked up a few things. These are things she likely knew all along, of which the teacher simply reminded her.

So, if something in this book lit you up, that wasn't me "teaching you something," that was you remembering or recognizing something that I was, let's say, "validating." If something, uh, anti-lit you up? That feeling of disagreeing with me was your artistic will asserting itself. (You put it on a leash and asked it to allow itself to be walked by me, but it could take only so much of that feeling of being yanked around against its natural inclinations.) That resistance is something to note and be glad of and honor. The road to that "iconic space" I mentioned at the outset (that place where you do the work that only you can do) is marked by moments of strong, even maniacal preference. (And defiance, orneriness, fascination, indefensible obsession.) What Randall

Jarrell said about stories holds true for the writers of stories: they "don't want to know, don't want to care, they just want to *do as they please.*"

It also holds true for readers of a story. Where else can we go, but the pages of a story, to prefer so strongly, react without rationalization, love or hate so freely, be so radically ourselves? You didn't need me to be here, to know what you thought of these stories. (But, as Carol Burnett used to say (sing): I'm so glad we had this time together.)

I want to thank you for allowing me to guide you rather bossily through the stories, for letting me show you how I read them, why I love them. I've tried to be as clear and persuasive as possible, telling you what you should be noticing, pointing out certain technical features, offering my best explanation for why "we" were moved in this place or that, and so on.

But all of that was just my dream, my mind dreaming as I read the stories, me relaying those dreams to you, you kindly agreeing to listen to my dream.

Now that we're done, I hope that some of what I muttered as I dreamed will stick with you (because those ideas were yours to begin with) and be useful, and that others (not so useful, not yours) will fall away, and that you'll be glad to see them go. Please know that I'll be glad to see you being glad to see them go. Because that's exactly how this is supposed to work.

One of the dangers of writing a book about writing is that it might be perceived to be of the how-to variety.

This book is not that. A lifetime of writing has left me with one thing: the knowledge of how *I* do it. Or, to be completely honest, a knowledge of how I *have done it.* (How I *will soon do it* has to remain a continual mystery.)

God save us from manifestos, even mine. ("An explanation does not go up to the hilt," said Tolstoy.)

The closest thing to a method I have to offer is this: go forth and do what you please.

It really is true: doing what you please (i.e., what pleases you), with energy, will lead you to everything—to your particular obsessions and the ways in which you'll indulge them, to your particular challenges and the forms in which they'll convert into beauty, to your particular obstructions and your highly individualized obstruction breakers. We can't know what our writing problems will be until we write our way into them, and then we can only write our way out.

A student once told me this story: Robert Frost came to a college to give a reading. An earnest young poet stood up and asked a complex, technical question about the sonnet form, or something like that.

Frost took a beat, then said: "Young man, don't worry: *WORK!*"

I love this advice. It's exactly true to my experience. We can decide only so much. The big questions have to be answered by hours at the desk. So much of the worrying we do is a way of avoiding work, which only delays the (work-enabled) solution.

So, don't worry, work, and have faith that all answers will be found there.*

We ended the previous section by agreeing to confine our expectations for fiction to this: reading fiction changes the state of our minds for a short time afterward.

But that may be a bit on the modest side. After all, as we've been seeing, reading fiction changes our minds *in particular ways,* as we step out of our own (limited) consciousness and into another one (or two, or three).

So, we might ask, how *are* we altered, in that "short time afterward"?

(Before I give my answer, let's just say, again, that there's no need, really, for me to do that. We know how our minds were changed as we read these Russians, because we were there. And we know, if we've been lucky enough to have other beautiful reading experiences in our lives, what those did for/to us.)

But I'll give it a try:

I am reminded that my mind is not the only mind.

I feel an increased confidence in my ability to imagine the experiences of other people and accept these as valid.

---

* Although . . . a few years later, a Frost scholar came up after an event and offered a gentle correction. What Frost had actually said (he said) was: "Young man, don't work: WORRY!" Well, that's true too. (Maybe worry can be a form of work.) But not *as* true (for me). But if it's true for you, I endorse that advice too. Go forth and don't work, WORRY!

I feel I exist on a continuum with other people: what is in them is in me and vice versa.

My capacity for language is reenergized. My internal language (the language in which I think) gets richer, more specific and adroit.

I find myself liking the world more, taking more loving notice of it (this is related to that reenergization of my language).

I feel luckier to be here and more aware that someday I won't be.

I feel more aware of the things of the world and more interested in them.

So, that's all pretty good.

Essentially, before I read a story, I'm in a state of knowing, of being fairly sure. My life has led me to a certain place and I'm contentedly resting there. Then, here comes the story, and I am slightly undone, in a good way. Not so sure anymore, of my views, and reminded that my view-maker is always a little bit off: it's limited, it's too easily satisfied, with too little data.

And that's an enviable state to be in, if only for a few minutes.

When somebody cuts you off in traffic, don't you always know which political party they belong to (that is, the opposite of yours)? But, of course, you don't. It remains to be seen. Everything remains to be seen. Fiction helps us remember that everything remains to be seen. It's a sacrament dedicated to this end. We can't always feel as open to the world as we feel at the end of a beautiful story, but feeling that way even briefly reminds us that such a state exists and creates the aspiration in us to strive to be in that state more often.

Would we have felt as fond of the real-life versions of Marya, Yashka, Olenka, Vasili, et al. as we now feel of their literary representations? Might we have dismissed them, failed to notice them at all?

They started out as notions in the minds of another person, became words, then became notions in our minds, and now they'll always be with us, part of our moral armament, as we approach the beautiful, difficult, precious days ahead.

Out the door of my writing shed are some things. What things? Yes, exactly. It's up to me to tell you, and in telling you, I will shortly be making them. How I tell them is what they'll be. Are those "shaggy sad redwoods, speaking of the long defeat that is life"? "Proud, magnificent red-brown friends of my working days, connecting me with innumerable generations past"? "A stand of redwoods"? "Some trees"? Depends on the day, depends on my mind. All these descriptions are true, and none of them is, at all.

There's a chair out there, holding open the door (it's hot and a fan in the doorway is blowing in some cooler air), and there's a hose I ran over here to water a plant, some kind of succulent, the exact name of which I don't know, that we bought last month at Home Depot, to which I try to whisper something encouraging as I come in here every morning. The hose is lying out there, pale green in the hot sun.

It is not, by the way, "greenish-looking, on this hot, sunny day." It's "pale green in the hot sun." Why? Because it's better that way. Why is it better? Because I prefer it.

Well, we can disagree about that. Above, as you read "pale green in the hot sun," did you see that hose? Your reading energy did something at that phrase. Were you in or out? With me or against me? Compelled slightly forward or held slightly back?

By that little tussle, you know I'm here. And I know you're there. That phrase is a little corridor connecting us, giving us a fragment of the world over which to tussle, i.e., connect.

There are many versions of you, in you. To which one am I speaking, when I write? The best one. The one most like my best one. Those two best versions of us, in a moment of reading, exit our usual selves and, at a location created by mutual respect, become one.

That's a pretty hopeful model of human interaction: two people, mutually respectful, leaning in, one speaking so as to compel, the other listening, willing to be charmed.

That, a person can work with.

I started this book, as I said at the beginning, with the realization of how important teaching these stories had been to me over the last twenty years. My intention was to get down on paper some of what I'd learned from them—to preserve those insights, I guess I'd say. As I worked with the stories, I found something else happening. Freed from the schedule of the semester, forced to specificity by the essay form, I found the stories opening up to me and challenging me in ways they never had before. They are, it turns out, even more wonderful than I'd believed all those years—more complexly made, more mysterious. And they threw my own work into relief: I see what the Russians did that I have, so far, failed to do.

It's been daunting and lovely to find that my chosen form contains so much potential and that I'm still so far from fulfilling it.

It's also made me feel this: these Russians did what they did so beautifully, there's no need for me, or anyone, to keep doing it.

Which is another way of saying that part of my job (part of your job) is to find new paths for the story form to go down; to make stories that are as powerful as these Russian stories but that, in their voice and form and concerns, are new, meaning that they respond to the things history has given us to know about life on earth in the years since these Russians were here.

These stories, as we've seen, work in a particular way. Ours will need to work differently, not only to distinguish them from the older works but so that they will speak to our time as freshly as these Russian stories spoke to theirs.

While writing this book, I turned sixty-one, and I found myself asking again and again, during the writing, why writing stories is important—if it's important enough to justify the time it takes, as I become keenly aware that time is precious and life is passing, and that, for sure, everything I want to do in this life is not going to get done, not at all, not ever, and that the end is going to come rushing up faster than I expect (even if it rushes up, per my plan, two hundred years from now, when I'm 261).

Writing this book turned out to be a chance to ask myself again, at length: "Do you still want to devote your life to fiction?"

And it turns out, I do.

I really do.

At the beginning of the first class of the semester I always ask my students to imagine themselves putting a parenthesis in front of everything I'm about to say (i.e., over the course of the semester) and preceding that parenthesis with the words "According to George."

At the end of the last class, I ask them to close the parenthesis and add the phrase "Well, anyway, that was all according to George."

You can close that parenthesis now.

I thank you, from the heart, for the investment of time and energy that has brought you this far, and hope, sincerely, that something in here will benefit you.

Corralitos, California
April 2020

APPENDICES

APPENDIX A

A CUTTING EXERCISE

EXERCISE, PART 1

Read the text below.

  Set a timer for five minutes.

  In that time, cut twenty words from that text.

  When finished, ask yourself these questions:

1. What did I cut?

2. Why did I cut it? (This will tell you something about your editing sensibility.)

3. Is the resulting piece better or worse?

Now do another round of the above.

  In fact, do round after round of the above, until you've cut the piece from its current length (600 words) to half that (300 words).

TEXT

Once there was a stolid friendly man named Bill. One day, Bill walked into the Department of Motor Vehicles, wearing a brown shirt and exuding a sort of paranoia. That is not usual, or inaccurate. The DMV makes anyone sane nervous. Bill's mind flip-flopped through a series of images that were as hazy as they were anxiety-producing. He saw himself in handcuffs. He imagined someone coming out of the back, with a list of all the cars Bill had bumped, scraped, or nicked with his door, in the various parking lots, over the fifty years of his life: first in Indiana, then California, and now, in Syracuse, New York, where, it seemed to Bill, they had the worst DMV ever, just in terms of provoking anxiety, angled, as it was, on a street of similar low buildings and factories that took a long time to find. And every time he had to find it all over again. He could never remember how he had found it the previous time, which was bad. The office had low ceilings and smelled of smoke, floor cleaning products, and human sweat. And yet there was always the same guy, mopping, mopping endlessly. It almost seemed as if he were mopping with a mix of cleaning product and human sweat, while smoking. But no: over his head was a sign: NO SMOKING. It was all so typical and bureaucratic, really. Everywhere in America were such public buildings: cheap to put up, probably, but incredibly expensive in the drain they exerted on the human psyche of the people forced to visit them. Bill made to approach the desk. But first he had to take a number from a woman with flaming red hair. She was sitting at a desk back by the front door, which Bill had just entered.

"Is this where I get that number thing?" Bill said.

"Yes," the woman said.

"Nice hair," Bill said.

"Are you being sarcastic?" the woman said.

Bill didn't know what to say. He had, yes, been being sarcastic, but now he saw that this was a bad move, just in terms of getting that number. Why was he always so sarcastic? What had this pale, clownish woman ever done to him? He felt even more paranoid. Images floated before his eyes—shapes, really: catastrophic, fetal, and celebratory wiggles and sparks, possibly being caused by an approaching migraine. The room swayed, eddied, then came back into focus. It was so hot.

The clown-woman gave him the number. Bill sat on a bench. A couple nearby was fighting. The woman was claiming the man didn't wash his rear end well, ever. The poor man looked humiliated. The woman was talking so loudly. The man was shriveled and old and defenseless. He literally held his hat in his hands. Bill glared at the woman. She glared back. Then the man glared at Bill. He made a menacing gesture with the hat in his hands. Now the couple was united, against Bill, and the man's unclean ass seemed to have been totally forgotten. This was always the way for poor Bill. Once he had intervened when a man was beating his wife, and the wife had turned on him, and the man had turned on him, and even some people passing by had turned on him. Even a nun had given him a gratuitous kick with her thick nun shoe. A robotic voice intoned Bill's number, which was 332. Bill approached the desk. To his surprise, he saw Angie, his ex-wife, working there, behind the desk. Angie looked more beautiful than ever.

(600 words)

DISCUSSION

Now, it's not the case that every piece of writing needs this level of cutting, but it's good to develop a feeling for how much cutting a piece of prose can tolerate before it gets worse.

This exercise is a way to discover your voice or, more exactly, your pace.

Imagine yourself standing naked in front of a mirror. Built into the mirror is an app that lets you add weight to the image, 5 pounds at a time. Crank it up to 500 pounds. How do you look? Dial it steadily down: 495, 400, 300, your current weight, past your current weight, down to, like, 60 pounds. Well, somewhere in there is your Ideal Body Weight.

You'll know it when you see it.

It's the same with prose. For each of us there's an Ideal Prose Pace. But very few of us write at that pace in a first draft. So we have to help ourselves find it. This exercise helps us get a taste of what our Ideal Prose Pace might be, by forcing us down through successive layers of strictness.

While you were doing the exercise, there probably came a moment when you lost your ability to know what to cut, because you didn't know what the goal of the rest of the piece was. You felt that you had to know where you were going in order to judge what was wheat and what was chaff. (That woman whose hair Bill insulted—is she going to be important later? If not, her bit could get pruned. On the other hand, if you really liked that exchange and decided to keep it in, that obliges you to give that woman a role later.)

But notice how far into the exercise you had to go before you felt that way. Mostly, you could find things to cut for other reasons. (What were those reasons *for you*? What, in prose, offends you? What delights you and inspires you to protect it?)

Extreme cutting like this is a gateway to voice. Let's say there are two phases in writing (although these tend to morph in and out of each other): *composition* and *revision*. We tend to associate voice with the first ("I just burst out my first draft in my true voice, singing out my spontaneous vision!"). But, in my experience, voice really gets made during the second phase—as we edit and, especially, as we cut. Most of us tend, in the first draft, to sing for too long, in ways that actually sound pretty similar to all of those other writers singing.

There are two ways to make a distinctive voice: we can put it in there in the first place or discover it by erasure. Either method, done to our taste, makes our prose more "like us." (And, of course, in a real writing session, we're going back and forth from one mode to the other, sometimes from second to second.)

There's something intelligence-increasing about compression. Our first pass at writing something is often loose and exploratory. "It always made me nervous, back in college, as, tired from the previous night of partying, I came into class and sat there in my usual seat near the window watching Professor Vader standing up there at the chalkboard as he did all sorts of proofs or calculations or just lectured, his black helmet hiding his face, his light saber hanging on his belt occasionally making these bright red sparks against the chalk ledge on which the chalk was kept when not in use." Well, that's a start. Cut down to something like "It made me nervous, watching Professor Vader at the chalkboard, his helmet hiding his face, his light saber occasionally making sparks against the chalk ledge," it's smarter than before and it's more considerate. The writer has sifted through that meandering initial exploration and brought forward what he's found in there that he feels is most vital.

If you cut a mediocre bit, just like that, you've got one less bit of mediocrity in your story. That's one benefit. (If you've got a piece of food in your teeth and you take it out, you're already that much more attractive.) But you've also created room for something better to be put in there (that part only applies to writing). Often, the excision will do something to the rhythm of the sentence that will encourage you to complete it in a different way, and this, in turn, will introduce some new fact into the story. If we revise "Sam was this big sort of dumb guy who I knew" into "Sam, big and dumb . . ."—well, already that's better. It doesn't suck yet. And when we take another run at that partial sentence, its tighter, post-cut state lets us see (and hear) what we have to work with. Try it: read that partial sentence out loud and see if some words don't come to mind with which to complete it. You're honoring rhythm there; some part of your brain knows what it wants to hear, and will supply something based not entirely on sense but also on sound.

"Sam, big and dumb . . . could, nevertheless, run."

Well, big, dumb Sam is now a runner and off he goes, all because we trimmed down our sloppy first attempt at describing him.

EXERCISE, PART 2

1. Think of a story you're currently working on, one that you feel is close to finished.

2. Take out page 4 of it (let's say) and *cut it in half,* as you did to my pages above. (It's easy to do on someone else's writing, harder to do on your own.) Students report that, having developed the habit on the practice piece, some of the "muscle memory" carries over when they try editing their own work.

APPENDIX B

AN ESCALATION EXERCISE

―――――――

EXERCISE

Set a timer for, let's say, forty-five minutes.

Now write a 200-word story. BUT the trick is: you get to use only 50 words to do it.

You'll discover your own way of keeping track of the word count; one approach is to make a running list. Say, for example, that your first sentence turns out to be "A cow stood in the field."

You write, at the bottom of the page, for reference:

1. a

2. cow

3. stood

4. in

5. the

6. field

Now you "have" those 6 words to use going forward.

When you hit 50 words, that's it: you have to start reusing words. (Let's allow plurals. So "cow" and "cows" count as the same word.)

The final product is to be *exactly* 200 words (not 199, not 201).

Ready? Go.

DISCUSSION

Most writers tend to write stories that are long on exposition but never ascend into the rising action (that is, they don't escalate). I've read entire student novels like this—pages and pages of brilliant exposition in which the tension never rises. I sometimes say that in the exposition we put a pot of water on the stove; getting the action to rise is making the water boil. (What we've been calling "meaningful action" is equal to the boiling water is equal to escalation.)

For reasons I don't understand, the stories produced using this exercise almost always have rising action. For certain students, they tend to be funnier and more entertaining and more dramatically shaped than those writers' "real" work.

If you like the piece you wrote—if it seems to have something your more seriously produced stories lack—you might pause here and ask what that is, exactly.

Why does this exercise work? I'm not sure. The constraints have something to do with it (the 50-word limit and the exacting—200, not 199, not 201—word count). When a person is doing this exercise, her attention is on those constraints, which means she's approaching things differently than she normally would. The part of her mind that would usually be thinking about her themes or preserving her style or the piece's goal or her politics is being kept busy counting words. Which allows another part of her mind to step forward, a less conscious, more playful part.

When I assign this exercise in class, I announce beforehand that everyone will be reading their story aloud afterward. This intensifies things. ("Depend upon it, sir, when a man knows he is to be hanged in a fortnight, it concentrates his mind wonderfully.") This brings out a natural performative streak that just about every writer I know has.

When I was a student at Syracuse, Doug Unger, a little fed up with how clever and "literary" the stories we'd been writing were, announced, just before a break in workshop, that during the second half we were each going to have to *tell* a story on the spot.

Talk about a nerve-filled break.

But compared to the stories we'd been submitting, the stories we told that night were, without exception, livelier and more dramatic and more infused with who we really were, richer with our real charms, the way we actually were witty in the world.

What is there to do with the little pieces that result from this exercise? They usually sound a little strange, Seussian. Once a student made a larger story out of several passes at this exercise; in each pass he used a different fifty-word set, but he kept the same characters throughout the longer story he made of those 200-word bits. Other students have used this exercise to generate a sort of starter piece, with good rising action, then relaxed the constraints and rewrote the story using as many "new" words as they wanted.

The beauty of this exercise is that it shows us that we usually walk around with a certain idea of the writer we are in our head. When we sit down to write, that writer is the one we start channeling. In that instant, our brain function changes. We're less open to what the story wants to do, to what that language generator inside of us wants to do. We're working within the narrow range of how we think we should write. This exercise shuts down that way of thinking by keeping it busy with the practicalities of the exercise, which leaves the rest of the mind asking, "Well, what else have we got?" That is: "What other writers might be in here?"

Maybe this exercise is a bit like dancing while drunk and filming it. In playback, we might catch a glimpse of something we don't normally attempt, but that we like. And if we like it, we might want to do it on purpose, later.

APPENDIX C

A TRANSLATION EXERCISE

One of the Russian writers I love most but couldn't include here (he's a twentieth-century Russian) is Isaac Babel.

Babel, like Gogol, is a writer for whom translation is key, because of the musicality of his prose. A more matter-of-fact writer—a writer whose effects depend on the juxtaposition of images and not so much on the precise wording of said images (like Tolstoy or Chekhov) is more immune to translation, we might say. If you're a stylist, as Babel is, you're more dependent on the translator doing what is, after all, an impossible job: making you sound and feel in English the way you sound and feel in Russian. Those of us who don't speak Russian can never truly know a stylistic master like Babel, but we can get a better feel for him by way of this exercise.

We can also, as you'll see, get a better idea of our own stylistic inclinations.

Here are five versions, by different translators, of a sentence I really love from Babel's story "In the Basement" (one of the greatest stories ever written on the touchy subject of class):

In verdure-hidden walks wicker chairs gleamed whitely.[*]

Wicker chairs, gleaming white, lined paths overhung with foliage.[†]

---

[*] Translated by Walter Morison: Isaac Babel, *The Collected Stories* (New York: Meridian, 1974).

[†] Translated by Boris Dralyuk: Isaac Babel, *Odessa Stories* (London: Pushkin Press, 2018).

White wicker chairs glittered in walks covered with foliage.*

Wicker armchairs dazzled white along green-shrouded promenades.†

In leafy avenues white wicker chairs gleamed.‡

Will the real Babel please stand up? He won't, he can't, he exists only in the original Russian. Does the Russian version have the Russian equivalent of that missing comma in the Morison translation that gives the sentence that rushed and hard-to-decipher quality that makes us want to read it twice and, thereby, affects the process by which words get converted into image? When a Russian reads this sentence in Russian, does she see *green path* first or *white chairs*? Is that green stuff, in Russian, foliage or verdure or shrouds of green or leaves, or what?

A good voice-finding exercise for any aspiring writer: rank the five translations above, best to worst.

When you're done, ask yourself: On what basis did I just now make that ranking? (Since I didn't suggest a basis on which to rank them, you supplied that, by way of some fundamental aspect of your artistic taste.)

Note that if you could do the ranking, this proves that you had a preference. Consider that this preference might have (must have) something to do with your innate sense of voice, i.e., that which you are going to be relying on in every sentence of your career.

We can take this exercise a step further: now make a "translation" of your own. The elements are plain: some white wicker chairs are reflecting light in a particular way while situated on some tree- and/or bush-containing paths. How would you put that across? With those elements stipulated, all that's left is to seek the best arrangement of those elements *per your taste*—that is, to supply (your) voice.

So try that here.

---

* Translated by Peter Constantine: *The Complete Works of Isaac Babel* (New York: W. W. Norton, 2002).

† Translated by Val Vinokur: Isaac Babel, *The Essential Fictions* (Evanston: Northwestern University Press, 2017).

‡ Translated by David McDuff: Isaac Babel, *Collected Stories* (New York: Penguin Books, 1994).

Now ask yourself: As I wrote my version, what was I honoring? That is, on what was I relying? How did I "decide" on that version?

What I just now learned about myself, when I tried out my own exercise, is that my mind first looks for a simple way through the data. I found myself scanning to see what verb I was going to use to avoid a passive-voice construction like "White wicker chairs *had been placed there* among the etc., etc." So: "were gleaming" became the cornerstone of the sentence. Then that became "gleamed." "White" seemed important (to contrast with all that green). I imagined myself looking at the scene. "White wicker chairs" felt good—that's a phrase that causes its subject to be seen. So: "White wicker chairs gleamed . . ." And then I asked: What is it that those chairs are gleaming *in*? I considered really going for it (they were gleaming "there in the verdure, the foliage, the leaves and low-hanging tendrils" but (1) that's a little more than Babel seems to have in mind and (2) it doesn't quite land; there's too much trouble (too many words) for too little payoff. The image is hard to see, and the sentence seems overstuffed. Better we should cut our losses and get out of the sentence, with the reader seeing, at least, WHITE and GREEN.

So:

"White wicker chairs gleamed in the green."

But my reaction, reading this, is: "Uh, what *green* are you talking about?"

"White wicker chairs, tucked into a foliage-thick promenade, gleamed."

Hmm. Not quite.

We don't know about the arrangement of those chairs (or how many there are), but I feel myself wanting to do something like "Three white wicker chairs faced vaguely but not exactly off in the same direction, looking distractedly off into the jungle that surrounded them, as if considering escape."

That sentence would be out of place in the Babel story, where this little description is part of a longer sequence, the purpose of which is to underscore that the character, a poor boy visiting the home of a rich classmate, is overawed by the wealth of the place.

And here we get to the real point of the exercise. Forget that the sentence is part of a Babel story and make it as good as you can. That new sentence, sitting there by itself, instantaneously starts dictating a whole story for itself, i.e., a story in which it would make sense.

In other words, our style (which we find by radical preference, in pursuit of "fun" or "cool" or "delight") results in a sentence, and that sentence has the DNA of a story in it.

"Three white wicker chairs looked out into the houseplant-jungle surrounding them as if contemplating escape."

If a person comes into the frame and sits down in one of those chairs, he has entered a world fraught with "desire for escape." Which is going to help us decide who he is. He might be someone longing to escape, he might be someone who has recently escaped. But he won't be—he can no longer be—just anyone. He's a man who walked into a story that has the idea of escape hovering around it, and he's not entirely free.

Acknowledgments

I'd like to begin by thanking Andy Ward, who has changed my life and art with his quiet wisdom, Zen-like precision, and generous view of the world. And I know I am just one of the many writers he has uplifted in this way, helping us become our best artistic selves with his tireless enthusiasm and advocacy.

Also, heartfelt thanks to Esther Newberg, my agent and dear pal, for believing in me and always representing me as I would represent myself, but with more zest, generosity, and imagination, since, unbelievably enough, 1992.

Thank you, too, to the amazing Bonnie Thompson, the Michael Jordan of copyediting, who made this book better in so many places, in so many ways.

Most especially, I am deeply grateful to my dear wife, Paula, and our daughters, Caitlin and Alena, and the way we have always been as a family, living and talking and dreaming as if there is no difference between literature and life, and as if devotion to the former can make the latter better.

For invaluable assistance as I wrote this book, thank you to: Val Vinokur, Mikhail Iossel, Jeff Parker, Alina Parker, Polina Barskova, Luba Lapina, Yana Tyulpanova, and Valeriy Minukhin. Thanks also to Lisa Nold, for revising/passing on that Einstein quote; Jon Fink, for the Frost story; Lynda Barry, for the enlightening visit she made to Syracuse all those years ago; Erika Haber, for an early and mind-blowing classroom visit that I've never forgotten, and that I've drawn on here, especially in my piece on Gogol; and Jonathan Dee, for turning me on to the Kundera quote in the essay on "Master and Man."

I'd also like to thank the following people who, over the years, taught me everything I know about writing and reading: My parents (who, from the beginning, gave me time to read and made me understand that it was a vital activity), Sheri Lindbloom, Joe Lindbloom, Jay Gillette, Michael O'Rourke, Richard Moseley, Charmazel Dudt, Sue Park, Douglas Unger, Tobias Wolff, Deborah Treisman, my students at Syracuse, and, going way back, Sister Carol Mucha and Sister Lynette at St. Damian School in Oak Forest, Illinois.

Many of the ideas in this book came from the people listed above and were absorbed into my understanding. Hard to say at this point what is mine and what is theirs. All value came from them, all errors from me.

Thanks, also, to Patrick Bierut and Kyle Nielsen, whose presence in my life made the world a warmer, saner place during the time I was working on this book.

I am very grateful to James and Anne Rasin for their wonderful last-minute hospitality during the finishing stages, in beautiful Cherry Valley, New York.

A special shout-out to Arthur Flowers, my recently retired and beloved fiction comrade over these twenty-plus Syracuse years. Every time I hear Arthur talk about writing in his loving and full-hearted way, it makes me grateful and proud to be part of our community of writers. Thanks, also, to my Special Narrative Discussion Pals, Dana Spiotta and Mary Karr, all my colleagues at Syracuse, and Dean Karin Ruhlandt, for her kindness to our program and her keen understanding of what it is we are trying to do.

Thanks to the translators of these stories, for allowing us to use them.

Finally, thanks again to you, dear reader, for all of your hard work, and let's strive to remember and live by the lovely contradictory mantra below, of juxtaposed Gogol quotes (from "How the Two Ivans Quarreled" and "Nevsky Prospect," respectively):

"It's dreary in this world, ladies and gentlemen."

(And yet):

"Marvelous is the working of our world!"

Texts

Chekhov, Anton. "In the Cart." In *The Portable Chekhov.* Translated by Avrahm Yarmolinsky. New York: Viking Portable Library, 1975.

Turgenev, Ivan. "The Singers." In *First Love and Other Tales.* Translated by David Magarshack. New York: W. W. Norton, 1968.

Chekhov, Anton. "The Darling." In *The Portable Chekhov.* Translated by Avrahm Yarmolinsky. New York: Viking Portable Library, 1975.

Tolstoy, Leo. "Master and Man." In *Great Short Works of Leo Tolstoy.* Translated by Louise Maude and Aylmer Maude. New York: Perennial Library, 1967.

Gogol, Nikolai. "The Nose." In *The Overcoat and Other Short Stories.* Translated by Mary Struve. Mineola, N.Y.: Dover Thrift Editions, 1992.

Chekhov, Anton. "Gooseberries." In *The Portable Chekhov.* Translated by Avrahm Yarmolinsky. New York: Viking Portable Library, 1975.

Tolstoy, Leo. "Alyosha the Pot." In *The Portable Twentieth-Century Russian Reader.* Translated by Clarence Brown. New York: Penguin Classics, 1985.

OTHER SOURCES CONSULTED

Gogol, Nikolai. *The Collected Tales of Nikolai Gogol.* Translated by Richard Pevear and Larissa Volokhonsky. New York: Pantheon, 1998.

———. *Dead Souls.* Translated by Richard Pevear and Larissa Volokhonsky. New York: Vintage Classics, 1997.

Gorky, Maxim. *Reminiscences of Leo Nikolaevich Tolstoy.* Translated by S. S. Koteliansky and Leonard Woolf. 1920. Reprint, Folcroft, Pa.: Folcroft Library Editions, 1977.

Hickey, Dave. *Air Guitar: Essays on Art and Democracy.* Los Angeles: Art Issues Press, 1997.

James, Henry. *The Art of Fiction*. 1884. Reprint, New York: Pantianos Classics, 2018.

Jarrell, Randall. Introduction to *Randall Jarrell's Book of Stories: An Anthology*. New York: New York Review Books, 1958.

Kundera, Milan. *Art of the Novel*. New York: Perennial Classics, 2003.

Kuzminskaya, Tatyana A. *Tolstoy as I Knew Him: My Life at Home and at Yasnaya Polyana*. New York: Macmillan, 1948.

Maguire, Robert. *Exploring Gogol*. Stanford: Stanford University Press, 1994.

Mamet, David. *True and False: Heresy and Common Sense for the Actor*. New York: Vintage Books, 1997.

Nabokov, Vladimir. *Lectures on Russian Literature*. New York: Harcourt Brace Jovanovich, 1981.

O'Connor, Flannery. *A Good Man Is Hard to Find and Other Stories*. New York: Harcourt, 1992.

Rezzori, Gregor von. *Memoirs of an Anti-Semite*. With an introduction by Deborah Eisenberg. New York: New York Review Books, 2007.

Terras, Victor, ed. *Handbook of Russian Literature*. New Haven: Yale University Press, 1985.

Tolstoy, Leo. "Alyosha the Pot." Translated by Sam A. Carmack. In *Great Short Works of Leo Tolstoy*. 2nd ed. New York: HarperCollins, 1967.

———. *The Death of Ivan Ilyich & Other Stories*. Translated by Richard Pevear and Larissa Volokhonsky. New York: Vintage, 2010.

Troyat, Henri. *Chekhov*. New York: Fawcett Columbine, 1988.

———. *Tolstoy*. New York: Dell, 1967.

———. *Turgenev: A Biography*. London: Allison & Busby, 1991.

Vinogradov, Viktor. *Gogol and the Natural School*. Translated by Deborah K. Erickson and Ray Parrot. Ann Arbor: Ardis, 1987.

Vinokur, Val. "Talking Fiction: What Is Russian *Skaz*?" *McSweeney's Quarterly Concern,* Fall 2002.

Zorin, Andrei. *Leo Tolstoy*. London: Reaktion Books, 2020.

Additional Resources

In the text, I've mentioned a number of stories and films. Additional resources related to these can be accessed at georgesaundersbooks.com/additional-resources.

Credits

PHOTO: © ZACH KRAHMER

GEORGE SAUNDERS is the author of twelve books, including *Lincoln in the Bardo,* which debuted at #1 on the *New York Times* bestseller list, won the 2017 Man Booker Prize for best work of fiction in English, and was a finalist for the Golden Man Booker, in which one Booker winner was selected to represent each decade, from the fifty years since the prize's inception. The audiobook for *Lincoln in the Bardo,* which features a cast of 166 actors, won the 2018 Audie Award for best audiobook. The story collection *Tenth of December* was a finalist for the National Book Award; it won the inaugural Folio Prize in 2013 (for the best work of fiction in English) and the Story Prize. Saunders has received MacArthur and Guggenheim fellowships and the PEN/Malamud Prize for Excellence in the Short Story. In 2013, he was named one of the world's one hundred most influential people by *Time* magazine. He has taught in the creative writing program at Syracuse University since 1997.